ARAB AWAKENING AND ISLAMIC REVIVAL

ARAB AWAKENING AND ISLAMIC REVIVAL

The Politics of Ideas in the Middle East

Martin Kramer

Transaction Publishers
New Brunswick (U.S.A.) and London (U.K.)

First paperback printing 2008
Copyright © 1996 by Transaction Publishers, New Brunswick, New Jersey 08903.

This book is printed on acid-free paper that meets the American National Standard for Permanence of Paper for Printed Library Materials.

Library of Congress Catalog Number: 96-18312
ISBN: 978-1-56000-272-7 (cloth); 978-1-4128-0767-8 (paper)
Printed in the United States of America

Library of Congress Cataloging-in-Publication Data

Kramer, Martin S.
  Arab awakening and Islamic revival : the politics of ideas in the Middle East / Martin Kramer.
      p. cm.
  Includes bibliographical references (p.   ) and index.
  ISBN 1-5600-272-7 (alk. paper)
      1. Nationalism—Arab countries—History.   2. Islam—20th century.
  3. Middle East—History—20th century.   I. Title.

DS63.6.K73   1996
320.5'4'09174924—dc20   96-183123
                                                                        CIP

To Bernard Lewis
master, mentor, mensch

Contents

Acknowledgments   vii

Introduction   1

Part I: Arabism and Friends

1. Arab Nationalism: Mistaken Identity   19
2. Arab Pen, English Purse:
   John Sabunji and Wilfrid Scawen Blunt   53
3. *Arabistik* and Arabism: The Passions of Martin Hartmann   63
4. The Sharifian Propaganda of Eugène Jung   87
5. The Arab Nation of Shakib Arslan   103
6. Ambition, Arabism, and George Antonius   111
7. Prisoner of Love: Jean Genet and Palestine   125
8. America's Arabists   133

Part II: Islamism and the West

9. "Islam is the Power of the Future"   141
10. Khomeini's Messengers in Mecca   161
11. Syria's Alawis and Shi'ism   189
12. Hizbullah: The Calculus of Jihad   209
13. Sacrifice and "Self-Martyrdom" in Shi'ite Lebanon   231
14. France Held Hostage   245
15. Islam and the West (including Manhattan)   255
16. Islam vs. Democracy   265

Conclusion   279

Index   287

Acknowledgments

This volume brings together sixteen separate but closely related studies, bound together by an introduction and conclusion. Chapter 9 is a new study; all other studies have been previously published, and are reprinted here by permission. Chapter 1 appeared in 1993 in *Dædalus*, a journal published by the American Academy of Arts and Sciences, in the issue entitled "Reconstructing Nations and States." Chapter 2 appeared in *The Islamic World From Classical to Modern Times: Essays in Honor of Bernard Lewis*, edited by C. E. Bosworth and others, and published by Darwin Press in 1989. Chapter 3 is a revised version of an article published by *Middle Eastern Studies*, a Frank Cass journal, in 1989. Chapter 4 appeared in *The Hashemites in the Modern Arab World: A Festschrift in Honour of the late Uriel Dann*, edited by Asher Susser and Aryeh Shmuelevitz and published by Frank Cass in 1995. *Middle Eastern Studies* published chapter 5 in 1987, and chapter 6 formed a part of *The Great Powers and the Middle East, 1919–1939*, edited by Uriel Dann and published by Holmes and Meier in 1988. *Commentary* published chapters 7 and 8 in 1994. Chapter 10 is an updated version of an article that appeared in *Religious Radicalism and Politics in the Middle East* edited by Emmanuel Sivan and Menahem Friedman and published by the State University of New York Press in 1990. Chapter 11 originally appeared in *Shi'ism, Resistance, and Revolution*, a collection edited by myself and published by Westview Press in 1987. Chapter 12 originally appeared in *Fundamentalisms and the State: Remaking Polities, Economies, and Militance*, edited by Martin Marty and R. Scott Appleby and published by the University of Chicago Press in 1993. Chapter 13, published here in a slightly abbreviated form, appeared in *Violence and the Sacred in the Modern World*, edited by Mark Juergensmeyer and published by Frank Cass in 1992. *Terrorism and Political Violence*, a Frank Cass journal, published chapter 14 in 1990, and *Commentary* published chapters 15 and 16 in 1993. I am grateful to the publishers of the above for their kind permission to reprint.

I wrote nearly all of these studies at Tel Aviv University's Moshe Dayan Center for Middle Eastern and African Studies, which I now direct. I am

vii

indebted to the two past directors, Itamar Rabinovich and Asher Susser, for opening wide space for thinking, research, and writing. I owe another debt to Martin Indyk and Robert Satloff, the previous and present directors of the Washington Institute for Near East Policy, who encouraged my broader inquiries into the nature of Islamism. I gratefully acknowledge Irving Louis Horowitz of Transaction Publishers, whose suggestions helped to give this book its final form. My gratitude goes also to my parents, Anita and Alvin Kramer, in whose wooded retreat I prepared this book for publication. Finally, I embrace in thanks my wife Sandra and our children, who stoically bore my long absences as I pursued leads wherever they led.

Introduction

For the Middle East, the old appellation of the Ottoman Empire—the "sick man"—still seems apt. The social and political order in the Middle East seems as afflicted today as it appeared to observers a century ago, and many of the symptoms have not changed. Paul Kennedy, author of *Preparing for the Twenty-First Century*, has provided the kind of trenchant summation perhaps only a complete outsider can dare to offer:

> Far from preparing for the twenty-first century, much of the Arab and Muslim world appears to have difficulty in coming to terms with the nineteenth century, with its composite legacy of secularization, democracy, laissez-faire economics, transnational industrial and commercial linkages, social change, and intellectual questioning. If one needed an example of the importance of cultural attitudes in explaining a society's response to change, contemporary Islam provides it.[1]

Some historians and political scientists of the Middle East would recoil at this hint of cultural determinism, and most Arabs and Muslims would blame colonialism instead. But the Arab and Muslim world's "difficulty in coming to terms" is undeniable.

This book is a critical assessment of two attempts to overcome that difficulty: Arab nationalism (or Arabism) and Islamic fundamentalism (or Islamism). Believers in each have tried to remake the modern Middle East into a seat of power and prosperity. So far they have failed, in many instances producing even more serious complications. While Arab nationalism seems finally to have been abandoned, Islamic fundamentalism remains the most widespread alternative to the resolute pragmatism of the "new Middle East." Whether it will prevail is one of the great preoccupations of our own *fin-de-siècle*.

But this is not a future study. It is a book about modern history and contemporary politics, looking back over a troubled Arab century and a difficult Islamic decade. Like Europe, the Middle East has been buffeted by ideologies. Admittedly, their effects have not been as devastating in the Middle East; Europe paid for its nationalism with two terrible world wars, and then paid again for its communism with over forty years of threat and

1

division. Ideology in Europe has had a greater capacity for destruction than ideology in the Middle East.

Yet if the failings of the Arab "awakening" and the Islamic "revival" seem smaller in comparison, this is largely thanks to restraints imposed by the West. It is usually argued that the oil extracted by foreigners, the military interventions made by foreigners, and the aid granted by foreigners have combined to make the Middle East dependent. But they may have also restrained a pursuit of utopias that could have pushed the Middle East over the edge long ago, into famines, gulags, and civil wars. As it is, parts of the region have been gutted or "cleansed" in the name of the Arab nation or Islam, from Kurdistan to Kuwait, from Lebanon to Sudan.

This is necessarily a book about illusion and disillusion, but even more, it is a series of studies in contradictions that finally became unsustainable. Arabism and Islamism purported to be authentic and original creations of Arabs and Muslims, but both owed much to foreign influences, romantic and radical. Both pretended to be liberating and unifying ideals, but their practice often produced oppression and division. Most of these contradictions have ended in a shattering of dreams, and sometimes of bodies. Each chapter picks up some discarded scrap of paper or shard of glass, and asks how the hope it represented came to nought.

The structure of this book is straightforward. An integrative chapter opens each of the book's two parts—one devoted to Arabism and the other to Islamism. Each integrative chapter is followed by seven more chapters on the particular origins or actual effects of Arabism or Islamism, in various times and places. This is not a seamless book of running narrative; its chapters are puzzle pieces, interlocking but separate. They can be assembled in more than one order, although the order suggested here seems the most logical to their author. The first part, on Arabism, revolves largely around personalities; the second, on Islamism, is structured around movements and events. The emphasis could easily have been reversed, but the sum would have been the same.

"Awake, O Arabs, and arise!"

The reign of ideology began with the spread of Arab nationalism. At the turn of the century, the Middle East was still largely the domain of the once-great empire of the Ottomans. It had been an empire defined by Islam but inhabited by peoples of many faiths and languages. Islamic tradition and local custom defined the relations between the empire's diverse peoples. As Western influence grew, however, the ideas of national self-determination began to make inroads—first among the subject peoples in the Ottoman Balkans, later among non-Muslim minorities in the Asian heartland, and finally among Muslims themselves. Thus was born Arab nationalism—the idea that the far-flung speakers of Arabic constituted a distinct nation, entitled to independence from "foreign" Turkish rule. Its enthusiasts called this the *Nahda*, the "Arab awakening": the stirring of the Arabs to their own vast potential, after centuries of supposed subjugation.

At first the idea took a liberal form. But then came World War I and the partition of the Ottoman Empire by the European powers, led by Britain and France. Zionism, still another new nationalism, took root in Palestine under the British umbrella. Arab nationalism became radical, both politically and socially. When most Arab states became independent after World War II, they adopted a war footing, and their sense of grievance took the form of an ideological fervor, sometimes tied to the personality cult of this century's great Arab figure, Gamal Abdul Nasser. The American socialist leader Norman Thomas attended a rally of the Arab National Movement in Beirut in 1958, and perhaps best summarized the content of this ideology. "I have a hard time understanding what Arab socialism means," he said. "But it seems to me that its slogan should be 'Liberty, equality, and revenge.'"[2]

In the end, Arab nationalism produced very little liberty, equality, or even revenge. Its heroes were military dictators who promised salvation, but Nasser, its great champion, was defeated on the battlefield in 1967. The appeal of Arab nationalism and pan-Arabism has been on the wane ever since, and the resulting void has been filled by an unstable mix of state loyalty, local patriotism, and Islamic particularism. There are a few in the Arab world, and also among Arab intellectuals in the bubble of Western academe, who still proclaim the revolutionary virtues of Arab nationalism. But in the Middle East, the idea seems as tired as its surviving souls, who convened in 1994 in a conference in Beirut. "From where I sat," an observer of this conference wrote,

the conferees appeared to represent an extinct tribe using strange words—indeed, a language incomprehensible in our time. Most of them had grey hair and stooping backs. Some needed canes to help them walk. Some had hearing aids and shaking hands that made it difficult for them to write, and others had difficulty getting the words out.

"Astonishingly," he added "none of this stopped them." But they were "blowing in a broken bagpipe."[3] Among the Arabs themselves, it is the poets who have most courageously declared the era over. In contrast, chapter 1 of this book employs prose to reassess Arab nationalism's lost moment in the Middle East.

Although Arab nationalism came to stand for resistance against the West, it relied heavily upon foreign ideas, often transmitted by sympathetic foreign friends. In fact, the "Arab awakening" was partly a wakening of the Arabs by foreign enthusiasts and romantics. Such foreign advocacy of the Arabs ran much deeper than the famous case of T. E. Lawrence. In the unfolding of successive Arab "awakenings," foreigners turn up in every act, to recite some of the most dramatic lines. The French social psychologist Gustave Le Bon told the Arabs they belonged to an ingenious race of conquerors. The English poet Wilfrid Scawen Blunt told them they alone practiced the pure Islam. The German Orientalist Martin Hartmann told them they enjoyed a cultural superiority over the Turks who governed them. The French publicist Eugène Jung told them they had been born to the art of self-government. The American philanthropist Charles Crane told them they would inherit the earth from a dissolute West. The British traveller Freya Stark told them they would achieve world power through unity. The British historian Arnold Toynbee told them they had been elevated by Clio, the French Islamicist Louis Massignon told them they had been graced by God. The British soldier John Glubb told them they were made for battle. The French novelist and playwright Jean Genet told them they were the stuff of dreams.

And these ideas found ways to Arab ears and eyes. The writings of these foreigners were cited, translated, and plagiarized. The task of appropriation began with two books of the early 1880s, Blunt's *Future of Islam* and Le Bon's *La civilisation des arabes,* that demonstrably inspired the first nationalists. Foreigners also became publicists for Arabism, as Hartmann and Jung did in the years before World War I. (They, too, wrote books: Jung's *Les puissances devant la révolte arabe* and Hartmann's *Die arabische Frage.*) Foreigners also sponsored nationalist journalism, including newspapers and books, exemplified by Crane's support in the 1930s for George Antonius, the author of *The Arab Awakening.* And often they arrived in Arab lands as prophets from afar, as Toynbee did in several visits to Nasser's Egypt in the early 1960s, where he lectured on the historical imperative of Arab unity. (The state-run publishing house disseminated his books and lectures in Arabic translation.)

The words of foreigners fed the nationalist imagination and provided crucial validation for the nationalist narrative. Millions of people had to be persuaded that they were Arabs—that as Arabs they had a great history and a greater destiny. Who had more persuasive power than this gallery of foreigners, who confirmed every historical premise of Arabism? Fouad Ajami has written of "illusions that outsiders come to fix onto a region they adopt—that not only will it find its own way but that it will help others as well...they are expressed and then imported by the people to whom they refer. Nature imitates art and such illusions become part of national self-delusions."[4] Wittingly or not, these foreigners acted as sorcerer's apprentices, performing sleights of hand and heart for the nationalist "awakening." Their scholarship and speculation made crucial contributions to the trilogy of Arabism, Arab nationalism, and pan-Arabism.

Arab historiography has largely omitted the doings of foreign friends from the nationalist narrative because they undermine Arabism's very claim to authenticity. In this book, they are presented in all their subversive variety. Five of the chapters on Arab nationalism uncover the involvement of foreigners of several nationalities—English, French, German, American—in the gestation and propagation of the Arab idea. Two chapters also consider the role of two self-professed Arabs who made some of the earliest effective Arab propaganda in the West.

Wilfrid Scawen Blunt, an English country squire, was the first foreigner to take up the cause of Arab independence. Blunt wrote in support of Arab separation from the Ottoman Empire and an Arab caliphate some thirty-six years before the Arab Revolt of 1916. And he got a hearing: Blunt was an amateur poet, explorer, and supporter of oppressed peoples who enjoyed easy access to the high policy circles of Victorian England. His literary advocacy of the Arab cause thus became famous.

But did he act to promote Arab separatism? Documents in a country records office in the south of England (separated from the bulk of Blunt's papers in Cambridge) provided the answer. For a number of years, Blunt subsidized John Louis Sabunji, a Syrian Catholic priest-turned-journalist who conducted a press campaign against the Ottoman sultan and in favor of an Arab caliphate. Chapter 2 is an exploration of this partnership, which lasted from 1880 to 1883. It was a curious liaison: Blunt was a romantic idealist, Sabunji a consummate opportunist. Their influence on the gestation of Arab nationalism is difficult to trace, but their propaganda anticipated all its early themes.

The nascent Arab cause found an even more persistent champion in

Martin Hartmann, a left-leaning German Orientalist. After completing a doctorate in philology, Hartmann served at the German consulate in Beirut from 1876 to 1887, where he cultivated many connections to the fathers of the Arabic literary revival. He later took a position as an Arabic instructor in Berlin, and became a dissident scholar who tried to break the monopoly of formalist philology on German Oriental studies. At the turn of the century, Hartmann launched a campaign to persuade his country-men that Germany should abandon its Ottoman alliance and support Arab independence. At the time, the Arab movement existed only as a rumor in Europe's capitals, and Hartmann gained a reputation as a visionary. During World War I, when Germany's link to the Ottoman Empire became a war alliance, Hartmann did a quick reversal, choosing German patriotism over his passion for the Arabs. But by this time, he had played no small role in posing "the Arab question" to Europe. Chapter 3 is a study of Hartmann's promotion of Arab independence years before the emergence of an Arab movement, based upon his own writings and papers.

The career of Eugène Jung, a French publicist on behalf of the Arabs, completes this trilogy of three early foreign friends. It is still impossible to say why Jung, a former French colonial official in Tonkin, took up the Arab cause. He had no experience in the Ottoman Empire or in any Arab land. Jung's enthusiasm seems to have been fired by Nagib Azoury, another Syrian Christian who arrived in Paris around 1904, and there published a book claiming that the Arab provinces were ripe for revolt. Jung gave himself wholeheartedly to Azoury's campaign, and they worked together during the decade between 1906 and 1916 to persuade France to champion the cause of Arab liberty.

The partnership of Jung and Azoury is a famous one, but it ended in 1916 with Azoury's death. Chapter 4 uncovers and assesses Jung's subsequent activities. In 1916 he found a new partner, a Syrian journalist in Paris, and together they published a newspaper that attempted to galvanize French support for the Arab Revolt of the Sharif Husayn and an independent Syria under Sharifian rule. (A unique set of the newspaper survives in the press annex of the Bibliothèque Nationale in Versailles, and it is the basis of this study.) French authorities censored the newspaper and ultimately closed it, but Jung persisted in his campaign right up to the postwar peace conference. Ironically, the Arab delegation snubbed him there, leading Jung to despair of the cause he had embraced. Jung personified the limits of the early foreign friends. He had more enthusiasm than influence, and he relied completely on the mediation of Syrian Christian journalists for his knowledge of Arab affairs. That said, Jung set a precedent of French sympathy for Arab independence which would be followed by a later generation of dissidents.

With the passage of friends like Blunt, Hartmann, and Jung, two men from Lebanon directly assumed the role of spokesmen for the Arabs in the West: Shakib Arslan and George Antonius. Between them, these two prolific polemicists repackaged the Arab argument in terms intelligible to foreign audiences, and some of their texts resonate to this day.

Chapter 5 considers the career of Shakib Arslan. Born to a notable Druze family in 1869, Arslan vigorously defended the Ottoman Empire right through the disaster of World War I. He then chose exile in Switzerland, where he worked for Arab independence from French and British rule between the wars. In particular, Arslan published a journal, *La Nation arabe*, which doggedly put the case for Syrian and North African independence before French public opinion. During World War II, Arslan placed his last bet on the Axis powers and he died in obscurity. But his propaganda between the wars contributed to the erosion of French resolve over Syria.

A similar fate awaited George Antonius, who defended the claims for Arab independence in the court of British and American opinion between the wars. Antonius, born a Greek Orthodox Christian in Lebanon, studied in Egypt and England, acquired the nationality of a Palestinian, and called himself an Arab. He was very much a cultural middleman, inhabiting the shifting ground between England and the Arabs, leaving many unsure of where he stood until publication of his book, *The Arab Awakening*, in 1938.

Antonius' book had a long and influential run as the authoritative account of Arab nationalism's origins and Britain's wartime promises to the Arabs. It was a brilliant study of considerable literary merit, with all the appeal of an exposé. However, it was not a history. Even the late Albert Hourani (upon inaugurating the Antonius Lectures at Oxford) conceded that Antonius "rarely quoted his sources or explained why, when they conflicted, he preferred one of them to another."[5] *The Arab Awakening* is ambivalent as history—an ambivalence shared, in a different way, by T. E. Lawrence's *Seven Pillars of Wisdom*, which covered some of the same ground.

Yet *The Arab Awakening* remains the bible of Arabism. There was a time when defenders of the book argued that it met all the criteria of history.

Many postmodernist readers claim that the maintenance of such criteria is hegemonic, and that all scholarship is connected to politics anyway. Yet Edward Said holds up *The Arab Awakening* as history once again; to dismiss Antonius' book as an "emotional and subjective *cri de coeur*" is to dismiss its "enormous contribution to knowledge." The book has "historical force," writes Said.[6] *The Arab Awakening*, almost sixty years later, apparently still provides too much comfort and assurance to permit its retirement from the canon.

In any case, chapter 6 deals not with the book but with the last years of Antonius' life. The last episode in Antonius' career demonstrated a confusion between idea and action, between the desirable and the feasible, that came to characterize an entire generation of Arab intellectuals. The attitudes that Antonius personified—a misreading of the force of Zionism, an intellectual intransigence dressed as a pursuit of justice, a dismissal of the very real differences among Arabs—ultimately proved the undoing of the "cause" he celebrated. This was a species of *trahison des clercs* of which Antonius was a forerunner.

In the last two chapters, the focus returns to Arabism's foreign friends. A glaring omission from the critique of Orientalism is the projection of Western homoerotic fantasy on the Orient. Like larger Orientalism, this sub-variety had its French and English styles. It was characterized by a passionate attachment to objectified Arab males, accompanied by a guilt-repelling anticolonialism. The French playwright Jean Genet, for all his unique genius, firmly belonged to this tradition. After a remarkable career as a playwright and poet, Genet turned into a political radical in the late 1960s, adopting the cause of the Black Panthers in America and then joining the Palestinian *fedayeen* in Jordan. Chapter 7 examines the playwright's immersion in the Palestinian cause.

As Genet admitted, his attachment to the Palestinian *fedayeen* had strong sensual overtones, and he invoked no logic in support of his emotional bond: "I defend the Palestinians wholeheartedly and automatically. They are in the right because I love them." This tone rather diminished Genet's effectiveness on behalf of Palestine. But he could convey something of Palestinian suffering in a vivid language, and so served as a counterweight in Paris to Jean-Paul Sartre and Michel Foucault, who preferred Israel's claims. (Foucault's own erotic fascination with the Arabs, most fully indulged during a year in Tunisia, did not resurface as political passion.) Genet regarded pan-Arabism as reactionary. But his political engagement on behalf of the Algerian revolution and North African immigrants in France suggested a broad investment of his "love" in the Arab world. Of all the foreign friends, Genet best personified the appeal of Arab causes on the very margins of Western culture. As it happened, the upheavals of the 1960s confused the center and the margins, making Genet one of the most formidable literary friends any Arab movement has ever had.

American support for Arab nationalism drew on a very different tradition, pioneered not by radical playwrights but by Presbyterian missionaries. Chapter 8 considers the rise and fall of the small groups of Americans who came to the Levant to proselytize among the Arabs, but then became proselytizers for the Arab nationalist cause in the United States. The sons of missionaries and educators became America's first diplomats in the Arab world, and their expertise proved indispensable as the U.S. succeeded Britain and France as the dominant outside power in the Middle East.

Arab nationalism had an impressive array of well-placed friends in mid-century America. But America has no stable policy class and no fixed political elite, and by virtue of the Arabists' long experience abroad they lost touch with politics at home. After the creation of Israel in 1948, some Arabists became self-appointed lobbyists for Arab governments or movements, and the term took on partisan connotations. Since the mid-1970s, many of the veteran Arabists have been eased out of the State Department, replaced by "peace processors" and diplomats with experience on both sides of the Arab-Israeli divide. Yet their influence lingers in subtle ways, most notably in an intellectual predisposition to appease radical Islam.

"Yes, he was a lover of Arabs" wrote Edward Said of Genet, "something not many of us are accustomed to from Western writers and thinkers, who have found an adversarial relationship with us more congenial."[7] In fact, Arab nationalists were thoroughly accustomed to the admiring gazes of Western writers and thinkers, from whom they borrowed many of their own self-exalting theories. Perhaps one more Arab grievance against the West should be that the West held up too flattering a mirror to Arab nationalist posturing, Nasserist heroics, and Palestinian bravado. Now that all have failed, a few Arabs are beginning the painful task of reconstructing their own image, looking not to their professed friends but to themselves. The outcome is far from certain.

Islam as Ideology

One reason for that uncertainty has been the rapid rise of Islamic fundamentalism, or Islamism, in the very space once occupied by Arab nationalism.

Islam, it has been rightly noted, is not an "ism." As a religion and a civilization, Islam has commanded vaster expanses of time and space than any modern ideology. Today it flourishes in countless forms, giving meaning to lives led in places as distinct as the immigrant quarters of Europe's cities, the villages and towns of Egypt, and the highlands of Afghanistan. Within every society, it takes multiple forms, from the high Islam of the great theological academies to the low Islam of the backroom mosques. In the realm of politics, it has been mobilized to legitimize differing and often rival political orders, each of which claims to embody the true Islam. But Islam resists possession. It is impossible to monopolize, and its survival and spread attest to its flexibility.

Yet in the hands of some of its present-day adherents, Islam has been remade into something militant and monolithic: fundamentalism, or what some prefer to call Islamism. This is very much an "ism," formulated not only as a religious and cultural preference, but as a modern ideology. Like modern ideologies, its exclusive claims draw stark lines in minds, and turn it rigidly against Islam's diversity, understood as deviation. And like all modern political ideologies, Islamism is obsessed with the acquisition of political power, and largely indifferent to the means used to acquire it. Chapter 9 follows that obsession from its origins to the present.

At the heart of each subsequent chapter is the same question: has the revival of Islam become the force of renewal it purports to be? The answer, demonstrated here across a wide range of movements and settings, is that Islamism appears to embody many of the same flaws as Arabism. In part, its ideas are an "Islamic" reworking of a secular radicalism, and its effect has been to give new life to old rationales for oppression, authoritarianism, and sectarian division.

In its very essence, Islamism is a reaffirmation of difference—not only between Muslims and non-Muslims, but between different varieties of Islam, and particularly between the earliest of Islam's choices, Sunni and Shi'ite. A long history of bigotry has divided them, and in our time it has now intruded even upon the pilgrimage to Mecca, as a result of two revolutions of religious fervor made by the House of Sa'ud and the Imam Khomeini. In 1987 the pilgrimage finally boiled over, in a bloody clash between Saudi police and Iranian pilgrims that left more than four hundred dead. Chapter 10 seeks the context of this incident, and finds it in the reawakening of sectarian identity which is the ominous shadow of a revived Islam. The pilgrimage continues to mutate, and the chapter follows the rivalry through the events of 1994.

Another inner controversy brought to the fore by Islamism involves the Islamic standing of Syria's Alawis (once known more commonly as Nusayris). Many of Syria's strongmen, and most notably its president, Hafiz al-Asad, hail from this sect, whose adherents number perhaps 12 percent of Syria's population. The concentration of power in Alawi hands coincided in the 1970s with a surge of Islamic sentiment among some of Syria's Sunni Muslims, who form Syria's overwhelming majority. These Sunnis painted the Alawis as non-Muslims; the Alawis, in response, sought out respected authorities in Shi'ite Islam who would declare them to be Muslims through and through.

Chapter 11 is an account of how that effort finally succeeded when a leader of Lebanon's Shi'ites, Sayyid Musa al-Sadr, gave his endorsement to the Alawis in 1973. The regime's suppression of a Sunni uprising in 1982 and the development of close Syrian ties with Iran have done still more to neutralize the issue of the Alawis' Islam. But the Alawi question lies in wait for that moment when the Alawis might finally show some weakness, or perhaps when Asad is called to his God—whoever that God might be. The persistence of the Alawi question provides more evidence of the ways in which Islamic revival has disinterred differences which new national identities were supposed to have buried for good.

The Shi'ite surge which followed Iran's revolution took yet another form in the birth and growth of Lebanon's Hizbullah, the "Party of God." The source of this Shi'ite energy will always remain a subject of debate. Was it the pent-up resentments of Lebanon's Shi'ites against other Lebanese? Then perhaps Hizbullah was a revolt against the very idea of Lebanon. Or was its source a Shi'ite hatred against the Israeli invasion and occupation of Lebanon in 1982, compounded by the entry of the U.S. and France as co-occupiers? Then perhaps Hizbullah was above all a reaction against foreign invaders. Or was that energy really Iran's own revolutionary power, transmitted to Lebanon's Shi'ites by Revolutionary Guards and zealous emissaries? Then perhaps Hizbullah was first and foremost a creature of Iran's making. These questions of input are difficult to answer.

Chapter 12 is concerned rather with Hizbullah's output: the violence in all forms that brought it such renown (and notoriety) during the 1980s.

For any movement that purports to restore Islamic law to its place in the world, violence poses dilemmas. There is no ethos of nonviolence in these movements, but there is a conviction that violence must be governed by the law. This chapter assesses a decade of choices made by one movement: the steep escalation of Hizbullah's violence in the mid-1980s, its gradual containment by the spread of Syrian power, and the movement's recent retreat into party politics. Hizbullah is no longer quite as unique as it once was; other Islamist movements, from Jerusalem to Algiers, kill foreigners, send "self-martyrs" to immolate enemies, and hijack aircraft. But their calculus is similar, and this study might be read as an introduction to Islamist strategy generally.

Perhaps the most devastating instrument in the hands of Islamist movements has been the "self-martyr," usually a young man prepared to go knowingly to his death in order to kill as many of a movement's perceived enemies as possible. The capacity to mobilize "self-martyrs" can assure an Islamist movement an impact far beyond its numbers, for a "self-martyr" is a logistical ace-in-the-hole, against which most conventional defenses are useless. Yet the tactic poses difficult problems of Islamic law, for it closely resembles the two forbidden acts of suicide and sacrifice. It requires careful calculation and a form of social selection, by which certain candidates are deemed appropriate for operations and others are not. The tactic, pioneered by Hizbullah, has now been emulated repeatedly by the Palestinian Hamas, and may become the tactic of choice for embattled Islamist movements.

Chapter 13 examines the dynamic of the competition between Hizbullah and its Shi'ite rival, the Amal movement, in mobilizing "self-martyrs" during the mid-1980s. The chapter suggests that this tactic not only compensated for the superior force of the foreign occupier. It also fed a sacrificial competition between two deeply antagonistic movements, which proved crucial to the preservation of the peace between them. The end of this competitive cycle was followed by a Shi'ite civil war between Hizbullah and Amal, as ferocious as any confrontation between Hizbullah and Israel. Even in the case of Hizbullah, the price of the Islamic revival also has been paid in Muslim blood shed by other Muslims—a development foreshadowed in the "self-martyrdom" operation, by which one Muslim consigns another to a certain death.

But this internecine conflict is only one face of the Islamist surge. The Islamists have also worked to resurrect the barriers between Islam and the West. It has been argued that the Islamist revolt is a rearguard action of besieged Muslims, who believe themselves under assault by Western power and Western ways. There is much truth to this analysis, and yet it is also true that some Islamists have understood their "defense" to include acts of political violence in the very heart of the West. Two chapters place in context the recent Islamist attempts to shake two great cities: Paris and New York.

Chapter 14 considers the shadowy war waged by Islamic Iran against France during the 1980s. At the heart of the war was a grim irony. France had thought itself far more clever than the United States in dealing with Iran's radical Islam. In 1978, France had offered refuge to Ayatollah Khomeini, who directed Iran's revolution from a Paris suburb. The French government of the day apparently thought that this would create a special bond of understanding between Paris and Tehran. It did not. When Iran saw French weaponry flowing into Iraqi hands during the Iraq-Iran war, the Islamic Republic took its grievance straight to the French public, first by abducting French nationals in Lebanon and then by setting off bombs amidst the shoppers in Paris.

Only the Iran-Iraq cease-fire bought a respite in the Iran-France confrontation. Since then, however, France has come to face an Islam even more threatening to its security, an Islam that challenges France's very identity. The turmoil in Algeria has begun to spill over into France. In 1994, Algerian Islamists hijacked an Air France flight to Marseille, with the apparent intention of destroying it over Paris. The image of French special forces storming the Air France jet (a crew member leapt from a cockpit window) contrasted sharply with the earlier image of Ayatollah Khomeini returning to Iran on another Air France jet (its pilot gently walked Khomeini down the steps to the tarmac). In fifteen years, the Islamic revival had returned on the very same wings. Ironically, the same French ministers who bartered with Iran in the 1980s promise a hard line on Algeria in the 1990s. But given the precedents described in chapter 14, French success in escaping compromise with resurgent Islam cannot be taken for granted.

Neither can the success of the United States, despite the separation afforded by a wide ocean. The World Trade Center bombing which shook New York City in 1993 was even more audacious than the Paris bombings. Had the bombing succeeded in collapsing one tower of the World Trade Center upon the other, some 50,000 persons would have perished. Chapter 15 locates the bombing at the junction of two processes: an Islamist resolve to carry the jihad for power into the heart of the complacent West, and the desire of millions of Muslims to enter and feed upon the cornucopia of the rich West. The U.S., as the seat of the West's greatest wealth and defender of the West's broadest interests, seems bound to draw more Muslim migrants—and more Islamist lightening. Ultimately, the battle for power in the Middle East will be decided on Middle Eastern ground, but deadly skirmishes in the great cities of Europe and the Americas already have become routine.

Despite these fiercely divisive forces, all unleashed by the Islamic revival in the Middle East and the West, many Western observers have hailed Islamism as the long-awaited quantum leap to reform, modernity, and democracy. Just as Arabism in its heyday found foreign friends and apologists, so does Islamism today. Chapter 16 surveys these views, and then allows the Islamists themselves to rebut them. It will fall to some future historian to document in detail the myriad motives of Islamism's foreign friends—from the structured optimism of the democracy theorists to the grim pessimism of the moral self-flagellants. What is already clear is a persistent tendency among some in the West to amplify the latest political passion in the Middle East with a passion all their own.

Political Religion

Pursue identity or pursue interests? According to the Tunisian historian Hichem Djaït (who will reappear in Chapter 1), the Arab-Muslim world has always been too predictable in its choice:

> For at least a century, the Muslim world has tended toward two principal goals in the course of its development: to participate in the modern world, but at the same time to demand recognition for its own special historical, cultural, and religious heritage. These two goals frequently converge; but they can also diverge. In fact, the search for recognition, through both nationalism and Islam, has always taken priority over everything else.[8]

The chapters of this book chronicle this single-minded search for recognition; its high costs are tallied in the conclusion. Recognition of one's "special heritage," whatever other satisfactions it may bring, cannot feed, clothe, educate, or employ—a simple truth for which the Arab-Muslim world now stands as a grim example. As the conclusion demonstrates, the futurist philosophers, from Francis Fukuyama to Samuel P. Huntington, do recognize that the Arab-Muslim world is "special," depressingly so. It seems impervious to the worldwide triumph of liberal democracy. It is heavily armed and poorly educated, and it remains susceptible to ideological excess in an age of pragmatism. Despite an Arab "awakening" and an Islamic "revival," much of the Arab-Muslim world still dreams.

There are some who believe that the Arabs cannot do without a dream, or at least a charismatic leader who will keep their heads raised well above their surroundings. "If the problem is to be overcome," wrote another foreign friend of Arabism, the late Malcolm Kerr, "it may be because a new and more dynamic set of ideas—a new political religion—will arise to take the place of the old. Perhaps this will be a new *Nahda*, less Western oriented and more authentically rooted than the old one."[9] The assumption here is that while the West has politics, the Arabs need "political religion," some comforting myth of authenticity that can legitimize change.

No doubt many Arabs do need "political religion," and some are finding it by politicizing even more thoroughly the religion they already have. But this Islam is already failing (a first book has appeared declaring *The Failure of Political Islam*[10]), and all the evidence of this century is that the politics of identity, any identity, can only divide and disappoint the Arab world. Among Arab intellectuals, there is a growing recognition that authenticity, whatever its gratifications, can also be a trap. "Such a society has no chance at all of ever flowering again," laments the Algerian writer Rabah Belamri. "It will no doubt continue to slumber amid all its tiresome idols, which it habitually goes on praising, and its sclerotic ancestral values, which it continues to exemplify; but that is about it."[11]

Still, such voices are themselves the sign of a stirring. Is the spell now finally broken?

Notes

1. Paul Kennedy, *Preparing for the Twenty-First Century* (New York: Random House, 1993), 208.
2. Quoted by Don Peretz, "Vignettes—Bits and Pieces," in *Paths to the Middle East: Ten Scholars Look Back*, ed. Thomas Naff (Albany: State University of New York Press, 1993), 246.
3. Fahmi Huwaydi, "The State of the Nation," *Al-Ahram*, 17 May 1994, quoted in *Mideast Mirror*, 17 May 1994. Huwaydi is an Islamist.
4. Fouad Ajami, *The Arab Predicament: Arab Political Thought and Practice Since 1967*, updated ed. (Cambridge: Cambridge University Press, 1992), 244–45.
5. Albert Hourani, *The Emergence of the Modern Middle East* (Berkeley and Los Angeles: University of California Press, 1981), 165.
6. Edward W. Said, *Culture and Imperialism* (New York: Knopf, 1993), 258.
7. Edward Said, "On Jean Genet's Late Works," *Grand Street* 9, no. 4 (Summer 1990): 34.
8. Hichem Djaït, "It's Time to Reverse the Condemnation of Salman Rushdie," in *For Rushdie: Essays by Arab and Muslim Writers in Defense of Free Speech* (New York:

George Braziller, 1994), 121.

9. Malcolm Kerr, "Arab Society and the West," in *The Shaping of an Arab Statesman*, ed. Patrick Seale (London: Quartet, 1983), 223–24.

10. Olivier Roy, *The Failure of Political Islam*, trans. Carol Volk (Cambridge: Harvard University Press, 1994).

11. Rabah Belamri, "The End of an Illusion," in *For Rushdie*, 67–68.

Part I

Arabism and Friends

1

Arab Nationalism: Mistaken Identity

Three lines of poetry plot the trajectory of Arab national consciousness. "Awake, O Arabs, and arise!" begins the famous ode of Ibrahim al-Yaziji, penned in 1868 in Lebanon.[1] George Antonius deployed the line as the epigraph of his influential book of 1938, *The Arab Awakening*, as the first utterance of a nascent Arab desire for independence from Ottoman rule.[2] "Write down, I am an Arab!" begins the renowned poem of resistance by the Palestinian poet Mahmoud Darwish, written in 1963 to assert an Arab identity denied by Israel and the West.[3] The poem immediately entered the Arab nationalist canon, to be recited from memory by a generation of schoolchildren. In the century that separated these two lines, millions of people gradually awoke and arose, insisting before the world and one another that they be written down as Arabs.

"Are we Arabs one big lie?" This line ends a poem of anguish written in the midst of the latest Gulf crisis by Nizar Qabbani, the most widely read contemporary Arab poet and critic.[4] Too much had gone wrong to sustain exclamation points of awakening and defiance; they were replaced by a question mark of doubt. Once half of Europe and a superpower had admitted to living a lie for most of this century, the Arabs could not suppress their own doubt any longer. Their god had also failed, spectacularly so. It had been called Arabism, or Arab nationalism, or pan-Arabism, and by the time Qabbani posed his question, it had been in full retreat for a generation.

At present, many Arabs have suspended their belief in the Arab nation, and now openly doubt whether there is a collective Arab mission. Those recently swept up by Islamic activism prefer to think of themselves first and foremost as Muslims, and do so without apology. At times, their lexicon has turned "the Arabs" into a derogatory label, implying wastefulness, incompetence, and subservience. Other Arabs plainly prefer to be known as Egyptians, Syrians, Jordanians, Moroccans—citizens of over twenty independent states, each with its own flag and own interests. Some have even taken to referring to themselves as Middle Easterners, in anticipation of an Arab-Israeli peace and a new regional order of cooperation modeled on Europe. A few intellectuals keep the Arab flame alive. Yet they are most often abroad, in London or Paris, where they command dwindling audiences of Third Worldists and "pro-Arabs." For a decade they have quarreled over whether pan-Arabism and Arab nationalism are simply in remission or beyond all resuscitation.

A sense of "Arabness" still persists. It has existed for as long as the Arabs have walked the stage of history, and it has been subject to negotiation by every generation for nearly a millennium and a half. In this generation, this sense of "Arabness" must come to terms with the growth of loyalty to separate Arab states, a burgeoning Islam, the global triumph of liberal democracy, the ascendancy of market capitalism, and the prospect of peace with Israel. All were anathema to Arab nationalism as it evolved over most of this century. "Arabness" can doubtless accommodate the new challenges, as it has always done. Arab nationalism, a modern creation of this century, may well disappear altogether under their impact.

But whatever the prospects of Arab nationalism, its history to this point represents one of the most remarkable instances of the rapid birth, rise, and decline of any modern nationalism. That history deserves a new telling, for it has not been invoked in the broader debate over the growing instability of identity that marks the end of this century. There was a time when Arab nationalism did enjoy a place of some prominence in the comparative study of nationalism, but later it became the domain of specialists, which was perhaps just as well. Arnold Toynbee and Hans Kohn, who first attempted to integrate Arab nationalism into some wider comparative framework, became its virtual partisans between the world wars despite their own reservations about nationalism in general. In a spirit of mea culpa—Toynbee's for British policy, Kohn's for Zionist—they accepted the most extravagant slogans of Arab nationalism as statements of sociological fact or incontrovertible moral claims, and saw none of the contradictions beneath its surface.

When the Arab states gained independence after World War II, these contradictions surged to the fore in all their complexity, and kept later theorists at arm's length. "No brief summary of the long and intricate history of the Arab world could hope to disentangle the forces which have shaped its states and peoples," wrote Rupert Emerson in scarcely concealed exasperation. "For a full-scale analysis it would be necessary to evaluate the whole record of Arab experience, including such matters as the tribal, sectarian, and other divisions, the effects of Ottoman rule, the machinations of the European powers, and the role of Islam and of the Arab language and culture."[5] In short, it was a job for someone else who knew it better. But even the comparativists who did know Arab nationalism quite well chose not to make it the pivot of their comparisons, perhaps for fear of losing the general reader in a labyrinth.[6]

The Arab case does remain a dauntingly complex one by the standards of Europe. The speakers of Arabic today number over 200 million, in a zone stretching from the Atlantic shores of Morocco to the Arabian Sea—a region that extends parallel to all of Europe from the Atlantic seaboard of Iberia to the Urals. No European nationalism has claimed a potential constituency as large, as far-flung, or as fragmented. It has never been easy to document the historical evolution of political consciousness across this zone, and a thinness persists in its study.

Nor did Arab nationalism originate as a straightforward reaction to Western imperial rule, of the kind familiar elsewhere in Asia and Africa. Some Arab peoples experienced over a century of direct Western rule, while others experienced none at all. As a result, Arab nationalism followed distinct courses of development in the Fertile Crescent, the Arabian peninsula, the Nile valley, and the North African coast. Each of these zones encountered the West on different terms, at different times. Variations on Arab nationalism multiplied, sometimes even inspiring separate classifications, such as Nasserism and Ba'thism, and even more arcane subclassifications, such as neo-Ba'thism. Many of these became rivals, even to the point of bloodshed. This has made it difficult to generalize about Arab nationalism, and treacherous to deploy such generalizations in the larger debate over nationalism.

The purpose in the following pages is not to attempt the treacherous. It is to attempt what Emerson wished, as a prelude to comparison: to trace the political trajectory of Arab nationalism plotted by the poets, to walk an idea briskly through its historical phases, and to characterize its relationship to those other ideas and identities that have appealed to "the speakers of the *dad*," that sound which is unique to Arabic. It is the story of a nationalism that arose fitfully, spread dramatically, then faltered and failed. It is an account of how millions of people imagined themselves to be Arabs and then, as though in a case of mistaken identity, claimed to have been someone else all along.

The Emergence of Arabism

Arabism first arose in the nineteenth century not as a direct reaction to Western rule, but as a critique of the state of the Ottoman Empire, whose reach had extended over most of the Arabic-speaking peoples since the early sixteenth century. For nearly four hundred years, these Arabic speakers had been fully reconciled to their role in the Empire. The seat of the Empire was in Istanbul, and its vast domains were administered in Ottoman Turkish. But the Ottomans professed Islam, as did the overwhelming majority of their Arabic-speaking subjects. Their state evolved as a partnership in Islam, embracing all of the Ottoman sultan's Muslim subjects, whatever language they spoke.

Those Muslims who spoke Arabic retained a pride in their language: God revealed the Qur'an in Arabic to an Arab prophet in the seventh century. They also celebrated the history of the early Arab conquests that carried Islam from the Oxus to the Pyrenees, and they took pride in their genealogies that linked them to Arabia at the dawn of Islam. But that very fidelity to Islam bound them to Muslims who spoke other languages and prided themselves on other genealogies, and who brought new vitality to the defense and expansion of Islam. Since the fifteenth century, the Ottomans showed precisely this vitality, harnessed to an Islamic zeal that had carried Islam to the very gates of Vienna. All the Muslim subjects of the Ottoman house saw themselves as participants and beneficiaries in this shared Islamic enterprise, and they drew no distinction between Arab and Turk.

But with the relative decline in Ottoman power, especially in the nineteenth century, the foundations of this symbiosis began to weaken. The great Ottoman carpet was being rolled up at both ends: by Europe's Great Powers, locked in imperial rivalry, and by the discontented Christian subjects of Ottoman rule in Europe, whose struggles for independence took a nationalist form. The Ottomans embarked on a succession of Westernizing reforms but eventually lost their footing in the Balkans, the Caucasus, North Africa, and Egypt. As the Empire dwindled, so did the confidence of its remaining subjects, and some discontent even appeared in the remaining Arabic-speaking provinces of the Empire, in Arabia and the Fertile Crescent—a discontent that would come to be known as the Arab "awakening."[7]

Many controversies still surround the nature and extent of this discontent, but it is generally agreed to have drawn upon two sources. First, there were the minority communities of Arabic-speaking Christians, much influenced by European currents, who worked to transform Arabic into a medium of missionary work and modern learning. From about the middle of the nineteenth century, their efforts did much to kindle interest in secular Arabic belles-lettres, through adaptation of Arabic to the modern conventions of the press, the novel, and the theater. The Arabic literary revival, centered in Beirut, did not translate immediately into Arab nationalism. But it did argue for the existence of a secular Arab culture, to which Christians and Muslims had supposedly contributed in equal measure. By elaborating upon this shared Arab legacy, the Christian minority sought to erode the prejudice of Muslim majority and to win Christians their full equality as fellow Arabs.

Arabism also arose from a second source. Rivalries had always absorbed the Arabic-speaking Muslim elite, especially in the keen competition over appointments to Ottoman government positions and bureaucratic sinecures. The grievances of those passed over for such spoils by Ottoman governors occasionally turned into the demand that Istanbul accord the Arabic-speaking provinces more autonomy in the conduct of their own affairs. As the twentieth century opened, this Arabism spread to all the major cities of the Ottoman Empire where Arabic was spoken, but it centered upon Damascus, where its adherents began to organize. While the Arabism of Muslims resembled that of Christians in its pride of language, it differed fundamentally in its deep attachment to Islam. It appealed to Muslims by arguing that the greatness of the Arabs resided in their privileged understanding of Islam. The Arabs, acting in the name of Islam, had created a great empire and civilization, and only the Arabs could restore Islam to its pristine grandeur. There was nothing secular about this assertion of Arab genius, which became closely associated with Islamic apologetics and reformism.

This "Arab awakening," Christian and Muslim, failed to produce a trenchant social criticism or a truly modern language of politics. Ultimately it would defeat itself by its apologetic defense of tradition and religion.[8] But it did go far enough to shake the confidence of some Arabic-speakers in the legitimacy of Ottoman rule. A few pamphleteers even tried to conjure up Ottoman fears (and foreign subsidies) by publishing tracts in the name of an "Arab movement." Most of these appeared in Europe, and some journals of opinion in Europe's capitals began to debate "the Arab question." The debate was premature. In 1907 the English traveler Gertrude Bell gave the commonplace assessment of these stirrings:

> Of what value are the pan-Arabic associations and inflammatory leaflets that they issue from foreign printing presses? The answer is easy: they are worth nothing at all. There is no nation of Arabs; the Syrian merchant is separated by a wider gulf from the Bedouin than he is from the Osmanli, the Syrian country is inhabited by Arabic speaking races all eager to be at each other's throats, and only prevented from fulfilling their natural desires by the ragged half fed soldier who draws at rare intervals the Sultan's pay.[9]

Yet by the eve of World War I, Arabism did begin to take a more palpable form against the two challenges of Turkification and Zionism.

Turkification threatened the cultural status quo. The Turkish-speaking subjects of the Ottoman Empire had been exposed to European-style nationalism, largely through its penetration into the Balkans. Turkish-speaking Muslims then began to construct for themselves a new identity as Turks, a trend strengthened by Western philologists and romantics who sought to establish the greatness of an ancient "Turanian" civilization.[10] As the Ottoman Empire stumbled, Ottoman authorities attempted to give the polyglot Empire more the character of a European nation-state by enforcing the use of Turkish at the expense of other languages, including Arabic. This policy, never fully implemented, caused some apprehension in the Arab provinces on the eve of World War I, and may have helped to rally the supporters of cultural Arabism to a political purpose.

Zionist settlement in Palestine threatened the political status quo. Ottoman authorities tolerated the influx of Jewish immigration in the belief that it would ultimately benefit the Empire, as it had in successive waves since the Spanish Inquisition. But not all of the sultan's subjects concurred, since this latest wave of immigrants saw the land on which they were settling not merely as a refuge but as a state in the making. As the pace of Zionist immigration and settlement increased, their immediate neighbors grew apprehensive about the looming possibility of dispossession. From the turn of the century, Ottoman policy toward Zionism became a matter of growing debate and criticism in the Arabic press.[11]

Arabism thus arose from a growing unease about the pace and direction of change. Yet, while the Ottoman Empire lasted, this Arabism did not develop into full-fledged nationalism. Its adherents pleaded for administrative decentralization, not Arab independence, and they had no vision of a post-Ottoman order. They imagined a solution in the form of an accountable government, and professed a vague admiration for the liberal democracies of the West, especially of France and England, although they had an imperfect grasp of the meaning behind the slogan of "liberty." Above all, they were practical. They did not indulge in dreams of Arab power. Their grievances, in the words of a critic of later Arab nationalism, "were local and specific; they related to the quality of government services or to the proper scope of local administration; and those who sought redress for such grievances were mostly men well known in their communities, able perhaps to conduct a sober constitutional opposition but not to entertain grandiose, limitless ambitions."[12] On the eve of World War I, they were probably still in the minority, outnumbered by Arabic-speaking Muslims and Christians who raised no doubt about the legitimacy of Ottoman rule, and even stood prepared to defend it.

The Arab Nation and the European Empires

World War I forced a choice upon the adherents of Arabism. After some hesitation, the Ottoman Empire entered the European war on the side of Germany, prompting Britain and France to fan every ember of dissent in the Empire. The Allies held out the prospect of independence for something they called "the Arab nation," and they eventually found a partner in a local potentate of Mecca, the Sharif Husayn. The Sharif had an ambitious vision of a vast "Arab kingdom" for his family, and in 1915 he secured commitments from Britain regarding its future independence and frontiers. In 1916, he finally raised the standard of revolt against Ottoman rule.

The Arab Revolt that began in Arabia had little to do with the Arabism that had emerged in the Fertile Crescent. It more faithfully expressed the dynastic ambition of the Sharif, and the enthusiasm for British guns and gold among Arabia's desert tribes. However, the Sharif's sons, the Emirs Faysal and Abdallah, also established contacts with the existing Arab societies in Damascus, and the revolt recruited dissident Arab officers who had deserted Ottoman ranks. These officers had attended Ottoman military academies, where they had imbibed the idea of the army as the "school of the nation" from the German officers who had trained and advised them. The revolt thus made for a volatile mix, whose diverse participants dreamed the different dreams of Arab kingship, desert anarchy, liberal constitutionalism, and military dictatorship. While the revolt lasted, they suspended their differences in the drive for independence.

In 1918, as the Ottomans retreated before British arms in Palestine, the

Arab Revolt culminated in triumph when Faysal led his followers into Damascus and there formed an "Arab Government." In 1919, he went to Versailles, where he asked that "the Arabic-speaking peoples of Asia" be recognized as "independent sovereign peoples," and that "no steps be taken inconsistent with the prospect of an eventual union of these areas under one sovereign government." Finally, in 1920, a "General Syrian Congress" declared the independence of a "United Kingdom of Syria" including the entire Levant, and proclaimed Emir Faysal king. From Damascus, an "Iraqi Congress" also proclaimed Iraq independent, under the kingship of the Emir Abdallah.[13]

An Arab nation had entered the game of nations, and from the outset, its members made far-reaching claims which ran up against other claims. Most notably, Britain had made wartime commitments to France and the Zionist movement. The first, the so-called Sykes-Picot agreement, secretly recognized most of the northern Levant as a zone of French privilege; the second, the Balfour Declaration, publicly supported a Jewish national home in Palestine. Britain also had strategic and economic interests in the territories demanded by the Sharif Husayn and his sons. The contradictory claims were sorted out in April 1920, at the San Remo conference, where Britain and France settled on the division of occupied Ottoman territory, which they planned to administer as separate League of Nations mandates. On the basis of these agreements, French forces drove Faysal and his followers from Damascus in a brief battle in July, and imposed French rule on Syria that would last for a quarter century. At the same time, Britain began to fulfill its commitment under the Balfour Declaration by opening Palestine to more extensive Zionist immigration and settlement. Arab violence against Jews first broke out in April, presaging the strife between Arab and Jew that would become a fixture of the British mandate for Palestine. In June, a widespread insurrection against the British broke out in Iraq, which the British suppressed by force.

Increasingly, Arab nationalists charged that Ottoman rule had been replaced by British and French imperialism, government even more alien than its Muslim predecessor. Britain did move to compensate the leaders of the Arab Revolt in 1921: it appointed Faysal as the king of Iraq in expanded borders, and carved an emirate of Transjordan out of the Palestine mandate, which it then exempted from Zionist immigration and turned over to Abdallah. But the Arab nationalists now nursed a deep grievance against Britain and France over the partition of the territories they wanted and the denial of independence in Palestine and Syria, which they believed had been promised to them. Arab nationalism, once inspired by the West's liberalism, began to redefine itself as a negation of its imperialism.

The Arab nationalist lament against the arbitrary partition of the Fertile Crescent had much validity. None of the new states was commensurate with a political community. Syria, Lebanon, Iraq, Transjordan, Palestine, Lebanon—these names derived from geography or classical history, and their borders largely reflected the imperial jostling for strategic position or oil.[14] Only the idea of Lebanon had some historical depth, since the Maronite Christians of Mount Lebanon maintained a strong sense of separate identity and had achieved some autonomy even in the late Ottoman period. But the Maronites were too few, and the borders of Lebanon drawn in 1920 by the French (at Maronite insistence) included large numbers of Muslims. Maronites would later attempt to manufacture the idea of a Lebanese nation, distinguished by a seafaring commerce and culture dating back to the Phoenicians—safely before the rise of any of Lebanon's contemporary religions. But the Maronites failed to persuade the Muslims in Lebanon that the idea of "eternal Lebanon" expressed anything more than the sectarian solidarity of the Maronites themselves. Half of Lebanon's population regarded their forced inclusion in Lebanon as still another trick of imperialism, as cruel as the other tricks the Arab nationalists thought had been played against them in 1920.[15]

But the idea of an Arab nation seemed just as arbitrary to most of its supposed members. It satisfied the makers and backers of the Arab Revolt, who regrouped in Iraq after their flight from Syria, and there established another Arab nationalist state. But in the fragmented societies of the Fertile Crescent, few persons were accustomed to regarding themselves as Arabs. As in Ottoman times, most continued to classify themselves by religion, sect, and genealogy. They were Muslims or Christians, Sunnis or Shi'ites, Maronites or Druzes, members of this or that clan, family, tribe, village, or urban quarter. They did not wish to be ruled by foreigners from over the sea, but neither did they desire to be ruled by strangers from across the desert, even if those strangers spoke Arabic. During the war, some of them had made their own diplomacy, to secure separate independence.[16] After the war, their allegiance proved difficult to win, as the Arab nationalists soon discovered. The Arab nationalist state under Faysal in Damascus proved to be chaotic, and his subsequent reign in Iraq rested on the bayonets of the British. In correspondence, the British called Faysal "The Great Imposed," a stranger to his subjects, who had been awarded a fragmented polity in arbitrary borders. The Arab nationalists in Faysal's entourage dreamed of a great Arab state, but it was all they could do to keep together the would-be Arabs whom they ruled.

Faced with masses of people who had not chosen to be Arabs, the Arab nationalists developed a doctrine that denied them any other choice. Between the wars, the Arab nationalists progressively discarded the French idea of the nation as a voluntary contract, formed by individuals to secure their liberty. Increasingly their nation resembled the German *Volk*, a natural nation above all human volition, bound by the mystery of language and lore. Only the unity of this nation could restore its greatness, even if the price of unity meant the surrender of freedom.

This struggle had to be conducted not only against imperialism, but also against the would-be Arabs themselves. Not all of them were eager to be Arabs, and some openly professed to be something else. In such instances, Arab nationalism assigned itself the task of educating them to an Arab identity, preferably by persuasion but if necessary by compulsion. According to Sati' al-Husri, Arab nationalism's first true ideologue and a confidant of Faysal,

> Every person who speaks Arabic is an Arab. Everyone who is affiliated with these people is an Arab. If he does not know this or if he does not cherish his Arabism, then we must study the reasons for his position. It may be the result of ignorance—then we must teach him the truth. It may be because he is unaware or deceived—then we must awaken him and reassure him. It may be a result of selfishness—then we must work to limit his selfishness.[17]

This ominous passage presaged the drift of Arab nationalism away from the liberal model of a voluntary community. "We can say that the system to which we should direct our hopes and aspirations is a Fascist system," wrote al-Husri in 1930, raising the slogan of "solidarity, obedience, and sacrifice."[18] The idea of the nation as an obedient army immediately appealed to the army itself, especially its officers. It went hand in hand with a growing militarism, and the belief that only the armed forces could rise above the "selfishness" of the sect and clan, enforcing discipline on the nation. Iraq pioneered this trend. The country became independent in 1930, and joined the League of Nations in 1932. Less than a year later, the army conducted a massacre of the Assyrian (Nestorian Christian) minority, accused of infidelity to the Arab cause. In 1936, a coup d'état established a thinly veiled military dictatorship, in the name of national unity. Finally, in 1941, a junta of colonels led Iraq into a war of "liberation" with Britain, which it promptly lost, and in the course of which the nationalists inspired a pogrom against the Jews of Baghdad.

Mistreated minorities, military strongmen, lost battles—in retrospect, Iraq's early experience of independence anticipated an entire era of Arab nationalism. Yet this nationalism, and its extravagant extrapolation, pan-Arabism, gained immensely in popularity from in the 1930s. Accelerated migration from desert encampment to settled town, from village to city, began to unloose primordial ties, diminishing resistance to nationalist ideology. With the expansion of education, Arab nationalist pedagogues indoctrinated masses of young people, from primary school through university. The spread of literacy and the growth of the Arabic press brought the message of Arab nationalism into every classroom, clubhouse, and coffee shop. In the public arena, Arab nationalism gradually achieved a firm hold on political discourse, and all other loyalties became unspeakable.[19]

It also began to spread beyond the Fertile Crescent, to include first Egypt, then North Africa. Arabic-speaking Africa had come under foreign rule earlier than Arabic-speaking Asia. France began colonization of Algeria in 1830 and occupied Tunisia in 1881, while Britain occupied Egypt in 1882. In every instance there had been resistance to foreign rule, but it had been formulated as local patriotism, in most instances strongly tinged with Islam. Until the 1930s, few Egyptians saw themselves as Arabs, and the earliest Arab nationalists did not include Egypt in their vision.[20] In North Africa, a large proportion of the population spoke Berber, and resistance to foreign rule took an Islamic form, since only Islam united its inhabitants. However, no definition of the Arab nation based on language could long exclude Arabic-speaking Africa, and the very geography of imperialism created a potential bond of solidarity between the Algerian and the Syrian, the Egyptian and the Iraqi. In time, a growing number of Egyptians and North Africans began to see themselves as Arabs. Paradoxically, the empires of Britain and France linked together Arabic-speaking lands that had enjoyed few if any organic ties in Ottoman times, inspiring for the first time the idea of an Arab world from the Atlantic Ocean to the Gulf.

At the time, the division of this world did not yet seem permanent, and the message of Arab nationalism, calling for the full independence and unity of all Arabs everywhere, did not seem completely contrived. After World War II, weary Britain and France began to divest themselves of the more troublesome portions of their empires. Syria, Lebanon, and Transjordan became independent. Egypt and Iraq, their independence effectively revoked by Britain during the war, began to renegotiate the terms of British withdrawal. Full independence for the great majority of Arabs seemed only a matter of time. It would be acquired piecemeal by individual states, but Arab nationalists hoped that an Arab commonwealth might emerge from this fluid situation. Elaborate plans for Arab unification proliferated.

But these plans quickly ran aground. By now each state possessed its own ruling elite, bureaucracy, flag, and anthem. Their proposals and counterproposals, for "Fertile Crescent unity," "Greater Syria," and "Arab federation," were schemes for self-aggrandizement.[21] After much Arab negotiation and British mediation, the independent Arab states established the Arab League in 1945, a compromise that recognized the distinct sovereignty of each of them. In the end, independence did not alter the map drawn by imperialism. The member states of the Arab League promised to assist one another, but none would sacrifice their prerogatives of sovereignty, which the Arab League charter meticulously upheld. In particular, Article 8 of the charter upheld the principle of nonintervention: "Each member state shall respect the systems of government established in the other member states and regard them as the exclusive concern of those states. Each shall pledge to abstain from any action calculated to change established systems of government."[22]

Yet the article of nonintervention, while sanctifying the status quo, pointed to its greatest weakness. Not all of these states and their rulers commanded the unencumbered allegiance of their citizens and subjects. By their own rhetoric, they admitted as much. They invariably justified their actions as advancing a larger Arab purpose, even when they were pursuing their own parochial purposes. Especially in the Fertile Crescent, states created without reason lacked the confidence to openly invoke reasons of state. The paradox could pass so long as Arab nationalism remained a loose mélange of slogans about independence and solidarity. But a growing number of intellectuals and officers, abhorring ambiguity, turned their Arab nationalism into a rigorous doctrine. They saw the Arab nationalism professed by rulers and states as posturing and began to argue the need for revolution. Their moment came when the fragile Arab order stumbled over Israel.

Arab Revolution

The rhetorical gap turned into a chasm in 1948, after the United Nations authorized the partition of Palestine into two states, one Jewish and one Arab. When the neighboring Arab states moved against Israel in 1948, they claimed to be fighting in concert, to uphold their brotherly commitment to the Arabs of Palestine. In fact they did just the opposite: each waged its own war to defend its own interests, each sought a separate modus vivendi with Israel. It was a hard-fought war, which ended with Israel in possession of even more territory than had been allotted to her by the United Nations, and with the Arab states as reluctant hosts to seven hundred thousand Arab refugees.

The events of 1948, like those of 1920, shifted the ground from beneath Arab nationalism. While the Arab states negotiated fitfully with Israel, disaffected intellectuals and officers began to stir. The intellectuals, exemplified by the Syrian historian Constantin Zurayk, leveled withering criticism against the conduct of the war, and made it difficult for Arab states to present 1948 as anything less than a rout. Then the officers moved, charging they had been stabbed in the back by politicians and senior commanders. Syria's old-guard nationalist leadership was turned out by a military coup in 1949; two more coups followed that year, with another in 1952, and yet another in 1954. Abdallah, who in 1949 renamed his kingdom Jordan, and in 1950 annexed the adjacent remnant of Arab Palestine as his "West Bank," was assassinated in 1951 for his dealings with Israel. The monarchy barely held on. In 1952, a group of "free officers," invoking Egypt's failure in the Palestine war and allegations of official corruption in its conduct, overturned the monarchy in a bloodless coup and established a revolutionary republic. By 1954, one of these officers, Gamal Abdul Nasser, had emerged as undisputed leader. In 1958, a sanguinary coup by more "free officers" destroyed the Iraqi monarchy, and the regicides established a "popular republic."

Arab nationalism, which became "anti-imperialist" after 1920, became "revolutionary" after 1948. The Palestine war had demonstrated that the Arabs, despite their formal independence, remained politically disunited, militarily weak, and economically underdeveloped. The failure could still be blamed on imperialism, and much Arab nationalist thought went into drawing images of a global conspiracy that allegedly implanted Israel to assure the West's continuing domination of the Arabs. But some intellectuals also began to suggest the existence of intrinsic weaknesses in Arab culture and society, arguing that these had made the task of the Zionists easier. The new champions of Arab nationalism, fiery young colonels, now promised a social revolution that would overcome these weaknesses and propel the Arab world to unity, power, and prosperity. In the spirit of the times, they usually defined this revolution as socialism—or, more precisely, Arab socialism, lest it be alleged that the changes were not authentically Arab in inspiration. Arab nationalism no longer meant only literary revival and anti-imperialism. It meant land reform, extensive nationalization, and five-year plans, all in the name of "the revolution." And if, in their new lexicon, Arab nationalists cast themselves as "revolutionaries," then their opponents could only be "reactionaries."[23]

The new dispensation took two parallel forms that became known as Nasserism and Ba'thism. Nasserism married revolutionary nationalism to the personality cult of Gamal Abdul Nasser, who enjoyed immense prestige in the Arab world after he pulled a political victory from the combined British, French, and Israeli attack on Suez in 1956. Nasserism combined a program of socialist-like reform with the idea that Egypt under the charismatic Nasser constituted the very heart of the Arab world, and had the resources and will to lead all Arabs to unity. A strong streak of pragmatism ran through Nasserism, which evolved from day to day while Nasser held power. It was too makeshift to constitute an ideology, and relied more on Nasser's warm glow than on any systematic doctrine. And while Nasser gave first priority to Egypt's Arab character, at times he made Egypt out to be Muslim, African, or Afro-Asian—whatever served his particular purpose. But it was precisely that ambiguity which made Nasser all things to all Arabs, and permitted Egypt to imagine herself to be the bridge of Arab nationalism, linking the Arabs of Asia and Africa in the march to unity.

Ba'thism tended to be more ideologically stringent, if only because its founders were Sorbonne-educated Syrians, mostly teachers hailing from minority sects, who had filled their spare time with academic debates and Nietzsche, Fichte, and Houston Stewart Chamberlain. They chose to call themselves the Ba'th, meaning resurrection, and they were "revolutionaries" as a matter of principle. Their constitution, adopted in 1947, announced that their goals could not be achieved "except by means of revolution and struggle. To rely on slow evolution and to be satisfied with a partial and superficial reform is to threaten these aims and to conduce to their failure and loss." The first of these goals was the creation of a single Arab state, since all differences among Arabs were "accidental and unimportant. They will all disappear with the awakening of Arab consciousness." And they regarded socialism as "a necessity which emanates from the depth of Arab nationalism itself."[24] As an early member attested, the Ba'th demonstrated all the characteristics of an ideological party: "Their interpretation of events was almost identical, but they did not trust one another; they loved the people, but hated the individual; they held the whole sacred, but they despised the parts."[25] The Ba'th spread its influence by penetrating the junior officer corps and eventually acquired power through military coups in both Syria and Iraq. The usual pattern was for the military wing of the local party to purge the civilian wing and install a military dictatorship, under the Ba'th slogan of "unity, freedom, socialism."[26]

Nasser and the Ba'th carried Arab nationalism to the summit of its achievements. Nasser's early gambles paid off because he was the first Arab nationalist leader who was positioned to play foreign powers against one another in a game he called "positive neutralism." When the Americans refused to finance the Aswan Dam, the Soviets came to his rescue. When his nationalization of the Suez Canal and backing of the Algerian uprising provoked an attack by Britain and France (in league with Israel), the United States came to his rescue. The Arab world, glued to these maneuvers through the now ubiquitous radio transistor, stood breathless before Nasser's high-wire act. The Ba'th in Syria longed to join it and pushed for negotiations with Nasser over unity. In 1958, the talks culminated in the birth of the United Arab Republic—a union of Egypt and Syria, offered to the Arab world as the first step toward a general Arab union. The names of Egypt and Syria disappeared from the map, replaced by a "southern region" and a "northern region." Arab nationalism reached its high-water mark during Nasser's first visit to Damascus, where he was greeted by wildly enthusiastic crowds. Other Arab leaders trembled as "Nasserists" filled the streets of their capitals to clamor for their long-awaited Bismarck. Lebanon invited American troops to stem the tide; Jordan accepted British forces. No Arab state seemed capable of withstanding the march of Arab unity on its own.

But in the end, it was the United Arab Republic that succumbed. The marriage of Nasser and the Ba'th turned into a struggle for domination within the camp of Arab nationalism. In this uneven contest, the Egyptians ran Syria like a colony—and a badly run colony at that. The union did not release some pent-up potential which only the combining of Egypt and Syria could tap. Quite the opposite: the union threatened to kill all productive initiative, especially in Syria, through the imposition of "Arab socialism." In 1961, a Syrian coup ousted Nasser's viceroy from Damascus and declared the union finished. The breakup demonstrated the salience of differences far too deep to be blown away by blithe slogans. There would be more negotiations between Nasser and the Ba'th in 1963, and more unity schemes and treaties. But there would never be a repeat of the United Arab Republic.[27]

In retrospect, the collapse of the Egyptian-Syrian union in 1961 marked the beginning of the long slide of Arab nationalism. The following year, Nasser contributed to its undoing by his massive intervention on behalf of the "revolutionary" side in Yemen's civil war. Everything Egypt did in Yemen, including aerial bombing and napalming, had the opposite of the intended effect. A British journalist who watched the Egyptians at work in Yemen was amazed by their ignorance and arrogance:

> It was one of the more piquant experiences of my post-revolutionary stay in Sanaa to be hailed by most of them with a chummy affability that implied as clearly as any words that they and I were somehow in this thing together as embattled representatives of civilisation in the midst of savagery. "What can you do with these people?" they would often laugh, in tones of vastly superior deprecation, "They are not like us, you see...." Having come directly from British colonial Aden I recognised the symptoms all the more easily. Creeping imperialism is a catching disease, and those Egyptians were only a step away from clapping their hands together and shouting, "Boy!" when they wanted service.[28]

In Yemen, as in Syria, vast differences overwhelmed any remote similarity, leaving Arab to wage war against Arab in a spirit of mutual incomprehension.

Nationalist theory had promised that unity would bring liberation from foreigners, but in the hands of actual practitioners it had become a whip of domination, wielded by some Arabs over others. The number of Arabs bearing its scars began to grow, as did the disillusionment. The Arabs, wrote one Syrian, were "like the inhabitants of an island who have been promised that the ship of deliverance will soon arrive. They have buried their tools and packed their meager belongings; but when the ship arrives, it is a slave boat."[29] The will to believe still remained strong in some quarters, but an edge of doubt began to show. Arab nationalism's supply of persuasive words began to dwindle. Its champions responded by making more frequent use of the persuasive prisons of Abu Za'bal and Tura near Cairo, Mezze in Damascus, and the cellars of the Nihayyah Palace in Baghdad.

The crisis finally broke in 1967. The Arabs may well have blundered into war with Israel that June, but once they were in the thick of it, they expected more than in 1948. Most assumed that they had been strengthened, not weakened, by nearly two decades of Nasser and the Ba'th, social revolution, and the militarization of politics, all under the banner of Arab nationalism and the struggle against Israel. Instead, they got less: a truly ignominious defeat, delivered in six days. Its territorial consequences included the Israeli occupation of East Jerusalem, the West Bank, and Gaza—all densely populated by Arabs—and of the Sinai and the Golan, two geographic buffers that had kept Israel at a distance from Cairo and Damascus. The defeat represented nothing less than "the Waterloo of pan-Arabism."[30] When Nasser offered to step down, the crowds filled the streets to demand that he continue as their leader. Through years of pounding indoctrination, Nasser and the Ba'th had managed to silence every other voice, and many only understood and spoke the limited language of Arab nationalism. But as defeat worked its way deep into the collective psyche, two other voices would be raised in opposition to Arab nationalism. One spoke the language of allegiance to individual states. The other spoke of loyalty to a universalist Islam.[31]

The Triumph of the State

Since their creation, individual Arab states had never hesitated to give priority to their separate interests. Yet they had been persuaded by their perceived lack of legitimacy to pledge formal fidelity to the Arab nation, and thus risked being dragged into crises generated by other Arab states, or being accused of breaking Arab ranks for staying out. As 1967 proved, however, such crises could deteriorate quickly into war, and exact a steep price in lives, territory, and prestige. Many of these states already lumbered under immense economic burdens. They did not have the means to assume the burdens of their neighbors, especially the weighty load of Palestine. Even mighty Egypt could no longer assume the sole custodianship of the Arab cause (an Egypt that sent tens of thousands of troops to defend the Arab cause as far away as Yemen, yet had difficulty feeding its own people at home). If these states were ever to set their own priorities, they would have to openly justify their separate existence, and demand the primary loyalties of their citizens and subjects.

Paradoxically, Egypt led the way again, this time under Anwar Sadat. Sadat launched an attack against Israel in October 1973, but this time Egypt fought a strictly Egyptian war for the return of the Israeli-occupied Sinai. Although Egypt waged the war in tandem with Syria, it quickly broke with Syria in the war's aftermath. By the decade's end, Sadat had given Israel a peace treaty in return for the Sinai. Sadat's recognition of Israel, his reliance on the United States, and his economic liberalization turned all the assumptions of Arab nationalism on their head—and Sadat offered no apologies for doing so. Instead, he made an explicit case for Egypt's right to chart its own course and address its own problems first. Sadat paid for his policies with his life, and Egypt was briefly ostracized for its peace with Israel. But other Arab states cautiously followed suit. More often than not, they now justified their choices by invoking Syrian, Jordanian, Saudi, or Iraqi national interests, not Arab national destiny. And by legitimizing themselves as states, despite their origins in imperial map rooms, they came that much closer to legitimizing Israel, despite its origins in Zionist drawing rooms.

For the first time, it became possible to criticize the myths of Arabism, and to see the differences among Arabs not as "accidental" but as living realities, even deserving of respect. Lebanon's most prominent historian, Kamal Salibi, criticized Arab nationalism for "deluding the general run of the Arabs into believing that the political unity they had once experienced under Islam was in fact an Arab national unity which they have subsequently lost, or of which they have been deliberately robbed." This made it "difficult for them to properly accommodate to the political realities of the present." Salibi called on intellectuals to

discount the erroneous Arab nationalist view of this history as a united national march that went wrong at some point, and correctly assess it as the parochial history that it normally was: an account of so many different Arab regional experiences of one kind or another, fitting more or less into a general pattern. No Arab country today need feel any guilt about accepting its actual existence as a willful or unwillful departure from an Arab national historical norm. It is only when the Arabs succeed in ridding themselves of the highly idealized Arab nationalist vision of their past that they will be able to live together in the modern Arab world as a coherent political community whose various members relate to one another constructively and without reserve.[32]

After 1967, this once-surreptitious view could be pronounced openly, and laid the intellectual foundation for the growing self-confidence of individual states.

But that self-confidence rested as much on power as persuasion. Despite their difficulties on the battlefield, these states had mastered the technologies of domestic surveillance. The regimes realized that defeat left them vulnerable, and resolved to forestall any dissent by using these technologies to make the state ubiquitous. The approach largely worked. Unlike the defeat of 1948, which inaugurated a bout of instability, the even more humiliating defeat of 1967 marked the beginning of an era of unprecedented stability, even immobility. The flood of oil income that followed the 1973 war also permitted regimes to buy off dissent. The state had not only become legitimate, it had become omnipotent. In the words of one Syrian intellectual, "The cancerous growth of the state has been accompanied by the increasingly diminished power of everybody and everything else, especially what some Arab thinkers and leaders enjoy calling 'The People.'" As a consequence, "Arab society is on the whole cancelled out as a reality of political significance in the reckonings of all Arab regimes."[33]

By the time communism collapsed, the Arab lands had become the last preserve of protracted one-man rule, and so they remain today. The king of Jordan has reigned now for forty years, the king of Morocco for thirty-two years. Libya's leader made his coup twenty-four years ago. The chairman of the Palestine Liberation Organization (PLO) has held his title for twenty-four years. Syria's president has held power for twenty-two years. Iraq's ruler has held sway over the country for twenty-two years, the last fourteen as president. The emir of Kuwait has reigned for fifteen years, the king of Saudi Arabia for eleven years. Egypt's president has held office for twelve years. Not one of these states could be categorized as a democracy, although after 1967 they laid unprecedented claims to the loyalty of their citizens and subjects, and intruded upon virtually every aspect of society.

Only Lebanon, the perennial exception, proved incapable of enhancing its legitimacy and its power over society after 1967. In this birthplace of Arab nationalism, social peace had come to depend on an equilibrium between the myths of "eternal Lebanon" and "one Arab nation." The Maronites agreed to march in step with the Arabs, so long as they could carry the flag of Lebanon; the Muslims agreed to parade behind the flag of Lebanon, provided the parade marched to an Arab cadence. By this understanding, Lebanon would supply intellectual rationales for Arab nationalism; others would provide the soldiers for its battles. For a time the equilibrium held, and Lebanon established a quasi-democratic public order and a free-market economy.

In times of regional crisis, Lebanon did its duty by words, and managed to dodge war with Israel. But after 1967, Lebanon began to lose its balance. The Muslims, wracked by guilt, demanded that Lebanon finally take up the Arab burden of Palestine, and open its southern border to attacks against Israel. The Maronites, awed by Israel's example, thought they could turn the state of Lebanon into something comparable: a small powerhouse, armed to the teeth, defiant of the Arab world around it. In 1975, the situation exploded in civil war, and Lebanon virtually disappeared under a checkered map of militia fiefdoms, crisscrossed by green and red lines. The only lines that did not count were Lebanon's borders, and both Syria and Israel entered the fray. When Israel invaded Lebanon in 1982, it worked even more feverishly with its Lebanese allies to remake the country in its image, but to no avail. Since 1989, Syria has tried to do the same, with more resolve and success.

Aside from Lebanon, all other states exercised more confident power over their societies, and more independence from one another. Before 1967, Arab nationalism appeared to drain states of their legitimacy. After 1967, its slippage seemed to produce a surge of legitimacy that strengthened both states and incumbent regimes. This strength had severe limitations: Arab states still could not stand up to powerful external enemies such as Israel. But they could ward off interventions by one another, and enforce their will over their own societies with an almost ruthless efficiency.[34]

The Challenge of Islam

The voice of Islam also bid to fill the silence left by Arab nationalism. Arab nationalists had always regarded Islamic loyalty as a potential rival, and had tried to disarm it by incorporating Islam as a primary element in Arab nationalism. Even the Christians among them went out of their way to argue that Arab nationalism complemented rather than contradicted the Islamic loyalties still felt by so many Arabs. "The power of Islam," affirmed Michel Aflaq, the founding ideologue of the Ba'th and a Christian by birth, "has revived to appear in our days under a new form, that of Arab nationalism."[35]

But many Muslim Arabs saw this as a confidence game, and regarded Islam and any form of nationalism as mutually exclusive. For Sayyid Qutb, the Egyptian ideologue of Islam who was executed by Nasser in 1966, Arab nationalism signified "spiritual decadence." If the Prophet Muhammad had so wished, he "was no doubt capable of setting forth a movement of pan-

Arab nationalism in order to unify the strife-riven tribes of Arabia." Instead, he called all of mankind, Arab and non-Arab, to submit to God. The Arabs thus enjoyed no privileged standing in Islam, of the kind claimed by Arab nationalism: "God's real chosen people is the Muslim community, regardless of ethnic, racial, or territorial affiliation of its members." Reflecting on early Islam, Qutb concluded that the "sole collective identity Islam offers is that of the faith, where Arabs, Byzantines, Persians, and other nations and colors are equal under God's banner." During his police interrogation, Qutb announced that Arab nationalism had "exhausted its role in universal history."[36]

The Islamic critique of Arab nationalism extended beyond its theory to its practice. Arab nationalism had erred in breaking the primary bond of Islam during the Arab Revolt—a bond that linked Arab and Turk. The Arab nationalists betrayed their fellow Muslims in order to side with the British, who naturally betrayed them—a just reward for those who placed their trust in unbelievers. The Arab nationalists then compounded their error by abandoning reliance on God and his divine law, in order to become liberals, fascists, and socialists, in mimicry of foreign ideological fashion. Moreover, while they professed respect for the faith of Islam, they filled their prisons with the truly faithful, whom they accused of subversion for preaching the word of God. Who did not doubt that the rout by the Jews, and the falling of Jerusalem into Zionist hands, constituted a punishment for straying from God's path? Did not Israel itself prove the power of religion and state combined?

This brand of Islamic loyalty enjoyed an immense appeal among the members of two underclasses. The first was composed of Shi'ites, who formed a majority in Iraq and Bahrein, the largest single confessional community in Lebanon, and important minorities in Saudi Arabia and the Arab Gulf states. Arab nationalism acknowledged them as fellow Arabs, but it glorified precisely that "golden age" of Arab history that the Shi'ites mourned as disastrous, during which their heroes were martyred by the very same caliphs lionized in Arab nationalist historiography. In the present, the institutions of Shi'ite Islam, and even many Shi'ite families, straddled the divide between the Arab states and Iran, so that many Shi'ites regarded Arab nationalism as an artificial division, incompatible with the Arab-Persian symbiosis of contemporary Shi'ism. After Iran's revolution in 1979, many Shi'ites in Arab lands identified so strongly with its success that they declared their allegiance to the revolution's leader, Ayatollah Khomeini, and repudiated both Arab nationalism and loyalty to the individual states in which they lived. Lebanon's Hizbullah took this the furthest, professing absolute obedience to the leader of the Islamic revolution, and denouncing "the Arabs" for self-worship and their capitulation to Israel.

The other underclass consisted of the tens of millions of indigents who had abandoned the countryside and flooded into the cities, and whose lot worsened as populations grew and oil incomes fell. In the slums and bidonvilles of Cairo and Algiers, not only did the doctrines of Arab nationalism sound obsolete, but the promises of prosperity made by states also rang hollow to those in the grip of grinding poverty and unemployment. In growing numbers, the dispossessed gave their loyalty to Islamic movements that employed a more familiar vocabulary and called for the reinstitution of Islamic law as the panacea for all political, social, and economic ills. These Islamic movements were prepared to work within existing states, but only as matter of convenience. They professed loyalty only to Islamic law, and committed themselves to fight for its implementation wherever possible, even in distant Afghanistan, where many thousands of Arab Muslims fought as volunteers against Soviet forces and their "atheistic" Afghan clients. For these believers, their political community did not end at the border crossing of any state, or even where Arabic ceased to be spoken. It extended to any place where Islam reigned supreme or had to be defended.

In the void left by Arab nationalism after 1967, two ideas of community thus competed for primacy. On the one side stood those who argued that the inhabitants of any one state constituted a distinct people in a political sense. Regimes championed this idea, for it legitimized their claim to act solely in the interests of the state—identified increasingly with one ruling group or one ruler. On the other side stood those who believed that all Muslims constituted a universal political community, standing above any narrower political authority. This idea suited opposition movements, since it denied legitimacy to virtually all existing regimes. An immense gap separated these two visions, but their adherents agreed on one point: Arab nationalism had failed irredeemably, having either been too broad or too narrow to satisfy the quest for identity.

Arab Nationalism Adrift

And what of the remaining Arab nationalists? After 1967, their numbers and influence steadily dwindled, except among intellectuals. Many intellectuals actually did live a pan-Arab reality. They wrote in Arabic for an audience that stretched "from the Ocean to the Gulf," and published in pan-Arab journals that circulated just as widely. They jetted from capital to capital for conferences on the state of the Arabs. They had one foot (and sometimes both) in the West, where the freest Arabic press and publishing houses did their business. In this rarified atmosphere, the myths of Arab nationalism could still be sustained. For the most part, these intellectuals did not regard the defeat of 1967 as a failure of their idea, but rather as a failure of its implementation by others, who were criticized for not being sufficiently radical or sufficiently ruthless. Much of the Arab nationalist "self-criticism" after 1967 pushed even further toward advocacy of violent change. But intellectuals lacked an Arab Bismarck who would revive an idea whose time had come and nearly gone. Nasser had faltered, and in 1970 he died. The Ba'th in Syria, after more twists and turns, came to rest in 1970 under Hafiz al-Asad, a master of realpolitik who put Syria above all. For lack of better alternatives, Arab nationalists fixed their hopes first on the Palestinians, and finally on Saddam Hussein.

The Palestinians were a desperate choice, since they themselves had largely despaired of other Arabs. At the height of Nasser's powers, they had allowed themselves to believe in him, and to see him as their redeemer. Nasser also prompted the creation of the PLO in 1964, under the auspices of the Arab League. But even before the Arab armies collapsed in 1967, Palestinians had begun to transform the PLO into an instrument of their own. The dominant Fatah component had no pan-Arab pretensions. Fatah demanded the moral support of the Arab states, and even extraterritorial zones of operation, especially along Israel's frontiers. It was prepared to fight to assure the independence of these bastions. But it promoted no message of Arab revolution, and it gave first priority to the establishment of a Palestinian "entity," presumably a state, which would fit into the existing Arab state system.[37]

But other Palestinian groups took a different course, announcing they would work to topple the "petty bourgeois regimes" of the Arab states as a stage in their struggle to liberate Palestine. This was the pan-Arab promise of the so-called Arab Nationalists Movement and its most flamboyant offspring, the Popular Front for the Liberation of Palestine (PFLP), both founded by students at the American University of Beirut. Their high-strung rhetoric and hijackings made them the heroes of many Arab intellectuals who, like their New Left contemporaries in the West, demanded "revolution" now.

The fedayeen, the Palestinian guerrillas in the rock-strewn hills opposite Israel, became the symbols of this struggle. Living on the edge and citing Mao and Guevara, they were celebrated in poetry and song by the pan-Arab intellectuals. But although the fedayeen sought to imitate the methods of guerrilla warfare that had succeeded elsewhere, they completely failed to liberate any part of Palestine or the Arab world, and they provoked Jordan's ruthless suppression in 1970. As Jean Genet recorded, the Palestinian "revolution" could be summed up in the phrase, "to have been dangerous for a thousandth of a second."[38] As the second passed, Arab nationalist enthusiasm for the Palestinian fringe waned, and even the fringe finally endorsed the mundane demand for a Palestinian state alongside Israel—one more Arab state, prepared to make one more compromise. "Our future is with Israel," the spokesman of the PFLP, Ghassan Kanafani, told a French academic in 1970—two years before his assassination by Israel. "Neither Europe, nor China, nor the Soviet Union, nor the Arab states, collectively or individually, are interested in us or would do anything decisive for us."[39] The Palestinian uprising that began in 1987 in the West Bank and Gaza was just that: a Palestinian uprising, relying not on the massive quantities of arms in Arab arsenals, but on stones and knives. The Palestinians would fight their own fight, in an effort to win the far more valuable sympathy of the West.

The choice of Saddam as the pan-Arab hero represented an even more desperate step. If anything, Saddam had done more than any modern Iraqi ruler to cultivate a specific Iraqi loyalty, drawing upon the legacy of ancient Mesopotamian civilization. In art, architecture, and poetry, the state encouraged the use of Mesopotamian motifs, and it lavished funds upon archaeological digs and restorations. Since no loyalties had survived from antiquity (which well predated the Arab conquest), all Iraqis could be accommodated by the Mesopotamian myth—Arabs and Kurds, Sunnis and Shi'ites. After Saddam blundered into war with Iran in 1980, Iraq billed herself as defender of the eastern Arab flank against the Persian hordes—all the better to justify the demand for war loans from Gulf Arab states. But Saddam was no ardent pan-Arabist, and in 1982 he dismissed the pan-Arab vision as an idea whose time had passed:

> The question of linking unity to the removal of boundaries is no longer acceptable to present Arab mentality. It could have been acceptable ten or twenty years ago. We have to take into consideration the change which the Arab mind and psyche have undergone.

> We must see the world as it is.... The Arab reality is that the Arabs are now twenty-two
> states, and we have to behave accordingly. Therefore, unity must not be imposed, but
> must be achieved through common fraternal opinion. Unity must give strength to its
> individual partners, not cancel their national identity.[40]

Those twenty-two states, on which unity "must not be imposed," included
Kuwait.

In 1990, Saddam's Iraq invaded Kuwait, declaring it a province of
Iraq. Possession of Kuwait would have filled the Iraqi treasury in per-
petuity (a treasury that held a cash reserve of $30 billion back in 1980
but groaned under a debt of more than $100 billion a decade later).
Significantly, Iraq did not formally justify its invasion as an act of Arab
nationalist unification. Iraq claimed that Kuwait belonged properly to
the state of Iraq, and that the annexation asserted an Iraqi legal right,
not an Arab moral claim. But Arab nationalists seized upon Saddam
as though he were a reincarnation of Nasser, and an improvement at
that, for being far more reckless and ruthless. While he lacked Nasser's
charm, he had oil, missiles, nerve agents, and nuclear potential—power,
he hinted, that would be put at the service of all the Arabs. He would be
their sword, much like the four giant swords he had cast for his victory
arches in Baghdad, dedicated at a ceremony in 1989 during which he
paraded upon a white horse.[41]

Hichem Djaït, the preeminent Tunisian historian, exemplified the euphoria of the intellectuals. In 1978, in a sober mood, he wrote that "it would
not be healthy to pin all hopes on achieving some sort of absolute unity,"
and that an attempt by any Arab state to use its power for that purpose
would be "not only dangerous but doomed to failure." No Arab state had
sufficient power to effect such unity, and no Arab could "entertain the notion that America, Europe, or Russia would allow so cohesive a unity to be
founded in the heart of the Old World."[42] The analysis makes perfect sense
to this day, yet Djaït threw it to the winds after Saddam annexed Kuwait.
Thanks to Saddam Hussein, he declared, "a new perspective is opening
up, that of unification. And Iraq is its pole and motor." If that meant war,
or even defeat, it still represented a start:

> I don't have to tell you, as Europeans, that your nations were born out of wars. In an-
> nexing Kuwait, Saddam Hussein has entered the dynamics of history. He was trying
> to make sure of a source of wealth for himself, material means. In addition, he was
> undertaking the beginning of the unification of the Arab world. Sometimes legitimacy
> is more important than legality.[43]

"Our goal let us seek by the edge of the sword / For our goals we pursue are thus surely secured." This verse from Yaziji's ode of 1868 anticipated the preference for coercion that ran beneath the surface of Arab nationalism. Once its slogans no longer swayed millions, Arab nationalism gave up even the pretense of persuasion, to worship raw power. But Saddam had not amassed enough of that power; despite incredible military expenditures, Saddam's Iraq, like the Palestinian fedayeen a generation before, could only be "dangerous for a thousandth of a second." In the end, Djaït was right when he wrote in 1978 that an attempt by any Arab state to force unity would be "doomed to failure." In battle, the Iraqi "motor" of unification immediately broke down, and the scenes of surrendering Iraqi soldiers and burned-out armored columns recalled nothing so much as the defeat of 1967. And in the end, Saddam was right when he said in 1982 that the "Arab mind and psyche" would not accept the imposition of unity or the removal of existing borders. Most of the Arab states joined the international coalition against him, to uphold a state system which had become their own, even if it originated long ago in an imperial partition. And it was not only Arab governments which rejected the invasion: the publics in the Arab coalition states, according to polls, never took Saddam seriously as a pan-Arab savior.[44] The Arab nationalists called 1991 a defeat of the Arabs as a whole, analogous to 1967. But it was not analogous. In 1967, three Arab states were defeated, Arab territory was lost to foreign occupation, and all Arabs felt humiliated. In 1991, only Iraq was defeated, the sovereignty of an Arab state was restored, and millions of Arabs in Casablanca, Cairo, Damascus, and Riyadh considered themselves the victors.

In the war's aftermath, the United States, the Arab states, and Israel moved to translate that victory into a new regional order that would represent the ultimate undoing of Arab nationalism. That order, Middle Eastern rather than Arab, would include Israel as a legitimate state among states, to be recognized by all Arab states following a negotiation of peace and a definition of Israel's borders. The new order would also include Turkey, and perhaps other states that wished to define themselves as Middle Eastern. The rationale for the idea of the Middle East, made most fully by some Cairo intellectuals, argued that the Arab nationalist vision had become anachronistic. It was ideological in a postideological age, and it pressed for continuation of a costly Arab cold war against Israel, although the Arabs could no longer count on any outside support following the end of the superpower cold war. The moment had come to shift priorities to the domestic agenda of economic growth, lest the Arab world sink under the weight of its swollen populations. As the unification of Europe seemed to demonstrate, the economic future belonged to regional formations composed of many nations. These cooperated to promote economic growth and collective security, relieving economies of the massive burden of military expenditure. Water, arms control, the environment, trade, tourism—these and hundreds of other issues could not be negotiated to a resolution by the Arabs alone. Arab states were also Middle Eastern states, and while they belonged to an Arab state system, they also belonged to a Middle Eastern regional order. The shape and content of that order would evolve over time; a first step would be the progress of Arabs and Israelis at the negotiating table.[45]

The idea of the Middle East as a framework of identity faces many obstacles. It has nothing like the depth of the idea of Europe. The Middle East is a term that was first put into wide currency by an American naval strategist, who in 1902 described it as "an indeterminate area guarding a part of the sea route from Suez to Singapore."[46] It remains a colorless and inaccurate term, but the idea of an Arab nation "from the Ocean to the Gulf" is no older, and the term Middle East passed long ago into common Arabic usage. Its translation into an organizing principle of regional relations would constitute the final triumph of the real map over the imaginary map. All now depends on adding the last touches to the real map—the mutually agreed borders that will define Israel.

Talking Democracy and Islam

Is it true, as Fouad Ajami wrote, that this signifies the "end of Arab nationalism"? Do its defenders, mostly in exile, inhabit "fortresses at the end of the road that are yet to receive the dispatches that all is lost and the battle is over"?[47] Arab nationalism has suffered yet another blow, and has retreated almost to its point of origin, inspiring a few societies and clubs in Beirut, and some newspapers and journals published in Europe. With the exception of Libya under the mercurial Mu'ammar al-Qaddhafi, no Arab state makes any pretense of championing Arab nationalism. Yet Arab nationalists have not lost hope that from their last fortresses, they might return triumphant to recapture the center. Did that not happen in the case of Iran, where an old ayatollah, banished to one of the last bastions of Shi'ite Islam, launched a revolution and swept to power? The return of political Islam from purgatory holds out hope to Arab nationalists that they might do the same. Their desperate gamble on Saddam failed, but there are other avenues of return, provided Arab nationalism can adapt to the changing spirit of the times.

Arab nationalism has never been totally averse to such adaptation. The core of its message has never changed, and remains the existence of one Arab nation, destined to be drawn together in some form of unity, and poised antagonistically against an array of external enemies. But in the past, Arab nationalism borrowed supplementary themes and vocabulary from liberalism, fascism, socialism, radicalism, and messianism. As the division of the Arab world became ever more established and recognized, this borrowing achieved less, so that Arab nationalism became ever more utopian in its presumptions. But given the immense economic and social problems that face Arab societies, there are Arab nationalists who believe that any moment might become a revolutionary one. They intend to be there.

Since the "defeat" of 1991, they have bid to stay in the contest by presenting Arab nationalism as the natural ally of democracy and Islam. In theory, Arab nationalism never required a commitment to either, and in practice it showed a strong preference for revolutionary dictators and a strong aversion to Islamic movements. In their prime, Arab nationalists had no qualms about banning political parties and executing Islamic activists, all in the name of Arab unity. That they now have fixed upon democracy and Islam is less a matter of conviction than convenience. They understand that the prevailing order has two weaknesses. First, it is not democratic. Its aging rulers, in power now for a generation, are under pressure from a populace that gets younger every year, and that yearns for a measure of political participation. Second, it is not legitimate in the eyes of the growing numbers of frustrated people who have filled the ranks of Islamic movements. They genuinely yearn for a measure of authenticity, which they believe can only be achieved by the creation of an Islamic state under Islamic law. Somewhere in the Arab world it is possible that a regime might succumb to one of these weaknesses. Arab nationalists hope to join the resulting fracas and perhaps emerge triumphant by championing either democracy or Islam or both.

From a reading of the leading journals of pan-Arab opinion, it appears that the slogan of Islam has been more difficult to sing. There is plenty of common ground with Islamic discourse, most notably in the shared conviction that the Arab world still suffers from imperialist domination and that Israel's presence must not be normalized. But Islam already has its champions, in the form of well-organized and disciplined mass movements, and these express almost no interest in an alliance with the discredited stragglers of Arab nationalism. The lengthy round-table debates among Arab nationalist intellectuals about their possible relationship with Islamic movements are not reciprocated by the Islamists, whose leaders have no need for guidance from others, especially those who once persecuted them.[48] Still, some Arab nationalist intellectuals, from their perches in Europe and America, have offered their intellectual services to the defense of Islamic movements before Western opinion—something Islamic movements have been ill-prepared to undertake themselves. This has created the foundations of a relationship, although not all Arab nationalists are pleased or prepared to become apologists for varieties of Islam which, only a few years ago, they denounced with all their polemical force.

In contrast, the slogan of democracy is easier to appropriate. There are no mass democracy movements, and while virtually every Arab regime now claims to be committed to democracy, their late conversion often seems less credible than that of the Arab nationalists themselves. And so the pan-Arab journals brim with articles, conference proceedings, and study-group reports on the methods and means of promoting democracy in the Arab world. The assumption underlying this sudden enthusiasm for political pluralism and free elections is that if the people were only allowed to express themselves, they would endorse the Arab nationalist program: greater Arab unity, repudiation of the United States, and withdrawal from the Arab-Israeli peace process.[49] This belief flies in the face of the existing attitudinal surveys that show a continuing shift of self-identification away from the Arab nation and toward either the state or Islam. The results of those relatively free elections held to date show a similar polarization between the party of the state and the party of Islam. No Arab nationalist parties have been a factor in these elections. And while there is a constituency for some elements of the Arab nationalist program, it clearly belongs to Islamic parties, whose platforms incorporate similar repudiations of American hegemony and Israel, but are couched in the language of Islam.

In these circumstances, the commitment of Arab nationalists to democracy remains as superficial as that of the Islamists and the regimes. It is deployed as a slogan for mass mobilization against the existing order, and then as a shield against the revenge of a triumphant Islam. But even as the Arab nationalists speak of democracy, their eyes remain fixed on the horizon, awaiting the next Nasser, the next Saddam—the man who will save the Arabs from themselves and unite them. Even now, when the slogan of democracy is on everyone's lips, half of the Arab nationalist intellectuals in a recent survey believe that Arab unity can only be achieved by force, not by democracy.[50]

But Arab nationalism, having lost almost everything, now has little to lose, and its endorsement of democracy and Islam has been made in just that spirit. That Arab nationalism should now cast itself as the defender of freedom and the faith is ironic. The irony is not lost on the Arabs themselves, who have a strong sense of history and long memories. They discarded Arab nationalism because it failed to keep its promise of power, even as it exacted an exorbitant price in freedom and faith. It was not the only utopian ideology to do so at the time. Perhaps the more useful comparison, when the perspective is longer, may be between Arab nationalism and Soviet communism: two great myths of solidarity, impossible in their scale, deeply flawed in their implementation, which alternately stirred and whipped millions of people in a desperate pursuit of power through the middle of the twentieth century, before collapsing in exhaustion—and stranding their last admirers in the faculty lounges of the West.

Notes

1. Ibrahim al-Yaziji, "Tanabbahu wa istafiqu" ("Awake and Arise").
2. George Antonius, *The Arab Awakening: The Story of the Arab National Movement* (London: H. Hamilton, 1938).
3. Mahmoud Darwish, "Bitaqa hawiyya" ("Identity Card").
4. Nizar Qabbani, "La buda an asta'dhina al-watan" ("I Must Ask the Homeland's Permission").
5. Rupert Emerson, *From Empire to Nation: The Rise to Self-Assertion of Asian and African Peoples* (Cambridge, Mass.: Harvard University Press, 1960), 126.
6. See, for example, Ernest Gellner, *Nations and Nationalism* (Ithaca, N.Y.: Cornell University Press, 1983); and Elie Kedourie, *Nationalism*, 4th ed. (Oxford: Blackwell, 1993).
7. First assessed by George Antonius, *The Arab Awakening*. For subsequent accounts, see Zeine N. Zeine, *Arab-Turkish Relations and the Emergence of Arab Nationalism* (Beirut: Khayat's, 1958); Sylvia Haim, *Arab Nationalism: An Anthology* (Berkeley and Los Angeles: University of California Press, 1962), pp. 3–72 (introduction); Albert Hourani, *Arabic Thought in the Liberal Age 1798–1939* (London: Oxford University Press, 1962; reprint, Cambridge: Cambridge University Press, 1983); C. Ernest Dawn, *From Ottomanism to Arabism: Essays on the Origins of Arab Nationalism* (Urbana: University of Illinois Press, 1973); Philip S. Khoury, *Urban Notables and Arab Nationalism: The Politics of Damascus 1860–1920* (Cambridge: Cambridge University Press, 1983); A. A. Duri, *The Historical Formation of the Arab Nation*, trans. Lawrence I. Conrad (London: Croom Helm, 1987); Bassam Tibi, *Arab Nation-*

alism: A Critical Inquiry, 2d ed., trans. Marion Farouk Sluglett and Peter Sluglett; (New York: St. Martin's Press, 1990); and Rashid Khalidi et al., eds., *The Origins of Arab Nationalism* (New York: Columbia University Press, 1991).

8. For the most systematic critique of the "awakening," see Hisham Sharabi, *Arab Intellectuals and the West* (Baltimore: The Johns Hopkins University Press, 1970). For its difficulties in creating a modern vocabulary of politics, see Ami Ayalon, *Language and Change in the Arab Middle East: The Evolution of Modern Arabic Political Discourse* (New York: Oxford University Press, 1987).

9. Gertrude Bell, *The Desert and the Sown* (London: W. Heinemann, 1907), 140.

10.   Turkish nationalism, inspired by Balkan nationalisms, in turn inspired much of the outlook of early Arab nationalism. On its genesis, see David Kushner, *The Rise of Turkish Nationalism, 1876–1908* (London: Frank Cass, 1977).

11. See Neville J. Mandel, *The Arabs and Zionism before World War I* (Berkeley and Los Angeles: University of California Press, 1976).

12.   Elie Kedourie, "Pan-Arabism and British Policy," in Elie Kedourie, *The Chatham House Version and other Middle-Eastern Studies* (London: Weidenfeld and Nicolson, 1970; reprint, Hanover, N.H.: University Press of New England, 1984), 213.

13.   On Arab politics in the immediate postwar period, see Zeine N. Zeine, *The Struggle for Arab Independence: Western Diplomacy and the Rise and Fall of Faisal's Kingdom in Syria,* 2d ed. (Delmar, N.Y.: Caravan Books, 1977).

14.   For the genesis of the names that filled the postwar map, see Bernard Lewis, "The Map of the Middle East: A Guide for the Perplexed," *The American Scholar* 58, no. 1 (Winter 1988–89): 19–38.

15.   The deep debate in Lebanon over the very definition of its history is considered by Ahmad Beydoun, *Identité confessionnelle et temps social chez les historiens libanais contemporains* (Beirut: Université libanaise, 1984); and Kamal Salibi, *A House of Many Mansions: The History of Lebanon Reconsidered* (Berkeley and Los Angeles: University of California Press, 1988).

16.   While the story of the Arab Revolt has been told many times, most famously by T. E. Lawrence and George Antonius, there are fewer accounts of the rival campaigns for separate independence in different parts of the Fertile Crescent. For a widening of the perspective, see Eliezer Tauber, *The Arab Movements in World War I* (London: Frank Cass, 1993).

17.   Quoted by William L. Cleveland, *The Making of an Arab Nationalist: Ottomanism and Arabism in the Life and Thought of Sati' al-Husri* (Princeton, N.J.: Princeton University Press, 1971), 127.

18.   Ibid., 163–65.

19.   On this evolution, see C. Ernest Dawn, "The Formation of a Pan-Arab Ideology in the Inter-War Years," *International Journal of Middle Eastern Studies* 20 (1988): 67–91.

20.   On the Egyptian debate over identity, see Israel Gershoni and James P. Jankowski, *Egypt, Islam, and the Arabs: The Search for Egyptian Nationhood* (New York: Oxford University Press, 1986).

21.   These plans have been considered in great detail by Yehoshua Porath, *In Search of Arab Unity 1930–1945* (London: Frank Cass, 1986).

22.   J.C. Hurewitz, *The Middle East and North Africa in World Politics: A Documentary Record,* 2d ed., vol. 2, *British-French Supremacy, 1914–1945* (New Haven, Conn.: Yale University Press, 1979), 736. For the development of inter-Arab relations in this period, see Bruce Maddy-Weitzman, *The Crystallization of the Arab State System, 1945–1954* (Syracuse, N.Y.: Syracuse University Press, 1993).

23.   For a contemporary discussion of the transition to ideological politics, see Leon-

ard Binder, *The Ideological Revolution in the Middle East* (New York: John Wiley, 1964).

24.   Translation in Haim, *Arab Nationalism: An Anthology*, 233–41.

25.   Sami al-Jundi, a member of the Ba'th from its earliest years who wrote a devastating account of the party, as quoted by Elie Kedourie, *Arabic Political Memoirs and Other Studies* (London: Frank Cass, 1974), 201.

26.   For the early history of the Ba'th, see Kamel S. Abu Jaber, *The Arab Ba'th Socialist Party: History, Ideology, and Organization* (Syracuse, N.Y.: Syracuse University Press, 1966); John F. Devlin, *The Ba'th Party: A History from Its Origins to 1966* (Stanford: Hoover Institution Press, 1976); and Kanan Makiya [Samir al-Khalil], *Republic of Fear: The Politics of Modern Iraq* (Berkeley and Los Angeles: University of California Press, 1989), 149–257.

27.   For this period, see Malcolm H. Kerr, *The Arab Cold War: Gamal 'Abd al-Nasir and His Rivals, 1958–1970*, 3d ed.(London: Oxford University Press, 1971); and P. J. Vatikiotis, *Conflict in the Middle East* (London: George Allen and Unwin, 1971).

28.   David Holden, *Farewell to Arabia* (New York: Walker, 1966), 101.

29.   Abdul Aziz Said, "Clashing Horizons: Arabs and Revolution," in *People and Politics in the Middle East*, ed. Michael Curtis (New Brunswick, N.J.: Transaction, 1971), 279.

30.   Fouad Ajami, "The End of Pan-Arabism," in *Pan-Arabism and Arab Nationalism: The Continuing Debate*, ed. Tawfic E. Farah (Boulder, Colo.: Westview Press, 1987), 98.

31.   The most thought-provoking account of the post-1967 crisis of Arab nationalism remains Fouad Ajami's *The Arab Predicament: Arab Political Thought and Practice Since 1967*, updated ed. (Cambridge: Cambridge University Press, 1992). Other works representative of the reassessments made by Arab intellectuals include Abdallah Laroui, *The Crisis of the Arab Intellectual: Traditionalism or Historicism?*, trans. Diarmid Cammell (Berkeley and Los Angeles: University of California Press, 1976); Samir Amin, *The Arab Nation* (London: Zed Press,1978); Hisham Sharabi, *Neopatriarchy: A Theory of Distorted Change in Arab Society* (New York: Oxford University Press, 1988); and Paul Salem, *Bitter Legacy: Ideology and Politics in the Arab World* (Syracuse, N.Y.: Syracuse University Press, 1994). For a variety of assessments by non-Arabs, see Michael Hudson, *Arab Politics: The Search for Legitimacy* (New Haven, Conn.: Yale University Press, 1977); Jacques Berque, *Arab Rebirth: Pain & Ecstasy*, trans. Quintin Hoare (London: Al Saqi Books, 1983); David Pryce-Jones, *The Closed Circle: An Interpretation of the Arabs* (New York: Harper and Row, 1989); and Olivier Carré, *Le nationalisme arabe* (Paris: Fayard, 1993).

32.   Salibi, *A House of Many Mansions*, 218, 231.

33.   Kamal Abu-Deeb, "Cultural Creation in a Fragmented Society," in *The Next Arab Decade: Alternative Futures*, ed. Hisham Sharabi (Boulder, Colo.: Westview Press, 1988), 165.

34.   The strengthening of the Arab state served as the theme of a multiyear project on "Nation, State and Integration in the Arab World," which generated four volumes of detailed studies. The most significant of these studies are collected in Giacomo Luciani, ed., *The Arab State* (Berkeley and Los Angeles: University of California Press, 1990).

35.   Michel Aflaq, *Fi sabil al-ba'th* (Beirut: Dar al-Tali'a, 1963), 55.

36.   Quoted by Emmanuel Sivan, *Radical Islam: Medieval Theology and Modern Politics* (New Haven, Conn.: Yale University Press, 1985), 30–32.

37.   On the evolution of this approach, see Moshe Shemesh, *The Palestinian Entity*

1959–1974: Arab Politics and the PLO (London: Frank Cass, 1988).
38.   Jean Genet, *Prisoner of Love*, trans. Barbara Bray (London: Picador, 1989), 239.
39.   Quoted by Olivier Carré, *Le nationalisme arabe*, 175.
40.   Quoted by Amatzia Baram, *Culture, History and Ideology in the Formation of Ba'thist Iraq, 1968–89* (London: Macmillan, 1991), 121. The book includes a detailed discussion of the issue of identity in Iraqi politics, and the genesis of the Mesopotamian myth.
41.   See Samir al-Khalil [Kanan Makiya], *The Monument: Art, Vulgarity and Responsibility in Iraq* (Berkeley and Los Angeles: University of California Press, 1991).
42.   Hichem Djaït, *Europe and Islam*, trans. Peter Heinegg (Berkeley and Los Angeles: University of California Press, 1985), 140–41.
43.   Quoted by Kanan Makiya, *Cruelty and Silence: War, Tyranny, Uprising, and the Arab World* (New York: Norton, 1993), 242. The second half of this work is devoted to the rush of Arab nationalist intellectuals to endorse Saddam Hussein before and during the Gulf crisis.
44.   David Pollock, *"The Arab Street"? Public Opinion in the Arab World*, Policy Papers, no. 32 (Washington: The Washington Institute for Near East Policy, 1992), 29–41.
45.   An example of this trend is the article by the Egyptian intellectual Lutfi al-Khuli, "Arab? Na'am wa-lakin sharq awsatiyin aydan!," *Al-Hayat* (London), 20 May 1992.
46.   Roderic Davison, "Where is the Middle East?," in *The Modern Middle East*, ed. Richard Nolte (New York: Atherton, 1963), 16–17.
47.   Fouad Ajami, "The End of Arab Nationalism," *The New Republic*, 12 August 1991.
48.   For an example of such a debate, see the proceedings of a roundtable of Arab nationalist intellectuals on the possibility of a nationalist-Islamist rapprochement, in *Al-Mustaqbal al-arabi* (Beirut) 161 (July 1992): 96–119.
49.   For a typical statement of this view, see As'ad AbuKhalil, "A New Arab Ideology?: The Rejuvenation of Arab Nationalism," *Middle East Journal*, 46 (Winter 1992): 22–36.
50.   The survey was conducted by researchers at Yarmuk University, and included almost one thousand respondents from several Arab countries. See *Al-Mustaqbal al-arabi (Beirut) 164 (October 1992): 27–33.*

2

Arab Pen, English Purse:
John Sabunji and Wilfrid Scawen Blunt

It is well known that the early Arabic newspapers, particularly those published by émigrés, could not bear their own weight financially. They were subsidized, usually in a secret way, by interested parties. Far from constituting open and sincere platforms of opinion, newspapers often amplified the views of silent benefactors, who were prepared to pay to see their political notions in print. In many cases it is difficult if not impossible to trace the fine lines linking journalists to their patrons. But without such evidence, the history of the Arab "awakening" becomes unintelligible, since the Arabic press provides the earliest proof for its existence.

In the annals of early Arab journalism, John Louis Sabunji occupies a position of minor eminence. A former priest of the Syrian Catholic Rite, Sabunji entered a turbulent career in journalism, publishing several Arabic newspapers in London and openly calling into question the Ottoman sultan's right to the caliphate. His newspaper *Al-Nahla* (The Bee), which he published in London from 1877, was one of the most influential of the early Arabic political journals, and one of the boldest.

Sabunji must have been a heavily subsidized journalist, as another study has suggested.[1] But the identity of his patrons was necessarily inferred, since none of Sabunji's relationships with his benefactors could be documented. Now a packet of Sabunji's letters sheds new light on his reluctant dependence upon one of his most important clients: the English Arabophile, Wilfrid Scawen Blunt.[2]

Egyptian Adventures

Sabunji's first employment in Blunt's service was not as a journalist, but as a tutor in Arabic to his wife, Lady Anne Blunt, in 1880. In this capacity,

Sabunji did more than instruct Lady Anne in the intricacies of the language. Her husband had just published a series of strongly anti-Turkish articles in *The Fortnightly Review*. The articles, which were later published together under the title *The Future of Islam*, proposed the severing of the Arabs from Turkish rule and the establishment of an Arab caliphate. Blunt was the first to challenge the traditional British support for Ottoman territorial integrity in Asia, and he prompted a spirited debate in London.

But as Blunt himself later wrote, his *Fortnightly Review* pieces "found their way, to some extent, in [Arabic] translation to Egypt."[3] Such translations were prepared by Sabunji and Lady Anne,[4] so that even in Sabunji's limited capacity as Lady Anne's tutor, he became swept up in Blunt's anti-Ottoman agitation. Early in 1881, while the Blunts were away in Arabia, Sabunji began his own campaign, in a newspaper appropriately called *Al-Khilafa* (The Caliphate). According to Sabunji, this newspaper consisted of "very strong articles against the Turks, their bad administration, and their claim to the title of 'El-Khelaphat.'"[5]

There is no evidence that Blunt subsidized this newspaper, although it echoed an indictment of the Ottoman caliphate made by Blunt himself. But after Blunt's return from Arabia, he did propose that Sabunji accompany him on his forthcoming trip to the Hijaz and the Yemen. Blunt would need the help of an interpreter, were he to get in touch with the "future leaders of reform and liberty in Islam" whom he hoped to identify.[6] Sabunji seemed the very best choice.

Although the two men apparently did not enter into a formal contract, Sabunji did set down terms in a letter to Blunt. Sabunji would not be Blunt's servant, but his "attaché interpreter," cooperating with Blunt "in your plan as much as it is in my power," in return for payment and a generous application of patronage. Blunt would cover Sabunji's travel expenses and provide him with £100 "so that I may settle some of my little affairs, before starting." Sabunji also asked Blunt "to procure for me an English passport, if it be possible; and I shall try my best to procure a Persian one, if the [Persian] Ambassador be in London before I leave." On their return to England, Blunt would offer Sabunji a remuneration left "entirely to your sound judgement, and well-known generosity. You and Lady Anne have always treated me kindly and with princely generosity." Finally, Sabunji asked that Blunt seek to "procure for me some appointment in the British Service, through your good recommendation and influence.... I am perfectly convinced, that there will be no lack of energy, or will in this matter on your part, if there will be any hope for success."[7]

The deal was done. Blunt set out for Arabia in November 1881, in his quest for men who might refashion Islam. But during a stopover in Egypt, he became fascinated by Ahmad Urabi, whose movement of military officers and Egyptian nationalists quickly won his sympathy and support. And at Blunt's side was Sabunji, his "attaché interpreter," who had a dual role. According to Blunt, Sabunji "had a real genius" for collecting information. On arrival in Cairo, he "was presently busy all the city over seeking out news for me, so that in a very few days we knew between us pretty nearly everything that was going on."[8] Sabunji also accompanied Blunt to his meetings with Egyptians, where Sabunji's role was that of translator, and he was at Blunt's side when Urabi first received this odd Englishman who so wholeheartedly embraced the Egyptian cause.

Indeed, so adeptly did Sabunji fulfill his mission that in June 1882, Blunt sent Sabunji to Egypt in his stead to conduct private diplomacy on Blunt's behalf. ("Sabunji is to go instead of me, and will do just as well.") For his trouble, Sabunji would receive £30 a month plus expenses, and left for Alexandria with a £100 advance and Blunt's explicit instructions.[9] Blunt's *Secret History of the English Occupation of Egypt* reproduces Sabunji's dispatches to Blunt, written during the crucial months of June and July 1882, and culminating in the British bombardment of Alexandria. Sabunji, dining at Urabi's table and sitting up late with the nationalist leaders, kept Blunt apprised of the mood in the nationalist camp, and supposedly transmitted Blunt's detailed advice to Urabi. In his book, Blunt expressed his great satisfaction with Sabunji's performance of his mission as "my representative":

> I could hardly have used more influence personally with Arabi and the other leaders than I succeeded in exercising through Sabunji. Sabunji was an admirable agent in a mission of this kind, and it is impossible I could have been better served. His position as ex-editor of the "Nahleh," a paper which, whether subsidized or not by Ismail, had always advocated the most enlightened views of humanitarian progress and Mohammedan reform, gave him a position with the Azhar reformers of considerable influence, and he was, besides, heart and soul with them in the national movement. As my representative he was everywhere received by the Nationalists with open arms, and they gave him their completest confidence. Nor was he unworthy of their trust or mine. The letters I sent him for them he communicated to them faithfully, and he faithfully reported to me all that they told him.[10]

It is striking, then, to read a rather disparaging comment on Sabunji's service in Edith Finch's biography of Blunt. Without providing details, she contradicts Blunt's clear testimony to Sabunji's reliability: "Although not able wholly to trust [Sabunji], Blunt used him for what he was worth, first as his teacher in Mohammedan thought, afterward as secretary and finally, in the time of the Nationalist uprising in Egypt, as his emissary." Indeed, according to Finch, Sabunji "turned out later to be something of an Oriental scallywag," although she accepts Blunt's assessment of Sabunji's trustworthiness during the crisis of 1882.[11]

From what seed did this distrust spring, from when did it date? The answers to both questions are to be found in a revealing letter from Sabunji to Blunt. Sabunji arrived back in London in late July or early August 1882. There he found his patron Blunt busily writing about the Egyptian drama, with a considerable emphasis upon his own mediation attempts during the crisis. Blunt's piece, entitled "The Egyptian Revolution: A Personal Narrative," was to appear in *The Nineteenth Century*, a leading London journal of opinion. Inevitably, Sabunji figured in the draft of this account, and Blunt was surprised to discover that this did not please Sabunji at all. True, Sabunji voiced no opposition when Blunt first mentioned the references to Sabunji in his narrative. But there soon followed a letter from Sabunji, seething with resentment at the possibility that his employment might become a matter of record:

> Since I left you, I have been thinking, whether it would be expedient or not, to have my name mentioned in the paper you are about to publish. After due consideration I came to conclusion that that portion of the narrative concerning myself, not only would not add any valuable strength to your argument, but it would weaken also [a] great deal my relations with my friends. Since you represent me in your narrative as a *hired* agent, to carry out your designs, you put me just in that same light in which my bitter enemies attempted to expose me with regard to Ismail. The difference in the eye of the public would consist only in the change of the name of the hirer. You know, however, that our agreement was a confidential one, and it was never meant to be published in the papers. Now, by your putting me before the public in such an unfavourable light of a *hired agent*, of a *tool*, as your narrative suggests, you simply confirm my enemies' former calumnies and pain my friends' hearts. What excellent recompense for my earnest and honest work! In a time like this, frothing with prejudices, and while the nation's passions have reached the apex of their effervescence, the most logical reasons and the most convincing proofs will produce no effect whatever. They would rather irritate than sooth. As to myself not being a British subject, nor an Egyptian, I need not give reason to anyone of my political doings, and nobody has any right to question me about my political views; hence, it would be useless to take upon yourself the responsibility of my political career. By doing so, you as an Englishman inconvenience yourself without doing any good to me as a stranger to both belligerent parties. But if you intend presenting the public with a complete and too naive narrative of your eastern politics, you might do so without mentioning the names of those who assisted you. The simple saying that you had carried on your political transactions with the leaders of the National party through the help of trustworthy Mohammadan & Christian friends would do just as well.[12]

This twisted logic for the suppression of the truth could not conceal what must have been Sabunji's reason for fearing its publication. Despite the fact that Blunt footed the entire bill for Sabunji's Egyptian adventures, and regarded Sabunji as his exclusive "agent," Sabunji must have presented himself in Egypt as an independent actor, working not in Blunt's employ but on his own. Indeed, nowhere in Sabunji's dispatches from Egypt did he give any indication that he had informed the Nationalists of his mission and its sponsor. Urabi once introduced him as "a friend of Mr. Blunt,"[13] but Sabunji obviously sat with the Nationalists as his own man, never making a clean breast of the fact of his employment. Blunt was indeed "too naive" to have assumed that Sabunji could have presented himself in Egypt as acting in Blunt's private service—a naiveté matched only by Sabunji's, for assuming that the notoriously indiscreet Blunt would not wish to publish his version of the Egyptian saga in full. It is Sabunji's prospect of being found out in a lie which gives his letter of protest a certain vulnerable poignancy.

Did Sabunji's failure to represent his position frankly to the Egyptians shake Blunt's confidence in his "emissary"? Blunt not only kept Sabunji but obliged him, omitting all reference to Sabunji from the article. Yet if Sabunji's Egyptian friends had not even known that he was in Blunt's service, then Blunt's own initiatives might well have been lost in transmission. If this likelihood occurred to Blunt, it remained an inner doubt. When he did write his *Secret History* years later, he made no allusion to Sabunji's self-misrepresentation. Indeed, Blunt's overwrought testimony to Sabunji's trustworthiness (on a page titled "Sabunji's Good Qualities") must have come to dispel any doubt as to Blunt's own influence upon Urabi and the significance of Blunt's mediation. Sabunji's letter now casts a shadow upon both.

Anti-Ottoman Journalism

Judith Lady Wentworth, in her embittered portrait of her father, averred that Blunt squandered a great part of her mother's fortune "in subsidies to the charlatans who besieged his door."[14] In addition to providing services of questionable value, Sabunji also sought outright subsidies from Blunt for his Arabic newspapers. Philippe de Tarrazi, author of the first history of the Arabic press, lists Sabunji's numerous patrons, who reputedly financed his no less numerous journals, but Blunt does not figure among them.[15] A begging letter from Sabunji to Blunt is therefore of great interest, not only for the light that it sheds upon their relationship, but for its detailed revelation of what it cost to publish an Arabic newspaper in exile. The letter was written in May 1882, at the height of Blunt's confidence in Sabunji, after their trip to Egypt but before Sabunji had been sent as Blunt's "emissary" to Urabi:

> Last year, you were kind enough to promise me, that you will, for this year, subsidize my paper by £100—. You see now, that I did all I could to make the paper attractive & interesting to the Arabs. This number has cost me £24—6—0, for 1000 copies. Here are the details:
>
> | | |
> |---|---:|
> | Front page | £6— 7—0 |
> | Five cuts | 4— 7—0 |
> | To the compositors of the Arabic types | 4—15—0 |
> | To the printer & paper | 5— 2—0 |
> | Postage | 3—15—0 |
> | | £24— 6—0 |
>
> The next number, of course, will not come to that much; It still will not cost less than £15—. So the expenses exceed my scanty means. Hence, I shall be very much obliged to you if would grant me the favour of £150— as a subsidy to my paper, which is, in some sense, yours too. I have been spending a great deal of money lately, & I feel in want of some help to be able to carry on this hard work.[16]

While the letter does not specify which of Sabunji's newspapers was in such dire need of a subsidy, information in the letter allows an accurate inference. Sabunji's *Al-Nahla* ceased to appear in late 1880. As we have seen, it was succeeded by *Al-Khilafa* in early 1881, but Tarrazi states that this was soon succeeded, also in 1881, by a newspaper entitled *Al-Ittihad al-arabi* (The Arab Union) of which only three issues appeared. As Blunt pledged his subsidy sometime in 1881, and was asked to make good his promise in 1882, it seems certain that Sabunji's begging letter refers to *Ittihad al-arabi*. This conclusion is supported by Sabunji's claim that he had done all that he could to make the paper "interesting to the Arabs."

Of this obscure newspaper, all that Tarrazi has to say is that it appealed to speakers of Arabic "to form one league against the Turks in all the Arab lands." When Sabunji saw that there was really no hope for such unity, he closed the newspaper after only three issues.[17] In content, then, *Al-Ittihad al-arabi* must have echoed Blunt's own ideas about the corruption of the Turks and the virtues of Arab independence from Turkish misrule. Sabunji's letter makes it clear that Blunt had indeed intended to support an Arabic newspaper meant to subvert Ottoman authority in Arab lands.

But less than a month after Sabunji's appeal, Blunt sent him to Egypt on a more important mission. The growing preoccupation of both Blunt and Sabunji with the affairs of Egypt must have been the real reason for the newspaper's closing: both set aside their anti-Ottoman agitation, in order to expound upon freedom for Egypt and the failings of British policy.

Blunt's revised position after the occupation of Egypt was that "the restoration of a more legitimate [i.e., Arab] Caliphate is deferred for the day when its fate shall have overtaken the Ottoman Empire. This is as it should be. Schism would only weaken the cause of religion, already threatened by a thousand enemies."[18] After the fall of Egypt, Blunt would not have supported a newspaper meant to aggravate precisely that schism.

Yet this did not end Sabunji's association with Blunt. "Sabunji remained in my employment till the end of 1883,"[19] in a capacity defined by Blunt as "my Oriental secretary."[20] Sabunji undoubtedly handled much of the Arabic correspondence and translations involved in Blunt's support for Urabi's defense. But Blunt may have backed one of Sabunji's other pursuits: there is indirect evidence for the irregular appearance of *Al-Nahla* in 1883, and for the inclusion in it of a laudatory biography of Blunt.[21] It seems not unlikely that Blunt would have subsidized the newspaper of his secretary, along the very lines suggested in Sabunji's earlier begging letter. *Al-Nahla* of 1883 would have differed from *Al-Ittihad al-arabi* of 1881–82 in criticizing British imperial policy rather than Turkish oppression of the Arabs. (Likewise *Al-Nahla* when it began to reappear regularly in April 1884.) Thus ended the anti-Ottoman and Arab separatist phase of Sabunji's journalistic career, a phase which coincided almost precisely with Blunt's own preoccupation with the same ideas. It seems likely that this embarrassing coincidence disqualified Sabunji and his newspapers from mention by George Antonius in *The Arab Awakening*, where early Arab nationalism is not allowed to spring from any but the purest of sources.

"Like a raven..."

Sabunji's last mission in Blunt's service was to accompany Blunt on a visit to Egypt and Ceylon, beginning in September 1883. Blunt had discovered that Sabunji's activities had created "so much suspicion" in the Foreign Office, and so resolved not to take him. After all, Sabunji had conducted himself a year earlier as a leading participant in Urabi's movement. But Blunt's arrangements for other assistance in Egypt fell through, "and I have consequently determined to take Sabunji. The fact is I should be very helpless without him, and if it should so happen that I could be of any good it would be as well to have him at hand." But Blunt made this assurance to Gladstone's private secretary: "I shall caution Sabunji to get into no mischief, and he has always acted as far as I am am aware squarely in his service with me."[22] This utter dependence upon Sabunji had led Blunt to overlook Sabunji's deceit of the previous year. But Blunt's vouching for Sabunji in this letter of assurance carried an important rider. Sabunji had served him squarely only "as far as I am aware," for Blunt could not dismiss the possibility that the Foreign Office had solid evidence to the contrary. During the fruitless Egyptian stopover, Blunt confined Sabunji to Port Said (although he "sent Sabunji like a raven from the Ark to get intelligence" in the town), and was happy to quit Egypt for Ceylon without Sabunji's getting arrested.[23]

Blunt had failed in his attempt to have the Nationalist leaders repatriated, and he brought no good news to the Egyptian exiles in Ceylon. Still, once in Colombo, "Sabunji went forth like the raven from the Ark, and did not any more return!"[24] Sabunji's stint in Blunt's service had come to an end. He would now tie his fate to Urabi's, in anticipation of an inevitable and triumphal return to Egypt.

As it happened, Sabunji quarreled with Urabi over the bill for Blunt's stay in Colombo, Urabi not agreeing to pay his share, or Sabunji having falsified the account of expenses, or both. Blunt had largely seen Urabi through Sabunji's eyes, yet now Sabunji charged that Urabi had "cunningly managed to deceive his best friends." Sabunji, in another agitated letter to Blunt, called Urabi "a pseudopatriot," a "degraded & ambitious ignoramus," "a bigamist and adulterer," and the "biggest liar I ever saw in my life."[25] It was an indictment of Urabi which Blunt, as Urabi's greatest defender, could never accept. "In spite of [Urabi's] faults and failings," wrote Blunt, "there is something great about him which compels one's respect. His faults are all the faults of his race, his virtues are his own."[26] Sabunji returned to London, where he was of much more value to Urabi's enemies than to Blunt.[27] His revived *Al-Nahla* of 1884 began a violent campaign against Urabi, of which Blunt would not have approved.

Sabunji's subsequent career warrants separate study, but it may be characterized as a quest for the perfect patron. He had hoped that Blunt could get him "some appointment in the British Service," but this had become quite impossible. Eventually he fixed his gaze upon Sultan Abdülhamid II, the arch-foe of Arab separatist dreams. When Blunt found Sabunji in Istanbul in 1893, his old friend was "in fine feather, having a permanent post as translator to the Sultan." The terms were enviable: "He gets £40 a month and a house at Prinkipo, and so is in clover."[28] Sabunji could not have found steadier employment, and he served his former nemesis from 1891 until a revolution cleared Yildiz Palace in 1909. By that time, Sabunji had lost even the appearance of a revolutionary, just as he had once shed his priest's cassock. Blunt dined with him in London in 1909, discovering that Sabunji had become "a Yildiz Palace spy, a little furtive old man dressed in black with a black skull cap on his head, a jewel in his shirt front and another jewel on his finger."[29]

Notes

1. See L. Zolondek, "Sabunji in England 1876–91: His Role in Arabic Journalism," *Middle Eastern Studies* 15 (1978): 102–15.
2. West Sussex County and Diocesan Record Office, Chichester, Acc. 5306, file 53 (hereafter: Blunt Letters). These are a portion of Blunt's papers, the bulk of which are in the Fitzwilliam Museum in Cambridge. I am grateful to the Right Honorable Viscount Knebworth for permission to examine the Chichester collection.
3. Wilfrid Scawen Blunt, *Secret History of the English Occupation of Egypt* (London: Unwin, 1907), 122. Elsewhere Blunt wrote: "My articles in the *Fortnightly Review* were translated while I was in Cairo [in 1881] and read and approved by my friends in the Nationalist press." Wilfrid Scawen Blunt, "The Egyptian Revolution: A Personal Narrative," *The Nineteenth Century* 12 (1882): 332.
4. Elizabeth Longford, *A Pilgrimage of Passion: The Life of Wilfrid Scawen Blunt* (London: Weidenfeld and Nicolson, 1979), 163.
5. Sabunji to Lady Anne Blunt, 25 May 1881, Blunt Letters.
6. Blunt, "The Egyptian Revolution," 328.
7. Sabunji to Blunt, 22 October 1881, Blunt Letters.
8. Blunt, *Secret History*, 163.
9. Ibid., 296, 298.
10. Ibid., 299.
11. Edith Finch, *Wilfrid Scawen Blunt, 1840–1922* (London: Cape, 1938), 122, 156.
12. Sabunji to Blunt, 9 August 1882, Blunt Letters.
13. Sabunji to Blunt, 18 June 1882, in Blunt, *Secret History*, 342.
14. Lady Wentworth, *The Authentic Arabian Horse and His Descendants*, 3d ed.(Canaan, N.Y.: Sporting Book Center, 1979), 74.
15. Philippe de Tarrazi, *Ta'rikh al-sihafa al-arabiyya* , 4 vols. (Beirut: Al-Matba'a al-adabiyya,1913–33), 2:250–53.
16. Sabunji to Blunt, 12 May 1882, Blunt Letters.
17. Tarrazi, *Ta'rikh al-sihafa*, 2:252–53.
18. Wilfrid Scawen Blunt, *The Future of Islam* (London: Kegan Paul, Trench, 1882), viii.
19. Blunt, *Secret History*, 299.
20. Wilfrid Scawen Blunt, *Gordon at Khartoum* (London: Swift, 1911), 45.
21. Zolondek, "Sabunji in England," 108.
22. Blunt to Edward Hamilton, 14 September 1883, in Blunt, *Gordon at Khartoum*, 572.

23. Blunt, *Gordon at Khartoum*, 51.
24. Wilfrid Scawen Blunt, *India under Ripon* (London: Unwin, 1909), 19.
25. Sabunji (Umballa) to Blunt (Allahabad), 6 January 1884, Blunt Letters.
26. Blunt, *India under Ripon*, 25.
27. *Al-Nahla*, 16 May 1884. Angry reference to this number of the paper is made by Urabi in a letter to Blunt, 23 June 1884, in file 2 of the Chichester collection.
28. Wilfrid Scawen Blunt, *My Diaries, Being a Personal Narrative of Events, 1888–1914*, 2 vols. (New York: Knopf, 1921), 1:102, 105. Tarrazi speaks of £50 a month, and a well-furnished house in one of the capital's best suburbs; Tarrazi, *Ta'rikh al-sihafa*, 2:74.
29. Blunt, *My Diaries*, 2:250.

3

Arabistik and Arabism:
The Passions of Martin Hartmann

The influence of European scholarship upon Middle Eastern nationalisms is a scarcely acknowledged one. The great work of retrieval and compilation done by European archaeologists and philologists served their own inquiring spirit. But the findings extracted from excavations, inscriptions, and manuscripts soon fed the imaginations of those who lived near the digs and spoke the modern forms of retrieved languages. European scholarship breathed life into silent ruins and established the ancient ancestry of languages still spoken in Eastern lands. Such scholarship did not create the discontent that spread through the Ottoman Empire in the late nineteenth century. It did stock a vast storehouse of scholarly findings that fed nationalism its grist.

Yet foreign scholars do not occupy any place of prominence in the conventional catalogue of influences which formed Arab nationalism. By most accounts, the Arabs bestirred themselves, or at least discovered the eclipsed greatness of their language and culture by their own labors. Still, it is impossible not to be struck by the similarity between many of the nineteenth-century theories propounded by European scholars in Arabic studies and the twentieth-century theories propounded by Arab nationalists. The greatness of pre-Islamic Arab civilization and the ingeniously Arab character of pristine Islam were ideas championed by some of these scholars years before similar ideas appeared in the writings of Arab nationalists. This loses the aura of pure coincidence when it is realized just how much of this scholarly and semischolarly material quickly found its way into Arab libraries. Perhaps the most influential of these works was Gustave Le Bon's *La civilisation des arabes*. The book was well known in the intellectual salons of turn-of-the-century Beirut and Damascus for its author's premise that the Arabs possessed a special genius, manifest in early Islam but later obscured by Persian and Turkish accretions.

A handful of these European scholars became so enamored of their theories that they themselves embraced a sort of Arab nationalism. One of them went so far as to call for the dismemberment of the Ottoman Empire and the restoration to the Arabs of their independence. He was Martin Hartmann, a brilliant if quixotic German student of Islam and Arabic, a socialist visionary, and one of the first truly disinterested foreign friends of Arab nationalism.[1]

Beirut and Berlin

Young Martin Hartmann, born the son of a Mennonite preacher in Breslau, had the attributes of a prodigy. In 1869, at the age of seventeen, he enrolled in university in his native city, and displayed a remarkable aptitude for languages. Later he completed advanced studies at Leipzig under Heinrich Leberecht Fleischer, the eminent Semiticist. Leipzig of a century ago boasted one of Europe's leading schools of Semitic philology, at a time when philology reigned supreme among Orientalist disciplines.[2] Young Hartmann received his doctorate in 1874 with a dissertation on pluriliteral forms in Semitic languages. No scholarly preparation could have been more remote from the living world of the Orient; Fleischer's school, in the words of one critic, resembled nothing so much as a tidy "French garden," from which Hartmann sprang like a "wild shoot."[3] Fleischer tagged Hartmann a "flighty youth,"[4] and at first opportunity the young man did fly: he made for Ottoman lands, in pursuit of a career far from staid academe.

In 1874, Hartmann arrived in Adrianople, where he spent a year as a private tutor. In March 1875, he proceeded to Istanbul, and there enrolled as a *jeune de langues* in apprenticeship for a career in dragomanry. Hartmann thus acquired a firm grasp of Turkish, the very practical language of Ottoman administration, as a supplement to his academic proficiency in Arabic. With these formidable credentials the polyglot Hartmann, then twenty-four years of age, earned an appointment as dragoman to the German consulate in Beirut. In 1876, he took up his post in the small Levantine port, where he remained for the next eleven years.

In Beirut, Hartmann's learning acquired the practical bent exemplified by his *Arabischer Sprachführer für Reisende*, a pocket-sized phrase book and word list that he published in 1880. The colloquial Arabic of the Beirut market served as Hartmann's model. His book is enlightening even now, for the conversational predicaments in which he situated the average German traveler and trader and for the prices of goods and services cited in hypothetical transactions. Hartmann made strictly mundane use of his mastery of Arabic during these years, a period closed by his publication of an Arabic translation of the German commercial code. Hartmann also undertook minor expeditions that were probably intended to gather information on economic conditions and topography. In 1882–83, he visited northern Syria, a journey that provided him with rich material for subsequent publications on the Aleppo region and the Syrian steppe.

Hartmann, in the judgment of one colleague, was transformed by his Syrian stay into a "passionate Turk-hater," in sympathy with "Arabs groaning under the Turkish yoke."[5] It was during this decade that he formed the prejudices and preferences that would last him a lifetime. Sweeping judgments as to the intrinsic character of peoples, past and present, were the currency of many respected scholars and travelers in Hartmann's time, and he unabashedly declared his preferences. He had nothing but contempt for "the Stambul Effendis and Hanums," and the Turkish peasantry struck him as "earnest but dumb."[6] The Egyptian was "intelligent and witty, but from his infancy extremely lazy, and as he becomes older he becomes hopelessly indolent."[7] The bedouin, with their incessant quarrels and lack of scruple, left Hartmann unmoved. He found nothing ennobling in the life of the desert.

But in the Syrian, and especially the Syrian Christian, Hartmann found that essential combination of intelligence and energy. "The Syrian is industrious, consistent, eager for knowledge, has always an object in view, is generally active, and never overawed."[8] Young Hartmann may have been involved in a romance with a Syrian Christian woman,[9] but he was no romantic. He firmly believed in the benefits of railways, industries, printing presses, and modern schools in Ottoman lands, and he offered no lament for the passing of old ways. The Syrians (and the Armenians in equal measure) shared his vision of steady progress along modern lines. He regarded both peoples as "the light of the Near East," and they earned his abiding sympathies.[10]

But those sympathies found no political outlet at the time. It was not Hartmann's duty to reflect or report on the politics of Syria. As the German consul's dragoman, Hartmann handled whatever local business had to be transacted in Arabic and Turkish, and spent most of his time on disputes that came before the commercial court in Beirut. The consul himself assessed provincial politics for Germany's ambassador in Istanbul. Hartmann occasionally substituted during a consul's absence from Beirut. In 1883, he wrote a despatch about local agitation against the Ottoman-appointed governor of Lebanon.[11] Yet he left no account of the other burning political issues that were debated in the same Beirut Arabic that he had studied so meticulously. Hartmann could and probably did know something about the spread of discontent in Syria following the outbreak of war between the Ottoman Empire and Russia in 1877. In Beirut, Damascus, Tripoli and Sidon, there were a few Arabic-speakers who secretly favored separation from the Ottoman Empire, a step advocated in anonymous placards that appeared on walls near Beirut's foreign consulates in 1880. Hartmann also knew Ibrahim al-Yaziji well, and later recalled having heard some of the subversive poetry composed by Yaziji in praise of the Arabs.[12] But Hartmann's views on the actual state and preferred fate of the Ottoman Empire were not yet a matter of record.

They would not be for some time. In 1887, Hartmann left Beirut for Berlin. Again he put his talent for languages to practical use, no longer in a distant province of a disintegrating empire, but in the confident capital of an ascendant one. To win her due share of world dominion, Germany needed many more men with knowledge of difficult and esoteric languages, a need German universities had failed to meet. Bismarck therefore ordered the establishment in Berlin of the Seminar für Orientalische Sprachen, which opened its doors in the autumn of 1887.[13] This institute sought to produce not more philologists, but to train aspiring diplomats, colonial officials, and missionaries in the languages of peoples beyond Europe. Unlike the university departments, it planned to teach living languages in their colloquial and dialectal forms. Hartmann's popular *Arabischer Sprachführer* had established his reputation as an authority on colloquial Arabic. With his many years of service to the Reich in Ottoman lands, he appeared eminently suited to the mission of the new school. Hartmann accepted an appointment as lecturer and began to teach Arabic in the autumn of 1887, the institute's very first academic year. In a letter to his friend Yaziji in Beirut, Hartmann wrote that his duties involved teaching Arabic fourteen hours a week.[14] Hartmann devoted his spare time to philological studies, with a special emphasis on metrics.

There was little in this portion of Hartmann's career to mark him a

political man. His youthful rebelliousness had been played out in a de-
cade-long Levantine adventure, and he now seemed settled in a routine of
teaching and philological research. Both activities agreeably immersed
him in Arabic. "Arabic is my second mother tongue and my love," he
later wrote. "I am more fluent in Arabic than in French or English."[15] His
inspirational abilities as a teacher of Arabic found ample confirmation in
the career of Ernst Harder, the editor of a Berlin newspaper and son of a
prominent Mennonite congregation leader in Elbing. Under Hartmann's
tutelage, Harder fell completely under the spell of Arabic, and devoted
himself to the full-time study of the language and literature. He later
became a professor of Arabic in his own right. In 1892, Hartmann married Harder's sister. After many years abroad, he had entered the fold of a
respected Mennonite family.

But in Berlin, Hartmann grew restless. His own notes for an autobiography described this early Berlin period as one of "groping."[16] His old
resentment against the narrow range of the philologists grew once he joined
their ranks, and finally overtook him after a visit he paid to Egypt and
Tripolitania in 1897, when he again immersed himself in the tumultuous
reality of the Orient. Did his academic colleagues not realize that a living
Arabic and a living Islam existed alongside the time-worn manuscripts?
Were these realities not worthy of scientific study as well, through methods
developed by pioneering sociologists?

It was the spell of the new sociology that captured Hartmann's imagination and made him perhaps the earliest critic of his own discipline. He
mounted his first siege, a modest one, in an editorial on the pages of the
Berlin *Orientalistische Literatur-Zeitung* in 1898. Teachers of Arabic
were lecturing in almost empty classrooms, he complained. Too often their
published works were dry recitations. Hartmann proposed to invigorate
the field by establishing a German outpost of Arabic studies in Jerusalem,
where students could learn Arabic in an authentic setting and apply their
knowledge of the language to many other disciplines.[17] Hartmann thus
took up the professional cross he would bear for the rest of his career: his
insistence on the necessity for scientific study of the contemporary history
and sociology of Islam. He repudiated Fleischer's old dictum that "there is
no salvation save in Arabic,"[18] calling instead for a "break with Semitics"[19]
and the creation of a chair for the "new science" of Islamology in Berlin's
university or in his own institute.[20] A similar movement had carried the day
at the Collège de France in 1902, but not without controversy. Hartmann's

proposal was bound to meet even stiffer opposition from the philologists who set the academic agenda of German Orientalism.[21]

In the same manner, Hartmann adopted a dissident stand within his own society, gradually embracing socialist ideas. He attributed the political tensions that divided the "high culture" of Europe to "the capitalist order," which concealed "egotistical aims" behind the "mask of nationality."[22] Hartmann attested to the decisive influence upon his own thought of the Munich jurist August Geyer, whose theories of differentiation among social groups resembled Marx's concept of class. An ambivalence toward established authority and privilege characterized Hartmann's mature judgments, and led him to devote disproportionate attention to "movements" opposed to economic and social oppression. Thus, Hartmann wrote at length on the barely audible complaints of women and workers in the Ottoman Empire; theirs was a struggle to reclaim the "democratic-social content" of "pure original Islam." In this direction Islam could and would be reformed; "new ideas" had undermined the "old orthodoxy," and their victory was inevitable.[23]

By trumpeting the inevitability of change, Hartmann soon found himself at odds with some of his conservative colleagues. Carl Heinrich Becker summarized Hartmann's work in this manner: "In the history of Islam, Hartmann seeks confirmation of his political opinions on state and society, and formulates his subjective value judgments in the terminology of modern radicalism." Although an enemy of scholasticism, Hartmann had succumbed to yet another set of scholastic dogmas in the course of elaborating a sociological system. The most dubious of these, opined Becker, was the domination of society by capital. By this emphasis on material categories, Hartmann overlooked the vital force of Muslim mysticism and indeed the power of religious belief in Islam, about which Hartmann had nothing to say and without which Islam simply could not be understood.[24]

Hartmann was not the sort to leave such charges unanswered. As a scholar, Hartmann claimed to have wrestled with the subjective moments that occur in all creative study. At the same time, he had a guiding vision of state and society that came to him only after much inner struggle. That vision was essentially sociological. Hartmann took offense at Becker's description of his approach as an expression of "modern radicalism." Radicalism in the abstract had no boundaries and belonged to no one party. Luther, Lessing, Schiller, Goethe, and Kant could all be tagged "modern radicals." The notion could not stand up to close scrutiny; it was a phantom conjured up to frighten children. Hartmann did admit to the influence of the new sociology and "sociography" upon his work, but he denied that this "system" represented a form of scholasticism, for its principles were not unalterable, and he cited his many travels as evidence of his demonstrated willingness to confront theory with "human documents."[25] The controversy between Becker and Hartmann embodied antagonisms which were at once personal, professional, and political. It was an unequal match. Becker, despite his youth, represented the Orientalist consensus of his day, and while he too later dealt in grand theories and sweeping generalizations, he did so in the more comfortably German fashion of the cultural historicist.

Hartmann's fascination with suspect sociology, his "modern radicalism," and his fiery personality combined to mark him as a dissident. The Dutch Orientalist Christiaan Snouck Hurgronje found Hartmann to be an "able man" of "unmistakable talent." But Hartmann also had a "wild" and "nervous" temperament, and his work was "disjointed." So convinced was Hartmann of the "narrow-mindedness" of his colleagues that his conceit shone through, and he came to regard himself as "the brightest star in the dim firmament of scholarship."[26]

Becker would later eulogize Hartmann as a tragic figure, saddled with bad judgment, an immoderate temperament, bizarre notions, and a mode of argumentation more like a preacher's than a scholar's. Still, behind Hartmann's "hatred for the church and the priesthood," Becker discerned "a seeker of God"; behind Hartmann's "tedious sociological scholasticism" lay "an unfulfilled yearning for inner harmony." Despite Hartmann's faith in historical materialism, he remained an idealist.[27] Becker did not seek the sources of these conflicts. Perhaps Hartmann's dissident idealism drew upon the traditional nonconformism of the Mennonite congregation. Perhaps his aggressively opinionated style, which so reminded Becker of a preacher, did owe something to a childhood spent in the world of the parsonage. In this controversial and volatile spirit, Arab nationalism found one of its first foreign champions.

An Arab Movement?

Hartmann dissented not only from the collegial consensus over the contours of his academic discipline. In the same moment he broke with prevailing wisdom about the resilience of the Ottoman Empire and the loyalty of its Arab Muslim subjects.

In his piece on the future of Arabic studies, published in 1898, Hart-mann sounded a note which would resound throughout his later writings. Syria, he claimed, was the land in which "Arab national feelings" were strongest, a land which had recently seen the development of a "specifically Arabic cultural life."[28] The following year, Hartmann made the point unequivocally in a piece devoted to the modern revival of Arabic literature and the growth of the Arabic press. In Hartmann's view, that revival had clear political implications. Strength through unity was indeed the cry of the hour in the Muslim world, but the Ottoman sultan could be ruled out as the focus of this quest for unity. Abdülhamid alone stood behind the campaign to have him recognized by Muslims everywhere as the defender of the faith. However, Islam, in Hartmann's view, was

> in its inner essence democratic, and even the strongest leaders of Islam's largest movements have occupied center stage not because of who they were, but as expounders of an idea. The Sultan as a pure representative of the Islamic idea can carry no weight. He is first a Turk, then a Muslim.

For the non-Turkish population of the Ottoman Empire, the regime was above all Ottoman, and the Ottomans, conquering with empty heart and mind, had brought nothing to Islam. Their craniums had been filled only with lust for blood and carnal pleasures. The Ottomans were not the pillars of Islam they appeared to be, for Islam needed no such pillars. As for the Muslims of other lands, many of whom professed a vague allegiance to the Ottoman sultan as a kind of universal caliph, they were not oblivious to the "glaring contradiction" between the Turkish way of government and "strict Islam." The Turk therefore "has no friends. In the Turkish empire he is detested by the Christians and the non-Turkish Muslims in the same measure, as that element who is averse to every genuine advance, who thwarts all efforts toward progress and knocks to the ground nearly every stirring of national awareness with shocking harshness and brutality."[29]

Istanbul could not master the driving force of Islam's great masses. But the revival of the Arabic language could. In Hartmann's view, literary Arabic had made tremendous strides as the common language of all Muslims. In Syria and Egypt, a literary renaissance had completely recast the language. In India it occupied an increasingly larger place in Muslim education. In Istanbul the Turks themselves realized Arabic's binding strength, and conducted their own pan-Islamic policy largely in Arabic.

In Arabic-speaking lands, the revival of Arabic had invigorated religious life, making religious reform possible and instilling in the Arab Muslim a sense of special pride in his nation. In Hartmann's view, Arabic and the Arabs were speedily regaining their place of primacy in Islam. He now averred that a sense of Arab cultural supremacy and resentment of Turkish misrule had created the climate for an "upheaval." "The seed has been sown," Hartmann announced. A "broad spectrum" of Arab opinion held this view as formulated by Hartmann on their behalf: "We Arabs no longer wish to be the slaves of the Turks. We wish to unite ourselves in an independent state, governed by ourselves, in our own language, according to our own customs."[30]

Hartmann did not claim that an organized movement existed. He took up that issue only when an Arab claimed that such a movement did exist and that it deserved external support to achieve the final aim of Arab independence. Negib Azoury provoked a spate of discussion in Europe with his publication of a small book entitled *Le réveil de la nation arabe dans l'Asie turque* in January 1905. Azoury's book was of no consequence among the Arabs themselves, and he later confided that the book sought not to describe Arab discontent so much as to create it. This it failed to do, but the message it carried to Europe had a greater impact. Here was an Arab author, a former Ottoman official, who claimed that the Arab provinces were ripe for revolt, and that a movement already existed that needed only the assent of Europe to bring about the final confrontation. The book won serious consideration in various foreign offices, and was reviewed in the prestigious policy periodicals of the day. Azoury first posed to Europe what soon became known as the Arab question.[31]

Hartmann had an answer to that question, which he felt compelled to offer following the appearance of Azoury's controversial book. The book itself, wrote Hartmann, was highly suspect. Azoury's prophecy that the struggle between Arabs and Jews for Palestine would prove decisive to the entire world struck Hartmann as a blatant sign of anti-Semitic motive, an impression strengthened by Azoury's promise of a forthcoming work entitled *Le péril juif universel: Révélations et études politiques*. Hartmann observed (correctly) that Azoury was a common family name among Syrian Jews, and speculated (wrongly) that Azoury himself might be an ex-Jew, whose work was an attempt to disown his origins.[32]

Yet Azoury's prejudices did not offend Hartmann as much as the alliances that Azoury urged upon the movement he purported to represent.

Azoury's book was written in French for a French audience, and directly appealed to those Frenchmen who were eager to gain an advantage for France at the expense of her European rivals. Azoury proposed to make the Arab national movement an agent of French influence in return for French support. "From a European point of view," wrote Azoury, "our independence conforms fully to French interests. If Syria and Mesopotamia remain in the hands of the Turks, within ten years all of Asia Minor will be a German colony."[33] Hartmann was outraged, certainly as one who had idealized the Arab cause, but also as a German with a jaundiced view of all reliance upon France. Azoury, he averred, imagined France to be a disinterested "good fairy," prepared to grant the Arab movement's every wish. But it was a delusion to think that the French would raise a finger or part with a centime for a free Arabia.[34] Hartmann had even harsher words for Azoury's French collaborator, Eugène Jung, whose book of 1906, entitled *Les puissances devant la révolte arabe*, was a deemed by Hartmann a "wretched, sorry piece."[35] These were the Arab movement's "false friends," whose activities brought "discredit" to the cause.[36]

Having dispensed with Azoury and his French collaborator, Hartmann took up the more consequential issue of the actual state of Arab opinion. It would be wrong, he warned his German readers, to see the Arab cause as one championed solely by intriguers and careerists. Resentment against Turkish rule ran deep and wide. The "Arabic-speaking masses of Asia and Africa" were "astir." But it was true that these masses had failed to form one alliance and recognize one of their own as leader. Hartmann attributed the lack of movement to the Arab dilemma of self-definition. "What is the 'Arab nation'?" Did these disparate elements, settled across North Africa and into Asia, indeed constitute one nation? "The worst enemy of the Arab is himself," answered Hartmann. The Arabs were "selfish, envious, quarrelsome," qualities that, throughout their history, had brought them under the domination of foreigners—first of Persians, then of "an inferior people," the Turks. With the fall of the Umayyads, Islam had ceased to be the religion of the Arab ethnos. A foreign religious autocracy devoted ostensibly to preserving the interests of Islam now held sway. The "dictatorship" of the "deranged" Ottoman sultan rested on religious fanaticism, which preached to Arab Muslims the hatred of unbelievers and foreigners. The reawakening of the Arabs to their identity began only with the literary revival authored mostly by Syrian Christians, who were by disposition "energetic, diligent, and persevering." Only they were truly free of the mind-shackling constraints of Muslim solidarity.[37]

But while Arab Muslims still clung to a tradition of self-abnegation in the name of Islam, even here there was "movement." Hartmann placed particular emphasis on an event that now occupies no place at all in retrospective accounts of early Arab nationalism: the uprising of 1904 against Ottoman rule in the Yemen. The new Imam of Yemen, Mahmud Yahya, had laid siege to the Ottoman garrison in San'a that year, forcing the Ottomans to withdraw and sue for peace. These Yemeni highlanders were "wild" and defiantly independent, and Hartmann did not rule out the possibility of their northward expansion into the Hijaz and even Syria, uniting Arabia under one rule. It was not clear to Hartmann whether Syrian Christians or Yemeni rebels would ultimately shape the Arab movement. But either could build on the eventual support of the discontented mass of Arab Muslims, who knew Turkish rule to be a "misfortune."[38]

Hartmann's very early claim that the Ottoman Empire had lost the loyalty of its Arab Muslim subjects could only arouse controversy. The prevalent political mood in Germany at the time was strongly Turcophile, a mood inaugurated by the celebrated visit of Kaiser Wilhelm II to Syria in the autumn of 1898. Such sentiment received crucial validation from other German observers who claimed that the Ottoman Empire most certainly did command the allegiance of its Muslim subjects. The German policy of professed friendship towards Islam rested on the assumption that Islam's true center resided in Istanbul, and that Turkish primacy in Islam stood uncontested. Hartmann's bold dissent raised eyebrows. It could only have damaged his simultaneous effort to have a chair of Islamology established in Berlin. The creation of such a chair required the backing of interested official circles, willing to force a door still held shut by academic purists. So it had been in France. But who could possibly be interested in lending the authority of an endowed chair to the kind of ideas Hartmann now propagated? Hartmann, in championing an unorthodox view regarding the health of the Ottoman Empire, demonstrably set aside self-interest.

A decade of these claims reached their culmination in 1908, with Hartmann's completion of a great grab-bag of archaeological, philological, and historical ruminations on Arabia, published as *Die arabische Frage*. This was a strangely proportioned book in which the notes occupied five times the space of the text. And it was strangely titled, since only a few pages were devoted to what was widely understood to constitute the Arab question. By this time, the Imam of Yemen had reached an accommodation with the Ottomans, so demonstrating himself to be of "small spirit." It would be wrong, Hartmann now wrote, to see the Imam's movement as an Arab nationalist one. Indeed, it seemed to Hartmann that the obstacles to the development of any independent, national Arab polity, "as the kernel of an Arab national state," were now "colossal." To think that these could be overcome by bombarding foreign governments with memoranda pleading for help was "the summit of naiveté." To all those who worked on behalf of the Arab cause, he offered this sobering advice: "Act with the courage of optimism, but without self-deception."[39]

Here was a telling sign of disillusionment, not with the undeniable justice of the Arab cause, but with the ability of the Arabs to ever see it to fruition. It stemmed, too, from Hartmann's growing realization that Arab Muslims still held firmly to the rope of Muslim solidarity. In the decade since he had first taken up the Arab cause, Hartmann had been unable to adduce any evidence for his claims concerning the shifting loyalties of Arab Muslims, and he eventually felt it necessary to modify them. It is noteworthy that Hartmann made no mention of Kawakibi's *Umm al-qura*, which he might have cited as evidence for the spread of Arab nationalism among Muslim thinkers. But Hartmann believed the British to be behind the appearance of Arab nationalist ideas in Egypt. From England's "ruthless power policy" had emerged the idea of an Arab state under the nominal rule of an Egyptian king, a state in which each constituent part would enjoy autonomy.[40] It was an idea that Hartmann regarded as a betrayal, for again it placed the Arab movement directly under the tutelage of an outside power. If he knew at all of Kawakibi's work or activities, he might well have dismissed them as a part of this scheme, which owed its life to foreign paymasters. By 1908, Hartmann had come to believe that Arab independence would follow only an arduous "step-by-step" process of enlightening Arab Muslim opinion.

In July 1908, Sultan Abdülhamid restored the Ottoman constitution, ending what Hartmann had long decried as Hamidian "tyranny and terror." The news from Turkey recalled for Hartmann the stirring days of 1876, when the disastrous Sultan Abdülaziz had been deposed and Sultan Abdülhamid had been persuaded to grant the first Ottoman constitution.[41] Hartmann had been a student of Turkish in Istanbul at precisely that time, and the restoration of the suspended constitution after more than thirty years seemed almost a personal invitation to reassess his position. Hartmann passed the months of September and October 1909 in Salonika and Istanbul, making notes along the way. The resulting book, published under the title *Unpolitische Briefe aus der Türkei*, made it clear that, for Hartmann, the revolution had failed, just as it had in his youth. It had produced mostly chaos and corruption, all portrayed in the book with an unbridled animosity.[42]

Among the revolution's many failures, Hartmann included its unwillingness to redress the grievances of the Ottoman Empire's Arab population. Everywhere Hartmann saw evidence for blatant discrimination against the Arabic language and its speakers. Even before his visit, he noted that Arab representation in the new parliament fell far short of the Arab share of the general population. He also learned of the founding in Istanbul of a Society of Arab-Ottoman Fraternity, and even secured copies of its publications in French and Arabic. The Society, composed of Arab parliamentary delegates and Arabs residing in the capital, did not preach separatism, but it did demand equality for the Arabs and their language. Hartmann cited an article in the Society's Arabic periodical which attacked the Turkish-language press for presenting the Arabs "in the filthiest way," a practice which gained currency during a press campaign against the hated Arab advisers of the sultan. All this, in Hartmann's view, simply hastened the day when "the Arab peasants," regarded so contemptuously by their Turkish overlords, would "give marching orders for good to the arrogant foreign pests."[43] As Hartmann later ascertained during his visit to Istanbul, the Society quickly broke apart on the rocks of internal quarrel.[44] But in its short life he saw the pattern for a future movement, assertive of Arab rights but free from dependence on any outside power.

For nothing so threatened Arab nationalism's prospects as the continued attempts to win it foreign support. Now another Syrian Christian, Rashid Mutran, busied himself in Paris, posing as the head of a committee "representing all the Syrians of Turkey and abroad," and issuing proclamations and a publication in order to win foreign backing. Hartmann recognized the "well-known trick" by which an upstart traveled about the capitals of Europe and created the illusion that he headed a movement. Hartmann thought Mutran was a fraud and said so.[45]

According to Hartmann, those truly working for national independence in Syria knew that its time had not yet come, and so preferred to operate within existing frameworks. Arab eyes were gradually opening to the fact that the Turks were "cunning and violent," and a clean break between "Ottomans" and Arabs would eventually occur. (The break-up of the Ottoman share into three states—Turkish, Kurdish, and Armenian—was only "a matter of time.") As for an interim strategy, Hartmann speculated freely about how the Arabs might wrest control from the Turks without rebellion or reliance on foreign powers. Against the Turks, the Arabs needed able allies within the Ottoman parliament; the people best suited for such an alliance, both by temperament and shared interests, were the Greeks of Asia Minor. Were the Arabs to join hands with the Greeks, and win the support of Jews, Armenians, and even a few Albanians and dissident Turks, the public administration and finance of the Ottoman Empire might be placed on an even keel.[46] But this cooperation would be no more than an interim arrangement. Arab independence, too, was only a matter of time.[47]

Return to Syria

Many years had passed since Hartmann had last set eyes on Syria's shores. Since coming to Berlin he had visited Cairo and Istanbul, and had gone on adventurous expeditions through the Libyan desert and Chinese Turkestan. But he had not been through Syria since his departure from Beirut in 1887, and what he knew about subsequent shifts in the mood of its peoples reached him by circuitous routes. Hartmann was an assiduous student of the Arabic press, which he followed as best he could under difficult circumstances. He knew something about the orientation and content of all the principle Arabic newspapers published in the Ottoman Empire and Egypt, although he could not follow them regularly and assessed many of them only on the basis of a few issues.[48] He conducted some correspondence with various editors of Arabic newspapers, including Jurji Zaydan and Khalil Sarkis, but the letters dealt strictly with literary matters. He also corresponded with German officials and consuls in the Levant and Anatolia, and with a few missionaries. But given Hartmann's long absence from the region, it had become difficult for him to speak authoritatively in his own country against a growing Turcophile sentiment, fed by German correspondents, travelers, engineers, and advisers who regularly traversed Syria. For lack of first-hand evidence, Hartmann even took to quoting these would-be authorities, when they confirmed his theories about the spread of Arab discontent.[49]

Hartmann finally resolved to return to Syria and to give an account of his journey in regular despatches to the *Frankfurter Zeitung*. In March 1913, he arrived in Haifa, and over the next five weeks visited Damascus, Beirut,

Hamah, Tripoli, Latakia, Homs, and Aleppo. The despatches were quickly published as a book entitled *Reisebriefe aus Syrien*, a valuable account of the state of Syria on the eve of the war.

Hartmann, viewing Syria with an eye for progress, could not but dwell upon the economic transformation of the country in the twenty-six years since he had last seen it. He recognized the tremendous significance of the new railroads, and declared Haifa "the city of the future," with its railhead and harbor. (There were also Zionist settlers there, but Zionism always seemed to Hartmann a utopian venture, of no political import.)[50] As for Damascus, Hartmann estimated that its population had more than doubled since his last visit in 1887, and while the atmosphere of the old marketplace had not changed, even the most modest residential streets had electric light. Beirut, a thriving center of commerce and education, had the look of a European city. All of this progress he attributed to the combination of foreign capital and local ability, and the growth had been in spite of onerous Ottoman policies.

But Hartmann concerned himself above all with charting changes in the political climate, and assessing the prospects for an Arab movement. He himself had no doubt about the ultimate aims of the "Stambul Effendis" and the ruling Committee of Union and Progress. They sought the Turkification of the Arabs through the "swindle" of "Ottoman nationality." For Hartmann, the very notion of an Ottoman identity seemed riddled with contradictions. The regime, in appealing to its Muslim subjects, emphasized religious allegiance to the Caliph; in appealing to non-Muslim subjects, it insisted they cast aside religious allegiance in favor of a secular loyalty to the sultan. In either instance, Ottomanization amounted only to Turkification, at the obvious expense of Arabic language and cultural expression.[51]

This Hartmann knew, but did the Arabs know it? His despatches were guarded. In Damascus he met with Muhammad Kurd Ali, "an extraordinary man" and editor of the newspaper *Al-Muqtabas*, which had published Arab grievances against attempts at Turkification and had been closed down in the past by the authorities. But Kurd Ali was "nervous and excited" during the meeting, which took place in the presence of others, and Hartmann did not find the setting conducive to a frank exchange.[52] One can well imagine Kurd Ali being circumspect in speaking with Hartmann, and Hartmann showing discretion in writing about their meeting. In any event, Hartmann attributed no views directly to Kurd Ali.

Once in Beirut, however, Hartmann began to formulate conclusions about the nature of "the Arab opposition to Turkish rule." This opposition took two forms, national and religious. In its national form, it obviously sprang from resistance to Turkification and administrative centralization. In its religious form, it arose from the resentment of pious Arab Muslims against the Young Turks, who stood for equal treatment of believers and unbelievers. Most Syrian Muslims did not understand that Arabdom would never have fallen as "booty" to the Turks had Arabic-speakers of differing religious faiths worked together. Few were prepared to work together now, and so the principal obstacles to true national consciousness were international bonds of religion, of the Maronite clergy and of what Hartmann called the international "church" of Islam. It was especially the internationality of Islam which "breaks the courage of the opposition to foreign rule." Arab national awareness was struggling toward maturity, toward victory over these other forces, and one could discern early signs of a break with the already weakened bonds of international religion. This had produced an Arab national spirit in Syria.[53] Now Hartmann looked forward to the day when a reformer of Islam would arise to finally sweep away "the entire debris of ritual" so that Arab Muslims might advance together with Arab Christians as one Arab nation.[54]

In mid-April, as Hartmann moved through northern Syria, important news reached him. The Ottoman authorities had moved against the Beirut Reform Committee, a group of local notables who had proposed a plan for administrative decentralization in January. This development was a welcome sign of discontent, although Hartmann thought the Beirut plan too modest.[55] An informant then gave him an account of the related activities of those Syrians belonging to the Ottoman Decentralization Party in Cairo, and Hartmann began to discern the contours of a wider movement linking Cairo, Beirut, and Damascus. This finally prompted him to question the wisdom of established German policy. Germany had withheld moral support for the subject peoples of the Ottoman Empire in accordance with a policy of "non-intervention," and she had systematically ignored Arab claims in deference to Turkish prestige. However, as the Arabs drew apart from the Turks, they were bound to seek assistance from foreign nations, and Germany stood to lose if she did not act. Germany's position in Syria was still sound, "despite all the intrigues against us," and Hartmann implied that a German effort should be made to extend support for legitimate Arab claims. Certainly the big German concerns operating in Syria should have demonstrated a measure of respect for the Arabic language. By way of annoying example, Hartmann noted that train information at the Aleppo station on the German-managed Baghdad railroad was offered only in Turkish and Armenian.[56]

But the remarkable point about Hartmann's Syrian journey was that he met no one who openly professed the idea of Arab separatism. When he met leaders of the Beirut Reform Committee, they were quick to assure him that they had no intention of undermining the caliphate of the Ottoman sultan, or challenging the inclusion of the Arab provinces in the Ottoman Empire.[57] Nor did the nervous Kurd Ali confide in him. It was not merely that Hartmann did not enjoy their trust. Obviously a German scholar writing for a newspaper could not expect these new acquaintances to share their innermost thoughts with him, but it also seemed to Hartmann that his Arab interlocutors had not yet convinced even themselves that reform could not work or that their only solution lay in independence. No one took schemes for an Arab caliphate seriously, and when the Sharif of Mecca was mentioned to a prominent Muslim supporter of reform in Beirut, Hartmann heard him dismiss the Meccan grandee as "a wretched simpleton" with a "wild" following.[58] And so while Hartmann did not alter his own view—that Turkish rule was "a succession of violations"[59]—he saw no Arab revolt on the horizon, and did not predict one.

While Hartmann probed for cracks in the Ottoman edifice, Germany committed itself still further to a policy of holding that edifice together. Hartmann obviously had done little to inspire the confidence of official circles with his writings, and it became clear to him that his efforts for establishment of a chair of Islamology in Berlin were bound to fail. He himself would remain a teacher of Arabic in what many scholars regarded as hardly more than a state-supported "Berlitz School" (or, in the uncharitable words of Becker, a "trade school for overseas routine").[60] It is impossible to tell from published sources just how Hartmann's criticisms of Turkish rule in Arab lands might have worked against him professionally. He had done much else to make himself an unacceptable candidate for such a chair. In print, Hartmann pointed an accusing finger at the narrow-mindedness of philologists and the inertia of Berlin bureaucrats, but unspecified "circumstances" did not permit him to speak "more openly."[61]

In the end, Hartmann simply set aside convention by acting as though he did occupy a chair. From the summer of 1910, he began to offer courses on Islamic culture, society, and theology. In January 1912 he and some like-minded colleagues founded the Deutsche Gesellschaft für Islamkunde, a scholarly society devoted exclusively to the study of contemporary Islam. Hartmann accepted the presidency of the new society, which exercised considerable influence through its journal, *Die Welt des Islams*.[62] On its pages, Hartmann continued to follow developments in Syria, particularly in his detailed reviews of foreign journals and books. In Beirut he had met the Viscount Philippe de Tarrazi, who had just published the first volume of his monumental history of the Arabic press.[63] Back in Berlin, Hartmann reviewed this essential source for the early history of Arabism, pronouncing again that the "religious bond" between Arabs and Turks was weak, and that the deep chasm between them remained unbridged.[64]

From Arabs to Turks

Then an unnatural transformation occurred. Becker put it delicately in his account of Hartmann's career. After 1914, "as regards the Turks, he turned from Saul into Paul." Hartmann's sudden enthusiasm for the Turks seemed "suspect" to some, wrote Becker, but the change was not for "lack of character; quick reassessments lay at the heart of his character."[65] Yet it was not the speed of the reassessment which seemed suspect. It was the timing, coming as it did precisely when Germany entered a war alliance with the Ottoman Empire.

While Hartmann sometimes wrote impulsively, his views on Turks and Arabs had not changed in any important respect since he first formulated them many years earlier. Hartmann certainly could not have continued to write about the Turks as he had written in the past, even had he wished to do so. Freedom of expression disappeared with the war, and no criticism of an ally could be tolerated in print. Yet Hartmann went still further, substituting adulation for ridicule. In recalling his devastating 1909 account of the new regime in Istanbul, Hartmann insisted that his *Unpolitische Briefe aus der Türkei* was mistakenly regarded as an anti-Turkish tract. "I have never felt animosity towards the Turks," he protested in 1916; the harsh words in the book had been directed only against individuals.[66]

During the war, Hartmann turned his talents almost exclusively to the study of Turkish literature and modern Turkish thought. But more than that, Hartmann began to write pieces that served Germany's war propaganda needs. Although they never approached Becker's war articles for sheer polemical distortion, they dealt with similar themes in a similar manner.

Most of Hartmann's pieces were published in two periodicals created especially for the purpose of convincing readers of German that the alliance with the Ottoman Empire served essential German interests and constituted a moral necessity.

Hartmann forged new friendships with the many Ottoman propagandists, Turkish- and Arabic-speaking, who arrived in Berlin during the war.[67] He did not comment on the disaster that soon befell some of his past Arab interlocutors. In the editorial offices of *Al-Muqtabas* in Damascus, he had conversed with Rushdi al-Sham'a, "a man in his forties with a round, rosy countenance," and Amir Umar al-Jaza'iri, "a tall, slender man of plain appearance."[68] Both were sentenced to death for treason by an Ottoman military court and were hanged in May 1915. In Beirut, Hartmann had fallen under the spell of Shaykh Ahmad Tabbara, a bold newspaper editor, "cheerful and strong and confident of victory," whom Hartmann regarded as "a shining example of Arab vigor."[69] He too met his end on the gallows. But other Arabs whom Hartmann admired, especially Muhammad Kurd Ali, stood solidly behind the Ottoman war effort. Their decision made Hartmann's choice still easier.

And Hartmann, too, had his allegiances. Despite his support for the Arab cause, he had refused to subject Germany's Eastern policy to trenchant criticism. He shared the wider German preoccupation with the "intrigues" spun by France, England, and Russia against the legitimate interests of Germany in Ottoman lands. He strongly disapproved of any form of Arab nationalist expression tainted by association with Germany's rivals in Europe. Now the Young Turks had shed their neutrality in favor of a German alliance at a crucial moment in the war, while Arab nationalists entered the not-so-secret embrace of Germany's enemies. Hartmann did not confuse his allegiances with his sympathies, and as a man too easily given to enthusiasm, he did his duty as a German not with dour resignation, but with the zeal of a true Turcophile. "Hartmann's present enthusiasm for Muslim prayer and the Turks is as distasteful to me as was his previous slander of them," wrote Hurgronje.[70] Hartmann spent his last days immersed in Turkish texts, and when he died after a short illness in December 1918, representatives of the Turkish colony of Berlin saw him laid to rest.[71]

From the turn of the century until the war, Martin Hartmann wrote and published as a friend of Arabism. His sympathy was forged by early personal experience and a dissident temperament that were shared by very few of his compatriots. But Hartmann was a lone friend in still another sense. If there had been an organized Arab movement in his time, it almost certainly would have sought him out. The diverse nationalist groups within the Ottoman Empire made a point of cultivating foreign friends in their struggle for foreign sympathy, and they had use for scholars as well as for statesmen. Hartmann would have been a valuable ally to such an Arab movement, for his imagination needed little stoking. As it happened, it was Hartmann who had to rush about Syria in search of a nationalism still without form. He found a "spirit" of Arabism, but did not know of the secret societies and the clandestine dealings. What he did see constituted a movement in its infancy. Arabism could not have known Hartmann, and so does not remember him. It arose too late, and then chose friends of lesser fidelity.

Notes

1. The most influential piece of writing on Martin Hartmann (hereafter MH) has been the compassionate but highly critical obituary written by Carl Heinrich Becker, "Martin Hartmann," in his *Islamstudien*, (Leipzig: Quelle & Meyer, 1932), 2:481–90, first published in *Der Islam* 10 (1920): 228–33. For other brief descriptions of MH and his work, see Lucien Bouvat, "Martin Hartmann," *Revue du monde musulman* 12 (1910): 530–31; Georg Kampffmeyer, "Martin Hartmann," *Die Welt des Islams*, o.s., 6 (1918): 67–71; Johann Fück, *Die arabischen Studien in Europa* (Leipzig: Harrassowitz, 1955), 269–73; Wolfgang Reuschel, "Zu Werk und Persönlichkeit des deutschen Arabisten Martin Hartmann," in *Arbeiterklasse und nationaler Befreiungskampf*, ed. Elmar Faber (Leipzig: Karl-Marx Universität, 1963), 159–66; W. van Kampen, "Studien zur deutschen Türkeipolitik in der Zeit Wilhelms II" (Ph.D. diss., Kiel University, 1968), 298–99; Ulrich Haarmann, "Die islamische Moderne bei den deutschen Orientalisten," *Araber und Deutsche*, eds. Friedrich H. Kochwasser and Hans R. Roemer (Tübingen and Basel: Erdmann, 1974), 59–63; Baber Johansen, "Politics and Scholarship: The Development of Islamic Studies in the Federal Republic of Germany," in *Middle East Studies: International Perspectives on the State of the Art*, ed. Tareq Y. Ismael (New York: Praeger, 1990), 87–88; and the introduction to *Islamkunde und Islamwissenschaft im deutschen Kaiserreich: der Briefwechsel zwischen Carl Heinrich Becker und Martin Hartmann (1900–1918)*, Abdoel-Ghaffaar: Sources for the History of Islamic Studies in the Western World, vol. 5, ed. Ludmila Hanisch (Leiden: Documentatiebureau Islam-Christendom, Faculteit der Godgeleerdheid, Rijksuniversiteit, 1992), 12–19, 21–24. This last item is a carefully annotated edition of MH's correspondence with Becker. For MH's bibliography, see Gotthard Jäschke, "Islamforschung der Gegenwart. Martin Hartmann zum Gedächtnis," *Die Welt des Islams*, o.s., 23 (1941): 111–21; *Die Welt des Islams*, o.s., 6 (1918): 86–87 (for MH's contributions to *Die Welt des Islams*); and *Islamkunde und Islamwissenschaft*, 129–48. The latter is comprehensive. MH's papers are located in the old library of the Deutsche Morgenländische Gesellschaft in Halle (Saale), Germany. They are cited here as MH Papers. The collection is uncatalogued; I am indebted to Ludmila Hanisch, who loaned me her private catalogue of the collection.
2. See Holger Preissler, "Arabistik in Leipzig (vom 18. Jahrhundert bis zur Mitte des 20. Jahrhunderts)," *Wissenschaftliche Zeitschrift der Karl-Marx-Universität Leipzig,*

Gesellschafts und Sprachwissenschaftliche Reihe 28, no. 1 (1979): 87–105.

3. Becker, "Martin Hartmann," 481.
4. Kampffmeyer, "Martin Hartmann," 69, as related to him by Nöldeke.
5. Becker, "Martin Hartmann," 483.
6. Such judgments pervade MH's *Der islamische Orient*, vol. 3, *Unpolitische Briefe aus der Türkei* (1910; reprint, Amsterdam: APA-Oriental Press, 1976), discussed below (and cited henceforth as *Unpolitische Briefe*).
7. A judgment formed during visits to Cairo; MH, *The Arabic Press of Egypt* (London: Luzac, 1899), 3.
8. MH, *The Arabic Press of Egypt*, 3–4.
9. MH received many love notes, probably in 1885, signed "Labibe Saber"; see MH Papers, packet 260.
10. MH's attachment to the Armenians also dated from his Beirut years, for it fell to him to arrange the placement of Armenian children in German orphanages after a massacre of Armenians at Urfa in 1882. MH, *Reisebriefe aus Syrien* (Berlin: Reimer, 1913), 102.
11. This and other occasional despatches from Hartmann are found in the German Foreign Office Archives as microfilmed by the University of California, National Archives Microcopy T-139, reel 275.
12. MH, *Unpolitische Briefe*, 173. A note from Yaziji to MH from 1880, MH Papers, blue file XI/2, mentions a loan of fifty francs which MH made to Yaziji.
13. The declaration establishing the Seminar, dated 6 August 1887, is preserved in MH Papers, blue file III/40.
14. MH (Berlin) to Ibrahim al-Yaziji, 21 December 1887, MH Papers, packet 141.
15. MH note of 17 August 1912, MH Papers, blue file I/1. The note concerns MH's meeting with Amin al-Rihani, with whom he spoke Arabic.
16. Undated autobiographical notes, MH Papers, blue file I/9.
17. MH, "Die Arabistik—Reformvorschläge," *Orientalistische Literatur-Zeitung* 1 (1898): 334–42.
18. MH, "Neue Bahnen der Orientalistik," *Beiträge zur Kenntnis des Orient* 1 (1902–3): 28–29. Fleischer had died in February 1888.
19. MH, "Les études musulmanes en Allemagne," *Revue du monde musulman* 12 (1910): 534–35.
20. A proposal that MH first made in his "Islamologie," *Orientalistische Literatur-Zeitung* 2 (1899): 1–4.
21. For the parallel controversy surrounding the establishment of a chair for "the sociology and sociography of Islam" at the Collège de France, see Edmund Burke, III, "La Mission Scientifique au Maroc," *Bulletin économique et social du Maroc*, nos. 138–39 (1979): 45–46. MH corresponded with Alfred Le Chatelier, first incumbent of the chair. In one letter, Le Chatelier revealed to MH that it had never been his intention to create such a chair. "My chair should have been a chair of African and Muslim Politics with a capital P—that is, history and doctrine. But the word 'politics' alarmed some people, who asked me at the last moment to change the title. So I invented 'sociography' and attached 'sociology' to it." Le Chatelier (Paris) to MH, 15 December 1912, MH Papers, packet 97.
22. MH, "Les études musulmanes," 536.
23. For MH's favorable view of Islamic reform, see his "Islam und Arabische," in his *Der islamische Orient*, vol. 1, *Berichte und Forschungen* (1900; reprint, Amsterdam: APA-Oriental Press, 1976), 14–18. MH knew the reformist Shaykh Muhammad Abduh, who sent him books, and MH's papers include a letter from an intermediary,

Edward Elias, conveying Abduh's regards. "He was just in Europe," wrote Elias of Abduh. "It would appear that travels in the West give great pleasure to our venerable shaykh." Elias (Cairo) to MH, 31 October 1893, MH Papers, packet 209.

24. C. H. Becker, "Islam," *Archiv für Religionswissenschaft* (Leipzig) 15 (1912): 535–36. In this review article, Becker criticized MH's popular *Der Islam: Geschichte—Glaube—Recht* (Leipzig: Haupt, 1909), which he thought had been hastily composed, doing only damage to Hartmann's reputation.

25. MH, *Islam, Mission, Politik* (Leipzig: Otto Wigand, 1912), iv–xvii.

26. *Scholarship and Friendship in Early Islamwissenschaft: The Letters of C. Snouck Hurgronje to I. Goldziher*, Abdoel-Ghaffaar: Sources for the History of Islamic Studies in the Western World, vol. 2, ed. P. Sj. van Koningsveld (Leiden: Documentatiebureau Islam-Christendom, Faculteit der Godgeleerdheid, Rijksuniversiteit, 1985), 179, 196, 200, 220.

27. Becker, "Martin Hartmann," 482–83, 490.

28. MH, "Die Arabistik," 336.

29. MH, "Islam und Arabische," 6–10; disparaging remarks on the Ottomans in MH, *Der Islam: Geschichte—Glaube—Recht*, 185–86.

30. MH, "Die Mekkabahn," *Orientalistische Literatur-Zeitung* 2 (1908): 5–6.

31. On Negib Azoury, see Elie Kedourie, "The Politics of Political Literature: Kawakibi, Azoury and Jung," in his *Arabic Political Memoirs and Other Studies* (London: Frank Cass, 1974), 107–23; Stefan Wild, "Negib Azoury and His Book *Le Réveil de la Nation Arabe*," in *Intellectual Life in the Arab East, 1890–1939*, ed. Marwan R. Buheiry (Beirut: American University of Beirut, 1981), 93–5; and Martin Kramer, "Azoury: A Further Episode," *Middle Eastern Studies* 18 (1982): 351–58.

32. MH, "Das neue Arabien," *Beiträge zur Kenntnis des Orient* 2 (1904–5): 15.

33. Interview with Azoury, *La République française* (Paris), 21 May 1905. The interview is in MH's copybooks. Elsewhere, Azoury was cautious not to burn Arab bridges to Germany. Kaiser Wilhelm II had erred in pursuing the friendship of the tyrannical Sultan Abdülhamid. Still, Germany's true interests lay not in Arab lands but rather in Anatolia. Azoury expressed the hope that the cause of Arab independence might yet win the Kaiser's sympathy. Negib Azoury, *Le réveil de la nation arabe dans l'Asie turque* (Paris: Plon-Nourrit, 1905), pp. 131–42.

34. MH, "Die Mekkabahn," 5. MH did have an indirect channel to Azoury: Edmond Fazy, a Parisian journalist and editor of *La République française*. Like MH, Fazy was strongly anti-Ottoman, as evidenced by his tract, *Les Turcs d'aujourd'hui, ou le Grand Karagheuz* (Paris: Paul Offendorff, 1898). Fazy took a keen interest in Azoury beginning in 1905, and interviewed Azoury several times for his newspaper. In 1907, Fazy attempted to persuade MH to reconsider his view of Azoury. MH replied with a scathing letter denouncing Azoury as a peddler of false information. MH also hinted that he had once known Azoury, but that "my friendship with him quickly ended" when he caught Azoury in lies; MH (Berlin) to Fazy, 27 May 1907, MH Papers, packet 3. Fazy replied that he still thought highly of Azoury, and urged MH to correspond directly with him; Fazy (Paris) to MH, 31 May 1907, MH Papers, packet 3. No correspondence with Azoury is preserved in MH's papers.

35. MH, "Die Mekkabahn," 5.

36. MH, *Der islamische Orient*, vol. 2, *Die arabische Frage* (1909; reprint, Amsterdam: APA-Oriental Press, 1976), 91. This volume is henceforth cited as *Die arabische Frage*.

37. MH, "Das neue Arabien," 94–95, 98–101.

38. MH, "Quid novi ex Arabia?" *Das freie Wort* (Frankfurt) 5 (1905): 257–59, 305–6.

MH's friend, Edmond Fazy, also shared this excitement over events in Yemen, in a series of articles he published in *La République française*, 18, 26 June 1905. The ultimate source of Fazy's enthusiasm, transmitted to MH, was none other than Azoury.

39. MH, *Die arabische Frage*, 88, 91–92.
40. Ibid., 559–61.
41. For MH's initial enthusiasm about the Young Turk revolution, see MH, *Die Frau im Islam* (Halle, 1909), 19.
42. The tone of MH's *Unpolitische Briefe* drew considerable fire in reviews and correspondence. The Russian Orientalist Vladimir Minorsky took MH to task in a letter: "Despite my respect for the opinions of others, I must say that such books, serving objectives which are *purely political* and not scientific, can only inflame passions and excite hatreds. You have spent thirty-five years studying Turkey. How much time did you spend forming your abusive generalizations about that country?" Minorsky (St. Petersburg) to MH, 16 October 1910, MH Papers, packet 155. See also packets 21, 51, and 123, which include more reviews and criticisms of the book, and MH's replies.
43. MH, "Der Islam 1908," *Mitteilungen des Seminars für Orientalische Sprachen*, Abteilung II, 12 (1909): 52–55.
44. MH, *Unpolitische Briefe*, 172.
45. For MH's discussion of Mutran, see MH, "Der Islam 1908," 56– 58, 106.
46. Ibid., 58–60.
47. MH, "Abdulhamid," *Das freie Wort* 9 (1909): 130.
48. A catalogue of MH's library is preserved in MH Papers, blue file IX/47. He owned a wide range of early Beirut newspapers and Ottoman provincial yearbooks. MH was supplied with this material largely by Jurji Sursuq, an employee of the German consulate in Beirut. Sursuq also collected the lyrics of the popular chants of Lebanon which MH studied. MH's papers include many letters from Sursuq decribing the political situation in bleak tones. "There is no repose in the Orient," he wrote in one letter. "There is no civilization in Islam." Sursuq (Beirut) to MH, 27 June 1909, MH Papers, packet 12.
49. In a typical instance, MH quoted an article by a German traveler, with whom he was obviously unfamiliar, as evidence that the Arabs in Palestine expected the revolt in Yemen to proceed northwards and free them from Ottoman rule; MH, "Das neue Arabien," 105, n. 15.
50. Not long after his return from Syria, the Zionist leader Nahum Sokolov came to visit Hartmann at his office, and began to explain to him the intricacies of Zionist and anti-Zionist politics. Hartmann professed indifference to the subject. There were only 12,000 souls in all the Jewish colonies, he noted; Tel Aviv, four years after its founding, had only 1,600 inhabitants. MH's notes of meeting with Sokolov, 23 December 1913, MH Papers, blue file II/3.
51. MH, *Reisebriefe*, xii, 66–67.
52. Ibid., 13–15.
53. Ibid., 24–25, 34–36, 45.
54. Ibid., 68.
55. For MH's discussion of the plan, see ibid., 39–43; and MH, "Die Vereinigten Staaten des Osmanischen Reiches," *Das freie Wort*, 13 (1913): 199–206.
56. MH, *Reisebriefe*, 91–95.
57. Ibid., 107–8.
58. Ibid., 108.
59. Ibid., 99.

60. Georg Kampffmeyer, "Das Seminar für Orientalische Sprachen zu Berlin," *Die Welt des Islams*, o.s., 8 (1923): 10–11.

61. MH, "Les études musulmanes en Allemagne," 533, 535.

62. Materials relating to the founding of the society are preserved in MH Papers, blue file IV/17.

63. MH, *Reisebriefe*, 106–7. For MH's subsequent correspondence about newspapers with Tarrazi, dating from 1913 and 1914, see MH Papers, packet 166.

64. *Die Welt des Islams*, o.s., 1 (1913): 246

65. Becker, "Martin Hartmann," 488.

66. MH, "Aus der neueren Osmanischen Dichtung," *Mitteilungen des Seminars für Orientalische Sprachen*, Abteilung II, 19 (1916): 129.

67. The importance of these friendships is mentioned by Becker, "Martin Hartmann," 488. MH even wrote a sympathetic introduction to a pro-jihad tract by one of these propagandists: Schaich Salih Aschscharif Attunisi, *Haqiqat Aldschihad, Die Wahrheit über den Glaubenskrieg*, trans. Karl E. Schabinger (Berlin: Reimer 1915), 1. For the circumstances surrounding the publication of this tract, see MH Papers, blue file VIII/1.

68. MH, *Reisebriefe*, 14.

69. Ibid.,110–12.

70. *Scholarship and Friendship in Early Islamwissenschaft*, 500.

71. Kampffmeyer, "Martin Hartmann," 67.

4

The Sharifian Propaganda of Eugène Jung

Most of the national movements that arose from the ruins of the Ottoman Empire entered the world of international politics without benefit of public relations. The support of European powers was something to be gotten through contacts with their official emissaries, and confirmed, if possible, in secret agreements. Few of these nationalist movements had the cross-cultural understanding or intellectual resources to influence European opinion or affect the climate of public debate over the merits of their causes. They opened no information offices, published no newspapers, lobbied no legislators or officials. Often they existed only as rumors in Europe's capitals. In the absence of an organized information apparatus, public debate in Europe was shaped by powerful interest groups, including colonial lobbies, that easily demolished the inarticulate or inaudible claims of the new nationalisms.

From the outset of their revolt against the Turks in 1916, the Sharif Husayn and his followers understood that their claim to Syria would be contested. Yet they could not muster the means to make a compelling public case in London or Paris. In the Sharifian bid for that part of southern Syria known also as Palestine, poor articulation constituted a formidable handicap.

Britain had conquered Palestine by force of arms, and quickly developed an imperial rationale for direct possession. The Zionist movement also utilized many of its best minds to mold British public opinion on the Palestine issue, and it was public opinion that served as Zionism's anchor against the shifting calculations of bureaucratic policymakers.

But there were fewer competing claims to the future of Syria north of Palestine. True, the battery of forces arrayed in favor of French control

---

This study was written in honor of the historian of the Hashemites, Uriel Dann. Alas, it is published in his memory.

over this part of Syria was impressive. They included French officials and strategists who feared British aggrandizement in the Levant if France did not act, clerical and cultural lobbies seeking to promote France's "civilizing mission," and commercial interests wishing to expand and consolidate French economic enterprise in Syria. They also included not a few Syrian Christians, who hoped to be saved from Muslim domination through the agency of French protection, and perhaps establish their own dominion.

Yet the preponderance of French opinion was indifferent to the expansion of France into Syria. It has even been argued that, had the French public ever debated the issue, it might have rejected the burden of Syria.[1] But the Sharifians could not have initiated that debate themselves. An effective case on their behalf could only have been made by an articulate Frenchman, someone who was a friend of the Sharifians and also knew the rules in the world of Parisian publicity-making. That role was filled by the curious figure of Eugène Jung.

Lobbyist for the Arabs

Eugène Jung was born in Bordeaux in 1863. The son of a noted general and parliamentary deputy, he enlisted in 1883, then joined the marine infantry as a junior officer and left for French Indochina in 1885. His administrative career at Tonkin culminated in his appointment as vice-resident of France in 1895, and as chancellor of the Residency in 1900. In 1901 he resigned and returned to Paris, where he lived from the proceeds of a plantation he owned in Tonkin.[2] He wrote occasionally on the problems of colonial administration in French Indochina, and published a number of plays at his own expense.

"On my return from Indochina, the unknown regions of Arabia attracted my attention," Jung later recalled.[3] His career at loose ends, Jung found new purpose in the prospect of an Arab awakening. He established his famous partnership with Negib Azoury, former Ottoman official and self-proclaimed leader of an Arab national committee, in Paris in 1905. Under Azoury's influence, Jung became an ardent supporter of Arab independence from Turkish misrule, publicizing Azoury's claim that the Ottoman Empire's Arab provinces were ripe for revolt. In 1906 Jung published a book, *Les puissances devant la révolte arabe*, urging France to support the Arab separatist movement that Azoury had described in a book of the previous year. From April 1907 to September 1908, Jung and

Azoury published a monthly in Paris, *L'Indépendance arabe*, which urged France to take up the Arab cause against Turkish oppression.

After the Young Turk revolution, Jung and Azoury suspended the paper in the hope that the new regime would allow greater Arab autonomy. These hopes, however, were quickly dashed, whereupon Azoury settled in Egypt and began to write for the newspaper *L'Égypte*. Jung served as Paris correspondent of the newspaper, which called for Arab freedom against the oppressive policies of the Young Turks. In secret contacts, Jung and Azoury also worked together to secure French financial and logistical support for an Arab rising against Ottoman rule. Although their campaign caused a minor stir in some journals of opinion, they never gained the confidence of French officials, who rebuffed each of their many overtures.

This propaganda was not Sharifian. In their prewar efforts, Jung and Azoury emphasized the role of secret Arab committees in Syria, on whose behalf they claimed to act. These mysterious committees would launch a revolt and lead the Arabs to independence. But the Sharif of Mecca did occupy a privileged place in their vision, for both of their books advocated the transfer of the caliphate to a descendant of the Prophet, who would rule the Hijaz and exercise a general spiritual authority over Muslims everywhere.

When the war broke out, Jung integrated this solution to the caliphate problem into his vision of Arab independence. On 7 November 1914, Jung wrote to the president of France offering his services in Asia Minor. Arab officers in the Turkish army were ready to revolt, Jung claimed; in order to activate them, France need only proclaim the Arab independence of Syria, Palestine, Mesopotamia, Hijaz, Asir, and Yemen, and "to name an Arab caliph at Mecca, with a specific territory like the Hijaz. My friends could provide the name of one who would be acceptable to all the Muslims."[4] In a memorandum of 21 January 1915, which Jung sent to French officials and parliamentarians, he argued that the caliphate "be transferred to an Arab descendant of the Prophet, to whom the Hijaz would be given as a temporal realm."[5] The Sharif of Mecca therefore occupied a privileged place in the scheme envisioned by Jung and Azoury, although his authority beyond the Hijaz would be strictly spiritual.

Jung thus could not contain his excitement when the Sharif finally raised the banner of revolt in June 1916. At last the cause of Arab independence, for which he had written countless articles and badgered dozens of officials, had found a champion. But Azoury's untimely death that same month deprived Jung of his Arab collaborator, whom he had always represented as his channel to the Arab movement. Jung could not do without a claim to such a channel, since he lacked the credential of first-hand experience in Arab lands. He did not delay. In August 1916 he found a new partner in the person of a Lebanese journalist, Ibrahim Salim al-Najjar (Naggiar).

Naggiar, born in 1882, was an established figure in Cairo's world of Syrian journalism. He founded his first publication, a weekly, in 1900; during the next few years he founded two other newspapers in Cairo and also corresponded for *Al-Ahram*. After the Young Turk revolution of 1908, Naggiar went to Istanbul as correspondent of the Cairo daily *Al-Muqattam*. While in Istanbul, he created an Arab club, and in 1911 he visited New York to form an Arab committee. He then returned to Istanbul, where he established more committees, as well as another newspaper. According to Jung, Naggiar was also among the founders of the Arab secret society known as Al-Ahd, and tried—unsuccessfully—to create ties between disgruntled Arab officers in Istanbul and the French embassy there.

In 1912, Naggiar returned to Lebanon, but he soon fled to Egypt because of Young Turk persecution, and there became an active member of the Decentralization Party. In 1915 he arrived in Paris and proposed the establishment of an Arabic newspaper to counter German propaganda. He first did some translating, and later contributed to *Al-Mustaqbal*, a newspaper established with official French subsidies under the editorship of Shukri Ghanim and Georges Samné, who both favored French guardianship over Syria. In September 1916, Naggiar fell out with Ghanim and Samné over editorial policy, quitting *Al-Mustaqbal* and offering his journalistic services to the Sharifians. He established a press agency which supplied French newspapers with news from the Hijaz, and he became the Paris political and literary correspondent of the Sharifian newspaper *Al-Qibla* of Mecca. He also continued to report for *Al-Muqattam* of Cairo, and sent despatches to *Al-Sha'b* of New York and *Al-Salam* of Buenos Aires.[6]

Initially, Jung and Naggiar wrote and elicited articles on the Arab cause in French journals of opinion, but they were dependent on the whims of editors at a time when their message required a steady outlet. This led Naggiar, together with Jung, to create a newspaper in French, entitled *L'Orient arabe*.[7] The new journal appeared irregularly in Paris, on the fifth and twentieth day of each month, beginning on 20 January 1917. The *directeur* of the newspaper was Ibrahim Naggiar; the *rédacteur en chef*, Eugène Jung. An identical arrangement had existed between Azoury and

Jung in publishing *L'Indépendance arabe* a decade earlier.

Each issue consisted of four pages on "political, economic and literary" matters. The first page usually carried statements of Allied principles by Allied leaders, as well as editorials and articles. The inside pages carried additional articles, and the last page, Arab news from various correspondents and press sources. Naggiar wrote many of the pieces in the newspaper, attacking the Turks and praising the Sharif Husayn, his officials and the progress of the Sharifian state. Jung contributed the editorials. Each issue carried an advertisement for Jung's book of 1906, as well as a notice to Syrian commercial agents with business in France urging them to contact the newspaper and avail themselves of its "special services" in placing orders with manufacturers. The newspaper declared that it "conformed to a widespread thought, long germinating in the minds of all Syro-Lebanese Arabs, of having a newspaper in Paris like those of all the oppressed nations who demand justice and liberty."[8]

For Jung, this neglect of French opinion represented a serious oversight on the part of the Arabs. "After 1916, while the Czechs, the Yugoslavs, the Poles, the Transylvanians and the Armenians had propaganda committees, informed the entire world of their desires, filled newspapers with interviews of their leaders, inundated politicians and intellectuals with their brochures, and interested businessmen in economic documents, the Arabs did nothing. They put faith in the justice of their cause."[9] This simple faith was particularly dangerous at a moment when Shukri Ghanim's Comité Central Syrien was working to convince French opinion that Syria cried out for French guardianship.

Jung and Azoury had always regarded Ghanim as the principal obstacle to French acceptance of the idea of Arab independence. When the Arab congress had been held in Paris in 1913, Azoury had informed Jung that Ghanim was in league with Turkish Decentralists and the Sabaheddine group, seeking an accommodation with Istanbul that fell short of Arab independence. "I am most pleased with this congress," Azoury had written to Jung, "because it will make all those persons there [in Paris] and throughout the Arab world aware of the inanity of any attempt at alliance or collaboration with the Turks. Then they will all come around to us."[10] On the eve of war, Ghanim had shifted from collaboration with the Turks to seeking protection by France. Refuting Ghanim's call for French administration of Syria required a much more determined effort in Paris. Ghanim's collaborator, Georges Samné, published a newspaper in French, the *Correspondance d'Orient*, which enjoyed the support both of the colonial lobby and certain officials at the Quai d'Orsay. If Jung and Naggiar wanted to enter the debate on an equal footing, they too needed a regular outlet for their views.

The Case for Syrian Independence

The campaign conducted by Jung and Naggiar in *L'Orient arabe* opened with the claim that the Arabs were just as worthy of independence as the peoples of Europe. In France, few thought that the Arabs were capable of self-government. Shukri Ghanim, for his part, persistently questioned the ability of the Arabs to govern themselves without sliding into anarchy and bringing about European intervention. But according to Jung, the Arabs had already proved themselves capable of mobilizing the human resources necessary for self-rule. "Their lack of discipline," wrote Jung, mocking Ghanim's dismissal of the Arabs, "has produced incontestable results in the military campaigns of the Hedjaz and Mesopotamia. Their lack of administrative and military manpower has been transformed into an organization of merit, thanks to all the Syro-Arab intellectuals in the Egyptian administration and to the thousands of Arab officers who have graduated from the great schools of Europe. Their religious fanaticism has permitted Christians to hold the highest posts at Djeddah and has prompted the King to proclaim freedom of religion explicitly." Criticism of the Arabs had "but one purpose: to justify a policy of expansion which Arab sentiment opposes in advance."[11] To illustrate these claims, Naggiar produced a series of laudatory articles about Sharif Husayn, and lavished praise on Fu'ad al-Khatib, the undersecretary of state for foreign affairs in the Hijaz government, whom Naggiar labeled "the Arab D'Annunzio."[12]

But if the Arabs gained independence, would not a fanatical Muslim majority oppress Christian minorities, who had traditionally looked to France for protection? Islam, Jung countered, was not a religion of fanaticism; it only became fanatic under certain conditions. In a number of tribes east of the Jordan, a mélange of Muslims, Catholics, and deists lived side by side without conflict. The Turks alone were responsible for such religious discord as existed among the Arabs.[13] But did Ibn Sa'ud not reject the claims of Sharif Husayn? No, announced Jung; the two chiefs had been reconciled: "There are no more rivalries. There is only one purpose: the Arab revival." The Arabs had taken on a "new life," wrote Jung; the "Arab soul" had been "transformed, almost made anew, through the adoption of modern ideas, the achievements of Western science and concepts of justice."[14]

Yet even if the Arabs deserved self-government and were capable of exercising it without oppressing minorities, did not Arab independence threaten to undermine France's position? How were French strategic, commercial, and cultural interests to be protected if the Arabs gained independence in Syria under Sharifian rule, especially in view of the total Sharifian dependence upon the British? French apprehension over British aggrandizement extended far beyond the colonial lobby to a broad public, sensitive to the issue of French prestige. The close collaboration between Great Britain and the Sharifians had created a distinct sense of exclusion among the French, so that even the few Frenchmen who actively favored the idea of Arab independence thought the Sharifians a weak vessel for the cause.

Jung responded that it was not too late to win the Arabs to the French side. In an article entitled "As Liberators, Not as Conquerors," Jung did praise Britain for its support of the Arabs: "England has rendered resounding homage to the expansive force of the Arab race. She has recognized that the Arabs have demonstrated themselves to be the equals of Europeans from both the intellectual and moral point of view, in every branch of industry and in the liberal professions."[15] But if France extended the same homage to the Arabs, the Arabs would reciprocate: "Is it not France that has always, from the first, supported the independence of peoples? Is not liberty a French word?"[16] Jung urged his countrymen to adopt a fair-minded policy:

> We have friends among [the Arabs]; guard them preciously. Be their good counselors, without any unjust thoughts; be their economic support, without ideas of monopoly. We will enjoy advantageous benefits, and will conserve our moral prestige in the eyes of the world. But, for the sake of God, reject the suggestions that conceal shameful purposes and serve evil ambitions. Be liberators, not conquerors.[17]

Jung did not rely exclusively on argument. He was also an amateur playwright with a flair—or perhaps a weakness—for the dramatic. This was vividly reflected in an article he wrote for the seventh issue of *L'Orient arabe*, titled "Au drapeau!" In the piece, Jung described the dream of an Arab officer, a fictitious hero named Baha-Eddine, who deserts the Turkish army to join his Arab compatriots in the Sharifian ranks. Here, Jung gives imaginative fantasy a free reign. The vision opens with Arab tribesmen galloping across vast expanses under a relentless sun, "their eyes ablaze with a feverish glow." They surge from the depths of the desert, driving out the Turkish troops. Long convoys, hastening to bring provisions to a population starved by the Turks, follow in their wake. Detachments of European armies arrive by sea.

> Arrayed before them are the Arab soldiers of the new caliph and great king, who have come from the lands of the south. In their midst is an imposing group of official persons gathered in full dignity—an extraordinary mélange of grey, green and blue uniforms, of black cloaks and white burnooses, with crosses and medals of gold that sparkle and dazzle.
>
> To the rear is the crowd.
>
> Silence descends.
>
> A high dignitary steps forth from the group and mounts a dais. He is a representative of the great American republic. In a lofty voice, quite clear, he reads: In the name of the free peoples of the world, it is proclaimed that the Arab world is free, that it is master of its destinies, that it will never again know oppression, that happiness, peace and wealth will bring about a rebirth of these beautiful lands, cradle of the world.
>
> The great Arab chiefs bow in acknowledgment.
>
> The trumpets sound their notes vibrantly; the musicians play the hymn of liberty, the Marseillaise; hurrahs ring out. A poignant emotion stirs hearts when, slowly, upon a mast chosen from the tallest ceders of Lebanon, an immense flag is raised which, when unfurled, reveals its shimmering colors: green, white, black! The green of the Prophet, the white of the Umayyads, the black of the Abbasids. Arabia has awakened; she has been restored to the world.[18]

In the early issues of *L'Orient arabe*, Jung urged French support for the Arab cause based upon the abstract concepts of liberty and justice. But when the prospect of French occupation of Syria became real, he stipulated a specific demand for Arab independence free of any French interference. Syria, he warned, must not be turned into another Tunisia. France's predominant position in Asia Minor could be assured without the complications of "an occupation full of perils," he wrote. "Our task is simple, from this day forth. Syria and Palestine want their independence. Only the Holy Places will remain internationalized, if this is insisted upon, although the rest of Palestine will neither understand nor accept this measure. These countries will be free, with a parliament, responsible cabinet ministers, and officials chosen among them and by them."[19] In an unsolicited report submitted to the French prime minister on 2 April 1917, Jung declared that the Syrians wanted "the greatest possible autonomy, including a constitutional regime, two chambers, a ministry responsible to both chambers and their own officials chosen by themselves from among themselves."

Under no circumstances could Syrians be subjected to the kind of regime that governed Moroccans, Tunisians, or Algerians.[20] At the same time, he urged the Syrians themselves to make provisional arrangements until such time as their affairs were institutionalized at a future peace conference. Meanwhile, Syrian Arabs outside the country "should openly declare the absolute freedom of the country and renounce before all the Allies any form of domination, be it a disguised or some other form of protectorate."[21]

L'Orient arabe, in advocating Syrian independence, also opposed Zionism, although this theme did not preoccupy Jung, who regarded French rather than Zionist ambitions as the principle obstacle to Arab independence. The newspaper carried a four-part series against Zionism, written not by Jung but by one of his French collaborators, which bore the title "Nécrologie: Le sionisme." Zionism was a threat, but one with no future; the series dismissed it as a mere creation of the Wilhelmstrasse. In later years, Jung would make amends for this underestimation of Zionism, attributing to the Jews a malignant and "occult" influence over Great Britain and the United States.[22] Yet he never claimed that France had succumbed to this menace. He directed his hostility at the French colonial lobby, determined foe of justice for the Arabs.

The Suppression of *L'Orient arabe*

Most of the passages quoted here were excised from the newspaper by the wartime censor. While the French authorities permitted the publication of *L'Orient arabe*, the censor cut statements deemed prejudicial to the future status of Syria. The censor ordered deletions from the very first issue, and the cuts became progressively more numerous, so that by the fifth issue the editors felt compelled to protest in print. The newspaper, they claimed, had been greeted "from the outset by an incomprehensible animosity that has expressed itself in numerous excisions. Why? For what purpose?" The journal "has not departed from the bounds of correct conduct. It has not raised diplomatic questions or made military assessments—though perhaps on this point it could have said some very useful things. It has not strayed into polemics." These "dictatorial" measures had only two plausible explanations: "They are the work either of an overly zealous subaltern, or of those loyal to a certain coterie known to us."[23]

At the same time, ominous rumors began to circulate that the newspaper received "very large sums of money" from "powerful friends"—a transparent reference to Britain. "Alas! Three times alas! *L'Orient arabe* has always had a poor little room for an office; its editors have lived from their writing in Job-like austerity." They had never touched a subsidy, and had never "extracted from others' pockets—oh, Robert Houdini!"—any sum, either for publishing or suppressing their views.[24] The French foreign ministry suspected Naggiar of being a paid agent of Britain,[25] a charge which he denied: "We received not a centime, not a sou, not only from abroad or from a foreigner, but for our work, our labors and our journalistic pains."[26] The only sum received from the British was the price of two subscriptions to the newspaper—one for the British embassy in Paris, the other for the Foreign Office in London.[27]

Just who financed the newspaper is not known. It certainly had subscribers, but Jung probably subsidized it himself. (He later published a number of his own books privately.) According to Jung, the enterprise suffered from a chronic lack of funds that made it impossible to put Arab propaganda in Paris on a proper footing, and he blamed the Syrian diaspora for not financing the defenders of Syrian independence. Syrians had done well in the United States, Egypt, Argentina, Brazil and Chile.

> But these people, rich and therefore powerful, did not offer financial support (or offered very little) to their representatives and defenders. Some did not have enough courage to begin the struggle; others thought only of their own affairs. Some were too young and had only ardor and good will; others awaited the outcome of the struggle before committing themselves. And all of them, even those living abroad, feared reprisals by the Turks against their near and dear ones.[28]

In the end, however, it was not censorship or accusations or deficits that brought the newspaper to ruin, but Naggiar's journalistic incompetence. On 13 August 1917, Naggiar was suddenly arrested and sent off to a detention camp near Mayenne in Normandy, and later transferred to Angers. His offense, according to the authorities, had been a cable sent by him to *Al-Muqattam* on 1 August, in which he reported that French prime minister Alexandre Ribot made a statement disavowing any French intention of occupying Syria. In fact, Ribot's statement dealt with French war aims in Europe, and made no reference to Syria.[29] The false item proved to be of considerable embarrassment to the French foreign ministry, and since Naggiar was an Ottoman national, the authorities punished him by arrest.

An issue of *L'Orient arabe* (the sixteenth) appeared on 20 October 1917, protesting Naggiar's detention. In an editorial, Jung admitted that Naggiar had made an error, but it warranted no more than a reprimand or the revocation of his press telegraph card. He certainly did not deserve to be sent to a concentration camp along with Turks and Germans. "Coastal Asia Minor is not French territory, and M. Naggiar has committed no crime of *lèse-patrie* by claiming independence for his country under the aegis of France," Jung wrote. The damage France had done to itself by his arrest was "incalculable." Jung met with Ribot on 22 September to plead for Naggiar's release and to explain his program, but to no avail. "Our conversation was long—and useless," he reported.[30] Jung concluded that he had been outdone by the conspiratorial forces of the colonial lobby and international financiers working in concert:

> Alas, we face a grouping of financiers, very international before the war and very Ottoman, which has designs on Syria, Lebanon and Palestine. Arrayed against us is a group of functionaries who covet positions (read M. Richard's subsidized book, *La Syrie et la Guerre)*,[31] and who had close relations with this world of finance before the war. And finally we have political personalities who aspire to high office. All of them, allied closely together, desire all legitimate opposition to be smashed; they want to succeed in their destructive task. They resort to all means, accusing us for no reason of pan-Arabism; they reproach us, without any proof, for receiving subsidies from certain of our Allies.[32]

The piece, which concluded with a pledge to continue publication despite Naggiar's arrest, was cut by the censor, but Jung sent uncensored copies abroad, whereupon the authorities promptly issued a three-month closure order against *L'Orient arabe*. Subscriptions lapsed and the newspaper did not reappear when the closure order was lifted. Ten months later, on 15 August 1918, the seventeenth and last issue appeared, again lamenting the arrest of Naggiar, who was still in detention. This issue, too, was censored. On 25 August the newspaper was banned indefinitely. It never appeared again.

The Lost Cause

With the closing of *L'Orient arabe*, Jung lost the principal weapon in his propaganda arsenal. The newspaper had given him an instrument, however imperfect, for initiating public debate. Without it, he had to fall back on lobbying behind closed doors, where he was least effective. He had become a familiar figure at the French foreign ministry during his partnership with Azoury, persistently advocating Arab revolt. Since the considered opinion of France's own representatives in the Arab lands had contradicted Jung's assertions, his views had ceased to carry any weight.

As a former colonial official, Jung could not be denied a hearing, and the foreign ministry granted him an occasional audience, which also enabled it to keep abreast of him. But Jung's message fell on deaf ears. Publicity, not diplomacy, was his strong suit; without a newspaper he lost his voice.

This did not prevent him from attempting to play a role in the diplomatic struggle that unfolded with the approach of the peace conference at Versailles. The young and inexperienced Emir Faysal arrived in Paris in December 1918 to represent Sharifian interests before heads of state and world public opinion. Jung hurried to see Faysal, and the Emir conveyed his father's regards to Jung. The Parisian publicist eagerly placed himself at Faysal's disposal. As Faysal had come to Paris without any supporting documents, Jung put together a dossier of Allied statements for use by the Arab delegation. But Jung wished to play a more active role, reminding Faysal that the visiting Arab was "unfamiliar with Western customs." Faysal would need to pursue a "combative" campaign to win public opinion, and to refute every charge against him, particularly the accusation that he was on Britain's payroll.[33] Jung clearly hoped that he himself would emerge as Faysal's public relations adviser, and thus serve as midwife to the birth of the independent Arab state that he had advocated a decade before the Sharifians raised the banner of revolt.

Instead, Jung suffered a devastating blow—not from his old opponents in the colonial lobby and the Quai d'Orsay, but from the Sharifians themselves. "Unfortunately," he wrote in his book, "Prince Faysal was quickly cornered by Syrians who had lived in France for many years, but whose experience was in the brasseries of the Latin Quarter rather than in political and diplomatic circles." Faysal's young Arab advisers were jealous of all those who wished to "speak the truth," and they plunged the delegation into a series of ill-conceived maneuvers. Faysal, complained Jung, made an additional mistake by appearing in Paris alongside T. E. Lawrence, whom the French regarded as a British agent despite his Arab garb.[34]

Spurned by the Sharifians at precisely the moment when his talents might have been put to use, Jung lost heart:

> Tired of fourteen years of struggles, unable (as I wrote to King Hussein) to accept being considered an intruder by Prince Faysal himself, having sustained too many wounds in this interminable struggle on behalf of the Arabs, seeing more and the more that the conflict would become acute and not wanting to be involved in it as a Frenchman, I left Paris for the Rhineland.[35]

The Arab delegation's snub completely undermined Jung's pretension that he enjoyed a privileged channel to the leaders of the Arab movement. His pride had been damaged. Although time and again he had suffered rebuffs by French officials, their rejection had never discouraged him from knocking on more doors. He attributed his setbacks to their misunderstanding of the Arab cause, not to their doubts about his own credibility. In his unabashed account of his failed lobbying in his two-volume *La révolte arabe*, Jung seemed completely unaware that he had been dismissed by the French foreign ministry as a nuisance. Yet when the Arab delegation turned their backs on him in 1919, Jung understood that it was his credibility, not his cause, that the Arabs doubted. He could maintain his pride in the face of rejection by financiers and high officials—enemies of Arab independence—but not by the Sharifians themselves. Jung remained in the Rhineland until 1923 and did nothing on behalf of the Sharifians at the moment of reckoning in 1920, when France dashed their Syrian dreams and illusions and occupied Damascus.

By the time Jung returned to Paris in 1923, his small window of opportunity had closed. The French and British had consolidated their positions in Syria and Palestine; Naggiar had left for Jerusalem, where he renewed his career in journalism.[36] During the following decade Jung again took up the cause of the Arabs and Islam, publishing half a dozen short polemical books. But Jung's advocacy lacked the sharp focus on Arab separatism and Sharifian primacy of the war years. In fact, his later work was clearly distinguished from his earlier writing by its increasingly pan-Islamic content. Jung's defense of Islam mirrored his growing awareness of the role of Islamic fervor in Arab nationalism—a fervor that his earlier propaganda, formulated in partnership with Syrian Christians, had completely ignored. There is no evidence that Jung established any formal partnership with Shakib Arslan, the Geneva-based Syrian exile whose influential French-language propaganda gave expression to Muslim protest against the denial of independence to Syria. But Jung echoed Arslan's message, calling for the restoration of the Arabs to their true place in history through adherence to Islam. Previously Jung had advocated Arab revolt against the Turks—a revolt that resulted in Arab subjugation under yet another imperialism, one that threatened their cultural integrity and, in Palestine, their actual possession of the land. Jung now sought to make amends, claiming that Islamic revolt had supplanted Arab revolt as the true cause of the hour.[37] This radical shift of emphasis could hardly have enhanced his credibility in his last years.

Jung does not figure in histories of French policy toward Syria, and in the few places where he is mentioned in histories of Arab nationalism, he appears only as Azoury's collaborator. In the end, he was doubly marginal. His efforts, however tireless, were too insubstantial to provoke a serious French policy debate over Syria. Those same efforts also failed to earn the appreciation of an Arab nationalist movement that was so self-absorbed that it did not know how to win or keep foreign friends. And so Jung's career as self-appointed champion of the Arab cause went unacknowledged by the very Arabs whom he sought to liberate. In his unrequited devotion, Jung typified the small group of foreigners who endorsed Arab nationalism even before it put forward its own claims. Their shared romanticism, dilettantism and alienation suggest that their political sympathy for the Arabs was a response to an inner need—that the "feverish glow" Jung saw in Arab eyes was actually a reflection of his own.

Notes

1. Christopher M. Andrew and A.S. Kanya-Forstner, *France Overseas: The Great War and the Climax of French Imperial Expansion* (London: Thames and Hudson, 1981), 29.
2. Police report on Jung, 2 December 1912, archives of the Ministère des affaires étrangères (Paris), Turquie: Syrie-Liban, nouvelle série, vol. 118.
3. Eugène Jung, *La révolte arabe*, 2 vols. (Paris: Colbert, 1925) 1:11.
4. Ibid., 106.
5. Ibid., 117.
6. For biographical details on Naggiar, see *L'Orient arabe* (Paris) (hereafter cited as *OA*), 5 September 1917; open letter from Jung to Clemenceau, *OA*, 15 August 1918. Naggiar's connection with Al-Ahd and his mediation with the French are mentioned by Jung, *La révolte arabe*, 1:32, 74. The newspapers which he founded in Cairo and Istanbul are listed in Yusuf As'ad Daghir, *Qamus al-sihafa al-lubnaniyya, 1858–1974* (Beirut: Al-Jami'a al-lubnaniyya, 1978), consult index.
7. A complete set of *L'Orient arabe* is preserved in the annex of the Bibliothèque Nationale in Versailles, near Paris. *L'Orient arabe* was subject to wartime censorship from the very first issue; the collection at Versailles includes both the censored and uncensored versions of most issues of the newspaper.
8. *OA*, 20 March 1917.
9. Jung, *La révolte arabe*, 1:13.
10. Text of letter from Azoury (Egypt) to Jung, received by Jung on 1 June 1913, in *OA*, 20 October 1917. The letter and Jung's commentary were excised by the censor. He later published it in *La révolte arabe*, 1:67–68.
11. Jung, "En libérateurs...pas en conquérants," *OA*, 5 April 1917.
12. Naggiar's article on Husayn in *OA*, 20 May 1917; on Khatib, *OA*, 20 January 1917.
13. Jung, "Questions de conscience," *OA*, 20 May 1917.
14. Jung, "L'Ame arabe," *OA*, 5 March 1917.

15. Jung, "En libérateurs...pas en conquérants," *OA*, 5 April 1917. The article owed its title to a proclamation by General Maude of 19 March 1917, when he led Allied forces into Baghdad.
16. Jung, "Le coeur de la France et de ses alliés," *OA*, 20 January 1917.
17. Jung, "En libérateurs...pas en conquérants," *OA*, 5 April 1917.
18. Jung, "Au drapeau!," *OA*, 20 April 1917.
19. Jung, "Concorde," *OA*, 5 and 20 June 1917.
20. Jung's report to the présidence du conseil, 2 April 1917, in Jung, *La révolte arabe*, 2:39.
21. Jung, "Concorde," *OA*, 5 and 20 June 1917.
22. E.g. Jung, *Les arabes et l'Islam en face des nouvelles croisades, Palestine et Sionisme* (Paris: L'auteur, 1931), 68–70.
23. *OA*, 20 March 1917.
24. *OA*, 5 September 1917.
25. Open letter from Jung to Clemenceau, in *OA*, 15 August 1918.
26. Naggiar to Jung, 5 October 1917, published in *OA*, 20 October 1917. In the letter, Naggiar asks Jung to get him a lawyer.
27. Jung, *La révolte arabe*, 2:41.
28. Ibid., 1:12–13.
29. Ibid., 2:58–60, for Jung's version of the episode.
30. Ibid., 62.
31. Henry Richard, a colonial official who had served in Africa, urged in his book of 1916 that Syria be placed under a French governor-general and French officials, and administered as "our spoils of war, just like German Togo and the Cameroons, conquered by our troops." For Jung's criticism of the book, see *La révolte arabe*, 2:23–24.
32. 32.*OA*, 20 October 1917.
33. Jung, *La révolte arabe*, 2:116–17.
34. Ibid., 2:121.
35. Ibid.
36. Naggiar was freed at the end of the war. His activities as a Sharifian propagandist ruled out journalistic activity in French-controlled Syria, and he settled in Palestine. In 1921 he established a daily newspaper in Jerusalem, the *Lisan al-arab*; see Yusuf Q. Khuri, *Al-Sihafa al-arabiyya fi Filastin, 1876–1948* (Beirut: Mu'assasat al-dirasat al-filastiniyya, 1976), 35. Later, he returned to Beirut and in 1939 founded and edited the daily newspaper *Al-Liwa*, which appeared (sporadically) until shortly after his death in 1957. See Daghir, *Qamus al-sihafa*, 236 (entry 1429). For Naggiar's role as a pioneer of Lebanese radio, see Yusuf As'ad Daghir, *Masadir al-dirasat al-adabiyya*, vol. 3, pt. 2 (Beirut: Al-Maktaba al-sharqiyya, 1972), 1316.
37. Jung, *L'Islam sous le joug* (Paris: L'auteur, 1926), 74.

5

The Arab Nation of Shakib Arslan

Shakib Arslan, the "Prince of Eloquence," was a master of self-promotion. As a publicist and self-publicist, Arslan kept his name in print between the world wars by producing a journalistic and literary corpus of formidable proportions: he wrote twenty books and two thousand articles. His polemical periodical, *La Nation arabe*, had an avid readership in Europe, among sympathizers and critics alike.

It is all the more striking, then, that Arslan should have eluded thorough study in the West, which he made his battleground for Islamic independence. William Cleveland, the author of the first Western biography of Arslan,[1] points to one explanation for this neglect: the Islamic unity championed by Arslan was defeated by secular nationalism. His efforts were spent in vain, earning him posthumous obscurity. To this one must add the unwillingness of Arslan's family to permit access to his voluminous papers. Even Arslan's Arab biographers, who were competent but never critical, failed to win their full cooperation. Neither did Cleveland, who was told in 1974 by Mayy Junbalat, née Arslan, that her father's papers had been sent off to Morocco, where they languish in government custody. To write a subject's life without his papers is an enterprise fraught with dangers. Yet Cleveland has met the documentary challenge with such resourcefulness that one doubts whether a radically different truth could ever emerge from Arslan's own papers. Their concealment has now become all the more pointless.

Shakib Arslan was a man of one vocation and many careers. Born in 1869 to a powerful Druze family in the Lebanese Shuf, he might have anticipated a long career as chief of a clan, defending the interests and honor of his kin and folk, and rallying them to arms whenever persuasion failed. This is precisely the role of Arslan's grandson, Walid Junbalat, who today guides the small Druze community of Lebanon in and out of confrontations with various militias, states, and world powers. Arslan did try his hand at chieftainship, mostly out of a sense of *noblesse oblige*. But his education, eloquence, and literary ability cultivated within him a sense of mission too ambitious to ever find satisfaction in the service of his sect. Arslan was touched at a precocious age by Afghani and Abduh, and drank from the literary fountains of Istanbul and Cairo while still a youth. In this heady world of ideas, he learned the dimensions of Islam's crisis, and fixed upon the Ottoman Empire as the last bulwark against the subjugation of Islamdom to an insatiable West. As the nineteenth century closed, Arslan chose as his vocation the defense of all Islam, becoming a fiercely patriotic Ottoman and a cosmopolitan pan-Islamist.

Cleveland adroitly sets the scene for that most fateful of Arslan's choices: his support for the Ottoman Empire's entry into a world war that would destroy it and send Arslan into permanent exile. Few Arabs rendered as many services to the Ottoman war party and its German ally as Arslan. His belligerent ardor was matched only by his contempt for those who plotted with the British to foment Arab revolt. A romantic intellectual without a dash of military judgment, Arslan adored the reckless Enver Pasha, whom he continued to serve after final defeat, during Enver's ill-fated exile in Berlin and Moscow.

Enver's demise cut Arslan adrift. In the prime of his own life, Arslan saw his empire divided, his military idols smashed, his homeland occupied by a foreign power. In his determined defense of Islam, he would have to draw up a new personal order of battle. While others continued the struggle on native soil, Arslan chose to pamphleteer on colonialism's doorstep, in Switzerland between the two world wars.

Agitprop in Geneva

It is here that Cleveland's sources become rich and his narrative vivid. Arslan took it upon himself to represent the Arabs before the League of Nations, and especially before the League's Permanent Mandates Commission. He held his formal brief from the fractious Syro-Palestinian Congress, but actually answered to no one in his campaign against the French and British mandates. He soon became a tremendous nuisance. Arslan bombarded the Mandates Commission with petitions, attended meetings of assorted oppressed peoples, hosted known agitators in his home, and published his views in any journal that would print them. Police and intelligence files bearing his name grew thick with reports of his doings and his intercepted mail. Cleveland makes thorough use of this material, particularly the files of the Swiss, who were compelled by French pressure to keep close a close watch on Arslan's activities. With Arslan's publication of *La Nation arabe*, beginning in 1930, his views found a regular and influential outlet, adding still more to his fame and notoriety.

Cleveland argues convincingly against the claim of Arslan's Arab biographers that Arslan embraced Arab nationalism during this period, and narrowed the aim of his campaign to Arab independence. In fact, there is overwhelming evidence for a deepening of Arslan's interest and involvement in the wider struggle of all Muslims against foreign rule. Arslan never made the full passage to Arabism, but formulated an all-embracing Islamic nationalism that included but transcended the Arab cause. *La Nation arabe* was misleadingly titled, for it carried dozens of articles on subjects remote from Arab concerns then and now.

It must remain an open question whether this unwillingness to give some focus to his struggle enhanced or diminished its effect. Arslan came to exercise a vast influence in North Africa, and tirelessly sought support in the wider Muslim world for the defense of Islam's western flank. This campaign reached its apex with his famous agitation against the Berber *dahir*, and much of Arslan's later reputation he owed to his success in exciting the Arab East over this dire threat to Islam in Morocco. On the other hand, he sank nearly as much effort into the cause of the Balkan Muslim minorities, whose plight (at the time) failed to fire the imagination of wider Islam. But for Cleveland, this Islamic nationalism is important as evidence for the underlying continuity in Arslan's values and beliefs, which made him a man of unvarying principle and integrity. He was no precursor, but he did reformulate the familiar message of Islamic solidarity in a rich language that many Muslims found inspiring.

Still, Arslan did not attempt to reformulate Islam itself, a point that Cleveland rightly underscores. Why this hesitation, in a man whose outspoken opinion knew no other limits? Cleveland suggests that Arslan lacked an interest in theology. But to this one must add Arslan's own awareness that his very standing as a believer was not beyond question.

It is not clear whether Arslan remained in any sense a Druze, having declared quite early that he regarded himself a Muslim like all Muslims. Even so, he was schooled in a climate of religious relativism, and was deeply influenced by radical reformers and freethinkers. Cleveland makes allowance for these influences in describing how Arslan presented Islam to others, but is too wary of his evidence to ask whether Arslan genuinely believed in Islam as religious logic. Did Arslan need the crutch of personal belief? In a chapter on Arslan's view of tradition, Cleveland seems poised to answer, but he chooses not to leap into the void, and one is left to draw the conclusion that Arslan was satisfied with his claim that modernity and belief could be reconciled.

But if evidence for religious doubt ever does come to light, as it did when Afghani and his papers became the object of critical scrutiny by scholars, the careful reader of this biography will not be surprised. Cleveland has warned us that Arslan preferred to leave the defense of Islam as a theological system to others. When Arslan wrote of Islam, he meant to evoke a sense of group solidarity that could inspire mass resistance to foreign encroachment. Religion was useful since it strengthened that solidarity, and infused it with power. This is a position that has been reconciled as often with agnosticism as with belief, and it is interesting that Cleveland offers no comment on the degree of Arslan's personal piety. From this account, it would seem that political integrity, not religious piety, was Arslan's strong card.

Philosopher and Kings

Yet how did he maintain this integrity when faced with the need to raise funds for his work? Subsidies kept Arslan afloat during these years, and he became indebted to many patrons. All of them had political aspirations, regarded him as a good investment, and expected a return on their money. Cleveland is quite right in determining that Arslan could not be bought by such subsidies. But Arslan became expert in misleading his patrons to believe that he could.

Consider Arslan's relationship with the ex-Khedive Abbas Hilmi II, one of Arslan's most important patrons between 1922 and 1931. There can be no doubt that Abbas wanted to use Arslan to build support for his bid for the throne of an independent Syria. Arslan knew it, but Cleveland maintains that it was Abbas who deceived Arslan, by concealing his true ambitions for close to a decade. Here Cleveland has relied upon Arslan's own published apologia that, like all of Arslan's accounts of his ties to patrons, smacks of self-justification. No added credibility is lent to this account by its appearance in Arslan's letters to Rashid Rida (released years ago for publication not by Arslan's family but by Rida's heirs). Truth in these letters is twisted by the fact that Arslan dreaded Rida's moral judgment even more than public ridicule. Theirs was not simply the intimate friendship described by Cleveland, but a relationship infused with moral and religious tension, and worthy of deep analysis.

For an accurate impression of Arslan's relationship with Abbas, one must turn elsewhere, to file 118 of the Abbas Hilmi Papers at Durham University Library. This file, which somehow eluded Cleveland, contains some 300 pages of Arslan's letters to Abbas, and here the picture becomes clear. Arslan massaged the ex-Khedive's vain ambition in a masterful way, leading his patron to believe that Arslan would declare himself for Abbas—when the right moment came. When Abbas finally made his bid, in 1931, and Arslan was called upon to return interest on Abbas's investment, he naturally defaulted. The relationship ended. Abbas could never have owned Arslan, but Arslan intentionally led him into thinking he could, an Arslanian ruse that the "Prince of Eloquence" would employ whenever it suited him.

Abd al-Aziz Ibn Sa'ud also extended his patronage to Arslan, and Cleveland accurately describes the many ways in which Arslan exalted the new king, by publishing praise of Ibn Sa'ud's regime at every turn. Cleveland tends to regard Arslan's attachment to Ibn Sa'ud as one of complete devotion, inspired by the Arabian monarch's Islamic fervor and martial prowess. Arslan was so enamored of his hero, claims Cleveland, that Arslan favored Ibn Sa'ud as head of a possible confederation of Syria, Iraq, and Arabia. Cleveland quotes a letter to Rida in 1931 in which Arslan declared that "I prefer no one over Ibn Sa'ud, not even Faysal."

Not even Faysal? Arslan's declaration to Rida that he preferred Ibn Sa'ud came in a letter written to persuade Rida that *Faysal* should have the throne; it was a rhetorical flourish, meant to disarm Rida's objections. In fact, Arslan's well-know flirtation with Faysal in the early 1930s led Ibn Sa'ud to cut off Arslan completely. Arslan revealed this in a letter that he wrote some years later to Haj Amin al-Husayni (preserved in a collection described below). When Arslan visited Faysal during the latter's stay in Bern in 1931, Arslan urged him to unify Syria and Iraq under one throne, on which Faysal would sit. "You needn't promote yourself," Arslan told Faysal. "We will handle the promotion." When Ibn Sa'ud got wind of Arslan's role in a scheme that would have greatly strengthened his rival, Ibn Sa'ud fumed against Arslan. "I lost all my standing with him," wrote

Arslan, "and he cut off relations with me. I had received heavy subventions from him because, the truth be told, he was generous to an extreme. And all this was lost because I called for the unification of Syria and Iraq; that is, I put general Arab interests before my personal interests." Khaldun S. Husry has published the gist of a remarkable letter by Arslan, in which he actually tried to convince Ibn Sa'ud that Faysal's occupancy of a combined Syrian-Iraqi throne was in Ibn Sa'ud's best interest! Ibn Sa'ud understandably could not follow this sort of logic, and shut off the money supply. With the failure of the confederation plan, Ibn Sa'ud relented, but Arslan admitted that he never again enjoyed the same standing with Ibn Sa'ud as before.

The episode confirmed how little personal devotion Arslan felt, even to his most generous patron. To advance his sacred cause, he needed the support of more powerful men, and brilliantly led them to believe they could guarantee his loyalty through their patronage. They inevitably felt cheated in the end. Much more remains to be done in exploring Arslan's alliances with Muslim rulers, for they resemble those of his reformist predecessor, Afghani, in their complexity and volatility.

In the Axis

Cleveland has worked from a more substantial dossier in reconstructing Arslan's most dangerous liaisons, with Nazi Germany and Fascist Italy. If the British and French were to be ousted from Muslim lands, popular resistance would never suffice. Arslan had seen popular revolts put down time and again. On his own initiative, he sought an alliance with great but disinterested European powers, who would guarantee Arab and Muslim independence in return for Arab and Muslim support in the event of a general war. Cleveland has drawn upon official German and Italian archives to follow the diplomatic dance that produced the understanding between Arslan and the Axis powers.

Obviously, Arslan's services were needed more by Italy than Germany, since Italy, colonizer of Libya, hardly had the image of a disinterested power in Muslim eyes. Arslan's campaign to cast Italy in a favorable light (for which the Italians showed their appreciation by occasional donations) opened Arslan to severe criticism, even by his admirers. But Arslan would not relent. Through his dealings with Mussolini, he had concluded that Italy's Mediterranean ambitions could help to rid the region of the British and French. Once that end had been achieved, Germany could be relied upon to check the Italian colonial impulse. With this in mind, Arslan assiduously cultivated old friends in the German Foreign Office, who thought it useful to hear him out from time to time. Those of his co-religionists who could not fathom the genius of this scheme, and so accused Arslan of selling himself for a few lire, became his worst enemies. Under the hail of their criticism, Arslan became obsessed with the defense of his personal integrity. Cleveland treats this most compromising of Arslan's liaisons with admirable insight and sensitivity, concluding that Arslan again acted on principles, which he again followed straight into disaster.

It was Arslan's last shred of sound judgment that kept his feet firmly on neutral Swiss soil during the war. Failing health and force of habit also made a move to Berlin or Rome unthinkable. But the Swiss authorities had become strict with him. They banned publication of *La Nation arabe*, and informed Arslan that he would not be readmitted if he left the country. Cleveland shows us an ailing and frustrated old man, sliding into debt and bereft of real influence.

It may prove possible to modify this assessment on the basis of a source that was beyond Cleveland's ken and reach when he conducted his research: the complete collection of Arslan's wartime correspondence to Haj Amin al-Husayni in Berlin exile. The Americans found these letters with the Mufti's other papers in Austria, where he had abandoned them during his flight from fallen Germany. The Israeli foreign ministry had the papers microfilmed in their entirety many years ago, and the materials were finally deposited in the Israel State Archives in 1984. The collection contains 370 pages of correspondence from Arslan to the Mufti, conveyed via the German diplomatic pouch.

Here we have Arslan's running commentary on the course of the war, and his tireless admonitions to the Mufti to pursue this or that line of political action. Arslan exercised an elderly mentor's influence over the Mufti, who kept Arslan going with occasional subventions. These letters also provide evidence, which Cleveland found lacking, for the wartime appearance of *La Nation arabe*. By 1943, four issues had been published in cooperation with the German Foreign Office. After an interruption, the journal reappeared in 1944 in Budapest, the product of the same collaboration. According to Arslan, the periodical carried many articles on such subjects as Muslim cooperation with the Axis powers and the "plots of the Jews." Cleveland's conclusion that Arslan published very little during the war must therefore be revised. Arslan's letters relate that one of the journal's wartime issues ran to one hundred pages, and that he wrote ceaselessly, despite his doctor's advice against such mental exertions.[2]

In concluding this balanced and elegant portrait of a controversial life, Cleveland chooses to regard Arslan's last few years until his death in 1946 as tragic. Arslan was "impoverished, ill, and ignored," and Swiss police reports "revealed an aging man living apart from his wife and son in a residence hotel, passing the days in tearooms with his newspapers, seeing few visitors other than his son, and spending an inordinate amount of time frequenting his bank." So he appeared from a distance, to those assigned to tail him. In a letter to the Mufti, however, we learn of an inner reflection that gave Arslan satisfaction during his last years. His enemies had "died in my lifetime.... I take no malicious joy in death, for I will die as they did. But God made allowance for me, that I might witness the deaths of those who incited aggression and made slander against me." A strange thought in which to find tranquility, and a stranger one to commit to writing, but perhaps not, for a Druze chieftain.

Notes

1. William L. Cleveland, *Islam against the West: Shakib Arslan and the Campaign for Islamic Nationalism* (Austin, Texas: University of Texas Press, 1985).
2. I have yet to discover copies of these wartime editions, which would have been published in very limited press runs in the last days of the war. They are not included in the reprint edition of 1988 by Archive Editions in four volumes.

6

Ambition, Arabism, and George Antonius

The world first learned the history of Arab nationalism from a book published in 1938. *The Arab Awakening* by George Antonius eventually became the preferred textbook for successive generations of British and American historians and their students. Yet few now would deny that *The Arab Awakening*, for all the appeal of its narrative style, is more suggestive of a sustained argument than a history.[1] "I have tried to discharge my task," wrote Antonius in the forward to his book, "in a spirit of fairness and objectivity, and, while approaching the subject from an Arab angle, to arrive at my conclusions without bias or partisanship." But Antonius did not pretend that his work met the highest standards of the historian's craft. *The Arab Awakening* he preferred to regard as the "story" of the Arab national movement, "not the final or even a detailed history."[2] And once the book was near completion in 1937, Antonius wrote that "my contribution should be one not merely of academic value but also of positive constructive usefulness."[3]

In this practical bent, he was encouraged by the very practical American patrons who financed his researches and owned all the rights to the book. One of these insisted that the writing of *The Arab Awakening* "is not an end in itself, but only a means to an end." It was

> an open question just how many problems are solved by the propagation of knowledge. On the other hand, writing a book is an excellent means of establishing a reputation for yourself. It helps you to reach into certain groups which you need to get into intimate contact with, and it gives you authority. In this limited sense, therefore, writing is a useful adjunct to your activities.[4]

These more urgent pursuits required that Antonius transform himself from observer into participant. Antonius himself wrote that

> my particular educational and vocational formation has fitted me to be above all a bridge between two different cultures and an agent in the interpretation of one to the other. I feel that this fitness, so far as it goes, enables me to be of use in the task of studying and

understanding the forces at work in the Near East, and of putting my knowledge and understanding to good account both as an interpreter and a participant. That is what I feel to be my true vocation in life.[5]

The Arab Awakening, then, was written not only to advance an Arab nationalist argument but to establish a reputation in pursuit of a career. That career consisted of casting aside pen and paper and pursuing political influence in a brisk dash across the Middle East—a "short story" of self-immolation that strangely presaged Arabism's own demise.

The Accidental Author

Antonius came late to authorship. Born in 1891 to Greek Orthodox parents in Lebanon, he had been raised in Egypt and schooled in England. After World War I, Antonius had found his niche in the civil service of Palestine, where he proved himself an able administrator in the education department. During the mid-1920s, he had experienced the exhilaration of high negotiations as an interpreter on loan to a British diplomatic mission in Arabia. Sir Gilbert Clayton, who headed the mission, treated Antonius as a partner and confidant—an experience that lifted Antonius above mundane administration and gave him a taste for politics.[6]

Still, it was only after his bureaucratic career had reached an impasse, in an acrimonious dispute over his advancement, that Antonius took up a pen. Had he wished, he could have joined his father-in-law, the publisher of a leading Cairo newspaper, who was eager to bring Antonius into his business. But a conventional career in Arabic journalism did not appeal to Antonius, and only briefly did he consider working as a reporter for the foreign press. For in 1930, an American newspaperman suggested to Antonius that he "do the Near East" for a new institute of international relations financed by a wealthy American, Charles Crane: "This is in general (financially and otherwise) far superior to any correspondent's job; it is dignified and important and the work is useful. If you definitely are leaving the government I don't think you could make a better arrangement than with Crane."[7] Antonius took a leave of absence and sailed for New York, where he signed an agreement with Crane's major-domo establishing Antonius as a fellow of the Institute for Current World Affairs (ICWA). His obligations over the next decade included researching and writing his book and accompanying Crane during the American's annual peregrinations in the region.[8]

Some who met Antonius during this decade thought him a man devoted to intellectual pursuits and committed to scholarship. He seemed preoccupied with the writing of his book, he corresponded with Western historians and orientalists, and he lectured at universities. His occasional forays into politics, wrote one admirer, "were all examples of people asking George to do something, not of his initiating anything. He was the exact opposite of a busybody. The sort of thing which he did take the initiative in was the big intellectual enterprise like the Arabic lexicon or an Institute of Arabic Studies. It was only occasionally, when a particularly glaring political gap presented itself, that he was moved to intervene." Others sought his mediation in their disputes, but "he did not himself seek the role."[9] Here was an assertion that only the most pressing of political exigencies could divert a reluctant Antonius from his scholarly pursuits.

But did Antonius welcome an academic career and the opportunity to pursue his work single-mindedly? In 1936, as *The Arab Awakening* neared completion, Crane learned that Columbia University sought to replace the recently deceased Semiticist Richard Gottheil. Crane immediately wrote to Nicholas Murray Butler, Columbia's president, to propose Antonius as a possible successor. Antonius "is still in the early forties," wrote Crane, "and might have a long and distinguished career at Columbia."

> He is of a fine old Greek family but says he cannot remember the time when he did not speak Arabic and French. He not only knows classical Arabic as well as any Arab, but speaks some ten or a dozen dialects of it. He has his doctor's degree both from Oxford and the Sorbonne. His English is quite the best Oxfordian.... As he is neither Jew nor Arab he is untouched by the deepest racial problems and carries very successfully an objective outlook.[10]

Antonius had not expressed any interest in departing so completely from his prior course. Nor could Antonius present the proper credentials, for he held no doctorate, either from Oxford or the Sorbonne, but had only a bachelor's degree in mechanical science from Cambridge. Yet Butler, perhaps too eager to satisfy so prominent and wealthy a figure as Crane, offered Antonius a visiting professorship for the 1936–37 academic year, in order to allow Columbia to take his measure. Antonius would not be expected to do any formal teaching, but would consult with students and faculty and would "help us to formulate our plans for the continuation of our work in Oriental languages and literatures."[11] The ICWA cabled this remarkable offer to Antonius in Jerusalem.

It would be idle to speculate how Antonius, atop Morningside Heights, might have influenced America's emerging vision of the Middle East. For Antonius did not wish to parlay *The Arab Awakening* into an academic position. He bombarded New York with cables asking for detail after detail on the responsibilities he would be asked to bear at Columbia, and the academic year began without him. Had he acted more decisively, Antonius might have thwarted an effort by Gottheil's widow and Jewish alumni to have the invitation to Antonius withdrawn. They were quick to point out to Butler that Antonius already had a reputation among Zionists as an Arab propagandist, and that Crane's representation of Antonius as "neither Jew nor Arab" widely missed the mark. Since Antonius had procrastinated, an embarrassed Butler still could retract the invitation without too much loss of face, once controversy loomed.[12] This episode, which reflected little credit upon any of the parties involved, underlined Antonius' ambivalence about the prospect of a career in scholarship, far from the political fray. Not for this had he labored.

In anticipation of the publication of *The Arab Awakening* in 1938, Antonius was summoned by his American patrons to formulate a program of further research. To the ICWA, he suggested a new program of study that committed him to a busy schedule of writing and publishing. He vaguely proposed to write "a comprehensive survey of my area," a project that he estimated would require five years to complete. At the same time, he would prepare some half dozen articles for publication each year.[13] But over two years later, the theme of this sequel still had not "taken final shape yet, not even in my mind. But the general lines are as I have already written to you, that it will take the form of a commentary, with examples drawn from the current problems of the countries of my area, on the moral and social issues which confront the world today."[14] There is not the slightest evidence in Antonius' own voluminous papers that he ever began to plan such a study.

"Suitable Work"

If not a sequel, then, what further pursuit appealed to Antonius? He briefly considered working as a paid advocate of the Arab case in London. As early as 1935, Antonius was reported to be "keenly interested" in the establishment of an Arab information office in London. But in his view, "the question of the expense and the financial support of such an office would be too important to be undertaken by only one party, and the mutual sharing of expenses by all parties would be out of the question, since no person equally trusted by the several mutually antagonistic groups could be found."[15] Nor did it seem likely that the remuneration could match his ICWA allowance, which was both ample and dependable.

Later, in January 1939, Antonius arrived in London to serve as secretary to the Arab delegations at the Round-Table Conference on the future of Palestine. This signaled his return to high politics, and one of his British opposites found him "a hard and rather pedantic bargainer" on behalf of the Arabs.[16] According to a British source, Palestinian Arab nationalist leaders even suggested that Antonius

> stay in London to look after the Arab Centre. He anticipated that this meant that the [Arab] Committee in Beirut were contemplating increased Arab propaganda in London. He would rather not accept this post until he had had a chance of learning their mind by travelling to the Near East, but he thought it quite possible he would return.[17]

But this, too, was not precisely what Antonius had in mind. Open identification with the Arab information effort would have made him an overt partisan and disqualified him from a further role as mediator and possible participant. Instead, he returned to the Middle East, where the anticipated outbreak of war seemed likely to provide him with an opportunity, as war had done for him twenty-five years earlier.

This time, it appeared to Antonius that his opportunity would arise in Beirut. There, in late 1939, he took a furnished flat, explaining that "while the war lasts there does not seem much to choose between residence in Beirut, Jerusalem or Cairo, save for the fact that the first is appreciably cheaper than either of the others." In April 1940, he reported that he did visit Cairo and Jerusalem, "to discover whether there might be some advantage in shifting my residence," but learned that "there is little to commend either as being preferable to Beirut."[18]

Beirut at this time, while perhaps cheaper than the other two cities, was also the site of considerable intrigue, the work of exiled Palestinian Arab nationalist leaders and local clients of rival European powers, and there is ample evidence that Antonius began to seek out opportunities in this cauldron. From the middle of 1940, he began a quest for wartime employment, a fact he belatedly confessed to the ICWA:

> I have offered my services in turn to the French, the British and the American authorities in my area, and I offered them without restriction as to locality or scope save for two stipulations, namely (1) that the work to be entrusted to me should be in my area, to enable me to continue to watch current affairs for Institute purposes, and (2) that it should be constructive work in the public service and not merely propaganda.[19]

The instrument of this effort was a memorandum "which I have drawn up on my own initiative in the belief that the public interest demands it," and which reviewed "the state of feeling in the Arab world in regard to the issues arising out of the conflict between Great Britain and the Axis Powers." Antonius submitted it first to the British.[20] The Arabs, Antonius maintained, were in a state of apprehension, "which is all the more striking as it is grounded not only upon distrust of Italian and German assurances but also upon uncertainty as to British and French intentions in respect of the political and economic future of those countries." The Arabs, then, were wavering, although in a cover letter Antonius made a protest of loyalty on his and their behalf. He himself believed in the value of Anglo-Arab collaboration,

> not only for its own sake but also as a means toward the upholding of those principles of freedom and the decencies of life, in the defence of which Great Britain is setting such a gallant example. My knowledge of Arab affairs enables me to state, with the deepest conviction, that the Arabs are at heart as attached to those principles as any other civilized people.[21]

He also determined that "there are throughout the Arab world an underlying preference for Great Britain as a partner and a willing recognition of the benefits that have accrued to the Arab countries from their past association with her."[22] (This was a very different approach from that which he had employed in the Round-Table Conference little more than a year earlier. There, speaking of the Italians, "who were always very friendly to the Arabs," he had warned that while he "did not wish his delegation to put themselves in the hands of any foreign Power," Great Britain "must not tempt them too much by being intransigent over the terms of our settlement.")[23]

The Arabs preferred Great Britain, claimed Antonius, but in order to secure active Arab collaboration, Great Britain necessarily would have to offer certain guarantees. This time there would be no secret pledges or covert undertakings of the kind Antonius had dissected in *The Arab Awakening*. Great Britain would issue a unilateral "enunciation of principles defining the attitude of the British Government towards Arab national aims," supporting the independence and unity of the Arabs, and among them the Arabs of Palestine. Then Antonius made this proposal, drawn from the experience of the previous war, and not without due consideration of his own predicament:

> I am of the opinion that there is a pressing need for the creation of a special British bureau in the Middle East, whose main functions would be to attend to political and

economic problems in the Arabic-speaking countries. The most suitable location for the bureau would seem to be in Cairo, but it should have branches in Jerusalem and Baghdad, and possibly in Jeddah and Aden, and a liaison agency in Whitehall. The head of the bureau should be a personality of some standing to whom a high military rank might be given, and he would have to assist him a small staff of carefully selected men who have experience of Arab problems and contacts in the Arab world. One of the functions of the bureau would be to establish close and widespread contact with persons of all shades of opinion in the Arab world, with a view to keeping its pulse on the movements of ideas, the reactions to military events and to Axis propaganda, the hardships caused by economic dislocation and the underlying grounds of discontent. Another function would be to put the knowledge thus collected to good use by studying possible remedies and devising practical suggestions.

Once armed with "all the relevant information," this agency would be in a position to make "comprehensive recommendations" as to the action required.[24] It was no doubt in connection with such a bureau, fulfilling precisely those tasks for which he felt himself uniquely gifted, that Antonius envisioned his own employment.

Antonius showed a draft of the memorandum to the high commissioner for Palestine, Sir Harold MacMichael, who saw through it. The document, he noted, "suffers from a touch of intellectual dishonesty, coupled, perhaps, with a certain lack of courage; neither is deliberate nor, I think, realised by the writer himself. The fact remains that the Memorandum is more of an essay by an ambitious writer, than a piece of constructive statesmanship."[25] At the Foreign Office, where evidence of Arab collaboration with the Germans and Italians accumulated at a rapid pace, readers of the memorandum found it "valueless" and "of little practical use."[26] As for Antonius himself, the British simply would not have him. According to an American who inquired after Antonius among British officials in the Middle East, they

did not trust Ant., because if put in an office he would be trying to run the whole office in a couple of days. While British recognize that he is in a sense anti-British with respect to Palestine, no one even suggests that Antonius is pro-Nazi with respect to the Arab movement as a whole. The lack of trust is simply on the point mentioned above, that he will be willing to fit in and cooperate, rather than run away with the whole show.[27]

The ambition Antonius had borne within him was now common knowledge. And as the author of a book on British policy in the last war with all the character of an *exposé*, he could hardly be made privy to the formulation of policy in this war. If Antonius had any questions regarding the British assessment of his reliability, British frontier authorities answered by searching his person and taking his papers on one of his crossings into

Egypt. "This was considered by A. an affront."[28]

Antonius then offered his talents to the Americans. To Wallace Murray, chief of the Division of Near Eastern Affairs at the State Department, Antonius also had written a lengthy, unsolicited letter sketching the "trends of public opinion" among the Arabs, along with an offer of his services:

> I am tempted to offer, if you should find this kind of letter of sufficient interest, to write to you again whenever my studies bring me to the point when I feel I can draw up useful conclusions. My address in Beirut is the Hotel St. Georges, but for the next few weeks I shall still be up in the hills. Perhaps the best way of getting a message to me would be to send it in care of the Consulate, with whom I am always in touch.[29]

This letter, virtually identical to his overture to the British but with recommendations for British policy removed, was apparently intended to evoke an American offer of employment. But the call from Washington never came.

Antonius had failed in his pursuit of an influential place in the Allied war machines. In November 1941, he wrote to the ICWA that "although I began offering my services over a year ago, I have not succeeded yet in finding some suitable work that would satisfy those two stipulations." He had some reason to believe that a proposal "of an acceptable nature" would be made "at no very distant date," but shared no details. There is no evidence in his papers for any Allied proposal of any kind.[30]

The Allies had spurned him, but Antonius would not relent. He now made a desperate bid to secure a place as an influential mediator between irreconcilable forces in Iraq. In April 1941 he arrived in the Baghdad of Rashid Ali al-Kaylani, where he appeared in the company of the exiled mufti of Jerusalem, Haj Amin al-Husayni. Antonius had an unqualified admiration for Haj Amin, who, as Freya Stark recalled, "had bewitched George Antonius as securely as ever a siren did her mariner, leading him through his slippery realms with sealed eyes so that George—whom I was fond of—would talk to me without a flicker about the Mufti's 'single-hearted goodness.'"[31]

By this time, Haj Amin and Rashid Ali had placed their trust in the Germans, and Haj Amin's private secretary already had conducted negotiations in Berlin on precisely how to put an end to the British presence in the Middle East. But for Freya Stark, and through her the British Embassy in Baghdad, Antonius tried to put an entirely different face on events. Antonius "admitted he had heard in Cairo that Rashid Ali is in German pay—but even if this had been so in the past, it did not follow it need be in the future." Antonius then proffered his services as a mediator.[32] Could Antonius have been so unaware of the sea of intrigue swirling about him in Baghdad that Rashid Ali's German links were known to him only by Cairo rumor? He supposedly wrote an account of the Baghdad events, but it does not survive.[33]

Antonius felt the first effects of a duodenal ulcer in Baghdad, and he returned to Beirut a sick man, a few weeks before the British campaign which purged Iraq of his associates. Things did not go well in Beirut:

> Shortly after, my persecution by the Vichy French and the Italian Commission began. At first they wanted to expel me, and later to put me in a concentration camp. It was only my illness in hospital and the intervention of the American Consul General (Engert) that saved me from the worst effects of that persecution.[34]

A short time later, Antonius returned to Jerusalem, thwarted and ill. He had failed in his pursuit of a kind of influence for which *The Arab Awakening* did not constitute a credential. And so thoroughly had he neglected to report his activities and submit expense accounts that the ICWA's director and trustees began to plan his dismissal. As early as August 1940, the ICWA's director had approached the Department of State to offer that "if Mr. Antonius' connection with his organization was likely to be in any way an embarrassment to the Department he would wish to dissolve the connection without any delay." American diplomats had no ill words for Antonius. But according to an American official, the ICWA's director still was "on the lookout for a young American who might be sent to the Near East to learn Arabic and who might eventually be in a position to serve as the Institute's principal representative in that area. He added that he would appreciate it if we would recommend to him any promising young American with an inclination to Near East Studies who might come to our notice."[35] Antonius had misjudged his employers, who feared that his political activities, about which he now told them next to nothing, might bring their work into disrepute.

Over a year later, their patience ran out. "The trustees of the Institute," wrote its director to the ICWA's lawyers,

> have a high regard for Mr. Antonius and wish to deal fairly with him, yet they have responsibilities that cannot be disregarded, especially in such conditions as now prevail. After all, he is not an American and he is in one of the most highly charged areas of the world. So in view of his failure to keep in close touch with the office and

be frank about his conditions and affairs, they have deemed it inadvisable to continue to finance him.[36]

The result was to leave Antonius financially embarrassed, and he wired New York repeatedly, demanding money and a reversal of the ICWA's decision. "When I decided to give up my career in the public service in 1930," complained Antonius, "I did so on the understanding that our agreement would be a permanent one, and that it was not liable to be terminated without valid cause. It is not easy at my age and in the midst of a world war to embark on yet another career."[37] The plea was disingenuous: Antonius had longed for another career ever since the publication of *The Arab Awakening*. But now he was without any employment at all, and had reached an impasse. As it happened, a complication of his illness claimed Antonius before idleness or debts, in May 1942. "Poor George Antonius," wrote Stark, "a gentle and frustrated man and my friend, was dying too, and soon lay in Jerusalem in an open coffin, his face slightly made up, in a brown pin-stripe suit, defeating the majesty of death."[38]

Of the later career of George Antonius, it can only be said that it showed more the effects of his ambition than his patriotism. He never doubted that he was too large for the clearly subordinate role suggested to him by Arab nationalist leaders, who would have kept him as a propagandist in London. His vain sense of "true vocation" would not concede that he had served his cause best as an author, and might serve it still better in a great university or in yet another book. To sit, pen in hand, even in the cause of an Arab Palestine, was a form of exile, which ended in a blind pursuit of political influence. And so the poet Constantine Cavafy's celebration in verse of a Syrian patriot is really most evocative near its conclusion:

> First of all I shall apply to Zabinas
> and if that dolt does not appreciate me,
> I will go to his opponent, to Grypos.
> And if that idiot too does not engage me,
> I will go directly to Hyrcanos.
>
> At any rate, one of the three will want me.[39]

Notes

1. The book has seen many reappraisals, the most important by Sylvia Haim, "'The Arab Awakening': A Source for the Historian?" *Welt des Islams*, n.s., 2 (1953): 237–50; George Kirk, "*The Arab Awakening* Reconsidered," *Middle Eastern Affairs* 13, no. 6 (June-July 1962): 162–73; Albert Hourani, "*The Arab Awakening* Forty Years After,"

in his *Emergence of the Modern Middle East* (Berkeley and Los Angeles: University of California Press, 1981), 193–215; and Liora Lukitz, "The Antonius Papers and *The Arab Awakening*, Over Fifty Years On," *Middle Eastern Studies* 30 (1994): 883–95.

2. George Antonius, *The Arab Awakening: The Story of the Arab National Movement* (London: H. Hamilton, 1938), 11–12.

3. Antonius (New York) to Walter Rogers (New York), 28 May 1937, file labeled "Antonius: Correspondence, Reports vol. II 1934–43," Institute for Current World Affairs Archive, Hanover, N.H. (hereafter cited as ICWA Correspondence).

4. John O. Crane (Geneva) to Antonius, 14 October, 1931, George Antonius Papers, Israel State Archives, Jerusalem (hereafter cited as ISA), file 65/854. John Crane was the son of Charles Crane, Antonius' patron, on whom see below.

5. Antonius (New York) to Walter Rogers (New York), 28 May 1937, file labeled "Antonius: Post-Staff Correspondence," Institute for Current World Affairs Archive (hereafter cited as ICWA Post).

6. On Antonius' earlier career in government service see Elie Kedourie, *Nationalism in Asia and Africa* (New York: World Publishing, 1970), 86–87; Bernard Wasserstein, *The British in Palestine: The Mandatory Administration and the Arab-Jewish Conflict 1917–1929*, 2d ed. (Oxford: Blackwell, 1991), 183–89; Liora Lukitz, "George Antonius, the Man and His Public Career: An Analysis of His Private Papers" (in Hebrew; master's thesis, Hebrew University of Jerusalem, 1978); Susan P. Silsby, "Antonius: Palestine, Zionism, and British Imperialism, 1929–1939" (Ph.D. diss., Georgetown University, 1985), 1–89; and idem, "George Antonius: The Formative Years," *Journal of Palestine Studies* 15, no. 4 (Summer 1986): 81–98.

7. Vincent Sheean (Sacramento) to Antonius, 21 January 1930, ISA, file 65/1961.

8. Text of seven-point agreement signed by Antonius and Walter Rogers, dated 9 April 1930 at New York, in ICWA Correspondence. The terms, generous by the standards of the day, stipulated a $7,500 personal allowance per annum, $2,500 in traveling expenses outside Palestine, and office expenses of up to $1,500 per annum.

9. Thomas Hodgkin, "George Antonius, Palestine and the 1930s," in *Studies in Arab History: The Antonius Lectures, 1978–87*, ed. Derek Hopwood (New York: St. Martin's, 1990), 86.

10. Crane (at sea) to Butler (New York), 12 June 1936, ICWA Correspondence.

11. Frank D. Fackenthal (New York) to Crane (New York), 28 July 1936, ICWA Correspondence.

12. Butler (New York) to Antonius (Jerusalem), 6 October 1936, ICWA Correspondence. This episode is discussed in more detail by Menahem Kaufman, "George Antonius and American Universities: Dissemination of the Mufti of Jerusalem's Anti-Zionist Propaganda 1930–1936," *American Jewish History* 75 (1985–86): 392–95.

13. Antonius (New York) to Rogers (New York), 28 May 1937, ICWA Post, for original plan.

14. Antonius (Beirut) to Rogers (New York), 30 December 1939, ICWA Correspondence.

15. E. Palmer (Jerusalem), dispatch of 9 March 1935, National Archives, Washington, D.C., RG59, 867n.00/237.

16. L. Baggalay minute of 12 April 1939, Public Record Office, London (hereafter cited as PRO), FO371/23232/E2449/6/31. According to Antonius, his appointment was the idea of Iraqi prime minister Nuri Pasha, whose suggestion enjoyed British support; Antonius (London) to Rogers (New York), 15 February 1939, National Archives, RG59, 867n.01/1466. For more on the role of Antonius at the conference, see Silsby, "Antonius," 242–92.

17. Memorandum of conversation by L. Butler on meeting with Antonius, 30 March 1939, PRO, FO371/23232/E2379/6/31. But Antonius "did not think very highly of the work of the Arab Centre. He thought that they had made some useful contacts with M.P.s in London, but that the 'atrocity' propaganda of the Arab Centre was a deplorable blunder." Memorandum of conversation by Downie on meeting with Antonius, 31 March 1939, PRO, FO371/23232/E2449/6/31.

18. Antonius (Beirut) to Rogers, December 30, 1939; Antonius (Cairo) to Rogers, 11 April 1940, ICWA Correspondence. His home in Jerusalem was not a consideration, for Antonius, according to an American diplomat, had "separated from his wife who is living in their house here." G. Wadsworth (Jerusalem) to Wallace Murray (Washington), 5 October 1940, National Archives, RG59, 811.43 Institute of World Affairs/15.

19. Antonius (Beirut) to Rogers, 25 November 1940, ICWA Correspondence.

20. Cover letter from Antonius (visiting Jerusalem) to High Commissioner for Palestine, 3 October 1940; and "Memorandum on Arab Affairs" of same date; both in PRO, FO371/27043/E53/53/65.

21. Ibid.

22. Ibid.

23. Memorandum of conversation by L. Butler on meeting with Antonius, 30 March 1939, PRO, FO371/23232/E2379/6/31.

24. "Memorandum on Arab Affairs," PRO, FO371/27043/E53/53/65.

25. H. A. MacMichael to Secretary of State for Colonies, 7 October 1940, PRO, FO371/27043/E53/53/65.

26. Minute page, PRO, FO371/27043/E53/53/65.

27. "Practically stenograph" of talk between McEwan and ICWA Fellow Samuel Harper, in letter from Harper (Chicago) to Rogers, 22 July 1941, ICWA Correspondence. Harper reported McEwan as saying that Antonius was "evidently living well and comfortably at the home of the wife of former president of Lebanon as I recall description of this aspect."

28. Ibid.

29. Antonius (visiting Jerusalem) to Wallace Murray, 4 October 1940, quoted at length in letter from Murray (Washington) to Rogers, 2 November 1940, ICWA Correspondence.

30. Ibid.

31. Freya Stark, *The Arab Island: The Middle East, 1939–1943* (New York: Knopf, 1945), 159.

32. Freya Stark, *Dust in the Lion's Paw: Autobiography, 1939–1946* (London: Murray, 1961), 79–80.

33. Antonius (Jerusalem) to John O. Crane, 12 February 1942, ICWA Correspondence, reports that he had sent a "long account" of his month in Baghdad to Rogers, "but I don't think it could have reached him." It did not.

34. Antonius (Jerusalem) to John O. Crane, 12 February 1942, ICWA Correspondence.

35. Memorandum of conversation with Rogers by J. Rives Childs, 14 August 1940, National Archives, RG59, 811.43 Institute of World Affairs/11.

36. Rogers (New York) to M. C. Rose of Baldwin, Todd & Young (New York), 21 May 1942, ICWA Correspondence.

37. Antonius (Beirut) to Rogers, 25 November 1941, ICWA Correspondence. Twenty years after the event, Antonius' widow wrote that in 1940–41, Antonius could not correspond as he was "under strict surveillance from the French Vichy Sûreté. I believe Mr. Rogers wrote in a way which very much disturbed George and he resigned from the Institute—as he said—because he could not send the reports to the Institute."

As to Rogers' attitude toward Antonius, "I felt it had added to his premature death." Katy Antonius (Jerusalem) to Richard Nolte (New York), 9 January 1962, file labeled "The Arab Awakening," Institute for Current World Affairs Archive. In fact, Antonius stopped filing regular reports before his move to Beirut and the fall of France, and his services were terminated against his protest. Within the ICWA, it was Rogers who had always been the most concerned about the political activism of Antonius, which he had tried to check a decade earlier; see Silsby, "Antonius," 115–18.

38. Stark, *Dust in the Lion's Paw*, 129.
39. "They Should Have Cared," in *The Complete Poems of Cafavy*, trans. Rae Dalven (New York: Harcourt Brace Jovanovich, 1976), 163. Cf. the verses of the poem quoted by Hourani, *"The Arab Awakening* Forty Years After," 214–15.

7

Prisoner of Love: Jean Genet and Palestine

On the morning of 19 September 1982, the French writer Jean Genet visited the Palestinian refugee camp of Shatila near Beirut. Two nights earlier, Israel had permitted its Lebanese allies to enter the surrounded camp, and they had massacred its Palestinian inhabitants. A walk through Shatila, wrote Genet, "resembled a game of hopscotch.... A photograph doesn't show the flies nor the thick white smell of death. Neither does it show how you must jump over the bodies as you walk along from one corpse to the next."[1]

Shatila inspired Genet to one last self-invention. He had been a thief and prisoner, then a world-famous novelist and dramatist. Now he would be reborn as a witness for the Palestinians. *Prisoner of Love*, his book-length memoir of the Palestinian *fedayeen*, appeared a month after his death in 1986.[2] This was the first new writing Genet had produced in years, rekindling an interest in his life and work. Edmund White's masterful biography more than satisfies that interest.[3]

Whatever White's intent, he has reminded us that Genet, rather than embodying some collective disorder of his time, acted largely upon his own disorder. White thus finally breaks the spell of Jean-Paul Sartre's long-winded speculation, *Saint Genet: Actor and Martyr* (1952). That book, which canonized Genet at the age of forty-two, purported to be an "existential psychoanalysis," based on Sartre's lengthy conversations with his subject: an abandoned child, vagabond thief, army deserter, and homosexual prostitute who wrote five remarkable books in prison that swept him to the summit of French letters. But as Sartre himself acknowledged, Genet practiced certain economies when it came to self-revelatory truth, and so White relentlessly seeks out corroboration. Many of the documents, it turns out, refuse to corroborate.

White first shows how thoroughly Genet's own version of his childhood—drawn in sharp lines of poverty and abuse—was a myth, an affectation given credibility by Sartre. Born in Paris in 1910, Genet had been abandoned by his unwed mother and made a ward of the state, but the carpenter's family entrusted with his care gave Genet ample attention and affection. Raised in a farming village, he was not made to work, prospered in school, had plenty of books, and scored high on examinations. Contrary to his later claim, he did not have to steal to survive. ("You couldn't call them thefts," recalls one classmate. "He took some pennies from his mother to buy sweets, all kids do that.")

The effect of these first chapters is to suggest that Genet largely fabricated a grim childhood to fit his chosen persona as renegade. Precocious and rebellious, the dandified Genet refused, as he put it, "to become an accountant or a petty official." And so he escaped from every apprenticeship, opting to become a petty thief. This eventually landed him in the notorious reform penitentiary at Mettray, a society of male outcasts governed by a counter-code of homosexuality, theft, and betrayal that Genet would later celebrate.

After stints of military service and desertions, Genet crossed Europe as a vagabond, and finally returned to Paris where he resumed his career of petty thievery and shoplifting, specializing in rare books. ("He may have been a thug," writes White, "but he was a highly literary one.") In the 1940s he was often in prison, where he wrote the novels and poems, beginning with *Our Lady of the Flowers*, which brought him to the attention of Jean Cocteau and the leading literary lights of Paris. They lobbied to save him from the life sentence of a repeat offender, and with the benefit of a pardon he settled into the role of the barely domesticated bad boy of French letters.

Genet's "resolute aestheticism" is an acquired taste. His arresting language consistently displays genius, an achievement all the more astonishing in an author who left school at the age of twelve. The themes celebrated in his work—theft, murder, homosexual eroticism—have the usual appeal of that which is deemed "scandalous." The frequent lack of narrative coherence adds an element of the absurd. White briefly considers each of Genet's works, but only to set them afloat on a river of detail about Genet's couplings and uncouplings, both intellectual and physical. This is dense biography—no bedroom door left unopened, no literary liaison left unexplored to its furthest implication.

From this mass of detail, though, White discerns a striking pattern. Genet invested himself completely in a succession of lovers and friends. He shared out his advances and royalties almost as soon as they were paid, setting up his favorites with houses while he lived in cheap hotels near train stations. But so many of Genet's intimates ended badly, often by their own hand, that even Genet began to wonder whether he cast a malevolent spell. That he could infect others with a particularly virulent nihilism would soon be demonstrated on the larger canvas of politics.

Panthers and Palestine

In wartime Paris, when Genet first appeared on the literary scene, he practiced an indifference to politics. He said and wrote nothing political, and took both a German soldier and a member of the Resistance as lovers. In 1952, Genet informed Sartre that "in politics nothing new can be contributed by a homosexual," since the significance of homosexuality was "a refusal to continue the world." He often repudiated political readings of his plays, maintaining that they occupied "a domain where morality is replaced by the aesthetics of the stage."

But the favorable reception of Genet's work owed a great deal to changes in the political weather. This is particularly true of his best-known plays, *The Balcony*, *The Blacks*, and *The Screens*, all written during the 1950s. Through allusions to democracy's corruption, racial oppression, and colonial domination, they tapped the growing self-doubt of France, Europe, and America. That *The Blacks* ran off Broadway for almost four years beginning in 1961 (with James Earl Jones in a leading role) can only be understood in the context of the rise of the civil rights movement. And even if *The Screens* was, in White's judgment, "more in praise of unregenerate individualism than of third-world nationalism," it could only be read as an indictment of the war in Algeria, and could only be staged in France fours years after de Gaulle pulled out of the war. Even then, angry demonstrators disrupted performances.

When his literary inspiration was finally exhausted, Genet sought in politics a fulfillment that had eluded him in art. His books, he declared, were "part of a dream, a daydream. And since I outlived this dream, this daydream, I had to take action in order to achieve a sort of fullness of life." But which action, and for whom? White observes that Genet thought politics "must be a purge of anger and not a reconciliation of differences." That could only mean violence.

Although Genet claimed to detest France, he found no "fullness" in its own purges of anger. (He showed up at the Sorbonne during the 1968 student uprising, but refused to address the crowd.) Abroad, however, conflicts seemed to embody the stylized contrast of black (men) against white (men) he had dramatized on the stage. "I wish I were Black," he told the American novelist William Burroughs after he visited Chicago to write up the Democratic Convention in 1968. "I want to feel what they feel." The fact that Genet spoke no passable English or Arabic only enhanced the aesthetic charge of the two causes he finally adopted: the Black Panthers and the Palestinians.

Genet's affair with the Black Panthers brought him briefly again to America in 1970. He visited some fifteen campuses, lecturing in support of imprisoned Panther Bobby Seale and rubbing shoulders with such radical celebrities as Angela Davis, Jane Fonda, and Allen Ginsburg. For a while, writing on behalf of the Panthers filled his void: "Literature, as I practiced it formerly, was gratuitous. Today it is in the service of a cause. It is against America." But Genet was never thoroughly taken by the Panthers, who were not the rigorous revolutionaries of his fantasy. Even before they broke up, Genet began his search anew; it now took him to an ungoverned corner of the kingdom of Jordan.

Genet's sensuality had long been stimulated by the Arab world, beginning with his service as a soldier in Syria and Morocco, but it was the dramatic pose of the Palestinians that moved him to action. Genet described himself as "enthralled" by the Palestinian hijacking of civilian airliners to Jordan in August and ("Black") September, 1970; a month later, he was with the *fedayeen* in northern Jordan, at the invitation of Yasir Arafat. The appeal of armed youths bordered on the erotic:

> The first two *fedayeen* were so handsome I was surprised at myself for not feeling any desire for them. And it was the same the more Palestinian soldiers I met, decked with guns, in leopard-spotted uniforms and red berets tilted over their eyes, each not merely a transfiguration but also a materialization of my fantasies.

Genet had found his redemption. He repeatedly returned to Jordan, logging some six months in the remote camps of the *fedayeen*. Genet freely described his bond with the Palestinians as an "irrational affinity," resting "on an emotional—perhaps intuitive, sensual—attraction; I am French, but I defend the Palestinians wholeheartedly and automatically. They are in the right because I love them."

Unfortunately for the Palestinians, Genet never developed their defense much beyond this. He detested King Husayn, who made war against the

Palestinian *fedayeen* in 1970, but did his passion confer more rightness on *his* Arabs than the lifetime devotion of, say, Glubb Pasha, British adviser to the king, who had commanded and lived among the Jordan's bedouin troops? "I went to the Arab countries in 1920 as an ordinary regimental officer in the British Army," wrote Glubb. "I stayed there for thirty-six years because I loved them."[4] Nor was Glubb alone. There are shelves of similarly enamored writing on armed Arabs in the hills and deserts east of the Jordan, beginning with T. E. Lawrence's *Seven Pillars of Wisdom*. It is still possible to read these texts as art, but no one thinks to trust them, and Genet's *Prisoner of Love* is no exception.

The Judgment of Israel

Genet did not love the Jews. Sartre wrote that Genet "played" at being an anti-Semite: "When he's cornered, he announces that he 'could never sleep with a Jew.' Israel can rest at peace." Sartre offered this explanation: "Since Genet wants his lovers to be executioners, he should never be sodomized by a victim. What repels Genet in Jews is that he finds himself in their situation." But like so much of Sartre on Genet, this speculation completely misses the mark. Genet thoroughly eroticized those other victims of French racism, North African Arabs; an Algerian high wire artist named Abdallah became his most enduring love, and he later would perceive the Jews as particularly ruthless executioners.

White stays closer to the evidence, but cannot decide. In his introduction to *Prisoner of Love*, White claimed that Genet, while anti-Zionist, was not anti-Semitic. Genet saw Israelis as "master manipulators of the media as well as of brainwashing techniques, but his objections are political, not racist. He attacks Israeli policies, not 'Jewish traits' (the very phrase is racist)."[5] In researching this biography, however, White did speak to Jews who heard Genet make offensive remarks, and this has persuaded him to pronounce the question of Genet's anti-Semitism "an open one." Still, in Genet's defense, White avers that Genet never published a single anti-Semitic word, and that he was tied by friendship to several Jews.

But Genet's offhand remarks and friendships are beside the point. For Genet, Jews represented the living affirmation of morality over aestheticism. He thought himself covered by what he called a "thick black layer of Judaeo-Christian morality," which he longed to strip away. The Palestinian struggle was very much his struggle precisely because Zionism, along with imperialism, were "the last incarnations of Judeo-Christian morality, which is itself the master of terms." When Genet wrote that "words are terrible, and Israel is a terrifying manipulator of signs," he meant both Israel in history and Israel the state.

Genet found even the alphabet of the Jews terrifying. Driving from Damascus to Israeli-surrounded Beirut in 1982, he sees Hebrew *signs*—"as painful as seeing Gothic lettering in Paris during the German occupation."

> Most of the letters were squat and rectangular; they read from right to left in a broken horizontal line. One or two had a crane-like plume on top: three slim pistils bearing three stigmata and waiting for the bees who'd scatter their age-old, nay primeval, pollen all over the world.[6]

Genet recalled first seeing these letters in childhood, carved in stone: the letters of the law, repelling a man who believed in no preexisting law, who affirmed that rules had to be invented by man, that they should be "more aesthetic than moral," and that his own rules "are against the rules, I mean against the law." Israel, armed with its law and its signs, seemed to Genet even more terrible than the imperialism it mimed; it was "a loathsome, temporal power, colonialist in a way which few dare to imitate, having become the Definitive Judge which it owes to its longstanding curse as much as to its chosen status"[7] For Genet, who had stood before many judges, Israel's judgment represented the definitive rap, which he could only beat by assimilating himself completely to the Palestinian struggle. He often said that the Palestinians did more for him than he for them. Indeed, they exonerated him.

In return, Genet gave the Palestinians bad counsel. Since Israel could always manipulate words and signs, Genet urged the Palestinians to use violence. Genet, for his part, would teach his own countrymen and Europeans in general not to "confuse the brutality of the Israelis with the violence of the Palestinians, which in my opinion in any case is good." In 1972, the terrorist Black September seized Israeli athletes at the Munich Olympics, an operation that ended in a blaze of gunfire and death. Genet blamed Israel: "This death of the Jews was desired by Israel. It was necessary that 'all Israel should lament,' that the 'Israelites should cry vengeance.'"[8] But to the Palestinians, he acclaimed the "perfect logic" of Black September's decision to carry the struggle to Europe. It was another example of Genet's drawing beloved friends to strategies of self-destruction: Israel quickly took retaliation to Europe, within months claiming the lives of two of Genet's dearest Palestinians, PLO representatives in Paris and Rome.

In the end, Genet failed to sway European opinion. His book on the Palestinians was delayed, and when in 1977 Genet extended his distinction between bad brutality and good violence to a defense of the Baader-Meinhof gang in Germany, it created a furor against him across Europe. From then until his death in 1986, he remained isolated, in the close company of a few Palestinian friends and a Moroccan vagabond, his last lover.

Beirut inspired one of Genet's last creative bursts. His "Four Hours in Shatila" displays all that was brilliant and flawed in his committed essays. The description is riveting, as the reader meanders with Genet among the bloated, blackened corpses, observing each in clinical detail, but his political speculations are blurred and skewed, and suggest no exit. Genet could convey something of Palestinian suffering, but he had no plan to alleviate it. Indeed, such suffering contributed to his own equilibrium. "I would like the world not to change so that I can be against the world," he said, and, "The day the Palestinians become institutionalized, I will no longer be on their side. The day the Palestinians become a nation like other nations, I will no longer be there."

This sentiment is still shared by many other foreign friends of the Palestinian cause. Theirs, too, is a suffocating love. Genet once called Lawrence of Arabia an imposter, whose supposed friendship toward the Arabs concealed his function as an agent of Western imperialism. But Genet, "prisoner of love," was perhaps the more insidious imposter: an agent of Western nihilism, urging freedom for the unfree, provided they forever remain prisoners of hate.

Notes

1. Jean Genet, "Four Hours in Shatila," *Journal of Palestine Studies* 12, no. 3 (Spring 1983): 4–5.
2. Jean Genet, *Prisoner of Love*, trans. Barbara Bray (London: Picador, 1989).
3. Edmund White, *Genet: A Biography* (New York: Knopf, 1993).
4. Sir John Bagot Glubb, *A Soldier with the Arabs* (New York: Harper, 1957), 37.
5. Edmund White, "Introduction," in Genet, *Prisoner of Love*, xi–xii.
6. Genet, *Prisoner of Love*, 269–70.
7. Genet, "Four Hours in Shatila," 16.
8. Jean Genet, "The Palestinians," *Journal of Palestine Studies* 3, no. 1 (Autumn 1973): 26, 27.

8

America's Arabists

On 18 January 1984, two men entered the campus of the American University of Beirut, known by generations of graduates simply and affectionately as AUB. In College Hall, the stately administration building, they approached Malcolm Kerr, the university's president and one of America's leading students of contemporary Arab politics. Kerr had left his professorship at the University of California in Los Angeles to guide AUB through the treacherous shoals of Lebanon's war. He returned to the Beirut campus literally as its son; he had been born in the university hospital fifty-two years earlier, to American parents who served on AUB's faculty.

Kerr was a quintessential Arabist, whose privileged knowledge of the Arabs derived from intimate familiarity and deep sympathy. "'Arab-Western relations' was *our* subject," he once wrote. But that morning, his own analysis of his subject proved fatally wrong: the two visitors shot him through the head, in the name of Islam.

In *The Arabists*, Robert D. Kaplan seeks to explain why such experts, despite the best of intentions and a close familiarity with the Arabs, showed a marked tendency to be fatally wrong.[1] As serving diplomats, they sometimes imperiled not only themselves but the interests of the United States. They were wrong when they argued that the U.S. had to choose between some twenty Arab states and one Israel. They were wrong when they endorsed Arab nationalism as the sole will of the Arab peoples. And they were spectacularly wrong when they portrayed Saddam Hussein as a man of reason, and then inadvertently flashed him a go over Kuwait.

With each miscalculation, more State Department Arabists were eased out of their slots, so that today they appear to be an endangered species. More decisive verdicts on their triumphs and failings will be passed by future historians who will have full access to the diplomatic archives, but Kaplan has rendered a great service by talking to these men now, before age and infirmity claim them.

Missionary Forebears

The origins of America's Arabists can be traced back to the nineteenth century, an age of Protestant missionary fervor and competition. Presbyterians and Congregationalists sent missions to those Ottoman provinces that would later be divided into Syria and Lebanon. Their religious preaching received a tepid response, but the missionaries opened modern schools, and these attracted eager students of every faith. The queen of this American empire of education was the Syrian Protestant College, established in 1866 on "the finest site in all Beirut," a promontory overlooking the Mediterranean.

"They went out to proselytize," wrote the late Elie Kedourie of the American missionaries, "and have stayed to sympathize." That sympathy took the form of support for Arab national sentiment. In the early years, this encouragement was almost inadvertent, the byproduct of missionary translations of the New Testament that helped to forge modern Arabic. In later years, however, the missionaries deliberately preached the gospel of national self-determination, and Woodrow Wilson's Fourteen Points proved to have a more potent appeal than the Bible.

In 1920, the Syrian Protestant College became the American University of Beirut. The change of name reflected the new mission of the school: the propagation of American values, through social service and nationalism. A year earlier, Howard Bliss, the college president, had gone to the Paris Peace Conference to plead the Arab case. Religion thus gave way to politics, and the American expatriates became one of Lebanon's most influential sects, allied especially to the Sunni Muslims and Greek Orthodox Christians in a shared allegiance to Arab nationalism.

Kaplan dwells on the story of the missionaries and educators because their sons became some of America's first Arabist diplomats. They were born and raised in Lebanon, and spoke some Arabic as their birthright. Perhaps the most dashing was Marine Colonel William Eddy, born in Sidon to missionary parents. Eddy became a wartime OSS operative in Tangier and an ambassador to Saudi Arabia, serving as translator at the famous summit between Franklin D. Roosevelt and King Ibn Sa'ud in 1945. The Foreign Service had no better way to secure competent Arabists, who were essential if the U.S. were to edge out rivals in the Arab world. Kaplan attests to the rare talents of men like Eddy, who proved indispensable in tasks requiring a sixth sense of local culture and firm grasp of a difficult language.

The Arabists, however, also brought the convictions of their fathers straight into the State Department. These included the belief that Arabs were becoming more like Americans with each graduating class of the mission schools and AUB. Good works, not conquest, had won for America an immense moral influence. The Arab world would become America's preserve the moment the U.S. government also endorsed the political cause of Arab independence and unity.

When the U.S. decided instead to support the creation of Israel in 1948, the Arabists felt abandoned. Eddy, for one, resigned, but others stayed on, nursing their resentment. In interview after interview, Kaplan's Arabists make it abundantly clear that they regarded American support for the creation of Israel as a tragic mistake, from which the region and America's stature have yet to recover.

Mistake or not, the Arabists aggravated its effects. Phillip J. Baram, in *The Department of State in the Middle East*, has shown that before Israel's creation, the Arabists wrongly led the Arabs to conclude that the U.S. had no interest in Zionism's success. Baram suggests that this

> self-deception and deception of the Arabs—as if, in the making of American foreign policy, Presidential, Congressional and domestic opinion counted for naught—was as much a cause of the Arabs' evolving hostility to the U.S. as the substantive fact that after the war American presidents did support the right of a Jewish state to exist.[2]

It would not be the last time Arabists misled Arabs over the direction of American policy, proving themselves as dangerous to their Arab friends as to their own department.

As Kaplan shows, the Arabists' peculiar talents could only be acquired at the price of prolonged isolation from a rapidly changing America—an isolation that a stint at Deerfield or Exeter, followed by Amherst or Princeton, did little to relieve. Ultimately that price became too steep, and after 1973, when Arab-Israeli "peace processing" required a broader empathy for Arabs and Jews, most of the Arabists of the old school had to go. Much of Kaplan's story is about how they were put out to pasture under the Nixon and Ford administrations, to be replaced by hybrid diplomats who knew their way not only through the Damascus market but across Dizengoff Street in Tel Aviv.

Some of these newcomers were professional peace-processors, others Kaplan describes as Arabists-lite. In any case, the formula worked, and the veteran Arabists were confounded. "Certainly," wrote Malcolm Kerr, "the United States has been far luckier than it deserved in managing to befriend Israel without sacrificing important interests in the Arab world." Luck indeed, for this immense triumph owed nothing to the old-school Arabists, and was achieved largely in spite of them.

Kaplan has told his tale with great verve and felicity of style—talents the Arabists themselves never mustered. Of the British Arabists, it can at least be said that they wrote tirelessly, even feverishly, to give some account of their deeds to a wider public. T. E. Lawrence's *Seven Pillars of Wisdom*, the self-serving outpourings of Gertrude Bell and Ronald Storrs, Wilfred Thesiger and Freya Stark—these writings commanded a vast and influential readership. America's Arabists have left no comparable literary legacy.

"Read, travel, read, travel, that's the way to go," Kaplan is told by William Eagleton, a former envoy to Iraq and ambassador to Syria (whom Francis Fukuyama, quoted in this book, remembers as "the one who always fed us horseshit about how Saddam was a potential moderate.") Eagleton's words sum up the difference between the British and American traditions: the British Arabists would write, travel, write, travel—ever with an eye to the public and posterity. The American Arabists largely subsisted on this borrowed intellectual capital. If they have been misunderstood, it is partly because they disdained getting ink under their nails.

The Arabists, then, is likely to stand as their monument for some time to come. All told, they have little cause for complaint. Kaplan displays a genuine admiration for the patriotism, courage, and expertise of many of his interviewees, who emerge from his brief portraits in all their decency and complexity. He has plainly been charmed by them, enough to exonerate them of the charge of anti-Semitism, which was often leveled indiscriminately by their critics. "In the long list of historical adversaries of the Jews," writes Kaplan, "the Arabists could easily claim to be the least noxious. The best of enemies, in other words."

In one Arabist, Kaplan even finds a hero: Hume Horan, the remarkable diplomat who, as ambassador to Sudan, finessed Operation Moses, the 1984 airlift of Ethiopian Jews to Israel. Horan, whose Arabic reportedly bested that of any of his contemporaries, described the Arabists as "the Pekinese orchids begot by an American superpower." Kaplan in turn calls *him* "the orchid of orchids," "the most advanced form of the Arabist species before it began going extinct." Kaplan's labored comparison between

Horan and T. E. Lawrence falls flat, but Horan, in addition to having achieved something of great value, recites the most penetrating lines in *The Arabists*, and leaves an appetite for more.

The Road to Kuwait

Then comes the antithesis: an Arabist who is held to embody all that went wrong in the tradition. In his hardest-hitting chapter, Kaplan zeroes in on April Glaspie, the last U.S. ambassador to Saddam Hussein and one of the last veteran Arabists. In her final audience with the Iraqi leader, she told him that the United States had "no opinion" on "your border disagreement with Kuwait." Iraq invaded Kuwait a week later.

The portrait of Glaspie is unsparing (she tried to be "twice as much of an old boy as the real old boys"); so too is the description of her performance in Baghdad as a "disgrace." Glaspie herself declined to be interviewed by Kaplan, and her defense has been left in this book to the veteran Arabists, who cast her as a victim of the Bush administration's indulgent Iraq policy. Kaplan is unconvinced, arguing that "she was a driver and a hard-core believer in this policy down to the very end."

This is a debate that will rage for years, even after historians have the documentary evidence. Nevertheless, Kaplan has made a compelling *prima facie* case against Glaspie, one that includes ample testimony from other diplomats that, whatever the precise genesis of American policy, this variety of Arabist, with her known weakness for Arab radicals, was in the wrong place at the wrong time. The episode leads inexorably to the conclusion that there are not many right places left in the Arab world, even for the most able survivors of the old guard.

Had Kaplan taken his research a step further, he would have noted the subtle exchange that has occurred between diplomacy and academe. The Arabists had to go because they could not adapt to the American role of making peace between Arabs and Israelis, but their decline in the Department of State has been accompanied by their ascendancy in departments of Arab, Islamic, and Middle Eastern studies. When Malcolm Kerr was turned away from the Foreign Service for health reasons, he went into the university. Now his second choice has become the first choice of a new generation.

In that light, Kaplan might have dissected the Middle East Institute in Washington, D.C., which has done more than any other institution to facilitate the transition from Arabist expertise to semischolarly authority. More recently, scholars who fled AUB during Lebanon's war have helped to transform major centers and departments in America into the last outposts of Arab nationalism. Some campuses, afflicted by an endemic Third Worldism or tempted by oil money, have provided hothouse conditions for the survival and spread of the views Kaplan examines. In these redoubts of tenured Arabism, the intellectual campaign against an Arab-Israeli settlement is already being waged. *The Arabists* is therefore unfinished: there is a crying need for a final chapter, perhaps entitled "The Retreat to the Academy."

And while no young diplomats would call themselves Arabists, the Department of State is not completely in the clear either. On the sidelines of the peace process, the last keepers of the Arabist flame pose as authoritative interpreters of Islamic fundamentalism. As they see it, radical Islam is the harbinger of a Protestant-like reformation, from which all Islam will emerge more democratic and more egalitarian. The radicals should not be fought, but gently guided to the light.

This is, of course, a political reworking of the unanswered prayer of missionary forebears for the conversion of the Muslims. Malcolm Kerr, whose wife eulogized him as "a non-religious missionary," was gunned down by just this kind of Islam. It remains to be seen whether such political evangelists can now persuade America to turn the other cheek yet one more time.

Notes

1. Robert D. Kaplan, *The Arabists: The Romance of an American Elite* (New York: Free Press, 1993).
2. Phillip J. Baram, *The Department of State in the Middle East, 1919–1945* (Philadelphia: University of Pennsylvania Press, 1978), 152, n. 27.

Part II

Islamism and the West

9

"Islam is the Power of the Future"

What is Islamic fundamentalism? Its contradictions seem to abound. On the one hand, it manifests itself as a new religiosity, reaffirming faith in a transcendent God. On the other hand, it appears as a militant ideology, demanding political action now. Here it takes the form of a populist party, asking for ballots. There it surges forth as an armed phalanx, spraying bullets. One day its spokesmen call for a jihad against the West, evoking the deepest historic resentments. Another day, its leaders appeal for reconciliation with the West, emphasizing shared values. Its economic theorists reject capitalist materialism in the name of social justice, yet they rise to the defense private property. Its moralists pour scorn on Western consumer culture as debilitating to Islam, yet its strategists avidly seek to buy the West's latest technologies in order to strengthen Islam.

Faced with these apparent contradictions, many analysts in the West have decided that fundamentalism defies all generalization. Instead they have tried to center discussion on its supposed "diversity." For this purpose, they seek to establish systems of classification by which to sort out fundamentalist movements and leaders. The basic classification appears in many different terminological guises, in gradations of subtlety. "We need to be careful of that emotive label, 'fundamentalism', and distinguish, as Muslims do, between revivalists, who choose to take the practice of their religion most devoutly, and fanatics or extremists, who use this devotion for political ends."[1] So spoke the Prince of Wales in a 1993 address, summarizing the conventional wisdom in a conventional way. The belief that these categories really exist, and that experts can sort fundamentalists neatly into them, is the sand on which weighty policies are now being built.

Islamic fundamentalism remains an enigma precisely because it has confounded all attempts to divide it into tidy categories. "Revivalist" becomes "extremist" (and vice versa) with such rapidity and frequency that

141

the actual classification of any movement or leader has little predictive power. They will not stay put. This is because Muslim fundamentalists, for all their "diversity," orbit around one dense idea. From any outside vantage point, each orbit will have its apogee and perigee. The West thus sees movements and individuals swing within reach, only to swing out again and cycle right through every classification. Movements and individuals arise in varied social and political circumstances, and have their own distinctive orbits. But they will not defy the gravity of their idea.

The idea is simple: Islam must have power in this world. It is the true religion—the religion of God—and its truth is manifest in its power. When Muslims believed, they were powerful. Their power has been lost in modern times because Islam has been abandoned by many Muslims, who have reverted to the condition that preceded God's revelation to the Prophet Muhammad. But if Muslims now return to the original Islam, they can preserve and even restore their power.

That return, to be effective, must be comprehensive; Islam provides the one and only solution to all questions in this world, from public policy to private conduct. It is not merely a religion, in the Western sense of a system of belief in God. It possesses an immutable law, revealed by God, that deals with every aspect of life, and it is an ideology, a complete system of belief about the organization of the state and the world. This law and ideology can only be implemented through the establishment of a truly Islamic state, under the sovereignty of God. The empowerment of Islam, which is God's plan for mankind, is a sacred end. It may be pursued by any means that can be rationalized in terms of Islam's own code. At various times, these have included persuasion, guile, and force.

What is remarkable about Islamic fundamentalism is not its diversity. It is the fact that this idea of power for Islam appeals so effectively across such a wide range of humanity, creating a world of thought that crosses all frontiers. Fundamentalists everywhere must act in narrow circumstances of time and place. But they are who they are precisely because their idea exists above all circumstances. Over nearly a century, this idea has evolved into a coherent ideology, which demonstrates a striking consistency in content and form across a wide expanse of the Muslim world.[2]

Fundamentalist Forerunners

The pursuit of power for Islam first gained some intellectual coherence in the mind and career of Sayyid Jamal al-Din "al-Afghani" (1838–97), a thinker and activist who worked to transform Islam into a lever against Western imperialism. His was an age of European expansion into the heartlands of Islam, and of a frenzied search by Muslims for ways to ward off foreign conquest.

In many respects, Afghani was the prototype of the modern fundamentalist. He had been deeply influenced by Western rationalism and the ideological mode of Western thought. Afghani welded a traditional religious hostility toward unbelievers to a modern critique of Western imperialism and an appeal for the unity of Islam, and while he inveighed against the West, he urged the adoption of those Western sciences and institutions that might strengthen Islam. Afghani spread his unsettling message in constant travels that took him to Cairo, Istanbul, Tehran, and Kabul. He visited Paris, London, and St. Petersburg as well, where he published and lobbied on behalf of revolutionary change.

A contemporary English admirer described Afghani as the leader of Islam's "Liberal religious reform movement."[3] But Afghani—not an Afghan at all, but a Persian who concealed his true identity even from English admirers—was never what he appeared to be. While he called for the removal of some authoritarian Muslim rulers, he ingratiated himself with others. While he had great persuasive power, he did not shrink from conspiracy and violence. A disciple once found him pacing back and forth, shouting: "There is no deliverance except in killing, there is no safety except in killing."[4] These were not idle words. On one occasion, Afghani proposed to a follower that the ruler of Egypt be assassinated, and he did inspire a supple disciple to assassinate a ruling shah of Iran in 1896. Afghani was tempted by power, and believed that "power is never manifested and concrete unless it weakens and subjugates others." Quoting this and other evidence, one Arab critic has argued that there is a striking correspondence between Afghani's thought and European fascism.[5]

Was Afghani a liberal or a proto-fascist? A reformist or a revolutionary? Was he the forerunner of those fundamentalists who plead their case in political ways? Or those who open fire on the motorcades of government ministers? Afghani was all these things, and one can only wonder how today's taxonomists (and with them, the Prince of Wales) would have classified him. Some fundamentalists still pose this same intractable dilemma of classification, although most of them have far weaker "liberal" and "reformist" credentials than had Afghani.

Between Afghani and the emergence of full-blown fundamentalism, liberal and secular nationalism would enjoy a long run in the lands of Islam. Europe had irradiated these lands with the idea that language, not religion, defined nations. In the generation that followed Afghani, Muslims with an eye toward Europe preferred to be called Arabs, Turks, and Persians. "If you looked in the right places," wrote the British historian Arnold Toynbee in 1929, "you could doubtless find some old fashioned Islamic Fundamentalists still lingering on. You would also find that their influence was negligible."[6] Yet that same year, an Egyptian schoolteacher named Hasan al-Banna (1906–49) founded a movement he called the Society of the Muslim Brethren. It would grow into the first modern fundamentalist movement in Islam.

The Muslim Brethren emerged against the background of growing resentment against foreign domination. The Brethren had a double identity. On one level, they operated openly, as a membership organization of social and political awakening. Banna preached moral revival, and the Muslim Brethren engaged in good works. On another level, however, the Muslim Brethren created a "secret apparatus" that acquired weapons and trained adepts in their use. Some of its guns were deployed against the Zionists in Palestine in 1948, but the Muslim Brethren also resorted to violence in Egypt. They began to enforce their own moral teachings by intimidation, and they initiated attacks against Egypt's Jews. They assassinated judges and struck down a prime minister in 1949. Banna himself was assassinated two months later, probably in revenge. The Muslim Brethren then hovered on the fringes of legality, until Gamal Abdul Nasser, who had survived one of their assassination attempts in 1954, put them down ruthlessly. Yet the Muslim Brethren continued to plan underground and in prison, and they flourished in other Arab countries to which they were dispersed.

At the same time, a smaller and more secretive movement, known as the Devotees of Islam, appeared in Iran, under the leadership of a charismatic theology student, Navvab Safavi (1923–56). Like the Muslim Brethren, the Devotees emerged at a time of growing nationalist mobilization against foreign domination. The group was soon implicated in the assassinations of a prime minister and leading secular intellectuals. The Devotees, who never became a mass party, overplayed their hand and were eventually suppressed. Navvab himself was executed, after inspiring a failed assassination attempt against another prime minister. But the seed was planted. One of those who protested Navvab's execution was an obscure, middle-aged cleric named Ruhollah Khomeini, who would continue the work of forging Islam and resentment into an ideology of power.

In the checkered history of Afghani, the Muslim Brethren, and the Devotees of Islam, clear patterns emerge. They saw foreign domination as a symptom of Muslim weakness, and its elimination as the key to Muslim power. Such domination could be attacked directly by jihad against foreigners, or indirectly by promoting an Islamic awakening. Those who gave priority to direct confrontation sometimes favored alliances with other nationalists who opposed foreign rule. In Afghani's anti-imperialist campaign, especially against the British in Egypt, he took all manner of nationalists as allies, including non-Muslims who became some of his most ardent disciples. The Muslim Brethren, who joined the attacks against the British presence in Suez Canal zone, had many ties to the Egyptian Free Officers who overthrew the monarchy in 1952, but their vision of an Islamic state eventually made them bitter enemies of the new regime. The Devotees of Islam, while thoroughly antiforeign, never collaborated with secular nationalists, whom they deeply distrusted. Whatever their strategies, however, they all worked to redress the gross imbalance of power between Islam and the West.

They also sought to replace weak rulers and states with strong rulers and states. Such a state would have to be based on Islam, and while its precise form remained uncertain, the early fundamentalists knew it should not be a constitutional government or multiparty democracy. Preoccupied with the defense of Islam and the acquisition of power, they preferred the strong rule of a just and virtuous Muslim. Afghani, the "Liberal," did not advocate constitutional government. His biographer, reviewing the famous Arabic newspaper published by Afghani in Paris, has noted that "there is no word in the paper's theoretical articles favoring political democracy or parliamentarianism." Afghani simply envisioned "the overthrow of individual rulers who were lax or subservient to foreigners, and their replacement by strong and patriotic men."[7] The Muslim Brethren in Egypt also rejected party politics. Banna demanded the abolition of all political parties in Egypt and the creation of a single Islamic party. Within this party there could be elections, but electoral campaigning would be limited, voting would be compulsory, and elections would be done by list, which Banna said would "liberate the representative from the pressure of those who elected him." Banna pointed to Stalin's Soviet Union as a model of a successful one-party system.[8] Navvab also allowed elections, but all representatives had to be "devout Muslims," who would be kept "under the supervision of an assembly of pious religious leaders in order to keep [their] activities in line with the Islamic provisions."[9] This preference for a strong, authoritarian Islamic state, often rationalized by the claim that Islam and democracy are incompatible, would become a trademark of fundamentalist thought and practice.

The pursuit of this strong utopian state often overflowed into violence against the weak existing states. These "reformers" were quick to disclaim any link to the violence of their followers, denying that their adepts could read their teachings as instructions or justifications for killing. Afghani set the tone, following the assassination of Iran's shah by his disciple. "Surely it was a good deed to kill this bloodthirsty tyrant," he opined, "As far as I am personally concerned, however, I have no part in this deed."[10] Banna, commenting on the assassinations and bombings done by the Muslim Brethren, claimed that "the only ones responsible for these acts are those who commit them."[11] Navvab, who failed in his one attempt at assassination, sent young disciples in his stead. For years he enjoyed the protection of leading religious figures while actually putting weapons in the hands of assassins.[12] (Only when abroad did he actually boast. "I killed Razmara," he announced on a visit to Egypt in 1954, referring to the prime minister assassinated by a disciple three years earlier.)[13] But despite the denials, violence became the inescapable shadow of Islamic fundamentalism from the outset—and the attempt to separate figure from shadow, a problematic enterprise at best.

The fundamentalist forerunners also determined that Islamic fundamentalism would have a pan-Islamic bent. The peripatetic Afghani took advantage of steamship and train, crossing political borders and sectarian divides to spread his message of Islamic solidarity. His Paris newspaper circulated far and wide in Islam, through the modern post. Egypt's Muslim Brethren also looked beyond the horizon. In 1948, they sent their own volunteers to fight the Jews in Palestine. Over the next decade, branches of the Muslim Brethren appeared across the Middle East and North Africa, linked by publications and conferences. Egyptian Brethren fleeing arrest set up more branches in Europe, where they mastered the technique of the bank transfer.

The fundamentalist forerunners even laid bridges over the historic moat of Sunni prejudice that surrounded Shi'ite Iran. Iran's Devotees of

Islam mounted massive demonstrations for Palestine, and recruited 5,000 volunteers to fight Israel. They were not allowed to leave for the front, but Navvab himself flew to Egypt and Jordan in 1953, to solidify his ties with the Muslim Brethren. Visiting the Jordanian-Israeli armistice line, he had to be physically restrained from throwing himself upon the Zionist enemy.[14] Navvab presaged those Iranian volunteers who arrived in Lebanon thirty years later to wage Islamic jihad against Israel.

From the outset, then, fundamentalists scorned the arbitrary boundaries of states, and demonstrated their resolve to think and act across the frontiers that divide Islam. The jet, the cassette, the fax, and the computer network would later help fundamentalists create a global village of ideas and action—not a hierarchical "Islamintern" but a flat "Islaminform"— countering the effects of geographic distance and sectarian loyalty. Not only has the supposed line between "revivalist" and "extremist" been difficult to draw. National and sectarian lines have been erased or smudged, and fundamentalists draw increasingly on a common reservoir for ideas, strategies, and support.

A resolute anti-Westernism, a vision of an authoritarian Islamic state, a propensity to violence, and a pan-Islamic urge: these were the biases of the forerunners of Islamic fundamentalism. No subsequent fundamentalist movement could quite shake them. Indeed, several thinkers subsequently turned these biases into a full-fledged ideology.

An Ideology of Revolution

In the middle of this century of ideologies, the fundamentalists set out to transform Islam into the most complete and seamless ideology of them all. All-encompassing Islamic law, based upon the Qur'an and the traditions of the Prophet Muhammad, constituted their ideological manifesto and program. Many of the provisions of that law had been remote ideals, enforced unevenly over the centuries by weak states. Now fundamentalists, recognizing the enhanced coercive power of the modern state, began to imagine that this law could be implemented in its entirety, and that this total order would confer hitherto unimaginable strength on the Islamic state. Fundamentalist ideology therefore insisted not only on power, but on absolute power—an insistence, admits one advocate of an Islamic state, that "has tended to make modern Islamists into proto-fascists, obsessed with dragging their compatriots kicking and screaming into paradise."[15]

Much of the ideological spadework was done by Mawlana Abu al-Ala Mawdudi (1903–79), the founder of the fundamentalist Jama'at-i Islami in Pakistan. His many writings, translated into every major language spoken by Muslims, provide a panoramic view of the ideal fundamentalist state. In this state, sovereignty would belong to God alone, and would be exercised on his behalf by a just ruler, himself guided by a reading of God's law in its entirety. As an ideological state, it would be administered for God solely by Muslims who adhered to its ideology, and "whose whole life is devoted to the observance and enforcement" of Islamic law. Non-Muslims, who could not share its ideology, and women, who by nature could not devote their entire lives to it, would have no place in high politics. Everything would come under the purview of this Islamic state. "In such a state," announced Mawdudi, "no one can regard any field of his affairs as personal and private. Considered from this aspect the Islamic state bears a kind of resemblance to the Fascist and Communist states," although Mawdudi rejected individual dictatorship, instead advocating a variety of one-party rule. Mawdudi was certain about what the Islamic state would not resemble: it would be "the very antithesis of secular Western democracy."[16] Mawdudi himself never had a sufficient following to make a concerted bid for power in Pakistan, but his writings exerted a wide influence over fundamentalists better positioned to act upon his vision.

Mawdudi's ideas were carried to their ultimate conclusion by an Egyptian Muslim Brother, Sayyid Qutb (1906–66). Qutb borrowed heavily from Mawdudi's vision of an Islamic state, but he broke new ground in his analysis of how to realize it. Mawdudi had written about the need for a "revolution" to create an Islamic state, but he believed this revolution had to be prepared by a long campaign of persuasion. Qutb, confined to one of Nasser's prison camps when he wrote his major work, was far more impatient. Islam was under assault, and redemption could not wait for a bloodless revolution. Qutb urged that a believing vanguard organize itself, retreat from impious society, denounce lax Muslims as unbelievers, and battle to overturn the political order. As Qutb put it, "those who have usurped the power of God on earth and made His worshippers their slaves will not be dispossessed by dint of Word alone."[17] Qutb thus transformed what had been a tendency toward violence into an explicit logic of revolution. He hardly had the chance to act on his theory, for he spent almost a decade in prison before his final arrest and execution. But later fundamentalists would return to his writings, to justify their own resort to force.

Qutb also placed the anti-imperialism of the early fundamentalists on an ideological footing. He attributed his own Islamic awakening to a period of more than two years spent in America from 1948. America repelled him on every level. It was, he claimed, a disastrous combination of avid materialism and egoistic individualism that commercialized women and practiced a ferocious racism. Qutb went still further, claiming that there existed something called "Crusaderism"—a systematic plan to eradicate Islam linking medieval Christianity, modern imperialism, and Western consumer culture. "Western blood carries the spirit of the Crusades within itself," wrote Qutb. "It fills the subconscious of the West."[18] Qutb's work would later prove crucial to the fundamentalist rationale that formal independence from the West had to be accompanied by a purging of Islam's own bloodstream of all Western cultural influence.

It was Ruhollah Khomeini (1902–1989) who finally wrote the ideological formula for the first successful fundamentalist revolution in Islam. Khomeini added nothing to fundamentalist ideology by his insistence on the need for an Islamic state, created if necessary by an Islamic revolution, but he made a breakthrough with his claim that only the persons most learned in Islamic law could rule: "Since Islamic government is a government of law, knowledge of the law is necessary for the ruler, as has been laid down in tradition." The ruler "must surpass all others in knowledge," and be "more learned than everyone else."[19] Since no existing state had such a ruler, Khomeini's doctrine constituted an appeal for region-wide revolution, to overturn every extant form of authority and replace it with rule by Islamic jurists. In Iran, where such jurists had maintained their independence from the state all along, this doctrine transformed them into a revolutionary class, bent on the seizure and exercise of power. Much to the astonishment of the world—fundamentalists included—the formula worked, carrying Khomeini and his followers to power on a tidal wave of revolution in 1979.

Khomeini also revalidated the anti-Western and anti-American credentials of fundamentalism. Qutb's idea of "Crusaderism" had worked particularly well in Egypt and the Levant, where the legacy of the Crusades could be resurrected from the depths of collective Muslim memory, but it did not speak to the people of Iran, a land untouched by the Crusades. Khomeini thus drew a striking metaphor to make the same point: America, historical heir to unbelief, was the "Great Satan." This posited an absolute conflict between Islam and the West, not just in history but in eschatology.[20]

It was dramatized by the seizure of the U.S. Embassy in Teheran and the 444-day detention of its staff. In fundamentalist ideology, political conflict with the West was transformed into a timeless cultural and religious conflict with the "enemies of Islam," led by America and represented on the ground by its proxy, Israel.

Not all of Khomeini's ideas had a full impact on wider Islam. His legitimation of rule by Islamic jurists proved difficult for other fundamentalist movements to assimilate, because it assumed such jurists were inclined to take an oppositional stand. In Sunni lands, Islamic jurists usually served the state, and Sunni movements therefore tended to coalesce under lay leaders. Likewise, while Khomeini's anti-Americanism struck a deep chord, the Soviet invasion of Afghanistan in 1980 diffused its impact. Sunni movements mobilized to wage an international Islamic jihad against the Soviets, and were even ready to cooperate temporarily with America to do so.

Khomeini's delegitimation of rule by nominal Muslims kings and presidents, though, found a powerful echo, and he demonstrated how a revolution might succeed in practice. Khomeini also showed how cultural alienation could be translated into a fervid antiforeign sentiment, an essential cement for a broad revolutionary coalition. Later it would be assumed that only "extremists" beyond Iran were thrilled by Iran's revolution. In fact, the enthusiasm among fundamentalists was almost unanimous. As a close reading of the press of the Egyptian Muslim Brethren has demonstrated, even this supposedly sober movement approached the Iranian revolution with "unqualified enthusiasm and unconditional euphoria," coupled with an "uncritical acceptance of both its means and goals."[21] Sunni doubts would arise about implementation of the Islamic state in Iran, but for the next decade, much of the effort of fundamentalists would be invested in attempts to replicate Khomeini's success and bring about a second Islamic revolution.

The attempts to make a second revolution demonstrated that fundamentalists of all kinds would employ revolutionary violence if they thought it would bring them to power. Frustrated by the drudgery of winning mass support, full of the heady ideas of Mawdudi and Qutb, and inspired by Khomeini's success, they lunged forward. From the wild-eyed to the wily, Sunni fundamentalists of all stripes began to conspire. A messianic sect seized the Great Mosque in Mecca in 1979. A group moved by Qutb's teachings assassinated Egyptian President Anwar Sadat in 1981. The Muslim Brethren declared a rebellion against the Syrian regime in 1982.

Another path of violence paralleled this one—the work of the half-dozen Shi'ite movements in Arab lands that had emerged around the hub of Islamic revolution in Iran. They targeted their rage against the existing order in Iraq, Saudi Arabia, Kuwait, Lebanon, and the smaller Gulf states. In Iraq, they answered Khomeini's appeal by seeking to raise the country's Shi'ites in revolt in 1979. In Lebanon, they welcomed Iran's Revolutionary Guards in 1982, first to help drive out the Israelis, then to send suicide bombers to blow up the barracks of U.S. and French peacekeepers there in 1983. Another Shi'ite bomber nearly killed the ruler of Kuwait in 1985. Some of Khomeini's adepts went to Mecca as demonstrators, to preach revolution to the assembled pilgrims. Others hijacked airliners and abducted foreigners. Khomeini put a final touch on the decade when he incited his worldwide following to an act of assassination, issuing a religious edict demanding the death of the novelist Salman Rushdie in 1989.

This violence was not an aberration. It was a culmination. From the time of Afghani, fundamentalists had contemplated the possibility of denying power through assassination, and taking power through revolution. Because resort to political violence carried many risks, it had been employed judiciously and almost always surreptitiously, but it remained a legitimate option rooted firmly in the tradition, and it became the preferred option after Iran's revolution emboldened fundamentalists everywhere. For the first time, the ideology of Islam had been empowered, and it had happened through revolution. Power for Islam seemed within reach, if only the fundamentalists were bold enough to run the risk. Many of them were. They included not just the avowed revolutionaries of the Jihad Organization in Egypt, but the cautious and calculating leaderships of the Muslim Brethren in Syria and the Shi'ite Da'wa Party in Iraq.

It was a seesaw battle throughout the 1980s. Nowhere was Iran's experience repeated. The masses did not ignite in revolution, the rulers did not board jumbo jets for exile. Regimes often employed ruthless force to isolate and stamp out the nests of fundamentalist "sedition." Fundamentalists faced the gaol and the gallows in Egypt. Their blood flowed in the gutters of Hama in Syria, Mecca in Saudi Arabia, and Najaf in Iraq. Yet fundamentalists also struck blows in return, against government officials, intellectuals, minorities, and foreigners. While they did not take power anywhere, they created many semiautonomous pockets of resistance. Some of these pockets were distant from political centers, such as the Bekaa Valley in Lebanon and several governates of Upper Egypt, but fundamentalists also took root in urban quarters and on university campuses, where Islamic dress for women became compulsory and short-cropped beards for men became customary. From time to time, impatient pundits would proclaim that the tide of Islamic fundamentalism had gone out, but its appeal obviously ran much deeper. Its straightforward solution to the complex crisis of state and society spoke directly to the poor and the young, the overqualified and the underemployed, whose numbers were always increasing faster than their opportunities.

After Iran's revolution and the subsequent revolts, it was impossible to dismiss the ideological coherence Islamic fundamentalism had achieved. It had succeeded in resurrecting in many minds an absolute division between Islam and unbelief. Its adherents, filled with visions of power, had struck at the existing order, turned against foreign culture, and rejected not only apologetics but politics—the pursuit of the possible through compromise. Fundamentalism mobilized its adherents for conflict, for it assumed that the power sought for Islam existed only in a finite quantity. It could only be taken at the expense of others: rulers, foreigners, minorities. Fundamentalists did not admit the sharing of this power, anymore than they admitted the sharing of religious truth, and although fundamentalists differed on the means of taking power, they were unanimous on what should be done with it. One observer has written that even in Egypt, where the fundamentalist scene seemed highly fragmented, the political and social program of the violent fringe groups "did not seem to differ much from that of the mainstream Muslim Brethren," and was shared by "almost the whole spectrum of political Islam."[22] This was true, by and large, for Islamic fundamentalism as a whole.

Repackaging the Islamic State

Yet at the same time, a younger generation of thinkers added crucial refinements to the ideology, adapting it to the times. Even fundamentalists could not reject the West in its entirety. The West, despite fundamentalist faith in its ultimate decline, continued to produce technologies and institutions that gave it immense power. Muslims, to acquire that power, had to import these tools or risk being overwhelmed completely. This next generation of thinkers imagined the Islamic state not so much as a bulwark against the West, but as a filter screening the flow of Western innovations and influences. This ideological filter would admit whatever might enhance the power of the Islamic state and reject whatever might diminish the unity and resolve of Islamic society. It took a different kind of fundamentalist leader to play this role—Muslims who knew the West's strengths and weaknesses first-hand, who had themselves come through the searing fire of its skepticism with their belief intact.

Sudan's Hasan al-Turabi (b. 1932) is the most notable representative of this successor generation. Coming from a strong religious background, Turabi took a doctorate in law at the Sorbonne from 1959 to 1964. Unlike Qutb, he was not altogether repelled by his sojourn in the lands of unbelief: "I was excited by the richness and precision of the French language, the culture, the history of the revolution, the relations between church and state, and the study of the different constitutions. I was not focused exclusively on my law studies. I went to the national library, I visited museums."[23] This unique formation has helped to transform Turabi into the *maître* of contemporary "Islamism," for he is presumed to know the West intimately enough to decide what should be borrowed and what should be spurned. His partnership with the military regime in Sudan, since 1989, has put him in the best position of any contemporary fundamentalist to implement an Islamic state.

Another member of this generation is Rashid al-Ghannushi (b. 1941), leader of the Tunisian fundamentalist movement.[24] Ghannushi took to the ideas of the Muslim Brethren while studying philosophy in Damascus, where he also witnessed the Arab debacle in June 1967. Ghannushi briefly continued his preparation in philosophy at the Sorbonne in the crucial year of the 1968 student uprising. By his own account, he read not only the works of Islamic philosophers, but Descartes, Bacon, Kant, Hegel, Schopenhauer, and Althusser.[25] But on his return to Tunisia, he preferred to teach the ideas of Mawdudi, Banna, and Qutb to an emerging fundamentalist movement. Ghannushi repeatedly ran afoul of the Tunisian authorities, and in 1989 choose voluntary exile. He is now a political refugee in Britain, where he plays the role of the foremost defender of Islamism in the West. His region-wide stature derives from the fact that he speaks knowingly from the belly of the beast.

A third figure of comparable stature, certainly among Shi'ites, is Sayyid Muhammad Husayn Fadlallah (b. 1936) of Lebanon. Fadlallah, born in Iraq of Lebanese Shi'ite descent, is a product of the Shi'ite academies of Najaf in Iraq. But even there, he was drawn to study the forbidden knowledge of philosophers and unbelievers, as he himself later hinted: "My studies, which were supposed to be traditional, rebelled against tradition and all familiar things."[26] Fadlallah arrived in Beirut in 1966, at a time when the city often mistook itself for an *arrondissement* of Paris. In this marketplace of ideologies, Fadlallah learned to package Islam in a highly competitive way. He, too, produced a nuanced argument for borrowing from the West while battling it. In the course of the 1980s Fadlallah became the oracle and mentor of Hizbullah, preaching dialogue and resistance in the same breath.

Turabi, Ghannushi, and Fadlallah did not rewrite the idea of the Islamic state developed by Mawdudi, Qutb, and Khomeini. They repackaged it. They understood that the young doubted whether the secular West really intended a crusade against Islam, and so they played down the themes of "Crusaderism" and the "Great Satan," substituting the more fashionable rhetoric of Third World anti-imperialism. This came naturally, for they had overheard the West incriminate itself during their own sojourns in and near its privileged academe. Their arguments for the inevitability triumph of Islam drew upon the dark prophecies of the West's decline which have emanated from European and American philosophers for a century. At the same time, they understood that many of the young had been influenced by notions of class struggle. This they incorporated by developing a terminology that referred to Muslims as the "dispossessed" of "the South."[27] Not surprisingly, fundamentalists even managed to find apologists among the West's own Third Worldists, who thought they heard an echo in the words pumped from Islamist pulpits. ("Because they hate us, they must be right," wrote a French writer in irony. "What a wonderful coincidence that the revelation of truth coincided with anti-imperialist struggle!")[28]

The genius of the new thinkers, though, was to create a climate that could sustain an altogether different analogy. They understood that many of the young had a sneaking or grudging admiration for the science and democracy of the liberal West. Thus, they claimed that elements of both could be selectively borrowed if this served to strengthen Islam. Without sacrificing any element of ideological principle, they worked to present Islamic fundamentalist movements as the functional equivalent of the "reform" movements of the former communist bloc.

This latest repackaging not only has brought new adherents to fundamentalist movements, but has persuaded a surprising number of the West's most hopeful observers of the Middle East that "Islam is the solution." They now argue that beneath a monolithic façade, Islamism has grown diverse, and carries the seed of the long-awaited reform of Islam. "Islam is now at a pivotal and profound moment of evolution," announces a journalist, "a juncture increasingly equated with the Protestant Reformation." "This is, indeed, the most exciting period in Islamic religious history since the twelfth century," gushes a professor.

But who are the "reformers" who supposedly are making the first breakthrough in seven centuries? Where are the pathfinding texts without which a "Reformation" is impossible? As one Western critic of Islamist thought observes, since the writings of the founders, compiled well before Iran's revolution, "there are nothing but brochures, prayers, feeble glosses and citations of canonical authors."[29] In works written a generation ago or more, Islamic fundamentalism became a coherent ideology, resting on a fixed canon. The road to redemption leads through the Islamic state of the kind envisioned by Mawdudi, Qutb, and Khomeini. Turabi speaks for nearly all fundamentalists when he dismisses the need for any further thought: "Those Muslims who venture to reform Islam because they are impressed by the Western Reformation.... did write a few books, but they did not go very far. They did not impress any Muslim."[30] For Turabi's generation, the intellectual work of thinking through an Islamic state has already been done. It is now a matter of repackaging the vision and mobilizing Muslims for its implementation. Turabi himself puts it best: Islamist movements are today "without elitism or obsession with quality." They represent "quantity and the people."[31]

So far, there has been no "reform," and certainly no "Reformation." While fundamentalist ideology has been refashioned at its edges, its core remains consistent and stable. A decade ago, Hasan Hanafi, another Sorbonne-schooled Islamist, described this irreducible and unalterable core:

> In the past, Islam found its way between two falling empires, the Persian and the Roman. Both were exhausted by wars. Both suffered moral and spiritual crises. Islam, as a new world order, was able to expand as a substitute to the old regime. Nowadays, Islam finds itself again as a new power, marking its way between the two superpowers in crisis. Islam is regenerating, the two superpowers are degenerating. Islam is the power of the future, inheriting the two superpowers in the present.[32]

A decade later, the Soviet Union is gone and the fundamentalists of Islam claim they pose the last ideological challenge to the last superpower. Ahmad Khomeini, son of the man who detonated the first explosion, summarized the fundamentalist point of view: "After the fall of Marxism, Islam replaced it, and as long as Islam exists, U.S. hostility exists, and as long as

U.S. hostility exists, the struggle exists."[33] This Islam, forged by a century of thought, claims the status of a world ideology. For fundamentalists, the proof of its validity will not be found in the number of souls it wins but in its empowerment of Islam.

Purge Before Power

To achieve that, of course, Islamism must first come to state power. Given the strength of existing regimes, its leaders must build coalitions with other groups if they are to stand any chance of breaking out of encirclement. And it is here that Islamism seems to be failing. The Islamic revival was perhaps most flexible at its outset, in the preaching of Afghani. He altered his message to accommodate a wide range of political alliances, and his biographer has rightly described his interpretation of Islam as "more 'progressive' than that of the modern revivalists—more open to new ideas and not concerned with reinforcing the Islam of the past."[34] Guile can sometimes compensate for a lack of flexibility: Khomeini's interpretation of Islam was not "progressive," but he struck just such a posture before the revolution, allowing him to forge a coalition of diverse forces. Because the Shah's state collapsed so fast, that coalition swept him to power before it unwound in recriminations and purges. A capacity for dissimulation, such as that so effectively cultivated in Shi'ite Islam, is an immense asset in the art of politics, and goes far to explain how leaders like Afghani and Khomeini found crucial allies.

In contrast, today's Islamists, certainly in the Arab world, are unwilling to suspend enough of their belief to find a common ground with potential partners. Their words and deeds frighten many Muslims, even those who long for change. The reason is violence—not against the West, but against other Muslims. Even in opposition, Islamist movements cannot resist the temptation to intimidate opponents, rivals, and even lukewarm supporters. The kind of purge Khomeini carried out once in power is being attempted by Islamist movements today, when it only serves to isolate them. Sayyid Qutb's idea of an unbelieving society, the basis of Islamism as ideology, is the congenital defect of Islamism as politics. Its deleterious effects can be seen in the continuing bloodshed between Islamic movements in Afghanistan, in the murder of intellectuals in Egypt, in the indiscriminate bombings against civilians in Algeria. Islamists claim they have been forced to follow the methods of the regimes they oppose, but if this is so, why should anyone prefer them? Regimes invoke the threat of Islamist "terror" precisely because there is a genuine dread of it in society at large. As a result, the Islamists have no allies, and without allies their chances of assuming power are slim.

There are some Islamists who know this, and who are trying (late in the day) to borrow a page from Khomeini's techniques of dissimulation. But for dissimulation to succeed, it must be consistent and seamless. As it is now practiced by many Islamists, dissimulation is no more than telling each audience whatever it prefers to hear. It is not too difficult to assemble these utterances and demonstrate their incompatibility. This is why Turabi, Fadlallah, and Ghannoushi, despite protestations of pluralism, create deep unease among liberals, leftists, nationalists, and feminists, who might have been allies. They overhear the full discourse on the Islamic state—a discourse in which one can hear democracy, free expression, and equal rights denounced as Western cultural imperialism.

Turabi is the only leading Islamist whose alliance-building has given him some access to power in Sudan, but his friends are generals and colonels. In the absence of other allies, the temptation of befriending the military may also prove irresistable to other fundamentalist movements. If so, Islamism will then have filled not only the same political space as Arabism. It will have made the same fatal choice. At some point, it dawned on the military partners of the Arab nationalist ideologues that they could do without the guidance of a Sati' al-Husri or a Michel Aflaq. They could formulate ideology for themselves, whenever needed. Likewise, generals and colonels who take leading Islamists as guides are likely to discard them, even as they appropriate their ideas and language. Perhaps this will be the next phase of Islamism, as men of theory are thrust aside by new military potentates, hungry for Islamic legitimacy. Libya's Mu'ammar al-Qaddhafi is perhaps the transitional man in this gradual shift from Arab to Islamist military rule.

But this is only speculation, and it is impossible to predict the future fortunes of Islamism. Of its many outcomes, only one seems absolutely certain. Like Arabism, Islamism may fail; and like Arabism, Islamism may fail at great cost, its adherents gradually becoming its victims. But by then, it will have launched a hundred careers and a thousand books. Of Marxism, it has been said that it failed materially everywhere but in Western academe, where its professors turned it into tenure and grants. Islamism seems destined to do the same.

Notes

1. H.R.H. The Prince of Wales, *Islam and the West: a lecture given in the Sheldonian Theatre, Oxford on 27 October 1993* (Oxford: Oxford Centre for Islamic Studies, 1993), 16.
2. For the two most comprehensive explorations of fundamentalist ideology, see Emmanuel Sivan, *Radical Islam: Medieval Theory and Modern Politics* (New Haven, Conn.: Yale University Press, 1985); and Nazih Ayubi, *Political Islam: Religion and Politics in the Arab World* (London: Routledge, 1991).
3. Wilfrid Scawen Blunt, *Secret History of the English Occupation of Egypt* (London: Unwin, 1907), 100.
4. Quoted by Elie Kedourie, *Politics in the Middle East* (New York: Oxford University Press, 1992), 274.
5. Aziz Al-Azmeh, *Islams and Modernities* (London: Verso, 1993), 85.
6. Arnold Toynbee, *A Journey to China* (London: Constable, 1931), 117.
7. Nikki R. Keddie, *Sayyid Jamal ad-Din "al-Afghani": A Political Biography* (Berkeley: University of California Press, 1972), 225–26.
8. Quoted by Richard P. Mitchell, *The Society of the Muslim Brothers* (London: Oxford University Press, 1969), 261–62.
9. Quoted by Said Amir Arjomand, "Traditionalism in Twentieth-century Iran," in *From Nationalism to Revolutionary Islam*, ed. Said Amir Arjomand (Albany: State University of New York Press, 1984), 210.
10. Quoted by Keddie, *Sayyid Jamal ad-Din "al-Afghani"*, 412.
11. Quoted by Mitchell, *The Society of the Muslim Brothers*, 70.
12. Farhad Kazemi, "The *Fada'iyan-e Islam*: Fanaticism, Politics and Terror," in *From Nationalism to Revolutionary Islam*, 169.
13. Mitchell, *The Society of the Muslim Brothers*, 126 n. 66.
14. Yann Richard, "L'Organisation des fedâ'iyân-e eslâm, mouvement intégriste musulman en Iran (1945–1956)," in *Radicalismes islamiques*, eds. Olivier Carré and Paul Dumont, 2 vols. (Paris: L'Harmattan, 1985), 1:29, 51.
15. Abdelwahhab El-Affendi, *Who Needs an Islamic State?* (London: Grey Seal, 1991), 87.
16. Quoted by Charles J. Adams, "Mawdudi and the Islamic State," in *Voices of Resurgent Islam*, ed. John L. Esposito (New York: Oxford University Press, 1983), 119–21.
17. Quoted by Gilles Kepel, *Muslim Extremism in Egypt* (Berkeley and Los Angeles: University of California Press, 1985), 55.
18. Quoted by Sylvia Haim, "Sayyid Qutb," *Asian and African Studies* 16, no. 1 (March 1982): 154.
19. Imam Ruhollah Khomeini, *Islam and Revolution: Writings and Declarations of Imam Khomeini*, trans. Hamid Algar (Berkeley, Cal.: Mizan Press, 1981), 59.
20. William O. Beeman, "Images of the Great Satan: Representations of the United States in the Iranian Revolution," in *Religion and Politics in Iran*, ed. Nikki R. Keddie (New Haven, Conn.: Yale University Press, 1983), 191–217.
21. Rudi Matthee, "The Egyptian Opposition on the Iranian Revolution," in *Shi'ism and Social Protest*, eds. Juan R. I. Cole and Nikki R. Keddie (New Haven, Conn.: Yale University Press, 1986), 263. Cf. Emmanuel Sivan, "Sunni Radicalism in the Middle East and the Iranian Revolution," *International Journal of Middle East Studies* 21 (1989): 1–30.
22. Raymond A. Hinnebusch, *Egyptian Politics under Sadat* (Cambridge: Cambridge University Press, 1985), 202–3.

23. Interview with Turabi, *Le Figaro*, 25 January 1994.

24. See Linda G. Jones, "Portrait of Rashid al-Ghannoushi," *Middle East Report* (July-August 1988): 19–24.

25. Interview with Ghannushi , *Maghreb Review* 2, no. 1 (1986): 33.

26. Interview with Fadlallah, Voice of Lebanon, 2 May 1992, quoted in *Foreign Broadcast Information Service Daily Report: The Middle East and South Asia* (hereafter cited as *FBIS*), 5 May 1992.

27. This tendency has been identified by Nikki R. Keddie, "Islamic Revival as Third Worldism," in *Le cuisinier et le philosophe: Hommage à Maxime Rodinson*, ed. Jean-Pierre Digard (Paris: Maisonneuve et Larose, 1982), 275–81. Keddie notes that "many current spokesmen of the Islamic revival have taken some of their ideas from non-religious third worldism," an influence so pervasive that "even a man so apparently separated for most of his life from Western currents of thought as Ayatollah Khomeini echoes third worldism (in fact often leftist third worldism)."

28. Pascal Bruckner, *The Tears of the White Man: Compassion as Contempt*, trans. William R. Beer (New York: Free Press, 1986), 33.

29. Olivier Roy, *The Failure of Political Islam* (Cambridge, Mass.: Harvard University Press, 1994), 60.

30. Transcript of remarks by Hasan al-Turabi before the Center for Strategic and International Studies, Washington, 12 May 1992.

31. Hasan Turabi, "Islam, Democracy, the State and the West," *Middle East Policy* 1, no. 3 (1992): 51.

32. Hassan Hanafi, "The Origin of Modern Conservatism and Islamic Fundamentalism," in *Islamic Dilemmas: Reformers, Nationalists, and Industrialization*, ed. Ernest Gellner (Berlin: Mouton, 1985), 103.

33. Speech by Ahmad Khomeini, 20 October 1991, quoted in *FBIS*, 21 October 1991.

34. Nikki R. Keddie, *An Islamic Response to Imperialism*, 2d ed. (Berkeley and Los Angeles: University of California Press, 1983), xx.

10

Khomeini's Messengers in Mecca

According to the tradition of Islam, Mecca during the annual Muslim pilgrimage is a city open to all Muslims, in which all forms of strife and bloodshed are forbidden. The peace of Mecca is a concept so rooted in Arabia that it even predates Islam, and was observed by sojourners in Mecca before the Arabian shrine became the center of Muslim faith.

But in 1987, Mecca became a site of unprecedented carnage when demonstrating Iranian pilgrims clashed with Saudi security forces in a bloody confrontation that claimed over four hundred lives. The Saudis and their supporters called the event a premeditated riot: violent Iranian demonstrators crushed themselves to death in a stampede of their own making. The Iranians and their sympathizers called it a premeditated massacre: the Saudis conspired to provoke and shoot Iranian pilgrims. The pilgrimage to Mecca, far from providing a respite from the conflicts that beset Islam, had itself become a point of confrontation between rival visions of Islam. The pilgrimage peace had been shattered by the brickbats and bullets of Muslims.

The disruption of the pilgrimage peace admitted multiple interpretations. It occurred at a moment of escalating tensions in the last phase of the Iranian-Iraqi war, following the American reflagging of Kuwaiti tankers and the introduction of foreign escorts in the Gulf. This foreign intervention, favored by Saudi Arabia and opposed by Iran, created an atmosphere of crisis between the two states. Yet the deterioration of the pilgrimage peace also reflected tensions dating back to Iran's revolution, an event that kindled a broader rivalry between Saudi Arabia and Iran over primacy in the Gulf and in Islam. That conflict had its remote origins in the great historical animosity of Wahhabism, the fount of Saudi Islam, to Shi'ism itself. Nor can the most recent pilgrimage strife be divorced from the history of mistrust between Shi'ite pilgrims and their Sunni hosts, a history that stretches back as far as the sixteenth century. At a still deeper level, the event echoed Sunni-Shi'ite animosities that had their origins in the seventh century, at the very dawn of Islam.

Even if it is allowed that the Gulf crisis triggered the violence of 1987, it was understood by Muslims in a larger historical context. Much of that understanding is implicit and unspoken, because it is essentially sectarian. Sectarian bigotry dare not speak its name openly. Like racial and ethnic prejudice in other societies, sectarian prejudice is not professed openly in the Muslim world. "They are now propagandizing and claiming that this incident was a war between Shi'ites and Sunnis," charged Ali Khamene'i, then the president of Iran, after the 1987 violence. "This is a lie! Of course there is a war; but a war between the American perception of Islam and true revolutionary Islam."[1] The pilgrimage controversy is not only one between Shi'ites and Sunnis, but neither is it one between Khomeini's truth and America's falsehood. It is a conflict that is simultaneously political and sectarian, that combines a present-day clash of interests with the historic clash of sects in Islam. Some of these sectarian differences touch upon the Muslim pilgrimage itself, and involve conflicting notions of sanctity and asylum. The aim of this essay is to explain the interaction of contemporary politics with the enduring prejudices that Saudis and Iranians still bring to Mecca.[2]

From Ottomans to Saudis

The pilgrimage ritual itself is not an issue about which Sunnis and Shi'ites have conducted an elaborate polemic. The bedrock of sectarian conflict has always been the matter of the Imamate—the question of legitimate authority in Islam—which is a matter of theological controversy outside the ritual sphere. Yet over time, theological differences were transformed into political, social, and cultural differences, and these infected both sects with bigoted lore about Shi'ite pilgrims and Sunni hosts. This was particularly evident after Sunni-Shi'ite differences took the form of Ottoman-Safavid armed conflict, beginning in the sixteenth century. That was perhaps the most divided century in Islamic history, marked by great wars of religion between Sunnis and Shi'ites. When the holy cities were under Sunni Ottoman rule, there were years in which the Ottomans denied entry to Shi'ites coming from Safavid domains. The Safavids reacted by trying to discourage the pilgrimage to Mecca and emphasizing the importance of Shi'ite shrines in their own domains.[3]

The Sunni corpus of libel is perhaps more readily documented, if only because it sometimes led to violent acts against Shi'ite pilgrims. At the root of the Sunni lore is the belief that Shi'ites feel themselves compelled to pollute the holy premises. Much evidence for Sunni belief in this libel exists both in Islamic textual sources and in European travel literature. This pollution was said to take a particularly repelling form: Burckhardt and Burton, the great nineteenth-century explorers of Arabia, both heard about attacks on Shi'ite pilgrims, prompted by the suspicion that they had polluted the Great Mosque in Mecca with excrement. According to Burton, "their ill-fame has spread far; at Alexandria they were described to me as a people who defile the Ka'bah."[4]

The Shi'ite libel was just as farfetched. It held that Sunnis did not respect Mecca as a sanctuary, and that the lives of Shi'ite pilgrims were forfeit even in these sacred precincts, where the shedding of blood is forbidden. Shi'ite pilgrims were indeed liable to humiliation at any time; as Burton wrote of Shi'ites on pilgrimage, "that man is happy who gets over it without a beating, [for] in no part of Al-Hijaz are they for a moment safe from abuse and blows."[5] Yet it would seem that, for the most part, Shi'ite pilgrims were as secure as other pilgrims, provided they exercised the discretion (*taqiyya*) permitted them by Shi'ite doctrine and conformed with the customs of their Sunni hosts. During the Ottoman period, the Iranian pilgrims' caravan also bought its security through a special tribute, paid both to desert tribes en route and to the guardians of the sanctuaries.[6]

Since toleration could be had at a price which Shi'ite pilgrims were prepared to pay, their lives were rarely as threatened as their dignity. The open manner in which Shi'ites observed Muharram in Jidda epitomized the tolerance of the late Ottoman years. When the Dutch Orientalist Hurgronje witnessed these ceremonies in 1884, he found the Ottoman governor in attendance. Hurgronje reported that the governor "not only drank sherbet but also wept piously."[7] Writing of his pilgrimage in 1885, an Iranian Shi'ite described the tolerance shown to Shi'ites generally:

> Previously, in Mecca the populace greatly persecuted the Iranian pilgrims who were Shi'ites, so they had to practice complete dissimulation. These days, because of the weakness of the Ottoman government and the European style civil law which is practiced there, and the strength of the Iranian government, this practice is completely abandoned. There is no harm done to the Iranians. No one would molest them, even if they did not practice dissimulation.[8]

Sectarian antagonisms were exacerbated, though, following the advent of Saudi rule over Mecca in 1924. The doctrinal divide that separated Ottoman Sunnism from Shi'ism seemed narrow in comparison to the chasm separating Saudi Wahhabism and Shi'ism. Wahhabi doctrine regarded Shi'ite veneration of the Imams and their tombs as blasphemous idolatry. The Wahhabi iconoclasts had earned lasting notoriety in Shi'ite eyes when they emerged from the Arabian desert in 1802 and sacked Karbala, the Shi'ite shrine city in Iraq. They slew several thousand Shi'ites on that occasion and desecrated the revered tomb of the Imam Husayn, whose martyrdom in the seventh century is the pivotal event in Shi'ite religious history. Those Shi'ites who perished became martyrs in the eyes of their coreligionists, sacrificed on the very site of Husayn's martyrdom.

When a revived Wahhabi movement swept through Arabia during the first quarter of this century, it appeared as hostile as ever to Shi'ism's most fundamental assumptions. The leader of the movement, Abd al-Aziz Ibn Sa'ud, when asked in 1918 about the Shi'ite shrines in Iraq, could still declare that "I would raise no objection if you demolished the whole lot of them, and I would demolish them myself if I had the chance."[9] He never had that chance, but he did besiege and occupy Medina, and his bombardment of the city produced a general strike in Iran and an uproar throughout the Shi'ite world. For while the pilgrimage (*hajj*) to Mecca holds the same significance for Sunnis and Shi'ites, the visitation (*ziyara*) to nearby Medina is of special significance for Shi'ites. The cemetery of al-Baqi', near the city, is the reputed resting place of the Prophet Muhammad's daughter Fatima and four of the Twelve Imams. It was the Shi'ite practice at this cemetery to pray for their intercession with God.[10] The Wahhabis, for whom prayer through these intercessors represented a form of idolatry, had leveled much of this cemetery in 1806, during an earlier occupation of Medina, but its domed tombs had been rebuilt by the end of the century. Now the Saudis, in their purifying zeal, again demolished the domes of al-Baqi', a move regarded by Shi'ites as desecration of their hallowed shrines.

The demolition created so profound a sentiment in Iran, especially in religious circles, that the Iranian government refused to recognize Ibn Sa'ud's rule. Instead, Iran demanded that a general assembly of Muslims be created to regulate the holy cities, while a Shi'ite conference convened in Lucknow, India, called upon all Muslims to use every possible means to expel Ibn Sa'ud from the Hijaz.[11] Denial of recognition was combined, in 1927, with a decision by Iran to forbid the pilgrimage to its nationals, as an act of protest against the alleged intolerance of the Wahhabis and their destruction of tombs.[12]

Still, the ban failed to discourage the most determined pilgrims from Iran, who continued to arrive via Iraq and Syria. And in a pragmatic step, Ibn Sa'ud moved to defuse the extensive Shi'ite agitation against him by a show of tolerance designed to win official Iranian recognition. Shi'ite pilgrims from Arab lands met with exemplary treatment during the year in which Iran imposed the ban, and Iran's *ulama* soon were demanding the restored right to perform the pilgrimage. In 1928, Iran lifted the pilgrimage ban, and in 1929 Iran and Ibn Sa'ud's kingdom concluded a treaty of friendship. Article 3 of the treaty guaranteed that Iran's pilgrims would enjoy treatment identical to that of pilgrims from other countries, and that they would not be prevented from observing their own religious rites.[13]

Iran's pilgrims came to enjoy a measure of toleration that reflected the pragmatism of Ibn Sa'ud on Shi'ite matters, an approach that also guided his policy toward his own Shi'ite minority in the east of his kingdom.[14] Ibn Sa'ud, in both hosting and ruling over Shi'ites, now asked only that they avoid public enactment of distinctly Shi'ite rituals. A pattern of tolerance thus seemed to have been established. It was not much tested during the 1930s, when Iran's own government imposed a virtual ban on the pilgrimage to Mecca, in order to conserve foreign exchange.[15] But other Shi'ites, especially from India, fulfilled the obligation with no difficulty, although they often expressed frustration at their inability to pray at graves and sites which had once been the focus of the Shi'ite pilgrimage.[16]

All the more striking, then, was a serious recurrence of the Sunni libel of Shi'ite defilement. In 1943, a Saudi religious judge ordered an Iranian pilgrim beheaded for allegedly defiling the Great Mosque with excrement supposedly carried into the mosque in his pilgrim's garment. Ibn Sa'ud remarked to some Americans that "this was the kind of offense which might be expected of Iranian." The verdict in local coffee houses held that "the Iranians always act that way."[17] The incident, which infuriated religious opinion in Iran, culminated in an official Iranian protest and a demand for payment of an indemnity. The Iranian press indulged in a campaign of anti-Wahhabi polemic shriller than anything published since Ibn Sa'ud's conquest of the Mecca. Once again, tales of Wahhabi barbarism were retold, and the story of the sacking of Karbala was recounted with anguish and embellishment. The government of Iran imposed another pilgrimage ban, which it only lifted in 1948, after the dust of controversy had settled.

The pilgrimage controversy became dormant again following the political rapprochement between Saudi Arabia and Iran during the 1960s, which was the outcome of shared apprehension over Egyptian-sponsored subversion. Theologians on both sides of the divide continued to publish intolerant polemical attacks and legal opinions directed against the rival reading of Islam. Yet the doctrinal disagreement was accompanied by a steady increase in the number of Iranian pilgrims, thanks to the introduction of a direct air service for pilgrims. The number of Iranian pilgrims rose steadily, from 12,000 in 1961 to 57,000 in 1972.

Revolution and Pilgrimage

This influx coincided with the appearance of an introspective and overtly political genre of Iranian writing on the pilgrimage. The radical Iranian publicist Ali Shariati, in his book entitled *Hajj*, sought deeper meaning in the Meccan pilgrimage in his quest for a solution to contemporary Islam's broader philosophical and political dilemmas. Shariati urged the pilgrims "to study the dangers and consequences of the superpowers and their agents who have infiltrated Muslim nations. They should resolve to fight against brainwashing, propaganda, disunity, heresy, and false religions."[18]

In 1971, several Iranians were arrested in Mecca for distributing a message to Muslim pilgrims from one Ayatollah Ruhollah Khomeini, at that time in Najaf, the Shi'ite shrine city in Iraq: "At this sacred pilgrimage gathering, the Muslims must exchange their views concerning the basic problems of Islam and the special problems of each Muslim country. The people of each country should, in effect, present a report concerning their own state to the Muslims of the world, and thus all will come to know what their Muslim brothers are suffering at the hands of imperialism and its agents." Khomeini then presented his own scathing "report" on Iran, describing it as "a military base for Israel, which means, by extension, for America."[19]

After 1971, hardly a year passed during which some Iranians did not distribute a similar message from Khomeini to Muslim pilgrims. The effort usually met with Saudi apathy, for the Saudis did not regard this preaching as directed against themselves. Khomeini worded his annual pilgrimage message in such a way as to appeal to Iranian pilgrims, and to alert other pilgrims to the "shameful, bloody, so-called White Revolution" of the Shah. Such propaganda was liable to complicate Saudi relations with the Shah's Iran, so Saudi authorities took measures against the more brazen distributors of Khomeini's messages, but the Saudis did not regard these few troublesome Iranians as a serious threat to their own standing as rulers of Islam's holiest sanctuaries. Khomeini himself performed the pilgrimage in 1973, without incident.

The truly radical feature of Shi'ite doctrine as expounded both by Khomeini and Shariati was their abrogation of the Shi'ite principle of discretion (*taqiyya*) during the pilgrimage, a discretion that had generally been reciprocated by Saudi tolerance. Khomeini now argued that a crucial obligation of the Muslim pilgrim was to "disavow the polytheists," in an essentially political rite focused on denunciations of America, Israel, and corrupt Muslim governments. By urging his followers to view the pilgrimage as a political rite, he set Shi'ites apart from other pilgrims, with serious consequences for the fragile tolerance that the Saudis had shown toward Shi'ite pilgrims. The new preaching upset the delicate balance that preserved the pilgrimage peace, by urging a line of action that implicitly underlined differences between Shi'ite pilgrims and Sunni hosts.

Following the Iranian revolution, Iran sought to act on the principles elaborated by Khomeini, by appealing directly to the Muslim pilgrims of other lands through political activity during the pilgrimage.[20] The process of politicization was gradual. In 1979, Iran's pilgrims engaged in only light propagandizing, and in 1980 Iran organized a much reduced pilgrimage, due to the outbreak of war with Iraq. But large demonstrations, resulting in violent clashes with Saudi police, first took place in 1981, when Iranian pilgrims began to chant political slogans in the Prophet's Mosque in Medina and the Great Mosque in Mecca. Saudi security forces acted against the Iranians in both mosques, and a subsequent clash in the Prophet's Mosque resulted in the death of an Iranian pilgrim. In 1982, the Iranian pilgrimage took an even more radical turn, when Khomeini appointed Hojjatolislam Musavi-Khoiniha as his pilgrimage representative. Khoiniha was the mentor of the students who had seized the United States Embassy in Tehran. Saudi police clashed with demonstrators whom he addressed in both Medina and Mecca. In Mecca he was arrested, and a speech delivered in Medina after the pilgrimage earned him expulsion as an "instigator."

This renewed conflict on the ground intensified the polemical debate over the pilgrimage. The debate was not a simple repetition of the old libels, if only because the intellectual climate of contemporary Islam is inhospitable to overt sectarian polemics. For most Muslims, it is no longer considered politic to dwell openly on the differences between Sunni and Shi'ite Islam. Indeed, merely to cite these differences is regarded by many as part of an imperialist plot to foment division in Islam. The new sectarianism takes a subtler form: Shi'ites profess their unity of purpose with Sunnis, but then declare that a major expression of Sunnism (in this case, Saudi Wahhabism) is a deviation from ecumenical Islam. Sunnis declare their acceptance of Shi'ites as Muslims, but then declare that a major expression of Shi'ism (in this case, Iran's revolutionary activism) constitutes a deviation from ecumenical Islam.

In this manner, sectarian prejudice is insinuated, even as the unity of Islam is openly professed. The new pilgrimage polemic insinuated the libels of yesteryear most perfectly in the brief correspondence between the Saudi King Khalid and Imam Khomeini in October 1981, at a time of violent clashes in Mecca and Medina between Iranian pilgrims and Saudi police.[21] Khalid compiled a revealing letter of protest to Khomeini, asking that Khomeini urge his followers to show restraint but strongly hinting that the Great Mosque had been defiled by blasphemous Iranian pilgrims. According to Khalid, Iranian pilgrims in the Great Mosque had performed their ritual circumambulations while chanting "God is great, Khomeini is great," and "God is one, Khomeini is one." There was no need for Khalid to elaborate on this charge. It was obvious that the Iranians' slogans constituted an excessive veneration of their Imam, a form of blasphemous polytheism. All this had aroused the "dissatisfaction and disgust" of other pilgrims, wrote Khalid to Khomeini.

In fact, Khalid's letter distorted well-known Iranian revolutionary slogans. Iranian pilgrims had actually chanted "God is great, Khomeini is leader." The Saudis had confused the Persian word for "leader" (*rahbar*) with the rhyming Arabic for "great" (*akbar*). The pilgrims' Arabic chant declared that "God is one, Khomeini is leader." Here, the Saudis had confused the Arabic for "one" (*wahid*) with the rhyming Arabic for "leader" (*qa'id*). There was a vast difference between the slogans as actually chanted by the Iranians, and the inadvertent or deliberate misrepresentations of Khalid. In the actual slogans, Khomeini is cast as a leader unrivaled in the world, but subordinate to an almighty God. In the slogans as reported by the Saudis, Khomeini is placed on one plane with God, a verbal pollution of Islam's holiest sanctuary. It was this familiar but disguised charge of Shi'ite defilement that the Saudis sought to level at Iran's pilgrims. The accusation gained credibility from the formerly widespread Sunni conviction that the Shi'ites are bound to pollute the Great Mosque.

In his reply to Khalid, Khomeini evoked the old Shi'ite libel, charging the Saudis with failing to respect the refuge provided by the Great Mosque. "How is it that the Saudi police attack Muslims with jackboots and weapons, beat them, arrest them, and send them to prisons from inside the holy mosque, a place which according to the teaching of God and the text of the Qur'an, is refuge for all, even deviants?" This was a decidedly Shi'ite reading of the meaning of the Great Mosque's sanctity, which owed a great deal to the concept of refuge (*bast*) which traditionally applied to Shi'ite shrines in Iran. Such shrines were indeed absolutely inviolable places of refuge, where any kind of malefactor could find asylum.[22]

Nothing could have been further from the Wahhabi-Saudi concept of the sanctity of the holy places. These were and are regarded as sites so sacred that no deviation at all may be allowed in their precincts. Only from a Shi'ite perspective did this Saudi concern for preserving the purity of the Great Mosque appear as blind disrespect. In 1979, when an extreme group of Sunni zealots took over the Great Mosque, the Saudis acted in good conscience to clear it of "deviants," relying upon a *fatwa* issued by over thirty men of religion who argued that it was permissible to dislodge the defilers even by force of arms. This decision enjoyed wide Muslim support beyond Saudi Arabia, and Khomeini's presentation of the Great Mosque as a place in which even "deviants" enjoyed absolute immunity could only be regarded as peculiarly Shi'ite, for it relied upon a Shi'ite concept of inviolable refuge that knows no parallel in Sunni Islam.

Differing concepts of sanctity also affected that part of the pilgrimage controversy played out in Medina. In 1982, Khomeini's representative to the pilgrimage chose the cemetery of al-Baqi' in Medina as the site for a series of demonstrations combined with visitation prayers. After the Saudi demolition of the shrines in the cemetery in 1926, al-Baqi' ceased to serve as a place of organized Shi'ite visitation, but after Iran's Islamic revolution, Iranian pilgrims began to recite prayers outside the high wall which the Saudis had built to seal off the cemetery. In 1986, in a concession to Iran's pilgrims, Saudi authorities allowed them access to the cemetery itself, and Khomeini's representative to the pilgrimage formally thanked Saudi King Fahd for permitting the return of Shi'ite pilgrims to the venerated site. This obsessive interest in al-Baqi' and other tombs, and the resort to the cemetery as a rallying point for pilgrims in Medina, reflected an especially Shi'ite notion of Medina's sanctity, and served to evoke past resentment against the Saudis for having defaced the memory of the Imams.

This heightened Shi'ite interest in Medina also owed a great deal to changes in the spiritual geography of Shi'ite Islam. After the outbreak of the war between Iran and Iraq, it was no longer possible for Iranians to visit the Shi'ite shrine cities in Iraq and the tombs of the Imams in their sacred precincts. For the great mass of Shi'ites, the pilgrimage to these sites in Iraq had taken precedence over the pilgrimage to Mecca and the visitation to Medina. Their inaccessibility greatly enhanced the significance for Iranian Shi'ism of the holy cities of Arabia. By 1988, over one million Iranians had made application to Iranian authorities to embark on the pilgrimage to Mecca and Medina.[23] As a result, al-Baqi' emerged again as a major Shi'ite center of pilgrimage, and mass prayer services were conducted there after Iran's revolution, not by the Saudi men of religion who manage the mosques in Mecca and Medina, but by visiting Shi'ite clerics.

The Pilgrimage Understanding

Such identifiably Shi'ite themes and methods of protest might have blinded other pilgrims to the political message of liberation Iran wished to convey during the pilgrimage. The fear that Iran's message might be dismissed by other Muslims as Shi'ite dissent was responsible for some of the ecumenical intonations of Khomeini's pilgrimage representatives and other Shi'ite clerics. Most notably, Khomeini's representatives instructed Iran's pilgrims to pray with all other pilgrims behind the Sunni prayer leaders in the Great Mosque and the Prophet's Mosque, lest they stand out for their Shi'ism rather than their political activism. This restraint, matched by a parallel Saudi restraint in dealing with Iran's pilgrims, left the impression that the pilgrimage controversy had been defused. The climate of confrontation dissipated in 1983; although tensions remained high, only minor incidents marred the pilgrimage peace over the next few years.

By 1986, it seemed that Iran and Saudi Arabia had reached a compromise permitting Iran to conduct a limited measure of political propaganda during the pilgrimage. By the informal terms of the pilgrimage understanding, Khomeini's pilgrimage representative was permitted to organize two pilgrims' rallies, the first in Medina and the second in Mecca, in areas removed from the holy mosques in each city. A number of understandings restricted the form and content of these demonstrations. Iran's pilgrims were not to import or display printed matter and posters of a political nature, and their slogans were to be directed only against the U.S., the Soviet Union, and Israel. Other Muslim governments and the host government were not to be criticized. This understanding allowed Iran's pilgrims to express their views, but enabled Saudi authorities to confine all demonstrating to two fixed events.

Yet not all of Iran's zealots accepted these limitations. In 1986, a group of Iranian pilgrims who opposed the strategy of moderation in dealing with Saudi Arabia arrived in the country with a large quantity of high explosives in their suitcases. Their apparent aim was to destroy the pilgrimage understanding reached between Iran and Saudi Arabia. The plot failed: Saudi airport authorities discovered the explosives and arrested over one hundred pilgrims upon their arrival. The episode embarrassed those Iranian leaders who had assured Saudi Arabia that the pilgrimage peace would be preserved, and they dissociated themselves from the plot by their silence while the Saudis detained the pilgrims for weeks. But the plotters did enjoy the support of one of the major factions in Iran, which opposed the pursuit of the any opening toward the Saudis and favored the aggressive export of the revolution. In the pilgrimage plot of 1986, it became clear that the pilgrimage peace was an unstable one, affected by the changing balance in Iran's internal power struggle.

The heightened political tensions of 1987 surrounding the introduction of U.S. naval forces into the Gulf also threatened the pilgrimage understanding. Saudi authorities were alarmed by a speech made at the beginning of July by Khoiniha, Khomeini's former pilgrimage representative. Khoiniha had presided over the most turbulent pilgrimage seasons. His replacement as pilgrimage supervisor and his appointment as prosecutor general in 1985 was probably intended to reduce the chances of confrontation in Mecca. But he remained a powerful figure in Iran and a champion of extremists who opposed all limitations on Iran's pilgrims. His speech was plainly provocative. This year, he declared, "a mere march or demonstration will not suffice." Iran should not simply "gather a certain number of people who might support the views of the Islamic republic." Khoiniha demanded that Saudi Arabia allow Khomeini's pilgrimage representative to enter the Great Mosque in Mecca for one night, and there conduct a referendum among the throngs of pilgrims over the decision of the emir of Kuwait to invite foreign escorts for Kuwaiti tankers. At the same time, Khomeini's representative would explain Iran's case in the Gulf war. "All we ask is that the Saudi government not oppose this, nor send its guards to the Great Mosque. Let us see what happens. We will try it for one year."[24]

Saudi authorities now had grounds to suspect that some of Iran's pilgrims might attempt a takeover of the Great Mosque, as a political maneuver to embarrass Saudi Arabia, Kuwait, and the U.S. Khoiniha's statement touched a raw nerve, and immediately elicited a warning from an unnamed official source in Saudi Arabia. The source noted that Saudi Arabia supported numerous other occasions for the expression of Muslim opinion on various matters, even during the pilgrimage, but such consultations in the Great Mosque would constitute an innovation in Islam, and "anyone who attempts to innovate in Islam will go to hell." Saudi Arabia would shoulder its responsibility for safeguarding the Islamic shrines in Mecca and Medina.[25]

Khoiniha's statement put the Saudi security apparatus on a high state of alert, and lent more credence to inevitable rumors that the Iranians planned a violent confrontation, but Khoiniha's demand did not figure in the negotiations between the Saudi ministry of pilgrimage affairs and Khomeini's official pilgrimage representative, Mehdi Karrubi. As Khomeini's spokesman, Karrubi asked only that Iran be allowed to conduct its demonstration in Mecca as in past years. An Iranian official even covered the route of the planned demonstration with a Saudi official, and it clearly ended a mile short of the Great Mosque.

But despite this understanding, the Saudi authorities remained deeply suspicious. On the eve of the Mecca demonstration, they pressured Karrubi to cancel the march, lest violence break out. Karrubi refused, and declared that "in the event of disorder and disruption, the responsibility for this will be fully with the Saudi government."[26] Two days before the planned demonstration, the Iranian media published Khomeini's annual message to the pilgrims. While longer and more high-strung than the messages of recent years, it did not constitute a major departure from the understanding regarding the pilgrimage itself. Khomeini included the customary plea to pilgrims that they "avoid clashes, insults, and disputes," and warned against those intent on disruption "who might embark on spontaneous moves."[27]

The Understanding Destroyed

The atmosphere in Mecca was charged with tension on 31 July, the day of the planned demonstration. Many units of Saudi security forces were in evidence throughout the city and at the Great Mosque, where the usual Saudi "morality" police were replaced by armed soldiers. For the first time, guards at the gate subjected entering pilgrims to full body searches and forbade pilgrims from carrying anything into the Great Mosque, including sun umbrellas and canteens.[28] These measures apparently reflected a Saudi intelligence estimate that an attempted Iranian takeover of the Great Mosque constituted a real possibility.

In the afternoon, the Iranian demonstration began in the usual fashion, with slogans and speeches. The march commenced upon the conclusion of the speeches; as in the past, it was led by *chador*-clad women and war invalids. At or near the end of the planned route, the march came upon a cordon of Saudi riot police and National Guardsmen who refused to allow the procession to go any further.

This dangerous situation became explosive in the wake of two developments. Apparently, some within the crowd of Iranian pilgrims chose this moment to echo Khoiniha's provocative demand, and called upon the marchers to continue to the Great Mosque. At the same time (or perhaps even earlier), unidentified persons in an adjacent parking garage began to pelt the Iranian demonstrators with bricks, pieces of concrete, and iron bars. This exacerbated the situation on the confrontation line between the pilgrims and the police, and both sides began to exchange blows, the police using truncheons and electric prods, the demonstrators using sticks, knives, and rocks.

Because Karrubi and the other Iranian officials had not positioned themselves at the head of the march, they had no control over the conduct of Iran's pilgrims at the crucial point of contact with Saudi police. During the ensuing confrontation, the Saudis backed down temporarily and the crowd surged forward. According to American intelligence sources, the tide was finally turned by reinforcements from the National Guard, who fired tear gas shells into the crowd and then opened fire with pistols and automatic weapons.[29] The Saudis later denied firing on the demonstrators or even using tear gas. They claimed that the dispersed demonstrators surged in retreat, trampling one another to death. According to official Saudi figures, 402 people died in the clash, including 275 Iranian pilgrims, 85 Saudi police, and 42 pilgrims from other countries. Iran claimed that 400 Iranian pilgrims died, and that several thousand were injured.

This reconstruction rests upon a selective reading of the contradictory accounts provided by Iranian and Saudi sources.[30] As no independent investigation will ever be conducted, important details will remain in doubt. But no evidence has been produced by Saudi Arabia or Iran to establish that the other side acted deliberately or with premeditation in order to provoke violence. The available evidence indicates that a group of undisciplined Iranian pilgrims, acting under the influence of at least one provocative statement by a leading Iranian official, wished to enter the Great Mosque as demonstrators. Saudi security authorities, who had been alerted to this possibility but lacked self-confidence in the face of provocation, employed deadly force to thwart the Iranian crowd.

While the actual events in Mecca remained shrouded by irreconcilable claims, there could be no doubt about the immediate effect of the deaths at Mecca in revalidating hoary prejudices. The accusations that flew in both directions after the incident had few parallels in their intensity. Saudi Arabia's interior minister, Prince Nayif bin Abd al-Aziz, relied upon Sunni prejudice when he charged that the real objective of the Iranian pilgrims was "to spoil the pilgrimage, because, as is known, the pilgrimage is done only if the Great Mosque is entered." Iranian "sedition" inside the Great Mosque would have made it impossible for other pilgrims to have carried out the required circumambulations in the Great Mosque. "The pilgrimage would have been spoilt."[31] There is no evidence that the Iranian demonstrators, even those who wished to carry their protest into the Great Mosque, intended to ruin the rite for other pilgrims, but by his charge Nayif sought to associate the Iranian demonstrators with the legendary Shi'ite "defilers" of the Great Mosque.

Iranian statements pandered to the belief still held by Shi'ites that the fanatic Saudis were driven by their own misguided beliefs to kill innocent Shi'ite pilgrims. Khomeini declared that the Saudi rulers, "these vile and ungodly Wahhabis, are like daggers which have always pierced the heart of the Muslims from the back," and announced that Mecca was in the hands of "a band of heretics."[32] Once more, the Saudis were transformed into what the speaker of the parliament, Ali Akbar Hashemi-Rafsanjani, called "Wahhabi hooligans." Rafsanjani recalled the nineteenth-century Wahhabi massacres (of Shi'ites) in Najaf and Karbala, the Wahhabi destruction of Islamic monuments in Medina (venerated by Shi'ites), and the Wahhabi burning of libraries (containing Shi'ite works). The Wahhabis "will commit any kind of crime. I ask you to pay more attention to the history of that evil clique so that you can see what kind of creatures they have been in the course of their history."[33] This represented a deliberate attempt to fuel a present crisis with the memory of past sectarian hatreds.

Following the Mecca tragedy, both Saudi Arabia and Iran conducted large-scale campaigns to influence Muslim opinion abroad. The Saudi government ordered its principal missionary organization, the Muslim World League, to convene an Islamic conference in Mecca in October 1987. More than six hundred supporters and clients of Saudi Arabia from 134 countries attended the conference, which was opened by Saudi King Fahd. As expected, the conference condemned Iran alone for the Mecca violence: Iran's government—a government "accustomed to terrorism and a thirst for Muslim blood"—"solely bears the responsibility for the outrage in God's holy mosque." The conference endorsed the measures taken by the Saudi authorities "to quell the sedition and to contain the fires of wickedness."[34] Iran immediately attacked the conference in Mecca as one more attempt by the Saudis to "buy the religion of Muslims."[35] Saudi Shi'ite opposition sources charged that the Saudis had spent $470 million on the conference, and that total expenses were liable to reach $700 million. The conference, far from being Islamic, had a narrowly Sunni, Wahhabi, and Saudi orientation, said its Iranian critics; it was a conference of men of religion who served the rulers, not the religion.[36]

The following month, Iran convened an "International Congress on Safeguarding the Sanctity and Security of the Great Mosque," under the auspices of the ministry of Islamic guidance and the foreign ministry. Rafsanjani, in addressing the three hundred participants from thirty-six countries, called for the "liberation" of Mecca and the establishment of an "Islamic International" that would govern Mecca as a free city.[37] Ayatollah Husayn Ali Montazeri, at the time Khomeini's successor-designate, met with the foreign guests and denounced the Saudis as "a bunch of English agents from Najd who have no respect either for the House of God or for the pilgrims who are the guests of God." Just as Jerusalem would be liberated from the "claws of usurping Israel," Mecca and Medina would be liberated from the "claws of Al Sa'ud."[38] A Sunni cleric at the conference apparently took the analogy still further, denouncing the Saudis as Jews. An Iranian conferee clarified the point: Iran did not label the Saudis Jews, but "even if we do not agree that you are Jews, your deeds are worse than those of the Jews. What you did to Muslims in the House of God has never been done to Muslims by the Jews."[39] The insinuation that the Saudis were Jews—the worst possible libel—echoed an old piece of Shi'ite bigotry that attributed Jewish origins to the Saudi ruling family.[40] The Tehran resolutions were repeated by Iranian-inspired seminars on the pilgrimage that subsequently met in Beirut and Lahore. The Saudis also convened supporting conferences elsewhere, most notably in London, where Saudi clients declared support for the use of force in quelling Iranian "sedition."[41]

The Three-Year Boycott

After the initial round of conferences, attention shifted to the next pilgrimage. The Saudis were reluctant to impose an outright ban on Iran's pilgrims, lest they open Saudi Arabia to the charge of denying Muslims the opportunity to fulfill a fundamental obligation of Islam. The Saudis, however, clearly sought to translate the tragedy into a far-reaching revision of the informal understanding that had come apart in 1987, and that had become a thorn in the side of Saudi security.

First, Saudi officials, citing wider Muslim support for their version of the 1987 tragedy, made it clear that no marches would be allowed again. The demonstrations Khomeini had attempted to introduce as part of the pilgrimage ritual—and which the Saudis had tolerated—would no longer be allowed.

Second, the Saudis moved to cut the number of Iran's pilgrims. Numbering 150,000 per year, they had come to constitute the largest national group. This move won full endorsement from the foreign ministers' conference of the Organization of the Islamic Conference, meeting in Amman in March 1988. That gathering placed the blame for the tragedy in Mecca squarely on the shoulders of Iran's pilgrims, and voiced support for Saudi measures to prevent a repetition of the violence. But most important, the conference supported a Saudi proposal to limit the number of pilgrims by establishing national quotas for pilgrims, based upon each country's population. The ostensible aim was to give Saudi Arabia a three-year interlude to expand and improve facilities in Mecca. While these facilities did need modernization, the most important effect of the planned quota of one thousand pilgrims per million population would be a drastic cut the number of Iran's pilgrims, from 150,000 to 45,000. The Saudis, of course, were fully aware of Khomeini's stand that any reduction in the number of Iran's pilgrims would result in an Iranian boycott of the pilgrimage.

Finally, to assure such a boycott, Saudi Arabia chose this moment to sever relations with Iran. Saudi Arabia had maintained relations with Iran through the confrontation of October 1987, despite the storming of the Saudi legation by a Tehran crowd and the resulting death of a Saudi diplomat. But in April 1988, Saudi Arabia severed relations, with the clear purpose of making it impossible for Iranian pilgrims to secure pilgrims' visas.

As expected, the Iranian government, with the sanction of a ruling by Khomeini, responded to the Saudi measures by boycotting the 1988 pilgrimage altogether. As expected, Iran accused the Saudis of preventing Muslims from fulfilling the fundamental obligation of pilgrimage. Any Muslim with the means to perform the pilgrimage was entitled to do so, claimed the Iranians; the Saudi implementation of a quota system demonstrated their incompetence.[42] In Khomeini's message on the first anniversary of the "massacre," he accused the "centers of Wahhabism" of "sedition and espionage." At Mecca in 1987, he said, "the sword of blasphemy and division, which had been hidden in the hypocritical cloak of Yazid's followers and descendants of the Umayyad dynasty, God's curse be upon them, had to come out again from the same cloak of Abu Sufyan's heirs to destroy and kill."[43] Whatever his intention, Khomeini's resort to this historical analogy constituted a sectarian allusion—despite his claim, in the very same message, that it was the U.S. and the Saudis who tried to portray the Mecca events as a sectarian clash. It would be his last word on the pilgrimage; Khomeini died less than a year later.

The boycott continued in 1989, but even in the absence of Iran, Sunni-Shi'ite tensions ran high. During July, two explosions in Mecca killed one pilgrim and wounded sixteen more. Saudi police speedily arrested over thirty Kuwaiti Shi'ites, and in September a Saudi executioner beheaded sixteen of them by sword in a public square in Mecca. The leader of the plot claimed to have acted on behalf of Iranians who presented themselves as officials of the Iranian embassy in Kuwait. The Saudis apparently were not persuaded that these Shi'ites had operated on highest Iranian authority, and did not accuse Tehran of involvement in the blasts. But the broadcasted confessions of the plotters seemed accusation enough.[44]

In April 1990, one hundred and forty deputies of the Iranian parliament issued an open letter, setting terms for the return of Iran's pilgrims. The parliamentarians demanded that the Saudis "apologize for their treachery to the meek Iranian pilgrims"; that Saudi Arabia pay blood money to the families of the Iranian pilgrims killed "unlawfully" by Saudi security security forces in 1987; that Saudi Arabia compensate Iranian pilgrims for "assets" seized from their caravans in the aftermath of that tragedy; that Saudi Arabia accept 150,000 Iranian pilgrims; and that these pilgrims be allowed to "disavow the polytheists"—that is, hold demonstrations.[45] Saudi Arabia rejected all these demands as so much cheek, and the boycott continued for a third year. During the pilgrimage itself, Ayatollah Ali Khamene'i, who had succeeded Khomeini as Iran's "leader" the previous summer, issued a message to the world's Muslims condemning the "despotic and traitorous rulers of the Hijaz" who had closed the door of the House of God on Muslim believers. "God's shrine is safe for U.S. advisors and oil company owners, but unsafe for selfless Muslims," Khamene'i lamented.[46]

An Understanding Renewed?

Contacts toward resolving the pilgrimage controversy nevertheless continued between Iran and Saudi Arabia as 1990 ended. In September, Saudi foreign minister Sa'ud al-Faysal met Iranian foreign minister Ali Akbar Velayati in New York to discuss the 1991 pilgrimage. Publicly, Sa'ud al-Faysal announced that "we are very eager to see the Muslim people of Iran travel to Saudi Arabia this year to perform their pilgrimage rituals."[47] Velayati expressed optimism that "our pilgrims will be able to perform the important religious-political *hajj* rituals this year."[48] Privately, Sa'ud al-Faysal reportedly offered to accept a larger number of Iranian pilgrims in 1991. The Saudi minister also proposed that the Iranians hold their rally but in a "fixed" place, without marching through the streets of Mecca. At that fixed point, Khamene'i's annual message could be read to the pilgrims, just as Khomeini's message had been read in the past. The Saudis repeated the offer during the Gulf Cooperation Council meeting in Qatar in December, which Iran attended as an observer. There Saudi Arabia reportedly proposed the figure of 90,000 Iranian pilgrims.

From the autumn of 1990, direct Saudi-Iranian talks took place on the highest diplomatic level, involving five meetings between Sa'ud al-Faysal and Velayati. Omani mediation helped to produce a written agreement, signed by the two foreign ministers in Muscat in March 1991. The agreement resolved the two outstanding issues that had divided Saudi Arabia and Iran. First, it set the number of Iranian pilgrims at 110,000, a figure later raised to 115,000. This was more than the annual quota of 45,000 that Saudi Arabia had set over a three-year period after 1987, a measure that produced a total Iranian boycott. Yet it was also less than the 150,000 Iranian pilgrims who had arrived annually through 1987. Second, Iran would be permitted to conduct one rally in a fixed place in Mecca, where a message from Khamene'i could be read to assembled pilgrims, as Khomeini's message had been read in the past. It was also understood that the rallied pilgrims would not criticize Muslim governments, although it was understood that they might chant the usual "Death to America" and "Death to Israel." The new agreement included an Iranian commitment to prevent any flow of demonstrating pilgrims from the rallying point. On this basis, the two countries renewed diplomatic relations, and the stage was set for the return of Iran's pilgrims to Mecca in 1991. Preparations for the pilgrimage went smoothly, orchestrated this time by a new pilgrimage representative, Muhammad Muhammadi-Reyshahri, one of Rafsanjani's own troubleshooters.

There was a complication, which emerged after the pilgrimage of 1991 was underway, involving the choice of a site for Iran's rally. The Saudis proposed a number of sites, all of them remote from the heart of Mecca and difficult of access. The Saudis clearly wished to place as much distance as possible between the rallied pilgrims and the center of the city. Iran rejected these sites, arguing that their location made it impossible for the rally to draw pilgrims from other countries. At the last minute, Saudi authorities relented and allowed the rally to gather in a square near the headquarters of Iran's pilgrimage representative, a site already at a good distance from the Great Mosque.

On the eve of the pilgrimage, Rafsanjani and Reyshahri made several statements that set a conciliatory tone for the pilgrimage, and at the last minute, Velayati himself arrived as a pilgrim. During his stay, he had two audiences with King Fahd, and three meetings with his Saudi counterpart, Sa'ud al-Faysal. "Saudi Arabia's conduct has been proper," he announced, "and we hope that in view of good understanding between Iran and Saudi Arabia we will see the pilgrimage rituals performed more splendidly than ever before in coming years."[49] After the pilgrimage, the two countries raised their diplomatic ties to the ambassadorial level. In addition, Saudi Arabia agreed to receive some three thousand Iranians a week over the next seven months, to perform the minor (out-of-season) pilgrimage (*umra*). There were 300,000 Iranians on the waiting list for this pilgrimage.

In 1992, the pilgrimage also passed uneventfully. Iran's leadership set the low key of the pilgrimage: Rafsanjani announced that the political aspect of the pilgrimage could not be allowed to have a negative effect on "other dimensions of the pilgrimage," which were presumably spiritual. In 1991, there had been "no problem," and Rafsanjani expressed hope that "excesses and extremes" would be avoided this year as well.[50] Ahmad Khomeini, son of the late leader of Iran's revolution, told departing pilgrims in a speech at his father's mausoleum that "disavowing the polytheists is not tantamount to opposition to the Saudi and similar governments."[51] Once again Rafsanjani's stalwart, Reyshahri, served as Iran's pilgrimage supervisor, and he closely followed the conciliatory lead of Iran's leaders, especially during the annual demonstration in Mecca. Some 3,500 Iranian pilgrims, with yellow ribbons on their arms, guided pilgrims to the demonstration site in front of the Iranian pilgrimage headquarters. Iranian sources put the crowd at 150,000 pilgrims. As agreed, the pilgrims confined their banners and chants to the familiar "Death to America" and "Death to Israel," making no criticism of the Saudis themselves. The Saudi police and security forces kept a distance of several miles from the demonstration.[52] There were no incidents, and Rafsanjani expressed his satisfaction: "Of course, I did not think that it was ideal, but it was a relatively good pilgrimage."[53]

An End to Demonstrations?

It seemed that Iran and Saudi Arabia had reached a final understanding on the extent of Iran's own use of the Meccan platform. The number of Iranian pilgrims, long a bone of contention, remained steady at 115,000, by mutual agreement. Reyshahri, who headed Iran's pilgrims, once again set a conciliatory tone as the 1993 season approached, reminding Iranians that "it would be the greatest sin if the dignity of Iranian pilgrims were to be cast in disrepute." He therefore called on Iran's pilgrims to pray with Sunni brothers in congregational prayer.[54] And Saudi-Iranian political relations were generally on the upswing. Velayati visited Saudi Arabia as the pilgrimage got underway, and there was even talk of a visit by King Fahd to Iran and a summit with Rafsanjani. There was no reason to expect any change in Meccan status quo, which provided for one Iranian rally in Mecca.[55]

On 27 May, the Iranians were to have held their annual rally for the "disavowal of the polytheists." This was the occasion for the usual chants and banners of "Death to America" and "Death to Israel," and the delivery of a message to the pilgrims from Iran's leader, Khamene'i. Much to the consternation of the Iranians, however, Saudi police threw up roadblocks around the rally site opposite the headquarters of the Iranian pilgrims, and they turned away pilgrims who arrived for the rally. Reyshahri protested that this violated the understanding between the two governments. "It was only due to my recommendation to have revolutionary patience, and also

due to the obedience of the pilgrims, that we were able to control their feelings, so as to make sure that no incident occurred."[56] The Saudis, though,
justified their action. They had always opposed such "unruly processions
interspersed with cheers and shouting of sensational slogans," and had
warned Reyshahri they would not be tolerated.[57] Saudi Arabia reiterated
its "categorical rejection of the staging of marches, gatherings, and demonstrations in general."[58] Shaykh Abd al-Aziz bin Baz, grey eminence of the
Saudi religious establishment, made a statement against Iran's "disavowal
of polytheists" march in particular, calling the practice a "groundless heresy" that could have "evil consequences."[59]

In a quick shift, Reyshahri rallied Iran's pilgrims five days later at their
caravan camp in Mina to hear Khamene'i's message, which he also had
broadcast in Arabic over loudspeakers.[60] According to the Iranians, the
Saudis quickly dispatched security forces to the site, but they were caught
by surprise and could only encircle the rally. The Saudis claimed they did
not notice any such gathering in the Iranian camp, but back in Mecca,
the Saudis put up a tight security cordon around the Iranian pilgrimage
headquarters once again, preventing pilgrims from entering or leaving.
Reyshahri left Saudi Arabia early, to protest the Saudi action.[61]

The Saudis did not seek a political confrontation with Iran, and immediately after the pilgrimage resumed their conciliatory tone. Yet they
also made it clear that the Iranian demonstration in Mecca, even in an at-
tenuated form, violated their monopoly on the politics of the pilgrimage.
Furthermore, Saudi Arabia had moved still closer to the U.S., and also
extended support to the American effort to resolve the Arab-Israeli conflict.
The kingdom's rulers saw even less reason to tolerate demonstrations that
featured chants of "Death to America!" and "Death to Israel!" In short,
Saudi Arabia sought the first opportunity to restore the pre-Khomeini *status
quo ante*, and finally acted when it was reasonably certain that Iran would
not launch a counter-campaign of Islamic vilification. They were right;
despite its protest, Iran backed down from confrontation. Even Ali Akbar
Nateq-Nuri, the speaker of Iran's parliament and a vocal critic of the Saudi
management of Mecca, chose to play down the incident: "We believe [the
Saudi decision] was due to pressure by others from outside, compelling
Saudi Arabia to prevent the rally. But this will not give way to a severance
in our relations. We should daily improve our ties with regional and neighboring countries, and we should mutually resolve bilateral issues."[62]

In 1994, the Saudis took still another step back from the prior understanding, by reducing the numbers of Iran's pilgrims by half. The Saudis read the situation accurately: Iran, groaning under a mountain of debt and short of foreign exchange, accepted the cut with muted protest. In Mecca itself, the Saudis repeated the maneuver of the previous year. On the eve of the planned Iranian demonstration, battalions of Saudi police surrounded the headquarters of the Iranian pilgrimage mission. Water cannons and armored personnel carriers were deployed around the mission; helicopters flew overhead. Reyshahri again cancelled the rally, opting instead for "ceremonies" at the Iranian pilgrims' camp in Mina.

The "disavowal of the polytheists" ceremony in Mecca, having been reduced from a march to a rally, existed no longer. Yet Iranian political figures responded with restraint. Both Khamene'i and Rafsanjani criticized Saudi policy, but they employed restrained language. Rafsanjani in particular called for renewed efforts to reach an understanding. "A *hajj* that means *hajj* to a Shi'ite can take place," said Rafsanjani. There was a need to find a formula "in which both our views and the views of the Saudis are catered for, and through which the Saudis' concerns will be alleviated."[63] As usual, the Iranian press took a harsher tone, but this did not resonate in public. The Saudi legation in Tehran requested and received police protection at the height of the Saudi "siege" of Iran's headquarters in Mecca, but at no point did any of Iran's leaders summon demonstrators into the streets of Tehran.

Iran clearly had lowered its profile over the pilgrimage. Saudi Arabia had acted to reduce the impact of Iran's pilgrimage, quantitatively and qualitatively; even as Iran protested these measures, it accepted them. In part, this reflected an Iranian desire to normalize relations with Saudi Arabia, but Iran's retreat from sectarian confrontation may have had an even more profound motive. As the 1990s unfolded, Iran's regime had become inwardly preoccupied with its own stability and survival. One threat to that stability, formerly dormant, was posed by Iran's own Sunni minority numbering somewhere between 12 and 18 percent of Iran's population. In 1994, the Sunni question suddenly burst upon Tehran in a dramatic way.

In January, authorities in the Shi'ite shrine city of Mashhad demolished a Sunni mosque, ostensibly as part of an urban renewal project. On 1 February, the populace of Zahedan, capital of the predominantly Sunni province of Baluchistan, reacted violently in antigovernment riots that left several dead and dozens wounded. On 20 June, a powerful bomb went off inside the packed prayer hall in the mausoleum of Imam Reza in Mashhad during

Shi'ite Ashura observances, killing twenty-six worshippers. Iran accused the Mojahedin-e Khalq, an opposition group, but widespread speculation attributed the bombing to Sunni militants. The sudden appearance of violent Sunni protest within Iran suggested that the sectarian sword cut both ways and that Iran also had sacred shrines of pilgrimage which could become Sunni-Shi'ite battlegrounds. The most important such shrine, in Mashhad, drew at least eight million pilgrims a year—the so-called "pilgrimage of the poor," an emotional substitute for the pilgrimage to Mecca.[64] Perhaps this realization contributed to Iran's accommodating posture in Mecca: after the domestic violence of 1994, Iran's interest lay not in fanning sectarian flames but in quenching them.[64]

But as the fifteen years since Iran's revolution have demonstrated, the revival of Islam has been more than a reassertion of Islam against the West. It has incited rival understandings of Islam against one another. The social and political earthquake of Islamism has not only opened the ancient fault line between believers and unbelievers. It has opened the fault line, just as ancient, between the two oldest traditions of Islam. Their holy places now echo with bombs and bullets. Indeed, more Muslim blood has been shed during the past decade in Mecca, Mashhad and Najaf, than in Jerusalem and Hebron. It is the revival of this clash of Islamic civilizations that may prove to be Islamism's most enduring legacy.

Notes

1. Khamene'i sermon, Radio Tehran, 6 August 1987, quoted in *BBC Summary of World Broadcasts: The Middle East and Africa* (hereafter cited as *BBC Summary*), 7 August 1987.
2. This study draws on the detailed narrative of international Islamic politics I have written for the annual *Middle East Contemporary Survey* (hereafter cited as *MECS*). For my accounts of the pilgrimage, see *MECS* 6 (1981–82): 284–88, 301–3; 7 (1982–83): 238, 249–51; 8 (1983–84): 175–77; 9 (1984–85): 161–64; 10 (1986): 149–51; 11 (1987): 172–76; 12 (1988): 177–85; 13 (1989): 182–84; 14 (1990): 189–91 (by Reinhard Schulze); 15 (1991): 191–93; 16 (1992): 216–18; 17 (1993): 116–17.
3. On the doctrinal shift from pilgrimage to visitation, see Said Amir Arjomand, *The Shadow of God and the Hidden Imam* (Chicago: University of Chicago Press, 1984), pp. 168–170. On Iranian pilgrims in Mecca, see Suraiya Faroqhi, *Pilgrims and Sultans: The Hajj under the Ottomans, 1517–1683* (London: Tauris, 1994), 134–39.
4. Richard F. Burton, *Personal Narrative of a Pilgrimage to al-Madinah & Meccah* (1893; reprint, New York: Dover, 1964), 2: 168, n. 1; John Lewis Burckhardt, *Travels in Arabia* (1829; reprint, London: Frank Cass, 1968), 168, 251–52.
5. Burton, ibid.
6. On these taxes, see H. Kazem Zadeh, "Relation d'un pèlerinage à la Mecque," *Revue du monde musulman*, no. 19 (1912): 159–60. Discriminatory levies continued to be

TABLE 10.1
Number of Iranian Pilgrims, 1979–1994
(to the nearest 5,000)

~~1979:~~	~~75,000~~
1980:	10,000
1981:	75,000
1982:	85,000
1983:	100,000
1984:	150,000
1985:	150,000
1986:	150,000
1987:	160,000
1988:	0
1989:	0
1990:	0
1991:	115,000
1992:	120,000
1993:	115,000
1994:	60,000

collected from Shi'ites until the late 1930s.

7. C. Snouck Hurgronje, *Mekka in the Latter Part of the 19th Century* (Leiden: Brill, 1931), 141.

8. Mirzâ Mohammad Hoseyn Farâhâni, *A Shi'ite Pilgrimage to Mecca, 1885–1886*, eds. and trans. Hafez Farmayan and Elton L. Daniel (Austin: University of Texas Press, 1990), 228–29.

9. Quoted by H. St. J. B. Philby, *Arabia of the Wahhabis* (London: Constable, 1928), 67.

10.   On the special place of Medina in Shi'ite Islam, see Dwight M. Donaldson, *The Shi'ite Religion* (London: Luzac, 1933), 142–51. On the cemetery's history, see *Encyclopaedia of Islam*, 2d ed., s.v. "Baki' al-Gharkad" (A.J. Wensinck-[A.S. Bazmee Ansari]). On Shi'ite worship there in Ottoman times, see Farâhâni, *A Shi'ite Pilgrimage*, 267–69.

11. *Oriente Moderno* 6 (1926): 310, 513–14, 610.

12.   *Oriente Moderno* 7 (1927): 91, 111–12.

13.   Text of treaty, *Oriente Moderno* 10 (1930): 105–6.

14.   The evolution of this policy is detailed by Jacob Goldberg, "The Shi'i Minority in Saudi Arabia," in *Shi'ism and Social Protest*, eds. Juan R.I. Cole and Nikki R. Keddie (New Haven, Conn.: Yale University Press, 1986), 230–46.

15.   The author of the British pilgrimage report of 1937 wrote of "the well-known reluctance of the Iranian Government to see good Iranian money spent outside Iran." A. C. Trott, "Report on the Pilgrimage of 1937," PRO, FO371/20840, reproduced in *Records of the Hajj: A Documentary History of the Pilgrimage to Mecca*, vol. 7, *The*

Saudi Period (1935–1951) ([Slough]: Archive Editions, 1993), 194.

16.   For examples of such complaints, see the documents reproduced in *Records of the Hajj*, vol. 6, *The Saudi Period (1926–1935)*, 415–32.

17.   As reported by James S. Moose (Jidda), dispatch of 24 February 1944, National Archives, Washington, D.C., RG59, 890f. 404/55. For reproductions of the the British reports, see *Records of the Hajj*, 7:529–59.

18.   Ali Shariati, *Hajj* (2d ed.; Bedford, Ohio: Free Islamic Literatures, 1978), 109. For more on the book, see Steven R. Benson, "Islam and Social Change in the Writings of 'Ali Shari'ati: His *Hajj* as a Mystical Handbook for Revolutionaries," *Muslim World* 81 (1991): 9–26.

19.   Khomeini's message, 6 February 1971, in *Islam and Revolution: Writings and Declarations of Imam Khomeini*, trans. Hamid Algar (Berkeley, Cal.: Mizan Press, 1981), 195–99.

20.   For a general discussion of this development, see R. K. Ramazani, *Revolutionary Iran: Challenge and Response in the Middle East* (Baltimore: Johns Hopkins University Press, 1986), 91–100, 111–12.

21.   Khalid-Khomeini correspondence, *Al-Nashra al-arabiyya lil-hizb al-jumhuri al-islami* (Tehran), 19 October 1981; and in *Sawt al-umma* (Tehran), 31 October 1981.

22.   *Encyclopaedia of Islam*, 2d ed., s.v. "Bast" (R.M. Savory).

23.   Figure given by Mehdi Karrubi, Tehran Television, 16 June 1988, quoted in *Foreign Broadcast Information Service Daily Report: The Middle East and South Asia* (hereafter cited as *FBIS*), 21 June 1988. The same need explains Iranian Shi'ism's rediscovery of the mausoleum of Sayyida Zaynab, the Imam Husayn's sister, near Damascus. A minor site of Shi'ite visitation in the past, it has been transformed into a major shrine, visited by thousands of Shi'ites from Iran and Iranian-backed Shi'ites from the Lebanese Hizbullah. Iran also has invested large resources in restoration of the still lesser shrine of Sayyida Raqiya, Husayn's daughter, near the Umayyad Mosque in Damascus. On these sites, see Biancamaria Scarcia Amoretti, "A proposito della communità imamita contemporanea di Siria," *Oriente Moderno*, n.s., 3 (1984): 193–201.

24.   Khoiniha's speech, Radio Tehran, 2 July 1987, quoted in *BBC Summary*, 4 July 1987.

25.   Saudi Press Agency (hereafter cited as SPA), 3 July 1987, quoted in *BBC Summary*, 6 July 1987.

26.   Radio Tehran, 30 July 1987, quoted in *BBC Summary*, 1 August 1987.

27.   Text of speech, Radio Tehran, 29, 30, 31 July 1987, quoted in *BBC Summary*, 31 July, 1, 3 August 1987. For a close content analysis of the message, see Michael Glünz, "Das Manifest der islamischen Revolution: Ayatollah Homeinis Botschaft an die Mekkapilger des Jahres 1407/1987," *Welt des Islams*, n.s., 33 (1993): 235–55.

28.   Fahd al-Qahtani, *Majzarat Makka: Qissat al-madhbaha al-su'udiyya li'l-hujjaj* (London: Al-Safa lil-nashr wal-tawzi', 1988), 27–28.

29.   Report on the assessment of American intelligence sources, *New York Times*, 6 September 1987.

30.   The most detailed eyewitness accounts from a pro-Iranian perspective include that of the Pakistani Shi'ite journalist Mushahid Hussain, which appeared in the *Washington Post*, 20 August 1987, and the several reports collected by Qahtani, *Majzarat Makka*, 77–107. Qahtani's book is an extensive survey of the event and the worldwide reaction to it. The Saudi director-general of public security, Gen. Abdallah bin Abd al-Rahman Al Shaykh, provided the most comprehensive Saudi account in a statement which prefaced a special Saudi documentary film on the incident, aired

on Saudi Television on 20 August 1987.

31.   Nayif's press conference, SPA, 25 August 1987, quoted in *BBC Summary*, 27 August 1987.

32.   Khomeini's message to Karrubi, Radio Tehran, 3 August 1987, quoted in *BBC Summary*, 5 August 1987.

33.   Rafsanjani's speech, Radio Tehran, 2 August 1987, quoted in *BBC Summary*, 4 August 1987.

34.   Conference communiqué, SPA, 15 October 1987, quoted in *FBIS*, 16 October 1987.

35.   *Al-Ahd* (Beirut), 23 October 1987.

36.   *Al-Thawra al-islamiyya* (London), October 1987.

37.   Rafsanjani's speech, Radio Tehran, 26 November 1987, quoted in *FBIS*, 28 November 1987.

38.   Montazeri's speech, Radio Tehran, 27 November 1987, quoted in *FBIS*, 29 November 1987.

39.   Emami-Jamarani's speech, 29 April 1988, quoted in *FBIS*, 2 May 1988.

40.   For a Shi'ite collection of alleged proofs of the Jewish origins of the Saudis, see Nasir al-Sa'id, *Tarikh Al Sa'ud*, vol. 1 ([Beirut]: Ittihad sha'b al-jazira al-arabiyya, n.d.): 392–403. I am indebted to Prof. Werner Ende for this reference.

41.   Report of conference, *Al-Sharq al-awsat* (London), 4 July 1988.

42.   Mehdi Karrubi, Tehran Television, 16 June 1988, quoted in *FBIS*, 21 June 1988.

43.   Khomeini's message, Radio Tehran, 20 July 1988, quoted in *FBIS*, 21 July 1988. Abu Sufyan was a member of the Prophet Muhammad's tribe who had originally opposed Muhammad. His son, Yazid, was responsible for the killing of the Imam Husayn. Another son, Mu'awiya, founded the Umayyad dynasty. The family and the dynasty are deemed usurpers in the Shi'ite reading of early Islamic history.

44.   On the bombing incident, see Reinhard Schulze, "The Forgotten Honor of Islam," *MECS* 13 (1989): 182–84.

45.   Text of letter, *Keyhan* (Tehran), 11 April 1990, quoted in *FBIS*, 24 April 1990.

46.   Khamene'i's message, Radio Tehran, 28 June 1990, quoted in *FBIS*, 2 July 1990.

47.   Sa'ud al-Faysal quoted by Radio Tehran, 30 September 1990, quoted by *FBIS*, 1 October 1990.

48.   Velayati quoted by IRNA, 4 October 1990, quoted by *FBIS*, 4 October 1990.

49.   Islamic Republic News Agency (hereafter cited as IRNA), 29 June 1991, quoted in *FBIS*, 1 July 1991.

50.   *Al-Alam* (London), 16 May 1992.

51.   Khomeini's speech, *Resalat*, 6 May 1992, quoted in *FBIS*, 1 June 1992.

52.   IRNA, 7 June 1992, quoted in *FBIS*, 10 June 1992.

53.   Rafsanjani's speech, Radio Tehran, 12 June 1992, quoted in *FBIS*, 15 June 1992.

54.   Radio Tehran, 10 May 1993, quoted in *FBIS*, 11 May 1993.

55.   *Al-Alam*, 12 June 1993.

56.   Radio Tehran, 27 May 1993, quoted in *FBIS*, 28 May 1993.

57.   Statement by "reponsible source," SPA, 2 June 1993, quoted in *FBIS*, 3 June 1993.

58.   SPA, 29 May 1993, quoted in *FBIS*, 1 June 1993.

59.   SPA, 2 June 1993, quoted in *FBIS*, 3 June 1993.

60.   Khamene'i's message, Iranian Television, 27 May 1993, quoted in *FBIS*, 28 May

1993.
61.   IRNA, 5 June 1993, quoted in *FBIS*, 7 June 1993.
62.   Nateq-Nuri's interview, *Middle East Insight*, July-August 1993.
63.   Rafsanjani's sermon, Radio Tehran, 20 May 1994, quoted in *FBIS*, 23 May 1994.
64.   See Nasrine Hakami, *Pèlerinage de l'Emâm Rezâ: Étude socio-économiques* [sic], Studia Culturae Islamicae 38 (Tokyo: Institute for the Study of Languages and Cultures of Asia and Africa, 1989).
65.   For the Sunni-Shi'ite strife of 1994, see "Sunnite 'reprisal' against Shiite sanctuary in Iran?" *Mideast Mirror*, 20 June 1994; and "The Coming Sectarian Conflict in Iran," *Mideast Mirror, 9 September 1994.*

11

Syria's Alawis and Shi'ism

In their mountainous corner of Syria, the Alawis claim to represent the furthest extension of Twelver Shi'ism. The Alawis number perhaps a million persons—about 12 percent of Syria's population—and are concentrated in the northwestern region around Latakia and Tartus. This religious minority has provided Syria's rulers for nearly two decades. Syrian President Hafiz al-Asad, in power since 1970, as well as Syria's leading military and security chiefs, are of Alawi origin. Once poor peasants, they beat their ploughshares into swords, first becoming military officers, then using the instruments of war to seize the state. The role of Alawi communal solidarity has been difficult to define, and tribal affiliation, kinship, and ideology also explain the composition of Syria's ruling elite. But when all is said and done, the fact remains that power in Syria is closely held by Alawis.[1]

This domination has bred deep resentment among many of Syria's Sunni Muslims, who constitute 70 percent of the country's population. For at the forefront of Syria's modern struggle for independence were the Sunni Muslims who populated the cities of Syria's heartland. They enjoyed a privileged standing under Sunni Ottoman rule; they, along with Syrian Christian intellectuals, developed the guiding principles of Arab nationalism; they resisted the French; and they stepped into positions of authority with the departure of the French. Syria was their patrimony, and the subsequent rise of the Alawis seemed to many of them a usurpation. True, Sunni Arab nationalists had put national solidarity above religious allegiance and admitted the Alawis as fellow Arabs. Still there were many Sunnis who identified their nationalist aspirations with their Islam, and confused Syrian independence with the rule of their own community. Alawi ascendence left them disillusioned, betrayed by the ideology of Arabism that they themselves had concocted.[2]

Some embittered Sunnis reformulated their loyalties in explicitly Muslim terms and now maintain that the creed of the Alawis falls completely outside the confines of Islam. For them, the rule of an Alawi is the rule of a disbeliever, and it was this conviction that they carried with them in their futile insurrection of February 1982. The Alawis, in turn, proclaim themselves to be Twelver Shi'ite Muslims. This is at once an interesting and problematic claim, with a tangled history; it cannot be lightly dismissed or unthinkingly accepted. It raises essential questions about religious authority and orthodoxy in contemporary Twelver Shi'ism, and it is complicated by the fact that Syria enjoys the closest and fullest relationship with revolutionary Iran of any state. The old controversy over the origins of the Alawis has been forgotten, and the contemporary Alawi enigma is this: by whose authority, and in whose eyes, are the Alawis counted as Twelver Shi'ites?

Schism and Separatism

The Alawis are heirs to a distinctive religious tradition, which is at the root of their dilemma in modern Syria. Beginning in the nineteenth century, scholars acquired and published some of the esoteric texts of the Alawis, and these texts still provide most of what is known about Alawi doctrine. The picture that emerged from these documents was of a highly eclectic creed, embracing elements of uncertain origin. Some of its features were indisputably Shi'ite, and included the veneration of Ali and the twelve Imams. But in the instance of Ali, this veneration carried over into actual deification, so that Ali was represented as an incarnation of God. Muhammad was his visible veil and prophet, and Muhammad's companion, Salman al-Farisi, his proselytizer. The three formed a divine triad, but the deification of Ali represented the touchstone of Alawi belief. Astral gnosticism and metempsychosis (transmigration of souls) also figured in Alawi cosmology.

These religious truths were guarded by a caste of religious shaykhs (*shuyukh al-din*); the mass of uninitiated Alawis knew only the exoteric features of their faith. An important visible sign of Alawi esoterism was the absence of mosques from Alawi regions. Prayer was not regarded as a general religious obligation since religious truth was the preserve of the religious shaykhs and those few Alawis initiated by them into the mysteries of the doctrine. Such a faith was best practiced in a remote and inaccessible place, and it was indeed in such rugged surroundings that the Alawis found refuge. For, as might be expected, Sunni heresiographers excoriated Alawi beliefs and viewed the Alawis as disbelievers (*kuffar*) and idolators (*mushrikun*). Twelver Shi'ite heresiographers were only slightly less vituperative and regarded the Alawis as *ghulat*, "those who exceed" all bounds in their deification of Ali. The Alawis, in turn, held Twelver Shi'ites to be *muqassira*, "those who fall short" of fathoming Ali's divinity.[3]

From the late nineteenth century, the Alawis were subjected to growing pressure to shed their traditional doctrines and reform their faith. The Ottomans had a clear motive for pressing the Alawis to abandon their ways. Alawi doctrine attracted much interest among French missionaries and orientalists, some of whom were convinced that the Alawis were lost Christians. The Ottomans drew political conclusions, and feared a French bid to extend France's religious protectorate northward from Lebanon to the mountains overlooking Tartus and Latakia. At the same time, the Alawis themselves could not but feel the effects of the Muslim revival that swept through Syria in the second half of the nineteenth century and the popular Muslim backlash against the Tanzimat. These two pressures combined to produce a reformist drive among a handful of Alawi shaykhs that enjoyed the encouragement of the Ottoman authorities. The result was some government-financed construction of mosques that were built almost as talismans to ward off the foreign eye. However, since the Ottoman purpose was to assimilate the Alawis, the formula of prayer in these first mosques was Sunni Hanafi, in accord with the predominant rite in the empire. The authorities had no reason to encourage the few reformist Alawi shaykhs to lead their coreligionists in any other direction.

All this produced few lasting effects. The influence of this early reformism was very limited, and most of the Alawi religious shaykhs would have nothing to do with it. The rapid turnover of Ottoman governors also meant that pressure upon the Alawis was not maintained. Since these governors could extract very few taxes from the Alawis, it seemed unsound fiscal policy to spend revenues on them. In the twilight years of the Ottoman Empire, the Alawis remained essentially as they had been for centuries, divided and unassimilated, with their esoteric doctrines still intact. Few Alawis had ever crossed the portal of a mosque.[4]

When the Ottoman Empire fell, the French claimed Syria as their share, and the Alawis found their new rulers eager to protect and patronize them. French policy was generally one of encouraging Alawi separatism, of setting Alawis against the Sunni nationalists who agitated for Syrian independence and unity. From 1922 to 1936, the Alawis even had a separate state of their own, under French mandate. Still, within their state, the Alawis remained the economic and social inferiors of Sunnis, and these relationships could not be undone by simple administrative decree. There was, however, one form of dependence that had to be broken, if the Alawis were to feel themselves equal to Sunnis. Ottoman authorities had imposed Sunni Hanafi law wherever their reach extended, a law administered by Sunni courts. Alawi custom had prevailed in Alawi civil matters, in which the Ottomans had no desire to intervene, but this custom had no legal standing. In the new order, a pressing need arose to give the Alawis recognized communal status, courts, and judges. This was a daunting task, for Alawi custom was too dependent upon traditional social authority to be reduced to codified principles and applied in the courts.

A solution was found in 1922, by importing the law and some of the judges. In that year, the French authorized the establishment of separate religious courts for the Alawis (*mahakim shar' iyya alawiyya*), and it was decided that they would rule in accordance with the Twelver Shi'ite school of law.[5] This school was as remote from Alawi custom as any other. Its principal advantage lay in the obvious fact that it removed Alawi affairs to separate but equal courts and placed Alawis squarely outside the jurisdiction of their Sunni neighbors and overlords. But since there were no Alawis sufficiently expert in Twelver Shi'ite jurisprudence to serve as judges, Twelver Shi'ite judges had to come up from Lebanon to apply the law.[6] The Alawis, then, were spared subordination to Sunni courts by embracing the Twelver Shi'ite school, but they were incapable of judging themselves according to its principles. Not a single Alawi had been to Najaf, to hear the lectures delivered in its academies by the recognized Twelver Shi'ite jurisprudents of the day. Yet there were a few Alawi shaykhs who did delve in books of Twelver jurisprudence, and these were soon given formal appointments as judges in Alawi religious courts. It seems likely that what prevailed in these courts was a very rough notion of Twelver Shi'ite jurisprudence, modified still further to accommodate Alawi custom.

In laying hand on the Twelver law books, the Alawi religious shaykhs had borrowed all that they cared to borrow from the Twelver tradition. These texts gave them a useful store of precedents for application in the narrow field of civil law, but in the weightier matter of theology, Alawi shaykhs clung to their own doctrine. They had no use for other branches of Twelver scholarship, and made no effort to put themselves in touch with Twelver Shi'ite theologians and jurisprudents elsewhere. Once Alawi judges were installed in the Alawi religious courts, Lebanese Twelver judges ceased to frequent the Alawi region, and the Alawis were content to remain cut off from the body of Twelver Shi'ism. As a result, Lebanon's Twelver Shi'ites were left completely in the dark about the beliefs of the Alawis.

This emerges from an anecdote about a visit to Latakia in the 1930s by Lebanon's preeminent Twelver divine, Shaykh Abd al-Husayn Sharaf al-Din of Tyre. To his host, a leading Sunni notable and *sayyid* of Latakia, he said: "I have come first of all to visit you and then to ask about the doctrine of the Alawis among whom you live. I have heard it said that they are *ghulat*."[7] In this curious scene, a Twelver Shi'ite inquired of a Sunni about the beliefs of an Alawi. In fact, the Alawi shaykhs were no more prepared to bare their doctrines to Twelver Shi'ites than to Sunnis. The Alawis had simply chosen to judge themselves, in their own courts, by the principles of Twelver Shi'ite jurisprudence. The religious shaykhs had not decided to submit their beliefs to the scrutiny of Twelver Shi'ites, or to recognize the authority of living Twelver divines.

Political separatism was compatible with Alawi religious esoterism and it won many adherents among the Alawi religious shaykhs, but as the French mandate wore on, nationalist agitation for Syrian independence and unity caused the French to falter in their support of Alawi separatism. Without unqualified French support, separatism did not stand a chance of success. Cautious Alawis instead began to seek Sunni guarantees for the fullest possible Alawi autonomy and equality in a united Syrian state. The Sunnis, in turn, wished to integrate the Alawi territory in a united Syria with the least amount of Alawi resistance. These interests converged in 1936 as Syria approached independence. To smooth the integration, some thought that a Sunni authority should recognize the Alawis as true Muslims, an expedient recognition that would serve the political interests of Alawis and Sunnis alike. In order for the recognition to have the desired effect, it would have to declare the Alawis to be believing and practicing Muslims.

The recognition came in July 1936, and took a reciprocal form. The Alawis themselves took two steps. First, a group of Alawi religious shaykhs (*rijal al-din*) issued a proclamation, affirming that the Alawis were Muslims, that they believed in the Muslim profession of faith, and performed the five basic obligations (*arkan*) of Islam. Any Alawi who denied that he was a Muslim could not claim membership in the body of Alawi believers.

Second, an Alawi conference held at Qardaha and Jabla submitted a petition to the French foreign ministry, stressing that "just as the Catholic, the Orthodox, and the Protestant are yet Christians, so the Alawi and Sunni are nevertheless Muslims."[8] At the same time, the Sunni mufti of Palestine, Haj Amin al-Husayni, issued a legal opinion (*fatwa*) concerning the Alawis, in which he found them to be Muslims and called on all Muslims to work with them for mutual good, in a spirit of Islamic brotherhood.[9]

There was more to this exchange than met the eye. The Alawi proclamation and petition did not renounce any of the esoteric beliefs attributed to the Alawis. Their very existence could not be divulged. It was widely believed that the Alawis kept some of their beliefs secret, and so their own public elucidation of their doctrine could not be expected to have much effect. Haj Amin al-Husayni's *fatwa*, however, was another matter since it issued from a prominent Sunni authority, in his dual capacity as mufti of Palestine and president of the General Islamic Congress in Jerusalem. Yet the *fatwa* also was problematic. Why did a Sunni authority in Jerusalem, and not in Damascus, act to recognize the Alawis? After all, there were no Alawis in Palestine, and Haj Amin had not made an independent investigation of their beliefs or rituals. Was he moved by a pure desire for ecumenical reconciliation?

It seemed unlikely. More to the point, Haj Amin had very close ties with those leaders of the pan-Arabist National Bloc who led the struggle for a united Syria. The pan-Arab nationalists in Damascus probably initiated the move, not Haj Amin, who was simply their obliging cleric. They obviously turned to Jerusalem because they could not extract comparable recognition of their Alawis from Sunni religious authorities in Damascus. These authorities apparently were not prepared to soil their reputations by declaring night to be day since they refused to regard the Alawis as Muslims. So when Syria's nationalists were pressed to provide Sunni recognition of the Alawis, they secured it from a dubious source. It would be accurate to say that in sealing this deal of recognition, both Alawis and Sunnis extended their left hands.

Excluded from all this were the Twelver Shi'ites, although there may have been an attempt to involve one of them as well: Shaykh Muhammad al-Husayn Al Kashif al-Ghita of Najaf. This ecumenical evangelist was keen to strike religious bargains with Christian, Sunni, and Druze, so long as these served the sublime political purposes of Arab unity. This was undoubtedly his motive in entering into correspondence with Shaykh

Sulayman al-Ahmad of Qardaha. Shaykh Sulayman held an exalted position among the Alawis. He was the spiritual leader of the majority Qamari section of Alawis and bore the formal title of "servitor of the Prophet's household" (*khadim ahl al-bayt*). A poet of reputation, he had been admitted to the Arab Academy in Damascus.[10] Yet he bore the responsibility of a master entrusted with all of the powerful esoteric teachings of the Alawi faith, and these he was bound to preserve from the prying divine from Najaf. Their correspondence was apparently never published and yielded no public gesture of recognition. Perhaps even Shaykh Muhammad al-Husayn realized that he had reached the limits of expediency.[11]

Certainly not a word of public comment on the standing of the Alawis was heard from Najaf or Qom, the great seats of Twelver Shi'ite learning. An open endorsement of the Alawis by a leading Twelver Shi'ite divine would have carried much more weight than the Alawis' own self-interested protestations, or the questionable *fatwa* from Jerusalem. How, though, could the leading lights in Najaf and Qom embrace the Alawis, when not one Alawi had attended their religious academies? When the works of the medieval Twelver theologians, still read and revered in these academies, described the Alawis as *ghulat*? When the news from Syria brought word that an epileptic, illiterate shepherd named Sulayman al-Murshid had unleashed a wave of messianic expectations among many Alawis, who acclaimed him a *nabi*, a prophet? On the one hand, much influence might be gained by laying claim to this community for Twelver Shi'ism; on the other, much authority might be lost by endorsing people of questionable belief. Recognition of the Alawi claim was obviously a matter that required exacting study in Najaf and Qom.

In 1947, Ayatollah Muhsin al-Hakim, the leading Twelver Shi'ite divine in Najaf, turned his attention to the Alawis. He wrote to Shaykh Habib Al Ibrahim, the Twelver mufti of the Lebanese Bekaa Valley, asking him to visit the Alawi region on his behalf, and to provide a first-hand report on their beliefs and ways. Shaykh Habib accepted the mission and traveled extensively among the Alawis, meeting with reformist shaykhs and offering religious guidance. The Lebanese emissary concluded that there was a clear need to send some intelligent young Alawis to Najaf, where they could engage in proper theological and legal studies under the masters. They would then return home radiant with knowledge to enlighten their brethren. Ayatollah Hakim agreed to bear the expense of this missionary effort, and twelve Alawi students left for Najaf in 1948.

In a short time, all but three of the students had dropped out. On their arrival in Najaf, they met with hostility from some of the Twelver Shi'ite men of religion, who set conditions upon their acceptance as Muslims and even demanded that they submit to purifying ablutions. In Najaf, the Alawi students found that they were still called *ghulat*, even to their faces. Years later, Ayatollah Hakim expressed his regret at this treatment, saying that "it seems this was the result of some ignorant behavior by the turbanned ones." Yet no one intervened at the time. The young students, cast into strange surroundings, could not bear these humiliations for long, and most returned home.[12]

No one suggested for a moment that older Alawi religious shaykhs be sent to Najaf. Instead, Shaykh Habib proposed the establishment of a local society to promote the study of Twelver Shi'ite theology and jurisprudence. In this manner, Alawi shaykhs could receive proper guidance in an organized framework. The Ja'fari Society, established in response to Shaykh Habib's proposal, had its headquarters in Latakia, and branches in Tartus, Jabla, and Banias. In addition to diffusing Twelver doctrine, the society undertook to construct mosques and lobbied for official recognition of the Twelver Shi'ite school by independent Syria. For with Syrian independence in 1946, the separate Alawi religious courts had been abolished, and Alawis were made to appear before Muslim religious courts that recognized only the Sunni schools.

The recognition sought by the Ja'fari Society was finally extended in 1952. Thereafter, the Twelver school was deemed equal to other recognized schools of law and its precepts could be applied by Muslim religious courts.[13] The Alawis, then, had won some formal recognition from the Syrian government, but they still had not received the endorsement of the Twelver Shi'ite authorities of Najaf and Qom. In fact, all of the recommendations made by Ayatollah Hakim's Lebanese emissary assumed that the Alawis were deficient in their understanding of true religion and still needing much knowing guidance.

In 1956, another Twelver Shi'ite emissary called upon the Alawis: Muhammad Rida Shams al-Din, a scholar at Najaf and a member of one of South Lebanon's most respected clerical families. His trip was funded by Ayatollah Mohammad Husayn Borujerdi, the very highest Twelver Shi'ite authority of the day, who had his seat at Qom and a large academy at Najaf. Ayatollah Borujerdi was very keen on Islamic ecumenism and invested much effort in pursuing a Sunni-Shi'ite reconciliation. Leading the Alawis back to the fold seemed an obvious motif for still another kind of ecumenical initiative, and Borujerdi was willing to bear the expense of a second group of Alawi students, who would study at his academy in Najaf.

The Lebanese emissary won an enthusiastic reception, and he immediately published a sympathetic account of the Alawis.[14] Nothing, however, came of the plan to bring a second group of students to Najaf. Memories of the ill treatment meted out to the first group were still fresh, but there may have been a more compelling reason. For in 1956, one of the remaining Alawi students from the first mission wrote a book about the Alawis, which was published in Najaf. While generally apologetic in tone, the book leveled some pointed criticisms at Alawi doctrine and the structure of Alawi religious authority. It was ignorance to deny the ignorance of Alawis in matters of religion, the student wrote. He denounced the "bloated army" of unschooled Alawi religious shaykhs who inherited their status and lived off tithes exacted from believers whom they kept in the dark.[15] If these were the sorts of ideas that the brightest Alawi students were bound to bring back from Najaf, then an unwillingness among the Alawi shaykhs to organize a second student mission would be perfectly understandable. No more Alawi students reached Najaf until 1966, when three came to study under Ayatollah Hakim. One of them reported that his group did not encounter the same visceral hostility that enveloped their predecessors.[16] By the late 1960s, however, Syria's ruling Ba'th party had entered upon a collision course with the rival Iraqi Ba'th party, and antagonism has generally plagued Syrian-Iraqi relations ever since. For Alawi students, Najaf was again beyond reach.

Several young Alawis preferred Cairo to Najaf anyway, and entered programs of religious studies at Al-Azhar. In 1956, an Azhar shaykh appeared in Qardaha with offers of scholarships for ten Alawi students.[17] With the establishment of the Egyptian-Syrian union in 1958, Alawis came under even greater Sunni pressure, and were encouraged to get their religious training in Cairo. There is no way of knowing how many Alawi students passed through Al-Azhar during those years and later, but they could not have been fewer than those who reached Najaf. Al-Azhar provided an education with an obvious Sunni bias and offered only rudimentary instruction in Twelver Shi'ite jurisprudence. Unlike the Najaf academies, though, Al-Azhar granted regular diplomas that were recognized in Syria, and this made it a very attractive alternative.[18] So the handful of Alawi religious shaykhs with wider education were divided in their attachments between Najaf and Cairo, between Twelver Shi'ism and Sunnism. This was the ambiguous situation in 1966, when power in Syria was seized by Alawi hands.

To Legitimize Power

The rise of Alawi officers to positions of influence and power put a sharp edge on the religious question. The new regime's radical economic and social policies stirred opposition, especially among urban Sunni artisans, petty traders, and religious functionaries. As the regime's base became more narrowly Alawi over time, opponents found it convenient to transfer the political debate to the highly emotive plane of religion. Those who did so argued that the regime's Arabism merely legitimized Alawi political hegemony; its socialism simply sanctioned the redistribution of Muslim wealth among the Alawis; and its secularism provided a pretext for stifling Muslim opposition. Fundamentalist opponents of the regime sought to draw the boundaries of political community in such a way as to exclude the Alawis and did so by relying upon their own exacting definition of Islamic orthodoxy.

This situation was rich in irony. The Alawis, having been denied their own state by the Sunni nationalists, had taken all of Syria instead. Arabism, once a convenient device to reconcile minorities to Sunni rule, now was used to reconcile Sunnis to the rule of minorities. The cause of Sunni primacy, once served by having the Alawis recognized as Muslims, now demanded that the Alawis be vilified as unbelievers.

In February 1971, Hafiz al-Asad became the first Alawi president of Syria. Rising from a poor Qardaha family, he played an important role in dismantling the old order and seized power by crushing an Alawi rival. His elevation to the presidency marked a turning point. The significance of this office in Syria had been symbolic rather than substantive, but the presidency had always been held by Sunnis, and its passage to an Alawi proclaimed the end of Sunni primacy. In January 1973, the government went still further and released the text of a new draft constitution. This document was also of symbolic significance, for it sought to legitimize the radical changes made by the regime. Its message was emphatic: unlike pre-Ba'th constitutions, this one did not affirm that Islam was the religion of state. This grievous sin of omission precipitated a crisis, as Sunni demonstrators poured out of the mosques and into the streets. General strikes closed down Hamah, Homs, and Aleppo. Asad, who was taken aback, proposed the insertion of an amendment in the constitution, stipulating that the president of the state shall be Muslim, but the situation actually deteriorated after Asad's offer. At issue was not the constitution, but Alawi hegemony. The violent unrest ended only with the entry of armored units into the cities.[19]

In 1973 the Alawi religious shaykhs stumbled over one another in their rush to affirm that the Alawis were Muslims, that they were Twelver Shi'ites through and through, and that other beliefs attributed to them were calumnies,[20] but these Alawi claims were in dire need of some external validation. Much had changed since 1936, and Sunni recognition would not do. The higher Sunni religious authorities in Syria had already knelt before Asad, and no one regarded them as capable of thinking or speaking independently on any issue. What was needed was some form of recognition from a Twelver Shi'ite authority, who could buttress the Alawis' own problematic claim that they were Twelver Shi'ites.

The solution appeared in the person of the Imam Musa al-Sadr.[21] By 1973, this political divine had made much progress in his effort to stir Lebanon's Twelver Shi'ites from their lethargy. His most impressive achievement had been the establishment of the Supreme Islamic Shi'ite Council (SISC), authorized by a 1967 law that declared the Twelver Shi'ites a legal Lebanese community in the fullest sense. With the establishment of the SISC, a question arose as to whether the small Alawi community in Tripoli and the Akkar district did or did not come under its jurisdiction. Numbering about 20,000, these Alawis in Lebanon were closely tied to those in Syria, and belonged to the same tribes. Although they were not recognized by Lebanese law as a distinct community, they generally tended their own affairs. The Alawis in the north of Lebanon had no historical ties to the Twelver Shi'ites in the south and east.

In 1969, Musa al-Sadr became chairman of the SISC and attempted to bring Lebanon's Alawis under his jurisdiction. A strong streak of ecumenism ran through Musa al-Sadr's highly politicized interpretation of Shi'ism. Even as he fought Sunni opinion over the recognition of Lebanon's Twelver Shi'ites, he did not stop preaching the necessity for Muslim unity. The uncomplimentary references to the Alawis in the Twelver sources would not have deterred him. He may also have been eager to extend his reach into the north of Lebanon. Inclusion of the Alawis, however few in number, would give him a constituency in a region where he had none.

But to bring Lebanon's Alawis under his wing, Musa al-Sadr first had to treat with the Alawi religious shaykhs in Syria. The dialogue began in 1969, and dragged on for four years. A statement by the SISC made only vague allusion to "difficult historical circumstances" and "internal disputes,"[22] but it was not hard to imagine what blocked an agreement. The Alawi religious shaykhs in Syria feared that their coreligionists in Lebanon might slip from their grasp, and they were also mindful that some Lebanese Alawis still hoped to secure official recognition of the Alawi community as separate and distinct from all others. The religious shaykhs probably never imagined that they would face a serious challenge issued by a Twelver Shiʻite divine from Lebanon. They had chosen Twelver Shiʻite law to guarantee their religious independence, not to diminish it. So they drew out the dialogue with Musa al-Sadr, withholding their assent.

Then came the Sunni violence of 1973 and the reiterated charge that the Alawis were not Muslims. The disturbances shook the Syrian Alawi elite, who then pressed the Alawi religious shaykhs to look differently at Musa al-Sadr's overtures. If Musa al-Sadr would throw his weight behind the argument that Alawis were Twelver Shiʻites, this would undermine at least one pillar of the Sunni indictment of the regime. Since the Alawis of Lebanon did not differ in belief from those of Syria, their formal inclusion in the Twelver Shiʻite community would constitute implicit recognition of all Alawis. For his part, Musa al-Sadr may have begun to realize that his recognition of the Alawis might bring political advantages that he had not previously imagined. The regime of Hafiz al-Asad needed quick religious legitimacy; the Shiʻites of Lebanon, Musa al-Sadr had decided, needed a powerful patron. Interests busily converged from every direction.

The covenant was sealed in a Tripoli hotel in July 1973. In a public ceremony, Musa al-Sadr, in his capacity as chairman of the SISC, appointed a local Alawi to the position of Twelver mufti of Tripoli and northern Lebanon. Henceforth, Lebanon's Alawis were to come under the jurisdiction of an appointee of the SISC. A delegation of Alawi religious shaykhs from Syria witnessed the event, and Musa al-Sadr delivered a speech justifying the appointment. Lebanon's Alawis and Twelver Shiʻites were partners since both had suffered from persecution and oppression. "Today, those Muslims called Alawis are brothers of those Shiʻites called Mutawallis by the malicious." What of the internal unrest in Syria? "When we heard voices within and beyond Syria, seeking to monopolize Islam, we had to act, to defend, to confront." Then Musa al-Sadr roamed still further afield: "We direct the appeal of this gathering to our brethren, the Alevis of Turkey. We recognize your Islam." The new mufti, Shaykh Ali Mansur, joined in the ecumenical oratory: "We announce to those prejudiced against us that we belong to the Imami, Ja'fari [Twelver] Shi'a, that our school is Ja'fari, and our religion is Islam." Nor did Musa al-Sadr lose the opportunity to call for an end to tension between Syria and Lebanon, which had resulted from a disagreement over the role of Palestinian organizations in Lebanon.[23]

The Alawi religious shaykhs in Syria had given the appointment their blessing, but this deal was done at the expense of another Alawi party: those Lebanese Alawis who wanted to preserve their separate identity, and perhaps win official recognition for their community. This opposition was championed by a group known as the Alawi Youth Movement. In a series of statements, the group maintained that the Alawis, while Twelver Shi'ites, were a separate community and deserved separate status under the law. The SISC was attempting to assimilate the Alawis against their will.[24] Tension in the Alawi quarter of Tripoli grew as the day of the ceremony approached, and when it arrived, security forces set up roadblocks at entrances to the city and the affected quarter. Opponents of the mufti's appointment held a rally that evening, featuring the inevitable demonstration of shooting into the air and a call to the community to boycott the new mufti.[25] Tension ran high for weeks afterward, and, in one instance, partisans and opponents of the new mufti even exchanged gunfire.[26] This internal dispute forced Musa al-Sadr to tread carefully, and the SISC issued a clarification, explaining that the purpose of the mufti's appointment was not to subsume the Alawis, but to provide them with a service that they lacked.[27]

Regardless of what happened in Tripoli, Syria's Alawis could claim to have Musa al-Sadr's endorsement. Did it amount to much? Musa al-Sadr did have extensive ties in Qom, his place of birth, and Najaf, where he had studied. His father had been one of the great pillars of scholarship in Qom. So it is interesting to note by what higher authority Musa al-Sadr claimed to act in the matter of the Alawis. His initiative, he declared, was part of his ecumenical work on behalf of the Islamic Research Academy, a Nasserist appendage of Al-Azhar.[28] This was one of those Sunni arenas in which Musa al-Sadr regularly appeared as part of his self-appointed ecumenical mission. Unlike other Lebanese Twelver emissaries to the Alawis, Musa al-Sadr did not represent a leading Twelver divine at Najaf or Qom. He acted solely in his official Lebanese capacity, with the sanction of an obscure academy in Cairo. For the embrace of 1973 was political, not theological. Syria's Alawis certainly did not plan to submit to Twelver authority, and Musa al-Sadr's move did not diminish their religious independence by a whit. They simply surrendered the small Alawi community of Lebanon, as one would force a marriage of convenience upon a reluctant daughter. Musa al-Sadr took the vow, and Hafiz al-Asad provided the dowry. Without that Syrian support, Musa al-Sadr's movement might not have weathered the storm that soon descended upon Lebanon.[29]

Still, the influence of Musa al-Sadr did wane following the outbreak of civil war. The Syrian regime, then, did not rest content with his endorsement, but sought to cultivate still another Shi'ite divine with an ambition as vaunting as Sadr's. This was Ayatollah Hasan al-Shirazi, a militant cleric from a leading Iranian-Iraqi family of religious scholars. In 1969, Shirazi's incendiary preaching in Karbala had led Iraqi security authorities to arrest and torture him. He fled or was expelled from Iraq in 1970 and soon found his way to Lebanon, where he had spent an earlier period of exile. There he began to gather a following, and like Sadr he received Lebanese citizenship by special dispensation in 1977.[30] A certain mystery enveloped Shirazi's affiliations, for he, too, seems to have enjoyed a friendship of convenience with Hafiz al-Asad. Asad must have recognized Shirazi's value as a possible card to play against both Iraq and Musa al-Sadr, should the need arise, while the exiled Shirazi desperately needed a patron.[31] It is not surprising, then, that Shirazi should also have made himself a champion of the Alawis, placing his coveted stamp of approval upon their qualifications as Twelver Shi'ite Muslims. Shirazi argued, in a preface to an Alawi polemical tract, that the beliefs of the Alawis conformed in every respect to those of their Twelver Shi'ite brethren, a fact which he had ascertained through personal observation.[32] Shirazi's explicit endorsement, combined with Sadr's, constituted a forceful argument for Alawi claims, but the obvious political expediency of this move rendered it as suspect as any previous endorsement. Shirazi, after all, was in exile, and in sore need of Syrian support. If he were to build his influence in Lebanon with Syrian backing, could he do less than Sadr had done? It is idle to speculate how this alliance might have unfolded: in May 1980, Shirazi was shot to death in a Beirut taxi.

As to the actual doctrines expounded by the Alawi religious shaykhs, it is impossible to know whether they underwent any change as a result of these embraces. Perhaps the younger, educated shaykhs formulated some sort of Alawi reformism and made a closer study of Twelver theology and philosophy. Perhaps their elders yielded on a few points of detail. In an esoteric faith, doctrinal controversies are kept in a closed circle of the initiated, and these held their tongues, except to assure their critics that they were Twelver Shi'ites.

Yet the question of religious doctrine was inseparable from that of religious authority, and here there was no change. Syria's Alawis did not recognize external authority, and they did not bind themselves as individuals to follow the rulings of the great living ayatollahs. On this crucial point, they differed from all other Twelver Shi'ites, and as long as they refused to recognize such authority, they could not expect reciprocal recognition by any divine of the stature of Ayatollah Abol Qasem Kho'i in Najaf, or Ayatollah Kazem Shariatmadari in Qom. It is worth noting that Ayatollah Shariatmadari, who had very broad ecumenical interests, did correspond with Shaykh Ahmad Kiftaru, Sunni grand mufti of Syria and faithful servant of the Syrian regime. Shaykh Ahmad even visited Qom during that tense summer of 1973, and one is tempted to speculate that he urged Shariatmadari to recognize the Alawis.[33] Shariatmadari, however, kept his silence, and made no gesture to Syria's Alawi religious shaykhs, who claimed so insistently to be his coreligionists.

The Impact of Iran's Revolution

In June 1977, Ali Shariati was laid to rest in Damascus, near the mausoleum of Zaynab. Regarded as something of an Iranian Fanon, Shariati offered a radical reinterpretation of Shi'ism, winning a devoted following and the scrutiny of SAVAK. When he died suddenly in London, his admirers charged foul play and arranged to have him buried in Damascus. The choice of Damascus as a place where Shariati's mourners might safely congregate was not accidental. After 1973, the Syrian authorities provided haven and support for numerous Iranians who were active in the religious opposition to the regime of the Shah. Musa al-Sadr, who officiated at Shariati's funeral, had much to do with encouraging these ties, since he openly collaborated with the Iranian religious opposition.

The Syrians, for their part, could not have imagined that this motley assortment of Iranian émigrés and dissidents might ever come to power in Iran. But it was no trouble to keep them, and they did have links to some leading Twelver Shi'ite clerics. If the endorsement of Ayatollah Shariatmadari could not be had, then perhaps that of Ayatollah Khomeini in Najaf might be secured. After all, Khomeini subordinated religious tradition to the demands of revolutionary action, and, like Musa al-Sadr, he needed influential friends. It is obviously impossible to know whether pursuit of such recognition for the Alawis played any role in the support given by the Syrian regime to the Iranian religious opposition. The Syrians may simply have wished to indulge Musa al-Sadr and defy the Shah. Still their support was steady, and in 1978, when Khomeini was forced out of Iraq and denied entry to Kuwait, he considered seeking refuge in Damascus before settling upon Paris.

The close relationship between Syria and the Islamic Republic of Iran was rooted in this early collaboration of convenience. A full account of Syrian-Iranian cooperation since 1979 would catalogue the stream of Iranian visitors to Damascus, and would mention Syria's tolerance of a contingent of Iranian Revolutionary Guards in Syrian-controlled Lebanon. It would explain Iran's silence in the face of pleas by the Sunni Muslim Brotherhood for moral support in its struggle against the Syrian regime, and it would consider how Islamic Iran justified waging ideological warfare against a Ba'thist, Arab nationalist regime in Iraq, while aligning itself with a Ba'thist, Arab nationalist regime in Syria. Common hatreds and ambitions inspired this expedient alliance between two incongruous political orders. The Iraqi regime was hateful to both Iran and Syria. In Lebanon, Iran realized that it could not extend support to its clients there without Syrian cooperation; Syria knew that without Iran it could not control those Lebanese Shi'ites who believed that they were waging sacred war against the West. A sense of shared fate, not shared faith, bound these two regimes together.

The Syrian relationship with Islamic Iran did enhance the religious legitimacy of Syria's rulers, but in a very subtle and indirect way. When these Twelver clerics—Khomeini's closest students and disciples—visited Damascus, they spoke only the language of politics. They did not utter any opinion on the beliefs, doctrines, or rituals of the Alawis, about which they knew no more than any other outsider. Instead, they spoke of political solidarity, appealing to all Muslims to set aside their religious differences, to unite to meet the threats of imperialism, colonialism, and Zionism. The Syrians, they argued, had made great sacrifices in the war against these evils. This particular commitment is the very essence of Islam in the minds of Iran's radical clerics, and they have not inquired further. To do so would only open a chasm between them and their self-proclaimed coreligionists.

Even so, the Iranian revolution has increased the pressure for religious reform within the Alawi community. In August 1980, Asad reportedly met with Alawi communal leaders and religious shaykhs at Qardaha. Asad called upon the religious shaykhs to modernize and make reforms and to strengthen the tenuous links of the community with the main centers of Twelver Shi'ism. To this end, two hundred Alawi students were to be sent to Qom, to specialize in Twelver Shi'ite jurisprudence.[34] These Qardaha gatherings are not open affairs, and it is impossible to determine the accuracy of this account, but once the star of Twelver Shi'ism had risen in Iran and Lebanon, the regime had every reason to press the religious shaykhs to compromise and to do their share to deflate the Sunni argument against Alawi primacy.

The departure of hundreds of Alawi graduates for the Qom academies would completely undermine the traditional structure of religious authority in the Alawi community. The old beliefs would wither; the new creed might not take root. Whether so many students have been sent out on their irrevocable course is impossible to say, for the consent of the religious shaykhs would not be given without long, procrastinating thought. But Hafiz al-Asad is waiting, and the guardians of Alawi faith may yet be made to sacrifice eternal truth to ephemeral power.

Notes

1. On the general issue of sectarianism in modern Syria, see Nikolaos van Damn, *The Struggle for Power in Syria: Sectarianism, Regionalism and Tribalism in Politics, 1961–1978* (London: Croom Helm, 1979); Itamar Rabinovich, "Problems of Confessionalism in Syria," in *The Contemporary Middle East Scene*, eds. Gustav Stein and Udo Steinbach (Opladen: Leske Verlag 1979), 128–32; Elizabeth Picard, "Y a-t-il un probème communautaire en Syrie?" *Maghreb-Machrek*, no. 87 (January-February-March 1980): 7–21; and Michel Seurat, *L'État de barbarie* (Paris: Seuil, 1989), 84–99. On the Alawis in society and politics, see R. Strothmann, "Die Nusairi im heutigen Syrien," *Nachrichten der Akademie der Wissenschaften in Göttingen*, phil.-hist. Kl. Nr. 4 (1950): 29–64; Moshe Ma'oz, "Alawi Officers in Syrian Politics, 1966–1974," in *The Military and State in Modern Asia*, ed. H.Z. Schriffrin (Jerusalem: Academic Press, 1976), 277–97: Peter Gubser, "Minorities in Power: The Alawites of Syria," in *The Political Role of Minority Groups in the Middle East*, ed. R.D. McLaurin (New York: Praeger, 1979), 17–48, Hanna Batatu, "Some Observations on the Social Roots of Syria's Ruling Military Group and the Causes for Its Dominance," *Middle East Journal* 35 (1980): 331–44; Mahmud A. Faksh, "The Alawi Community of Syria: A New Dominant Political Force," *Middle Eastern Studies* 20 (1984): 133–53; and

Daniel Pipes, *Greater Syria: The History of an Ambition* (New York: Oxford University Press, 1990), 166–88.

2. On Sunni opposition to Alawi primacy, see Hanna Batatu, "Syria's Muslim Brethren," *MERIP Reports* 9, no. 12 (November-December 1982): 12–20; Umar F. Abd-Allah, *The Islamic Struggle in Syria* (Berkeley, Cal.: Mizan Press, 1983); Thomas Mayer, "The Islamic Opposition in Syria, 1961–1982," *Orient* 24 (1983): 589–609; and Raymond A. Hinnebusch, *Authoritarian Power and State Formation in Ba'thist Syria* (Boulder, Colo.: Westview Press, 1990), 276–300.

3. For the main features of Alawi religious doctrine and organization, see René Dussaud, *Histoire et religion des Nosairis* (Paris: Bouillon, 1900); *Encyclopaedia of Islam*, 1st ed., s.v. "Nusairi" (Louis Massignon); Heinz Halm, *Die islamische Gnosis: die extreme Schia und die Alawiten* (Zurich: Artemis Verlag, 1982), 284–355; Matti Moosa, *Extremist Shiites: The Ghulat Sects* (Syracuse, N.Y.: Syracuse University Press, 1988), 255–418; and Fuad I. Khuri, *Imams and Emirs: State, Religion and Sects in Islam* (London: Saqi Books, 1990), 136–41, 198–202. For a compendium of hostile Twelver references to the Alawis, see the clandestine publication of the Syrian Muslim Brotherhood, *Al-Nadhir*, 22 October 1980.

4. On Ottoman-sponsored mosque construction for the Alawis, see Mahmud al-Salih, *Al-Naba al-yaqin an al-alawiyyin* (Damascus, 1961), 134–37; and Strothmann, 51.

5. *Oriente Moderno* 1 (1922): 732; 4 (1924): 258–59.

6. On the appearance of Lebanese judges in the Alawi region, see *Encyclopaedia of Islam*, "Nusairi," and Jacques Weulersse, *Les pays des Alaouites*, vol. 1 (Tours: Arrault, 1940), 261.

7. Ali Abd al-Aziz al-Alawi, *Al-Alawiyyun* (Tripoli [Lebanon]: n.p., 1972), 43.

8. Texts in Munir al-Sharif, *Al-Muslimun al-alawiyyun*, 2d ed. (Damascus: Dar al-umumiyya, 1960), 106–8.

9. Full texts with translations in Paulo Boneschi, "Une fatwà du Grande Mufti de Jérusalem Muhammad Amin al-Husayni sur les Alawites," *Revue de l'histoire des religions* 122, no. 1 (July-August 1940): 42–54; nos. 2–3 (September-December 1940): 134–52.

10. On Shaykh Sulayman, see *Al-Irfan* (Sidon) 28 (1938): 520–21, 648.

11. Although he may have yielded to temptation after all. According to the same Alawi source, Shaykh Sulayman managed to secure from Najaf a license (*ijaza*) as an interpreter of law (*mujtahid*) although he never set foot in the Shi'ite shrine city; see Salih, *Al-Naba al-yaqin*, 138. This could only have been at the instance of Shaykh Muhammad al-Husayn. But there is no corroboration for this report in other Alawi published sources.

12. On the first student mission, see Alawi, *Al-Alawiyyun*, 38–41; Muhammad Rida Shams al-Din, *Ma'a al-alawiyyin fi Suriya* (Beirut: Matba'at al-insaf, 1956), 48–50; and *Al-Irfan* (Sidon) 37 (1950): 337–38.

13. On the Ja'fari Society, see Shams al-Din, *Ma'a al-alawiyyin*, 50–52; Alawi, *Al-Alawiyyun*, 41–42; text of the official decrees recognizing school, ibid., 47–49.

14. On Borujerdi's role, see Shams al-Din, *Ma'a al-alawiyyin*, 19, 43.

15. Ahmad Zaki Tuffahah, *Asl al-alawiyyin wa-aqidatuhum* (Najaf, 1957), 5, 52–53.

16. Alawi, *Al-Alawiyyun*, 41.

17. Shams al-Din, *Ma'a al-alawiyyin*, 36–37.

18. Among the Alawi Azhar graduates was Shaykh Yusuf al-Sarim, who became one of Latakia's leading religious shaykhs. Although his orientation was said to be strongly Sunni, he was assassinated by the Muslim Brotherhood in August 1979.

19. On the crisis of 1973, see John J. Donohue, "La nouvelle constitution syrienne et ses détracteurs," *Travaux et jours*, no. 47 (April-June 1973): 93–111; and Abbas Kelidar, "Religion and State in Syria," *Asian Affairs*, n.s., 5, no. 1 (February 1974): 16–22.

20. See the resolutions of the Alawi religious shaykhs, and other statements in the pamphlet *Al-Alawiyyun, shi'at ahl al-bayt* (Beirut: n.p., 1972); also *Al-Hayat*, 4 April 1973.

21. See Fouad Ajami, *The Vanished Imam: Musa al Sadr and the Shia of Lebanon* (Ithaca, N.Y.: Cornell University Press, 1986).

22. Statement by Supreme Islamic Shi'ite Council, *Al-Hayat*, 6 July 1973.

23. *Al-Hayat*, *Al-Nahar*, 7 July 1973; see also *Middle-East Intelligence Survey* 1, no. 10 (15 August 1973): 77–78.

24. Statements by Alawi Youth Movement, *Al-Nahar*, 7 July 1973; *Al-Hayat*, 20 July 1973.

25. *Al-Nahar*, 7 July 1973.

26. *Al-Nahar*, 18 July 1973.

27. *Al-Nahar*, 6 July 1973.

28. Statement by Supreme Islamic Shi'ite Council, *Al-Nahar*, 6 July 1973. On the Academy, see Jacques Jomier, "Les congrès de l'Académie des Recherches Islamiques dépendant de l'Azhar," *Mélanges de l'Institut Dominicain d'Études Orientales du Caire* 14 (1980): 95–148.

29. It is interesting to note that the endorsement of the SISC was reaffirmed by Shaykh Muhammad Mahdi Shams al-Din after Musa al-Sadr's disappearance. According to Shams al-Din, "there are no religious sects within the Shi'ite community. When we speak of Alawis or Isma'ilis, this signifies regional, historical denominations based on political allegiances and not religious differences. The Ja'faris or Shi'ites are absolutely indivisible, and they all share the same belief in the Twelve Imams." *Magazine* (Beirut), 15 December 1979.

30. On Shirazi, see *Tariq al-thawra* (Tehran) no. 25 (Rajab 1402): 10–11; *Rah-e enqelab* (Tehran), no. 29(Jumada I-II 1403): 25–29, where mention is made of his view of the Alawis as brethren of the Shi'a. I owe these references to Prof. Amatzia Baram.

31. On Shirazi's role in Lebanon and his Syrian ties, see *Arabia and the Gulf*, 16 May 1977.

32. *Al-Alawiyyun, Shi'at ahl al-bayt*, preface.

33. On the visit, see *Al-Hadi* (Qom) 2, no. 4 (August 1973): 182–83.

34. According to Seurat, *L'État de barbarie*, 89.

12

Hizbullah: The Calculus of Jihad

Of the many fundamentalisms that have emerged within Islam during recent years, perhaps none has had so profound an impact on the human imagination as Hizbullah—"the Party of God." This movement of Lebanese Shi'ite Muslims gained both fame and infamy within months of its first public appearance in 1982, by its resort to ingenious forms of violence. Hizbullah's progression from suicide bombings to airline hijackings to hostage holding made it an obsession of the media and the nemesis of governments.

For a time, Hizbullah seemed invincible, dealing blow after blow to the "enemies of Islam," and creating islands of autonomous fundamentalism in Lebanon. Hizbullah held the attention of the world. Armies of journalists besieged the press secretaries of Hizbullah's leaders. Satellites crisscrossed the blackness of outer space above Hizbullah's bases, searching for the tracks of its adherents. Diplomats and mediators shuttled around the globe, seeking deals that would check or conciliate Hizbullah. More than any other fundamentalist movement in recent history, Hizbullah evoked the memory of the medieval Assassins, who had been feared in the West and Islam for their marriage of fierce militancy to destructive deeds. Like the Assassins, Hizbullah gave rise to an immense lore, and much confusion.

That Hizbullah owed its impact to its violence is beyond any doubt. Although it grew into a social movement, it never commanded the means or manpower necessary to seize power in Lebanon. Hizbullah's appeal remained limited to perhaps half of one sect, in a small and vulnerable state inhabited by many other sects. As for resources, Hizbullah reportedly disposed of an estimated annual budget of $100 million, smaller than that of many an American university. The movement owed its reputation almost solely to its mastery of violence—a violence legitimated in the name of Islam. This legitimation may be fairly described as Hizbullah's

209

most original contribution to modern Islamic fundamentalism. Hizbullah's vision of an Islamic state and society was derivative, but its methods for inspiring and rationalizing violence displayed a touch of genius.

This violence is subject to interpretation from any number of analytical and disciplinary vantage points, but any approach must necessarily settle on the core issues of cause, intent, and effect. Why and in what circumstances did the adherents of Hizbullah resort to force? What did they intend to achieve by their acts? What were the effects of their violence? These are large questions, and the evidence is scattered at best. The purpose here is not to provide confident answers, but to chart the islands of existing knowledge where answers might be found. The point is to better understand the unique predicament of Hizbullah—unique even within contemporary Islam. Nevertheless, the experience of Hizbullah may illuminate the passage of other fundamentalist movements into violence, a passage for which there are examples in every great tradition.

Shi'ite Fundamentalism in Lebanese Context

Hizbullah's militancy must first be set in context. But which context? There is the 1,400-year legacy of Shi'ism, a legacy of martyrdom and suffering, resting on an ancient grievance: the belief that Islamic history was derailed when political power passed out of the hands of the family of the Prophet Muhammad in the seventh century. In the subsequent course of history, Shi'ism has sometimes erupted as a form of protest against the existing order in Islam; at other times it has retreated into an other-worldly preoccupation with messianic redemption. This inner tension in Shi'ism, and Lebanon's place in it, have been explored in a growing literature.[1] The themes addressed there, especially the crisis that confronts all contemporary Shi'ism, are the necessary prelude to any appreciation of Hizbullah.

Here it is more appropriate to dwell on the narrow but rich Lebanese context of Hizbullah. Many works of reportage and scholarship now attest to the power of modern grievance among Lebanon's Shi'ite Muslims. Their pattern of settlement reflected a history of persecution, from which they had found refuge in redoubts along the eastern shore of the Mediterranean. The Shi'ites felt secure and free in the mountains of what is now the south of Lebanon and the plains of the Bekaa Valley, tucked between two high ranges. But when the impact of the West struck Lebanon in modern times, the isolated Shi'ites felt it last, and they were slow to modernize. When

Lebanon became independent in 1943, the Shi'ites were the despised stepchildren of a state governed by (and for) Maronite Christians and Sunni Muslims.[2]

The Shi'ites have been rushing breathlessly to catch up ever since. Demographically, they soon surpassed every other sect. In the thirty-five years between 1921 and 1956, the Shi'ite population had risen from 100,000 to 250,000, but its percentage of Lebanon's total population remained steady at about 19 percent. Yet in the twenty years between 1956 and 1975, the Shi'ite population tripled, from 250,000 to 750,000, bringing the Shi'ites to about 30 percent of the total population.[3] The large size of the Shi'ite families, coupled with Christian emigration, had produced a dramatic rise in the Shi'ite proportion of Lebanon's population. The Shi'ites had become Lebanon's largest single confessional community, surpassing the Maronite Christians and Sunni Muslims.

The Shi'ites, though, could not close the social and economic gap. Some did shake the legacy of poverty and ignorance, and forced open Beirut's worlds of commerce, administration, and education, but many more flocked from their villages to the great Lebanese capital to sweep the streets and hawk on corners. The angriest of Shi'ites joined the revolutionary movements that swept Lebanon in the 1960s and 1970s, especially those founded and led by Palestinians, who were even angrier. Other Shi'ites who still held out hope for reform created their own communal movement to promote their interests, under the leadership of a progressive cleric and middle-class professionals. After the outbreak of the Lebanese civil war in 1975, this movement created a militia known as Amal ("Hope"), which adopted a largely defensive posture in the fighting.[4]

But geography trapped the Shi'ites in the withering crossfire of the shoot-out that pitted the Palestinian organizations in Lebanon against the Maronite-led Lebanese Forces and Israel. Hundreds of thousands of Shi'ites became refugees, first from Maronite-Palestinian fighting in 1976, then as the result of the first Israeli invasion of South Lebanon in 1978. A quarter of a million refugees poured into the squalid southern suburbs of Beirut, which they transformed into a massive village, reeking of garbage and open sewage.[5] By 1982, the storehouse of Shi'ite grievance had filled to overflowing, and Amal could scarcely manage it.

For some years before 1982, a few voices, mostly of Shi'ite clerics, had raised a slogan very different from Amal's call for reform. These voices pronounced the death of Lebanese confessionalism and urged the transformation of Lebanon into an Islamic state. Not only did they demand rule by Muslims, who now constituted a majority of Lebanese, but they claimed that only an Islamic government could restore peace and independence to Lebanon.[6] Few persons in the jaundiced world of Lebanese politics took this promise of an Islamic utopia seriously, even within the Shi'ite community. After the Islamic revolution in Iran in 1979—a revolution that swept a white-bearded Shi'ite cleric to power on a tide of revolutionary rage—the idea of an Islamic state suddenly seemed real to many Shi'ites, and even urgent. The events of 1982, including the Israeli occupation of the Shi'ite south, the massacre of Palestinians by Maronite militiamen in league with Israel, and the deployment of American and French troops near the Shi'ite slums of Beirut, convinced many Shi'ites that they stood to become the victims of history once again.

As the vice closed ever tighter, the Shi'ite community finally cracked. A faction of Amal bolted, and the defectors left in their hundreds for the Bekaa Valley. They were accompanied by several fervent young Shi'ite clerics, whose minds burned with visions of a Lebanon purified by Islamic revolution. There the Lebanese Shi'ites joined hands with a contingent of a thousand Iranian Revolutionary Guards, who had come to do battle with the "enemies of Islam" now assembled in Lebanon and to spread the revolutionary message of the Imam Khomeini. Together they seized a Lebanese army barracks on a hill in the Bekaa Valley and transformed it into a formidable fortress, ringed by anti-aircraft emplacements and bristling with antennae. This base, and several smaller installations in its vicinity, would become the nucleus of an autonomous zone, governed by the precepts of Islam. The new formation took the name of Hizbullah—the "Party of God"—after a verse in the Qur'an (V, 56): "Lo! the Party of God, they are the victorious."[7]

Hizbullah thus issued from a marriage of Lebanese Shi'ites and Islamic Iran, and grew to become the most influential Shi'ite fundamentalist movement outside Iran. Herein lies a paradox. Iran's Islamic revolution first targeted the Shi'ite populations of the countries immediately adjacent to Iran or across the Persian Gulf: Iraq, Kuwait, Saudi Arabia, Bahrain, and Afghanistan. Some of these states had large Shi'ite populations that were in ready reach. Yet Iran's revolution ultimately had its greatest impact in Lebanon, the most westward and remote outpost of the Shi'ite world, and home to only 2 or 3 percent of the world's Shi'ites outside Iran. Despite the distance from Iran, Lebanon seemed to magnify the signal of Iran's revolution many times over, generating a Shi'ite fundamentalism that marched stridently to Iran's cadence. (Lebanon also produced the only Sunni fundamentalist movement that unashamedly embraced Iran as its model, the Tawhid movement in Tripoli.)

The paradox had a ready explanation: Lebanon's civil war amplified the effect of Iran's revolution. The collapse of the state and the resulting violence had taken a tremendous toll on Shi'ite society, producing demographic, social, and economic dislocations that dwarfed the simple discrimination suffered by Shi'ites elsewhere. Many hundreds of thousands of Shi'ites had been made into destitute refugees, in a country without a functioning state, in a capital city without operational municipalities and services. On the scale of human distress, Lebanon's Shi'ites could not be surpassed by Shi'ites elsewhere, and their hopelessness made them the most receptive of all Shi'ites to the siren calls that issued from Iran.

Just as important, the gate to Lebanon lay wide open. Iraq and the Arab Gulf states, while closer to the torch lit by Khomeini, also had the will and means to extinguish local sparks of sympathy with Iran's revolution. Iraq went to war to do so; Saudi Arabia and Kuwait launched cold wars against Iran, which included the arrest and deportation of thousands of Iran's Shi'ite sympathizers. In Lebanon, however, there was no one to arrest or deport those sympathizers, or even to keep Iran's zealots from entering Lebanon in force to join hands with their Shi'ite admirers. "The biggest obstacle to starting Islamic movements in the world is the people's attachment to governments," declared Islamic Iran's first ambassador to Lebanon, "but since the republic of Lebanon does not have much power, there is no serious obstacle in the way of the people of Lebanon."[8] Syria, which exercised a state-like authority in parts of Lebanon, was willing to accept any help against the hostile foreign forces entrenched in its Lebanese backyard: Syria allowed a supply line of support to run from Iran through Syria to Lebanon's Shi'ites. The absence of effective government, and the ease of Iranian access to Lebanon, created hothouse conditions for the rise of Iranian-inspired fundamentalist movements in Lebanon, a situation unique in the Middle East.

The Partisans of God

Those Lebanese Shi'ites who rallied around the banner of Islam in the summer of 1982 came from many different walks of life, but they all bore a double grievance. Not only did they feel threatened by outside enemies—the "satans" against whom Khomeini railed—but they also seethed with resentment against the Amal movement and its allies in the Shi'ite clerical establishment.

At the forefront of the new movement were young clerics, all drawn from the same narrow age group. They shared the stigma of inadequate preparation for their chosen profession. The fault was not theirs. Like their elders, they had gone to the Shi'ite shrine cities in Iraq to acquire the best credentials at the best theological academies, but in the 1970s the Iraqi security authorities decided to expel most foreign Shi'ite students, and several hundred returned to Lebanon empty-handed. The Shi'ite clerical establishment then spurned them, and they became became a disgruntled mass, uncertain of their allegiance. When Iran's emissaries arrived in the Bekaa Valley in 1982 and issued the clarion call to make a revolution, these young clerics rushed to pledge their loyalty to Khomeini and assume positions of leadership in Hizbullah.

Iran's emissaries also reached out to the great Shi'ite clans of the Bekaa Valley. They had long felt themselves excluded from the higher echelons of Amal, which drew its leaders from the south of Lebanon. Yet the Shi'ites of the Bekaa had recently enjoyed an unprecedented prosperity, the result of a trade in illicit drugs that had flourished since the collapse of central authority. They now sought a vehicle to legitimize their new status and found it in Hizbullah, which accorded them a disproportionate place in its leadership and turned a blind eye to the original source of their wealth. The first two incumbents of the office of secretary-general, Hizbullah's highest office, were clerics who hailed from the Bekaa Valley: Shaykh Subhi al-Tufayli and Sayyid Abbas al-Musawi.

Hizbullah also fed upon another grievance against Amal. Many young Shi'ites had joined Palestinian organizations during the 1970s, usually to escape poverty. When Israel forced the Palestinian organizations out of Lebanon in 1982, these Shi'ites lost their paymasters. In a blunder Amal would come to regret, it failed to make room for these Shi'ite orphans of the Palestinian revolution, scorning them for their service in a cause that had brought misery to South Lebanon. In contrast, Iran's emissaries held no grudge against them. Indeed, many of these same Iranians had been trained in Palestinian camps before the Islamic revolution, and they saw Palestinian service as a commendable credential. They now offered the unwanted Shi'ite militiamen jobs, weapons, and a sense of divine purpose. These Shi'ites joined enthusiastically and rose quickly through the ranks.

The brilliant commander of Islamic Jihad, Hizbullah's clandestine branch, would be a graduate of long Palestinian service: Imad Mughniyya.

Iran's emissaries even recruited successfully from within Amal. The established Shi'ite militia had grown brittle over the years, and some of its junior commanders concluded they had no prospects for advancement. When Iran offered Amal's malcontents some of the most senior command positions in the new movement, they jumped at the opportunity. Hizbullah even incorporated a faction called Islamic Amal, comprised of disaffected Amal veterans and led by Husayn al-Musawi.

Finally, Hizbullah won followers among the many tens of thousands of Shi'ites who had no stake in existing communal institutions. Many were impoverished refugees from the south who had crowded into the southern suburbs of Beirut. They had suffered terribly, and they regarded Amal and the Shi'ite clerical establishment as ineffectual defenders of the Shi'ite interest. Iran's emissaries moved quickly to offer food, jobs, loans, medicine, and other services to the teeming masses of impoverished Shi'ites in Beirut's slums. In return, they gave Hizbullah their loyalty. The senior cleric often named as the spiritual mentor of Hizbullah, Sayyid Muhammad Husayn Fadlallah, personified their grievance. His native town in the south of Lebanon abutted Israel and had often been emptied by fighting. He relocated to a Shi'ite slum in East Beirut, but lost his first pulpit in Maronite-Palestinian fighting in 1976 and arrived as a refugee to Beirut's southern suburbs. There, like other refugees, he began anew, without the help of the Shi'ite establishment. The mosque he built and guided would become the hub of Hizbullah in the city.[9]

From this account, it is clear that Hizbullah met some very mundane needs among its adherents. Yet it also made some very severe demands. The most fundamental of these demands was the obligation to "strive in the path of God." This is the literal meaning of jihad, interpreted in Shi'ism as a willingness to sacrifice in defense of Islam. Hizbullah's strength resided in its ability to harness a hundred grievances to one sublime purpose, and to persuade its downtrodden adherents of their own hidden strength—the strength of sacrifice.

To Right a World

One compelling idea forged a movement from these fragments of broken humanity, from the diverse grievances of thousands. It resided in a holistic vision that ingeniously transformed every kind of despair, injustice, and suffering into the product of one great crimp in the world. Muslims had abandoned Islam. Seduced by the falsehoods of others, they had cast aside the only known certainty in this world: the divine revelation of the Prophet Muhammad. The more they doubted this revelation, the further they fell from grace. Now they had lost all power to defend themselves, and their enemies preyed on their wealth, territory, and lives. Only by returning to Islam could Muslims right the world and set human history on the course intended by God.

The great return to Islam was already underway, led by the Imam Khomeini. By his appearance, he had begun to banish the darkness that enveloped the believers. Beneath his evocation of Shi'ite symbolism, his message had a dualistic simplicity: all that was truly Islamic was pure; all that was demonstrably foreign was impure. If the pure did not root out the impure, then the impure would prevail. The message touched a deep chord in Iranian culture, amplifying more prosaic grievances. Ultimately Khomeini succeeded in turning the Iranian people into a cauldron of righteousness. He promised to overturn the faithless regime of the Shah, purge society of hypocrites and corrupters, and cut the tentacles of the foreign powers that gripped Iran's destiny. He kept his word. The Shah fell, the accused hypocrites faced imprisonment or execution, and every trace of American influence vanished. Khomeini had created the first Islamic fundamentalist state.

Lebanon's Shi'ites watched his performance with amazement. Some began to believe that his medicine could cure Lebanon as well. Hadn't Lebanon's Muslims been corrupted by foreign ways? Didn't foreign powers control the destiny of the country? Hizbullah ultimately rested on an analogy between Lebanon and Iran—an analogy that defied vast disparities in the size and populations of the two countries, and in their geostrategic positions and resources. In the eyes of some, Lebanon now appeared like some remote extension of Iran, linked by a shared fealty to one man. Hizbullah's program, conveyed in its "open letter" of February 1985, declared that the movement "abides by the orders of the sole wise and just command represented by the supreme jurisconsult who meets the necessary qualifications, and who is presently incarnate in the Imam and guide, the Great Ayatollah Ruhollah al-Musawi al-Khomeini."[10] Khomeini became the only source of legitimate authority, and by their allegiance to him, the Shi'ites of Hizbullah ceased to be Lebanese. "Some say we are Muslim Lebanese," noted Husayn al-Musawi. "No! We are Muslims of the world and we have close links with other Muslims of the world."[11] "We do not work or think within the borders of Lebanon," declared Shaykh Subhi al-Tufayli, "this little geometric box, which is one of the legacies of imperialism. Rather, we seek to defend Muslims throughout the world."[12]

Hizbullah's vision was as grand as Lebanon was small. Its goals exceeded even the transformation of Lebanon into an Islamic state. The establishment of an Islamic state in Lebanon "is not our demand," said Husayn al-Musawi. The aim was not Islam in one country but the creation of an "all-encompassing Islamic state" that would absorb Lebanon.[13] An almost apocalyptic messianism animated this vision of a sweeping triumph of Islam. Islamic revolution had first occurred in Iran, but it was not Iranian. As one of Hizbullah's leading clerics declared: "The divine state of justice realized on part of this earth will not remain confined within its geographic borders, and is the dawn that will lead to the appearance of the Mahdi, who will create the state of Islam on earth."[14] This evocation of the Mahdi, the messianic figure in Islamic eschatology, suggested that the world had entered upon the last days and that redemption might by imminent.

In this vision, Hizbullah had the heroic role of purifying a province of Islam. "We are proceeding toward a battle with vice at its very roots," declared Hizbullah's manifesto. "And the first root of vice is America." The manifesto announced that "the Imam Khomeini, our leader, has repeatedly stressed that America is the cause of all our catastrophes and the source of all malice.... We will turn Lebanon into a graveyard for American schemes."[15] Once the Americans were ousted, their agents would fall as well. "We will bring down the Maronite regime just as we brought down the Shah in Iran," promised the chief of staff of the Revolutionary Guards to his Lebanese listeners—although he could only address them in Persian.[16] Finally Hizbullah was charged with the most daunting task of all: driving Israel from Lebanon and then from existence. Israel was "the cancer of the Middle East," said Sayyid Abbas al-Musawi. "In the future, we will wipe out every trace of Israel in Palestine."[17]

This grandiose vision served the deepest needs of the most alienated of Lebanon's Shi'ites. Through their membership in Hizbullah, the clerics, commanders, and the common followers of the movement could escape narrow allegiances and embrace a vast cause that transcended the boundaries of family, clan, sect, and state. Through an affiliation with Hizbullah, the individual ceased to be Lebanese, Shi'ite, Arab—a member of a disadvantaged sect in a small war-torn state populated by many different sects.

Through the agency of Hizbullah, the poor village boy or slum-dweller became a true Muslim, a member of a religious-political community spanning three continents, and a soldier in a world movement led by the Imam Khomeini for redressing the imbalance between Islam and infidelity. This was a mission above human history, a task of eschatological significance. A sense of divine purpose accounted for Hizbullah's appeal and eased its resort to violence, not only in Lebanon but throughout the world.

But to remake the world, the adherents of Hizbullah first had to remake themselves. The adherents of Hizbullah had to undergo a spiritual transformation if they were to muster the inner strength necessary for sacrifice—the kind of sacrifice without which the weak could not overcome the strong. The Iranian Revolutionary Guards brought with them to Lebanon the fire that had made the revolution in Iran. Sayyid Abbas al-Musawi, Hizbullah's secretary-general from 1991 until his assassination by Israel in 1992, was a cleric who had passed some time in higher theological studies in Najaf. He also took the first training course offered by the Revolutionary Guards in 1982. Of the two experiences, his training with the Guards had the greater impact:

> I recall one of the sights I can never forget. We were awakened at night by the weeping of the brethren Guards during the night prayer. Is this not the greatest school from which one can graduate? I also recall when one of the brethren Guards gave a weapons lesson. Suddenly, after he had given all the explanations, he put the weapon aside and swore an oath saying: "All I have explained to you will not help you; only God can help you." He began to talk about belief and reliance on God.... When I joined the Guards and sat with the brethren in the first course they gave in the Bekaa Valley, I felt I derived immense benefit. I felt I had truly penetrated genuine Islam. If this is how I felt, as someone at an advanced level of schooling, then how must the other youths have felt who filled the ranks of the Guards?[18]

Sayyid Muhammad Husayn Fadlallah called this transformation the "rebellion against fear." The great powers inspired fear among the oppressed, who had no more than "children's toys" to mount their opposition, but by conquering their own fear, through acceptance of the virtue of martyrdom, the oppressed could evoke alarm and fear among their oppressors.[19] In a short span of time, the first adherents of Hizbullah had overcome that fear. "The school of the Islamic Revolutionary Guard made the Muslim youths love martyrdom," said Abbas al-Musawi. "We were not surprised at all when, shortly after the arrival of the Guards, a Muslim youth in Lebanon smiled at death while carrying with him 1,200 kilograms of explosives."[20]

The Revolutionary Guards passed the torch to Hizbullah's clerics.

Their new role found symbolic representation in the arming of clerics at Hizbullah's rallies. They would stand in a row at the head of marches, awkwardly gripping AK-47s and M-16s, occasionally wearing the added accessory of an ammunition belt. They delivered funeral orations over dead fighters while brandishing rifles. In fact, clerics were not expected to bear arms in combat. The clips in the paraded weapons were probably empty, but the bearing of arms constituted a visual allusion to the preaching of the clerics. It reminded witnesses not that clerics sometimes took up arms but that they guided those who did.

Violence and Virtue

The blinding light of Lebanese Shi'ite anger, focused through the lens of Iran's Islamic zeal, set a fire. To understand the impact of that violence, it must first be characterized. A day-by-day chronology of the violence employed by Hizbullah during its first decade would be long indeed—too long to bear repetition.[21] But most of it fell into these four categories:

1. Campaigns meant to rid the Shi'ite regions of Lebanon of all foreign presence. Assassinations of individual foreigners escalated into massive bombings, some of them done by "self-martyrs," which destroyed the American embassy and its annex in two separate attacks in 1983 and 1984, the barracks of American and French peacekeeping troops in two famous attacks on the same morning in 1983, and command facilities of Israeli forces in the occupied south in 1982 and 1983. Hundreds of foreigners died on Lebanese soil in these bombings, the most successful of which killed 241 U.S. Marines in their barracks. These operations, combined with other lesser actions, forced American and French forces into a full retreat from Lebanon. As one Hizbullah leader put it, they "hurriedly ran away from three Muslims who loved martyrdom."[22] This violence also pushed Israeli forces back to a narrow "security zone" in the south.[23] "The Israeli soldier who could not be defeated was now killed, with an explosive charge here, and a bullet there," said Fadlallah. "People were suddenly filled with power, and that power could be employed in new ways...it deployed small force and a war of nerves, which the enemy could not confront with its tanks and airplanes."[24] Hizbullah continues to launch frequent attacks against Israeli forces and their Lebanese ally, the South Lebanon Army, in the "security zone." "Our goal is not the liquidation of [South Lebanon Army commander] Antoine Lahad in the border zone," said Sayyid Abbas

al-Musawi. "Our slogan is the liquidation of Israel."[25]

2. Operations intended to lend support to the efforts of Iran during the Iran-Iraq war. Before Hizbullah's emergence, its Shi'ite fundamentalist precursors launched a violent campaign against Iraqi targets in Lebanon, culminating in the destruction of the Iraqi embassy in Beirut in a 1981 bombing. The campaign later spread to Kuwait, where Hizbullah's Islamic Jihad bombed the American and French embassies and other targets in 1983, in an effort to compel Kuwait to abandon its support of Iraq. This violence peaked in a series of paralyzing terror bombings in Paris in 1986, meant to force France to abandon its policy of supplying Iraq with arms. The cease-fire between Iran and Iraq in 1988 brought this campaign to an end.

3. Operations meant to free members and affiliates of Hizbullah who had been captured by enemy governments in the Middle East and Europe. These operations included the hijacking of an American airliner in 1985 to secure the freedom of Lebanese Shi'ites held by Israel, and two hijackings of Kuwaiti airliners in 1986 and 1988 to win freedom for Lebanese Shi'ites held by Kuwait for the bombings there. The hijackers killed passengers in each of these hijackings, to demonstrate their resolve. In addition, Islamic Jihad and other groups affiliated with Hizbullah abducted dozens of foreigners in Lebanon, mostly American, French, British, and German citizens, for the same purpose. Some of these foreigners would later be traded for American arms needed by Iran in the Gulf war, but the motive for the wave of abductions remained the release of Hizbullah's imprisoned fighters elsewhere. The longest-held hostage spent over six years in captivity. Most of the hostages were freed; a few died in captivity.

4. Battles waged against the rival movements over control of neighborhoods in Beirut and villages in the south. In 1986, Hizbullah clashed repeatedly with the Syrian Social Nationalist Party over control of routes leading from the Bekaa Valley to the south. And beginning in 1988, occasional skirmishes with Amal escalated into war. Over one thousand Shi'ites, many of them noncombatants, died in this intra-Shi'ite fighting, which persisted despite numerous cease-fire initiatives. In the course of the battles, Hizbullah perpetrated several atrocities and assassinated two prominent leaders of Amal. Hizbullah usually enjoyed the upper hand in fighting, but it was denied the fruits of victory by Syrian intervention. The fighting ended in late 1990 with a cease-fire mediated by Syria and Iran.

In what way did this violence reflect its origins in a fundamentalist movement? Violence in Lebanon did not constitute a deviation. Indeed, it had become the norm. Long before the appearance of Hizbullah, Lebanon had become a land in which guns spoke louder than words. To do battle was not a matter of choice but of survival, and in some respects, Hizbullah's violence followed well-worn paths in Lebanon—paths blazed first by the Palestinians in the early 1970s and followed by various militias in the late 1970s. The commanders of Hizbullah were veterans either of Palestinian service or the Amal militia, and they often took pages from both books.

Nor could the "self-martyrdom operations," which Hizbullah pioneered, qualify as a strictly fundamentalist mode of operation. Groups in Lebanon that were not fundamentalist, religious, or Shi'ite quickly imitated this method. In terms of the number of casualties inflicted by such operations, Hizbullah undoubtedly deserved place of primacy. Hizbullah employed the method first, and enjoyed the advantage of surprise, but in terms of the number of operations—and the number of "self-martyrs"—pride of place went to the imitators: the secular, nationalist organizations that operated in Lebanon under Syrian auspices. A study that summarized the major round of "self-martyrdom operations" from their inception in 1983 through the end of 1986, found that Shi'ite organizations perpetrated only seven of the thirty-one attacks. Pro-Syrian organizations carried out twenty-two attacks, most notably by the Syrian Social Nationalist Party (ten attacks), and the Ba'th Party (seven attacks). (These operations were all directed against Israel and the South Lebanon Army.)[26]

It was also obvious that Hizbullah's collective choices regarding the extent and intensity of its violence had a clear political rationale. Hizbullah was also a political movement, and indeed saw politics as an inseparable part of religion. When it employed violence, it did so for political and not ritualistic purposes—to bring it closer to power. In making its choices, Hizbullah weighed benefits against costs. Violence drove enemies into retreat and created a zone of autonomous action for Hizbullah, but it simultaneously invited punitive retaliation and at times created political complications for Iran. Fadlallah fairly described the guiding principle of Hizbullah: "I believe that in all cases violence is like a surgical operation that the doctor should only resort to after he has exhausted all other methods."[27]

The calculus of politics, however, is not driven by a universal logic. It is conditioned by cultural values. Hizbullah did not simply seek power; it sought power in order to implement Islamic law. That goal had to be pursued within the law of Islam, as understood by its interpreters among the clerics. "The Muslim fighter needed answers to many questions," said Shaykh Abd al-Karim Ubayd, a Hizbullah cleric who would be made famous after his abduction by Israel in 1989. "Is resistance to the occupation obligatory on religious grounds? What about the question of self-martyrdom? The law has an answer to these examples, which therefore are not political questions so much as legal questions, and here lies the role of the cleric." Only he could provide answers; without his essential contribution, there could be no legitimate violence, since "these questions cannot be answered by the military commander, especially for the believing fighter, who must turn to a cleric who is enthusiastic, responsive, and committed to resistance."[28]

On the one hand, submission to Islamic law freed Hizbullah from non-Islamic moral constraints. Hizbullah felt no need to justify its acts by other codes. Its struggle was a jihad, a form of sacred warfare regulated solely by Islamic law. (Hence the choice of Islamic Jihad as the name for Hizbullah's clandestine branch.) It made no difference to Hizbullah's adherents that jihad remained associated with fanaticism in the historical consciousness of the West. They did not seek the favor of world public opinion and addressed their justifications solely to Muslim believers.

On the other hand, jihad had its requirements. The Islamic law of war is the codification of a moral sensibility. While it is open to some interpretation, it is not infinitely elastic. Some of its provisions compel violence—acts of punishment or resistance—but other provisions forbid violence against persons afforded protection by the law. The believing public had to be persuaded that Hizbullah's actions were not criminal but "in the nature of a jihad, launched by the oppressed against the oppressors."[29] The clerics, as interpreters of law, constantly subjected Hizbullah's selection of targets and techniques to the judgment of this law.

In doing so, they forced Hizbullah to resist two powerful temptations of its Lebanese environment. First, Hizbullah sometimes threatened to deteriorate into one more sectarian militia devoted to battling other sectarian militias. "Parties and movements and organizations begin as great ideas," warned Fadlallah, "and turn into narrow interests. Religion starts as a message from God and struggle, and turns into the interests of individuals and another kind of tribalism."[30] That deterioration had to be fought. The clerics never ceased to remind the movement of its divine mission and to urge the expansion of the jihad to confront the "global infidelity" of foreigners. Second, Hizbullah occasionally seemed poised to imitate the sectarian militias, by employing wholly indiscriminate violence. The clerics never ceased to insist that the jihad not harm innocents. To be worthy of Islam, the struggle had to be global in conception, but discriminating in execution.

In retrospect, some of Hizbullah's acts of violence met these demanding criteria; some did not. It soon became clear that in the real world, violence could rarely be pure. A few acts approximated the ideal, such as the earliest bombings by "self-martyrs" against foreign forces in Lebanon. These targeted armed, foreign intruders and so constituted legitimate jihad in the defense of Islam. The use of "self-martyrs" assured that these attacks achieved pinpoint precision—an unusual technique for Beirut, where exploding cars usually killed indiscriminately.

Yet even here, a problem of Islamic law arose, since some innocents did die in these attacks: the "self-martyrs" themselves. Suicide is prohibited by Islam, and the question of whether their deaths did or did not constitute suicide tugged at the consciences of Hizbullah's clerics. As long as the attacks succeeded so dramatically, the clerics suppressed all doubt, but the question resurfaced when subsequent attacks began to produce lower yields in enemy casualties. "The self-martyring operation is not permitted unless it can convulse the enemy," said Fadlallah, "the believer cannot blow himself up unless the results will equal or exceed the [loss of the] soul of the believer. Self-martyring operations are not fatal accidents but legal obligations governed by rules, and the believers cannot transgress the rules of God."[31] The clerics ultimately banned such operations, and they gradually ended. (For more on this issue, see chapter 13.)

Other acts generated even more controversy. Abductions of innocent foreigners divided Hizbullah's clerics. Some came out clearly against the practice, which they criticized as a violation of Islamic law. Other clerics justified the hostage-holding as an unfortunate but necessary evil. However, even these showed some hesitation, so that the hostage-holders often had to provide their own justifications, communicated through hand-scrawled missives to the press. Ultimately, the debate over the Islamic legality of hostage-holding did not produce a repentant release of hostages. They were usually freed when it served Iran's purposes, in moves governed by the ethic of the marketplace rather than Islamic law. The debate, though, did put the perpetrators of these acts in the moral docket, before the only constituency that mattered: believers in the primacy of Islamic law. It is possible also that hostage-holding would have been practiced even more extensively had this debate never taken place, although no one can say this for certain.[32]

Finally, some acts could not be defended from the point of view of Islamic law. True, France supplied Iraq with the weapons that killed Iran's faithful in the Gulf war. Striking at French interests would show the solidarity of true believers. Yet the bombings that shook Paris in 1986, killing at random in shops and trains, represented acts of sheer terror that Hizbullah's clerics could never have defended. Thus, the Lebanese Shi'ite plotters, who came from within Hizbullah, took care not to claim the bombings for Islam and even enticed a hapless Tunisian recruit to plant the bombs. Both distancing measures reflected a certain knowledge that the bombings constituted terror by *any* definition, Western or Islamic. Perhaps for this reason, the Paris bombings remained an isolated instance, although Hizbullah possessed the capability to launch similar campaigns abroad, and was reported ready to do so on many occasions.[33]

Hizbullah's war with Amal also caused deep anguish among the clerics, for it involved the killing of Shi'ites by Shi'ites. Of course, it could be rationalized: Amal had conspired with the enemies of Islam, within Lebanon and abroad. It denied the global leadership of Islamic Iran and protected Israel by barring Hizbullah's way to the south. Yet Hizbullah's clerics were not completely persuaded that these deeds justified killing, and they persisted in calling the struggle a "dissension," a *fitna*, rather than a sacred war, a jihad. This did not stem the fighting, but if Amal had to be fought, then it had to be done quickly and in a spirit of regret. At one point, at the height of the fighting, the clerics could no longer look away, for fighters in the field had taken to mutilating corpses in Lebanese fashion—a method used to inspire terror in the enemy. The men of religion issued a religious edict against the practice.

In the end, Hizbullah's violence could not help but demonstrate the movement's contradictory character. Hizbullah was Islamic by day, Lebanese by night. What seemed right in the mosques did not always work in the alleys. Hizbullah's clerics had to know when to avert their eyes from the compromises between the ideal and the real. Was this hypocrisy? There were some principles, even of Islam, that the poor could not afford; if the poor did not have smart bombs, then who would deny them the blunt weapons at hand? "The oppressed nations do not have the technology and destructive weapons America and Europe have," said Fadlallah:

They must thus fight with special means of their own.... [We] recognize the right of nations to use every unconventional method to fight these aggressor nations, and do not regard what oppressed Muslims of the world do with primitive and unconventional means to confront aggressor powers as terrorism. We view this as religiously lawful warfare against the world's imperialist and domineering powers.[34]

Yet even Fadlallah drew a line: sacred ends could not be achieved *only* by profane means. There always had to be some aspects of Hizbullah's struggle that approached the exacting standards of the law. Usually there were. At one moment, a guard might beat a hapless foreign hostage to discourage thoughts of escape, but that could be rationalized if, at the same moment, a fighter of the jihad prepared himself to court death by assaulting an Israeli army patrol. "There is evil in everything good and something good in every evil," reasoned Fadlallah.[35] Even a fundamentalist movement preoccupied with purity had to acknowledge its own impurities—and strive to cleanse itself, even as it cleansed the world around it.

The Impact of Hizbullah

During the decade between 1982 and 1992, Hizbullah's violence made an indelible impression on the world, and its name passed into common parlance. Yet Hizbullah's vision of a new age receded from grasp. By the end of the decade, the triumph of Islam in Lebanon, the further spread of Iran's revolution, and the liberation of Jerusalem all seemed more remote than ever. Lebanon inched toward a Syrian-guaranteed peace based on (revised) confessionalism—a reform, not a revolution. Islamic Iran, still smarting from wounds sustained in a failed war with Iraq, turned toward domestic reconstruction. Arab states, Lebanon among them, sat down with Israel in direct talks to discuss a possible peace. Had Hizbullah chased the horizon?

No one could say for certain, but none could deny that Hizbullah had become one of the realities of Lebanon and the region. Hizbullah did not have the means to turn the world upside down, but it had fought and bought its way to the hearts of perhaps as many as half of Lebanon's politically active Shi'ites. Hizbullah had played an instrumental role in driving foreign forces out of Lebanon and continued a tireless campaign against Israel in the south. It had rendered some service to Islamic Iran by its abductions of foreigners and had also secured the release of many of its own imprisoned members. It had defeated its Shi'ite rivals in one confrontation after another, earning the respect of friends and the fear of enemies. Above all, it had initiated a return to Islam—a gradual process of inner transformation whose results no one could predict.

Still, the world had changed in profound ways while Hizbullah made itself secure. Old ideologies broke under the weight of economics; old conflicts moved toward resolution. Even some of the leaders of Islamic Iran urged that the revolution turn a corner, and move from confrontation to cooperation with the West. Fadlallah helped his listeners accept the fact. "Like all revolutions, including the French revolution, the Islamic revolution did not have a realistic line at first," he said. "At that time it served to create a state, it produced a mobilization, a new religious way of thinking and living, with the aim of winning Muslim autonomy and independence from the superpowers." But "the new phase which should now be reached is the normalization of relations with the rest of the world."[36] To speak of the Islamic revolution like any other revolution, to speak of accepting the world as it is—at first these ideas found little echo among Hizbullah's other clerics, but soon they also would concede that Hizbullah, too, would have to turn a corner. The release of the last Western hostages in 1992 indicated that the reassessment was well under way.

Fadlallah had warned against the limits of violence. The Palestinians in the 1970s had also stunned the world with their violence—and had nothing to show for it. To avoid such an impasse, Hizbullah would have to move to a new phase: the struggle for ideas. This would be a different kind of jihad, requiring perseverance and patience, for Hizbullah had taken only a first step:

> We work to arrive at a result from within the objective and actual circumstances, some of which we ourselves must work to create, while others we must await with the passage of time. We see that these conditions do not exist in the Lebanese reality at the present stage, and in the immediate stages to follow—this, despite the spread of the Islamic spirit which transformed Islam into a pressure force on political reality.[37]

Hizbullah began to fashion a new strategy for this jihad over hearts and minds. At home in Lebanon, it became more committed to grass-roots social activism and more willing to substitute the slogan of democracy for the slogan of revolution. Elsewhere in the region, Islamic movements bid for power as political parties, not as revolutionary conspiracies, and they enjoyed a remarkable success. Might this not work in Lebanon? After all, Shi'ite and Sunni Muslims constituted a clear majority in the country.

Hizbullah began to demand a general referendum on the question of an Islamic state. In an ironic twist, Hizbullah cast itself as a champion of democracy; the "Party of God" began to evolve slowly into a political party, a *hizb*, whose clerics spoke more like candidates.[38]

Hizbullah also transformed its own vision of its regional role. During the 1980s, the movement had looked east toward Islamic Iran, anticipating a victory against Iraq and the creation of an "all-encompassing Islamic state." That dream had been shattered, but another arose to replace it. Hizbullah's leaders noticed how Mediterranean Islam began to gain social and political momentum in the 1980s—in Algeria, Tunisia, Egypt, Jordan, and among the Palestinians. Islamic movements in these countries also sought the transformation of secular state and society into Islamic state and society. Mediterranean Islamic activism is largely Sunni, as are the great majority of Muslims in the Mediterranean basin, but its attitude to Shi'ism was usually dispassionate, and it now contained pockets of open sympathy for Iran's revolution as a genuine expression of Islam, from Tunisia's "Renaissance" Islamic party to the Palestinian Islamic Jihad.

Hizbullah sat astride a point where two powerful winds of Islamic reassertion converged—one from the west, the other from the east. And it soon established itself as the mediating bridge between Mediterranean Islam—the Islam of the Algerian Islamists and the Palestinian Jihad groups—and the stalled but still potent Islam of Iran. In short, Hizbullah sought to play the classic Lebanese role of middleman—to stay afloat by mediating the contact between two parts of the Muslim world separated by language, culture, and space. This kind of mediation is precisely the Lebanese art, and it is the way Lebanon has found its place and livelihood in the world. Hizbullah bid to become the bridge between Shi'ism and Sunnism, Iran and the Arabs, the Gulf and the Mediterranean.

Were Hizbullah to become such a bridge, its role would change profoundly. The fighting vanguards of Islamic revolution would become the talking mediators of ideas. Lebanon would cease to be the ground of contention; instead, Hizbullah would assist the struggle of others, by becoming a regional amplifier of Islamic Iran's message. It now remained to be seen whether Hizbullah would prove as adept in persuasion as in coercion, whether its words would topple the structures that its bombs had only shaken.

Notes

1. See Abdulaziz A. Sachedina, "Activist Shi'ism in Iran, Iraq, and Lebanon," in *Fundamentalisms Observed*, eds. Martin E. Marty and R. Scott Appleby (Chicago: University of Chicago Press, 1991), 403–56 (with extensive bibliography).
2. Many aspects of the history of the Shi'ites in what is now modern Lebanon remain obscure. For general appreciations, see Mounzer Jaber, "Pouvoir et société au Jabal Amel de 1749 à 1920 dans la conscience des chroniques chiites et dans un essai d'interprétation," (thése 3e cycle, University of Paris IV, 1978); Monika Pohl-Schö-berlein, *Die schiitische Gemeinschaft des Südlibanon (Gabal 'Amil) innerhalb des libanesischen konfessionellen Systems* (Berlin: Klaus Schwarz, 1986); and Ghaleb el Turk, "The South," in *Lebanon and Its Provinces: A Study by the Governors of the Five Provinces*, ed. Halim Said Abu-Izzedin (Beirut: Khayat, 1963), 49–71.
3. On the voluntary movement of Shi'ites to Beirut before the outbreak of the civil war in 1975, see Salim Nasr, "La transition des chiites vers Beyrouth: Mutations sociales et mobilisation communautaire à la veille de 1975," in *Mouvements communautaires et espaces urbains au Machreq* (Beirut: Editions du CERMOC, 1985), 87–116.
4. For the history of the Shi'ite awakening in Lebanon, see Fouad Ajami, *The Vanished Imam: Musa al Sadr and the Shia of Lebanon* (Ithaca, N.Y.: Cornell University Press, 1986); Augustus Richard Norton, *Amal and the Shi'a: Struggle for the Soul of Lebanon* (Austin: University of Texas Press, 1987); Andreas Rieck, *Die Schiiten und der Kampf um den Libanon. Politische Chronik 1958–1988*, Mitteilungen des Deutschen Orient-Instituts, no. 33 (Hamburg: Deutsches Orient-Institut, 1989); and Majed Halawi, *A Lebanon Defied: Musa al-Sadr and the Shi'a Community* (Boulder, Colo.: Westview Press, 1992). Article-length studies that consider important aspects of the awakening include Thom Sicking and Shereen Khairallah, "The Shi'a Awakening in Lebanon: A Search for Radical Change in a Traditional Way," in *Vision and Revision in Arab Society, 1974*, CEMAM Reports, no. 2 (Beirut: Dar al-Mashreq, 1975), 97–130; Talal Jaber, "Le discours shi'ite sur le pouvoir," *Peuples méditerranéens*, no. 20 (July-September 1982): 75–92; Salim Nasr, "Mobilisation communautaire et symbolique religieuse: L'Imam Sadr et les chi'ites du Liban (1970–1975)," in *Radicalismes islamiques*, eds. Olivier Carré and Paul Dumont, 2 vols. (Paris: L'Harmattan, 1985), 1:119–58; Elisabeth Picard, "De la 'communauté-classe' à la 'Résistance Nationale.' Pour une analyse du rôle des Chi'ites dans le système politique libanais (1970–1985)," *Revue française de science politique* 35 (1985): 999–1027; and Shimon Shapira, "The *Imam* Musa al-Sadr: Father of the Shiite Resurgence in Lebanon," *Jerusalem Quarterly*, no. 44 (Fall 1987): 121–44.
5. On the forced movement of Shi'ite refugees to West Beirut and the southern suburbs after 1975, see Salim Nasr, "Beyrouth et le conflit libanais: Restructuration de l'espace urbain," in *Politiques urbaines dans le monde arabe*, eds. J. Metral and G. Mutin (Lyon, 1984), 287–305.
6. On the emergence of this trend, see Chibli Mallat, *Shi'i Thought from the South of Lebanon* (Oxford: Centre for Lebanese Studies, 1988).
7. On the emergence of Hizbullah and the role of Iran, see these studies by Martin Kramer: *Hezbollah's Vision of the West*, Policy Papers, no. 16 (Washington: The Washington Institute for Near East Policy, 1989); "The Moral Logic of Hizballah," in *Origins of Terrorism: Psychologies, Ideologies, Theologies, States of Mind*, ed. Walter Reich (Cambridge: Cambridge University Press, 1990), 131–57; "Redeeming Jerusalem: The Pan-Islamic Premise of Hizballah," in *The Iranian Revolution and the Muslim World*, ed. David Menashri (Boulder, Colo.: Westview Press, 1990), 105–30; and my annual essays for the *Middle East Contemporary Survey*, commencing with vol. 8 (1983–84). See also R. K. Ramazani, *Revolutionary Iran: Challenge and Response in the Middle East* (Baltimore: Johns Hopkins University Press, 1986),

175–95; Yves Gonzales-Quijano, "Les interprétations d'un rite: célébrations de la 'Achoura au Liban," *Maghreb-Machrek*, no. 115 (January-February-March 1987): 5–28; Shimon Shapira, "The Origins of Hizballah," *Jerusalem Quarterly*, no. 46 (Spring 1988): 115–30; Andreas Rieck, "Abschied vom Revolutionsexport? Expansion und Rückgang des iranischen Einflusses im Libanon 1979–1989," *Beiträge zur Konfliktforschung* (Cologne) 20, no. 2 (1990): 81–104; and Augustus Richard Norton, "Lebanon: The Internal Conflict and the Iranian Connection," in *The Iranian Revolution: Its Global Impact*, John L. Esposito, ed. (Miami: Florida International University Press, 1990), 116–37.

8. Interview with Hojjat al-Islam Fakhr Rouhani, *Ettela'at* (Tehran), 9 January 1984.

9. On Fadlallah, see Martin Kramer, "Muhammad Husayn Fadlallah," *Orient* 26, no. 2 (June 1985): 147–49. Some of Fadlallah's theoretical writings, mostly from the 1970s, have been examined by Olivier Carré, "Quelques mots-clefs de Muhammad Husayn Fadlallâh," *Revue française de science politique* 37 (1987): 478–501; and "La 'révolution islamique' selon Muhammad Husayn Fadlallâh," *Orient* (Opladen, Germany) 29, no. 1 (March 1988): 68–84. Both have been reprinted in Olivier Carré, *L'Utopie islamique dans l'Orient arabe* (Paris: Fondation nationale des sciences politiques, 1991).

10. *Nass al-risala al-maftuha allati wajjahaha Hizbullah ila al-mustad'afin fi Lubnan wal-alam* (Open Letter from Hizbullah to the Disinherited in Lebanon and the World) ([Beirut], 16 February 1985), 6.

11. Interview with Husayn al-Musawi, *Kayhan* (Tehran), 27 July 1986.

12. Speech by Shaykh Subhi al-Tufayli, *Al-Ahd* (Beirut), 10 April 1987. *Al-Ahd* is the weekly newspaper of Hizbullah.

13. Interview with Husayn al-Musawi, *Al-Harakat al-Islamiyya fi Lubnan* (Beirut: Dar al-Shira', 1984), 226–27.

14. Speech by Sayyid Hasan Nasrallah, *Al-Ahd*, 7 February 1986.

15. *Nass al-risala al-maftuha*, 9, 17.

16. Speech by the chief of staff of the Revolutionary Guards Corps, delivered in the Imam Ali Mosque in Baalbek, *Al-Anwar* (Beirut), 9 February 1988.

17. Interview with Sayyid Abbas al-Musawi, *La revue du Liban* (Beirut), 27 July 1985.

18. Interview with Sayyid Abbas al-Musawi, *Al-Ahd*, 16 October 1987.

19. Interview with Fadlallah, *Al-Nahar al-arabi wal-duwali*, 21 July 1986.

20. Interview with Sayyid Abbas al-Musawi, *al-Ahd*, 16 October 1987.

21. For chronologies of Hizbullah's campaign, see the section on "Shiite Terrorism" in the annual *Middle East Military Balance*, published by the Jaffee Center at Tel Aviv University, and also the U.S. Department of State's annual *Patterns of Global Terrorism*. For a comprehensive account of Hizbullah's hostage holding, see Maskit Burgin et al., *Foreign Hostages in Lebanon*, memorandum no. 25 (Tel Aviv: Jaffee Center for Strategic Studies, August 1988). Hizbullah's violence is also described in a number of accounts by journalists from the Western countries targeted by Hizbullah's violence. From the American vantage point, see Robin Wright, *Sacred Rage: The Wrath of Militant Islam* (New York: Simon and Schuster, 1986); John Wolcott and David C. Martin, *Best Laid Plans: The Inside Story of America's War Against Terrorism* (New York: Harper and Row, 1988); and Larry Pintak, *Beirut Outtakes: A TV Correspondent's Portrait of America's Encounter with Terror* (Lexington, Mass.: Lexington Books, 1988). From the French vantage point, see Xavier Raufer, *La nébuleuse: Le terrorisme du Moyen-Orient* (Paris: Fayard, 1987); Yves Loiseau, *Le grand troc: Le labyrinthe des otages français au Liban* (Paris: Hachette, 1988); and Gilles Delafon, *Beyrouth: Les soldats de l'Islam* (Paris: Stock, 1989). There are already many published first hand accounts by former hostages.

22. Interview with Sadiq al-Musawi, *Al-Nahar al-arabi wal-duwali*, 28 July 1986.
23. See W. A. Terrill, "Low Intensity Conflict in Southern Lebanon: Lessons and Dynamics of the Israeli-Shiʿite War," *Conflict Quarterly* (Fredricktown, New Brunswick) 7, no. 3 (1987): 22–35.
24. Al-Sayyid Muhammad Husayn Fadlallah, *Al-Muqawama al-islamiyya fil-Janub wal-Biqa al-Gharbi wa-Rashayya: tatalluʿat wa-afaq* (Beirut: n.p., 1984), 11.
25. Speech by Sayyid Abbas al-Musawi, *Al-Safir* (Beirut), 23 September 1986.
26. Ariel Merari, "The Readiness to Kill and Die: Suicidal Terrorism in the Middle East," in *The Origins of Terrorism*, ed. Walter Reich (Cambridge: Cambridge University Press, 1990), 204–5.
27. Interview with Fadlallah, *Monday Morning* (Beirut), 15 October 1984.
28. Interview with Shaykh Abd al-Karim Ubayd, *Al-Safir*, 28 July 1986.
29. Interview with Husayn al-Musawi, *Kayhan*, 29 July 1986.
30. Friday sermon by Fadlallah, *Al-Nahar* (Beirut), 27 July 1985.
31. Speech by Fadlallah, *Al-Nahar*, 14 May 1985.
32. For the debate in Hizbullah over hostage-holding, see Kramer, "The Moral Logic of Hizballah," 149–56.
33. After this article was written, Hizbullah played a role in a series of devastating bombings against Israeli and Jewish targets in Buenos Aires. See Martin Kramer, "The Jihad Against the Jews," *Commentary*, October 1994, 38–42.
34. Interview with Fadlallah, *Kayhan*, 14 November 1985.
35. Fadlallah Friday sermon, *Al-Ahd*, 5 December 1985.
36. Interview with Fadlallah, *La Repubblica* (Rome), 28 August 1989.
37. Interview with Fadlallah, *Al-Shiraʿ* (Beirut), 18 March 1985.
38. After this paper was written, Hizbullah proceeded to participate in Lebanon's 1992 parliamentary elections, and did send members to the country's parliament. For details on this development, see A. Nizar Hamzeh, "Lebanon's Hizballah: From Islamic Revolution to Parliamentary Accommodation," *Third World Quarterly* 14 (1993): 321–37.

13

Sacrifice and "Self-Martyrdom" in Shi'ite Lebanon

On 11 November 1982, a gas explosion gutted an eight-story building used by the Israeli occupation forces in Tyre in south Lebanon. In the conflagration, sixty Israeli soldiers and fourteen others died. The Israeli authorities announced that the blast was the result of an explosion of gas balloons, although there was considerable speculation that the attack had been a deliberate bombing. Indeed, Islamic Jihad claimed credit for the explosion, announcing that it had been produced by time bombs it had infiltrated into the building. Little more was said until May 1985, when Hizbullah's Islamic Resistance gave a different account, claiming that the building had been demolished by an explosive-laden car driven by a "self-martyr." The announcement attributed the act to Ahmad Qusayr, a fifteen-year-old from Dayr Qanun al-Nahr, a Shi'ite town about ten miles inland from Tyre in south Lebanon.[1]

It is impossible even now to pronounce definitively on the origin or authorship of the explosion. Yet if the claim of the Islamic Resistance is true, then the Tyre attack of 1982 may be said to have initiated the tactic that made Hizbullah both famous and dreaded. The "self-martyring" operations took the following form: an individual would take the wheel of a truck or car loaded with high explosives, position that vehicle alongside a target, and detonate the explosives while still in the vehicle. In the resulting explosion, the driver was certain to die. The explosion also inflicted damage on the target, although its effect could not be predicted. The most destructive attack by Islamic Jihad, less than a year later, claimed 241 American lives in Beirut. Other attacks claimed fewer casualties, and sometimes only the life of the driver.

Although such attacks were devised by Hizbullah, other Lebanese organizations soon sponsored similar operations, including Hizbullah's

Lebanese Shi'ite rival, the Amal movement. The first such operation by Amal took place on 17 June 1984, when a Lebanese car approached an Israeli military patrol in south Lebanon. As the patrol and the car met, the driver of the car detonated high explosives packed in the vehicle, killing himself and wounding a number of Israeli soldiers. Credit for the operation was immediately claimed by the Amal movement, which identified the "self-martyr" as Bilal Fahs, a seventeen year old from the town of Jibshit, near Nabatiyya in south Lebanon.

Those who claimed credit for these operations represented them as straightforward acts of war. Hizbullah's attacks were directed against American, French, and Israeli targets in Lebanon; Amal's operations targeted Israeli forces in Lebanon. Yet from the outset, this classification posed problems. For while the operations were no doubt conceived as acts of war, and therefore as politically purposeful, their very structure suggested sacrificial rite. The perpetrators went deliberately to their deaths; the planners deliberately sent the perpetrators to their deaths.

There was another paradox. By these acts, Shi'ites seemed united in a struggle against foreign invaders and aggressors. Yet beneath this apparent unity, it seemed as though Hizbullah and Amal had entered into a competition. In their boastful presentations of these attacks, both Hizbullah and Amal sought to amass greater credibility as promoters of sacred struggle—in the number of attacks launched against foreign intruders, in the number of claimed enemy casualties, and in the number of martyrs offered to the cause. Far from displaying unity, the escalating attacks seemed to point to an intensified rivalry with Shi'ite ranks. The two movements, Hizbullah and Amal, were waging a *competitive* guerrilla war against the Western presence in Beirut and the Israeli presence in south Lebanon.

This struggle culminated in the withdrawal from Lebanon of the United States and France and the retreat of Israel to a narrow zone in south Lebanon. To most observers, this represented an instance of successful and unified resistance against an onerous foreign occupation. Few noticed the evidence of imitative rivalry that drove the sacred war forward, and that channeled the growing antagonism between Hizbullah and Amal into competitive displays of violence against intruders.

The rivalry reached its apex in the "self-martyring" operations which were initiated by Hizbullah and subsequently imitated by Amal. No aspect of the struggle had the same effect upon the Shi'ite community as these operations, which thrilled, fascinated, and repelled at once. This was particularly true of the two operations cited above—one by Hizbullah and one by Amal—that first introduced the technique in the struggle against Israel in south Lebanon. The attacks against the United States and French contingents of the Multinational Force in Beirut were far more deadly, but the anonymity of the bombers, preserved to this day, established a distance between the community and the acts. However, the poster visages of the two "self-martyrs" who allegedly brought the method to the south are readily recognized throughout Shi'ite Lebanon. So too is the lore behind the visages, and within that lore are grains of evidence that open new possibilities of interpretation. This is true even if the actual identities of the "self-martyrs" cannot ever be independently established. The following biographical fragments, stripped of embellishment, convey the essential information.

The Short Lives of Two Martyrs

Ahmad Qusayr, named by the Islamic Resistance as the youth responsible for the Tyre attack in 1982, was born in 1967. He had an unexceptional childhood. Ahmad left school after fifth grade and went to work for his father, who ran a fruit and vegetable stall in Dayr Qanun al-Nahr. He then went to Saudi Arabia where he worked for three months as a hospital orderly to save money. Upon his return, he began to drive a pick-up truck bought by his father, from which he sold produce. Ahmad would also go regularly to the mosque for prayer, and help to decorate and clean it. Like most local boys, he also enjoyed hunting and the outdoors.

Ahmad did not become a fighter himself, but he fell under the influence of young men who were fighters. He began to run small errands for them, such as smuggling arms and tracking the movements of Israeli patrols while he delivered produce. Then he began to drive the pick-up to Beirut, leaving before sunrise and returning after sunset, without offering explanations. His father, who saw that he was not carrying produce on these trips, assumed he was running weapons. Then one day he borrowed his father's passport and transferred the registration of his truck to his father's name. He disappeared a few days before the operation, plunging his family into worry; his father went to Beirut to find him. Perhaps he had been kidnapped, perhaps he was being held by Christian militiamen. His parents learned of Ahmad's mission only when Hizbullah revealed his "self-martyrdom" two and a half years after the operation.[2]

Bilal Fahs, who carried out Amal's first "self-martyring" operation in 1984, was born in 1967 to an impoverished family. His father sold vegetables from a cart, and lived in a one-room cinder block house on the edge of Jibshit. Bilal's mother separated from his father a few months after Bilal's birth; the father remarried and had more children, crowding the house beyond endurance. Bilal spent most of his days in the room of his paternal grandmother. Bilal's father had not registered his marriage to Bilal's mother with the religious courts, which have jurisdiction in Lebanon over civil status. Bilal therefore did not receive an identity card, and could not be admitted to school, although he did learn to read and write. He drifted between Jibshit and the southern suburbs of Beirut, where he had aunts and uncles, and he did some occasional fighting on behalf of Amal. Eventually he became a bodyguard to Amal leader Nabih Birri. A year and two months before the operation, he became engaged, but encountered bureaucratic difficulties in legally marrying because his existence was not registered and he had no card to establish his identity. The dynamic young prayer leader in Jibshit tried to help him straighten out the matter with the religious courts, but the outcome of this intervention is unknown.

Bilal's fiancée later said that during the three months before the operation, she saw a change in Bilal. He spoke at length about the prayer leader of Jibshit, killed allegedly at the hands of the Israelis, and listened to every item of news about the resistance in the south. He carried photographs of martyred fighters, read some Islamic books, and watched war movies and films about Islam. In his last letter, addressed to Amal leader Birri, he wrote: "I will that my brothers in the movement all join hands in the jihad enjoined upon us the Imam-Leader [Khomeini], and that we will persevere however many obstacles there might be, under the leadership of the giant fighter of the jihad, brother Nabih Birri."[3]

This evidence, like all evidence, raises at least as many questions as it answers. Like all evidence, it is incomplete, and perhaps it changes nothing. It is still possible to represent these "self-martyring" operations as a straightforward extension of war, and the product of the tactical acumen of their planners. Given the fundamental asymmetry of power between the two Shi'ite movements and their adversaries, the techniques of guerrilla warfare and "self-martyring" operations constituted a tactical response ideally suited to their limited resources. It is also possible to continue to represent them as acts of individual self-sacrifice, inspired by hatred of foreign intruders, religious vision, vengeance, or psychological disorder.

Such interpretations have been suggested not only for these operations, but for comparable instances at other times and places in Islamic history.[4]

But knowing the identities of the "self-martyrs" (or at least their alleged identities) while not banishing other interpretations, does suggest new possibilities. The one that emerges with the least coaxing is the existence of a social dimension of sacrifice in the operations. This dimension is still partly obscured from view, for the biographical accounts completely conceal the identities and methods of those who sponsored the "self-martyrs." The moment we become acquainted with Ahmad Qusayr and Bilal Fahs, however, we realize that while "self-martyrs" sacrificed themselves, they were also sacrificed by others. They were selected, prepared, and guided toward their "self-martyrdom," a fact admitted in a general manner in the announcements published by sponsoring organizations after the operations. The "self-martyring" operations combined self-sacrifice and sacrifice, and blurred the distinction between the two. It is not at all certain that the two elements can now be separated for purposes of analysis. The sacrificial dimension, though, was most transparent in a simple truth about the operations: the "self-martyrs" were not self-selected, but had to meet criteria that were socially and culturally defined.

The precise criteria for selection were never made explicit, but the selected "self-martyrs" shared a number of characteristics that were valued above others. First, they had to be male. That this constituted a form of selection became evident in 1985, when a Syrian-backed nationalist party launched a wave of similar operations that included several women, among them Shi'ites. The laws of sacred war in Islam do not permit women to serve as combatants, and for Hizbullah or Amal to have employed women in these operations would have undermined their character as sacred acts of war. This position was explained by one of Hizbullah's clerics:

One of the nationalist women asked me, does Islam permit a women to join in military operations of the resistance to the occupation, and would she go to paradise if she were martyred? The jihad in Islam is forbidden to women except in self-defense and in the absence of men. In the presence of men, the jihad is not permissible for women. My answer to this woman was that her jihad was impermissible regardless of motive or reason. She could not be considered a martyr were she killed, because the view of the law is clear. There can be no martyrdom except in the path of God. That means that every martyr will rise to paradise. I do not deny the value of the nationalist struggle (nidal) against Israel, but the jihad of women is impermissible in the presence of men. I do not deny women of the right to confront the enemy, but we must ask whether all of the nationalist men are gone so that only the women are left, or whether their men have become women and their women have become men.[5]

This position was confirmed after the "self-martyrdom" of Bilal Fahs, when his fiancée sought to "join him in paradise" by undertaking an operation similar to his. Despite well-publicized efforts, she found no cleric prepared to declare her sacrifice permissible.

Second, the "self-martyrs" had to be old enough to be deemed individually responsible for their acts, yet too young to have incurred the obligations of marriage. Their sacrifice could not be left open to the criticism that it had infringed upon the rights of parents or the claims of wives and children, from whom the planning of the act would have to be concealed. On the one hand, this meant that persons below a certain age could not be recruited. One of Hizbullah's clerics, asked whether young persons could fight without permission of parents, answered: "When the plan establishes the necessity of their going out to fight, then going out is obligatory, and the agreement of the two parents is not necessary. If their going out is not necessary in the framework of the plan, then they must consult with the two parents."[6] Since "self-martyrdom" did not demonstrably require a minor for operational purposes, and no parent would knowingly consent to participation of a son in such an operation, the employment of minors was virtually forbidden. Given the fact that death was assured in such operations, the same ban was extended to husbands and fathers. The sacred war of which the "self-martyring" operations were a part did include married men with families, some of whom were killed, but the "self-martyring" operations required more stringent limits. Given the early age of marriage in Lebanese Shi'ite society, this placed a low ceiling on the age of possible candidates. The remaining window of opportunity was correspondingly small. Ahmad Qusayr at 15 still lived at home, and was almost too dependent to qualify; Bilal Fahs at 17 was already engaged to be married, and almost too attached to qualify.

Third, the "self-martyr" could have no ties to anyone who might consider himself socially responsible for avenging the death against its sponsors, which would be conceivable were the operation to fail tactically. Ahmad Qusayr had no older brother, while Bilal Fahs was the sole product of a dissolved marriage without legal standing, and lived as an outcast. The lack of fundamental social ties—to responsible parents, dependent wives and children, avenging brothers—rendered both of these "self-martyrs" acceptable candidates for operations.

Finally, those selected for "self-martyrdom" had to have a minimal measure of pious intent, and no traits understood in surrounding society as signs of emotional disorder. This was usually demonstrated in a published will and the testimony of parents and friends. While the "self-martyr" obviously would have to be someone susceptible to suggestion, he could not be suicidal. If he were, his death would smack of exploitation, not devotion.

Selection of the "self-martyr," which is done secretly but on behalf of all, is thus a social and cultural selection. When the "self-martyring" operations are understood as collective rather than individual acts—as sacrificial acts—the dynamic of sacrificial competition becomes clear. That competition took place on the level of sponsorship, as Hizbullah and Amal sought to demonstrate their capacity for mobilizing the many resources necessary for the operations. The operations, far from demonstrating Shi'ite unity, proved to be a powerful indicator that a once-united community was rapidly heading toward civil war.

What were the origins of this escalating competition? Before Hizbullah's appearance, virtually all of Lebanon's Shi'ites identified with Amal, subsuming their profound differences under the mantle of a charismatic leader, Sayyid Musa al-Sadr. To carve a niche for itself, Hizbullah had worked upon those differences, splitting families, neighborhoods, villages, and towns along existing lines, and infusing ideas into existing rivalries and feuds. Hizbullah raced through Lebanon like a hundred rivers along the dry beds of division that break the Shi'ite landscape of Lebanon. The potential for reciprocal violence was enhanced by the influx of arms, provided to Amal by Syria and to Hizbullah by Iran. On more and more occasions, in local settings, small-scale violence erupted in the form of gunfire and kidnapping between Amal and Hizbullah.

For the first five years of Hizbullah's growth, that violence was contained and conflagration avoided. The clashes remained expressions of endemic local feuding that sought shelter in the distinction between Amal and Hizbullah. The much more consistent element in the relationship between the fraternal movements was imitative rivalry. They competed in professing their fealty to Khomeini, in distributing aid, in organizing marches, and in covering walls with posters. As the rivalry intensified, however, the pursuit of a balance became ever more fundamental to the preservation of peace—and ever more difficult to achieve. When Hizbullah took the dramatic and unprecedented step of launching "self-martyring" operations, Amal had no choice but to do the same. The sacrifice of Ahmad Qusayr (and the still unnamed "self-martyr" of Islamic Jihad who did a comparable operation a year later) sealed the fate of Bilal Fahs. Amal, too, would have to recruit and dispatch "self-martyrs."

It was at this point that the (obligatory) sacred war began to fade at its edges into (forbidden) sacrificial rite. Perhaps the first casualty of the competition was operational planning, which became less thorough as Hizbullah and Amal (soon joined by leftist and Syrian-sponsored parties) worked to outbid one another in the frequency of their operations. The sacrifice was no longer expected to obtain immediate results; "self-martyrdom" was presented increasingly as its own reward. Thus, for the Amal movement which sent Bilal Fahs to his death, the fact that he killed no one did not detract from the value of his sacrifice as a counterpoint to the sacrifice of Ahmad Qusayr. The monument that Amal erected to Bilal served the double function of commemorating the "self-martyr" and reminding the community that his sponsors commanded the resolve and resources to sacrifice him for the good of all.[7]

At the same time, Hizbullah and Amal sought to elevate the standard of the sacrificial "self-martyrs," by selecting slightly older youths who had more thorough religious and ideological commitment, and who had demonstrated the depth of their commitment by past participation in conventional operations. One such instance was the bombing organized by Hizbullah on 19 August 1988 that sacrificed a most promising cadre, Haytham Subhi Dabbuq, from Tyre. Dabbuq was twenty at the time of his operation. He had joined Hizbullah's Islamic Resistance at the age of fourteen, later participated in conventional operations, and once had been wounded. After graduating high school in 1986, he visited Iran, where he underwent religious and advanced military training.[8] From the point of view of selection, Dabbuq was the ideal "self-martyr." From a military standpoint, it was unfortunate that his operation failed to kill any Israelis, but his death had its own redemptive quality and demonstrated Hizbullah's willingness to sacrifice its most promising young recruits. As purer "self-martyrs" were offered for fewer immediate results, the measure of sacred war in the operations diminished, and that of sacrifice increased.

Yet the lives of the "self-martyrs" were a small price to pay for the Shi'ite peace. For these operations served to forestall the outbreak of fratricidal violence from within. The competitive cycle of sacrifice, done in the name of Islam, averted a competitive cycle of violence among adherents of Islam, between Hizbullah and Amal. The jihad, while liberating the believers from foreign intruders, also postponed the incipient *fitna*—the destructive strife that threatened Lebanon's Shi'ite community from within.

Rulings For and Against

Lebanon's Shi'ite clerics provided the legitimation of this balancing mechanism. They assured the "self-martyr" and his sponsors that his sacrifice enjoyed the highest sanction. According to one of Hizbullah's leading clerics,

> those who blew up the [U.S.] Marines headquarters and the Israeli military governate in Tyre [Ahmad Qusayr] did not martyr themselves in accord with a decision by a political party or movement. They martyred themselves because the Imam Khomeini permitted them to do so. They saw nothing before them but God, and they defeated Israel and America for God. It was the Imam of the Nation [Khomeini] who showed them this path and instilled this spirit in them.[9]

In addition to the role of the clerics in reassuring the "self-martyrs" themselves, the support of the community depended largely upon the verdict of clerics on the admissibility of the operations. Since Hizbullah and Amal entered the sacrificial competition also to win a larger share of Shi'ite allegiances, the sanction of the clerics was valued by both. It was widely understood that the "self-martyring" operations were religious acts, but only in an emotional sense. Religious feeling had helped to generate them, but in a raw and dangerous form with strong sacrificial overtones. They could be made *Islamic* only by sanctification, which takes the form of reconciliation between the act and abstract principle, done by those qualified to interpret sacred law.

The Shi'ite clerics had no difficulty in urging armed resistance to perceived enemies, and indeed did everything in their power to encourage it. They achieved this, at least in part, by the transference of Shi'ite anguish from self to other. That anguish found its most vivid ritual expression on Ashura, the annual Shi'ite day of mourning for the seventh-century martyrdom of the Imam Husayn at Karbala. There were some whose zeal for ritual self-flagellation on Ashura landed them in hospital, especially in Nabatiyya in the south, where the practice had the longest tradition in Lebanon. Hizbullah's spiritual mentor, Sayyid Muhammad Husayn Fadlallah, sought to transform such self-immolation into the immolation of others, when he called upon self-flagellants to desist from the practice and join the resistance against Israel:

> Do you want to suffer with Husayn? Then the setting is ready: the Karbala of the south. You can be wounded and inflict wounds, kill and be killed, and feel the spiritual joy that Husayn lived when he accepted the blood of his son, and the spiritual joy of Husayn when he accepted his own blood and wounds. The believing resisters in the border zone are the true self-flagellants, not the self-flagellants of Nabatiyya. Those who flog

themselves with swords, they are our fighting youth. Those who are detained in [the Israeli detention camp in] al-Khiyam, arrested by Israel in the region of Bint Jubayl, they are the ones who feel the suffering of Husayn and Zaynab. Those who suffer beatings on their chests and heads in a way that liberates, these are the ones who mark Ashura, in their prison cells.[10]

This kind of argument abolished a vital distinction, transforming struggle against the self—the ritual purpose of self-flagellation—into struggle against the other. Following the initial successes of the "self-martyrdom" operations, Shi'ite clerics were inclined to do the same, this time abolishing the distinction between death at the hands of others and death at one's own hands. Fadlallah argued that if the aim of one who destroyed himself in such an operation "is to have a political impact on an enemy whom it is impossible to fight by conventional means, then his sacrifice can be part of a jihad. Such an undertaking differs little from that of a soldier who fights and knows that in the end he will be killed. The two situations lead to death; except that one fits in with the conventional procedures of war, and the other does not."[11] In another formulation, he determined that "the Muslims believe that you struggle by transforming yourself into a living bomb like you struggle with a gun in your hand. There is no difference between dying with a gun in your hand or exploding yourself."[12] "What is the difference between setting out for battle knowing you will die *after* killing ten [of the enemy], and setting out to the field to kill ten and knowing you will die *while* killing them?"[13] There could be no more thorough endorsement of a technique that seemed to border two forbidden acts: sacrifice and suicide.

Yet the ratio of ten to one could not be guaranteed, and when it dropped precipitously, the sacrificial dimension of the operations came into clearer focus. At that point, although operations continued to contribute to the inner equilibrium of the community, they lost their value as acts of war. On that score, some Shi'ite clerics began to reason that the "self-martyring" operations had lost their Islamic justification. A failed military tactic now threatened to degenerate into a purely sacrificial rite; when it appeared more sinful than saintly, it had to be stopped.

The Shi'ite clerics therefore issued a conditional ban. According to Fadlallah, "we believe that self-martyring operations should only be carried out if they can bring about a political or military change in proportion to the passions that incite a person to make of his body an explosive bomb." He deemed past operations against Israeli forces "successful in that they significantly harmed the Israelis. But the present circumstances do not favor such operations anymore, and attacks that only inflict limited casualties (on the enemy) and destroy one building should not be encouraged, if the price is the death of the person who carries them out."[14] "The self-martyring operation is not permitted unless it can convulse the enemy. The believer cannot blow himself up unless the results will equal or exceed the [loss of the] soul of the believer. Self-martyring operations are not fatal accidents but legal obligations governed by rules, and the believers cannot transgress the rules of God."[15]

This ruling undermined the sacrificial cycle that had bound up Hizbullah and Amal in a competitive race to produce "self-martyrs." A few more operations were launched, at very wide intervals of time, but the field was largely left to smaller factions, whose sponsorship of additional operations did not threaten either Hizbullah or Amal.

Civil War

Yet the de-escalation of the sacrificial cycle between Hizbullah and Amal did not end their fraternal rivalry. Indeed, when the cycle was broken, the violence turned inward upon Lebanon's Shi'ites, in the form of a fratricidal war.

On one morning in January 1989, several Shi'ite villages in the area known as the "Apple Region" of south Lebanon became a killing ground. In the early hours before dawn, a group of several hundred Hizbullah fighters, with photographs of Khomeini affixed to their chests, entered the villages by surprise, but this time their targets were not Israelis. Instead they sought out sleeping adherents of the rival Amal movement. In the darkness of the night, a massacre ensued. Some of the victims were shot; others had their throats cut. In a few instances, the killing engulfed the families of the victims. This was later confirmed when photographers and cameramen entered the villages. One villager, choking back tears and standing over a pool of blood in his garden, told of how two masked men of Hizbullah had seized a member of Amal and slaughtered him "like a sheep." Clerics in Beirut had to issue rulings prohibiting the deliberate mutilation of bodies.

"The day will never come when Shi'ites fight one another," Fadlallah had declared only a year earlier. Those who saw the rivalry and predicted fighting did not understand the Shi'ite community, he said. It had multiple mechanisms of mediation, and a strong taboo against shedding Shi'ite blood.[16] Was he sure Hizbullah and Amal would not fight? "I'm one hundred percent sure," he had replied.[17] Not only was Fadlallah wrong. His own endorsement of the "self-martyring" operations had helped to make a fatal suggestion: that one Muslim might legitimately consign another to death in the name of Islam.

For two years, Lebanon's Shi'ite community descended into *fitna*—internal strife, the antithesis of sacred war, pitting brother against brother. As Israel withdrew to a narrow belt in south Lebanon, Hizbullah and Amal contested the ground they had liberated, and the conflict that had always existed between them threatened to rise up and gut the Shi'ite community itself. The fratricide began in early 1988. Then came assassinations: one of Hizbullah's clerics was shot dead in an ambush done by Amal, two of Amal's foremost leaders in the south were gunned down in their car by Hizbullah. The weekly newspapers of both movements repeatedly published photographs of the bullet-torn bodies of the slain leaders. For sheer ferocity, these recurrent clashes matched any conflict between militias from different confessional communities. Clerics in the community appealed for an end to the conflict and banned the killing of Muslims by Muslims, but to no avail.

The revolution in Lebanese Shi'ism now threatened not the world, but the Shi'ites themselves. The violence was perhaps that same violence which attended the birth of Shi'ism. It had been suppressed and subsumed, until all that remained was the sacrifice of tears, shed once a year for the martyrdom of the Imam Husayn. But by the 1980s, that violence had broken free of the bonds of pious restraint. Self-repentance yielded to self-flagellation, then to sacred war and individual "self-martyrdom." With the passage to fratricide, some in Lebanon's Shi'ite community shed the last restraint.

The successive rounds of bitter fighting ended only after a thousand Shi'ites had died. Syria and Iran negotiated a truce in late 1990, and it has held, but the scars remain. In 1993, Fadlallah claimed that "extensive cooperation and coordination" had been established between Hizbullah and Amal. But he also admitted that "some time is needed before all the residual negative sentiments that surfaced due to the conflict can be erased."[18] Vengeance was the deepest of these "residual negative sentiments," and it became the ever-present shadow of the Shi'ites. It remained to be seen whether the Shi'ites of Lebanon would ever again be completely free of the temptations of self-immolation, and the threat of self-destruction.

Notes

1. Ahmad Qusayr's identity was first revealed in Hizballah's weekly newspaper, *Al-Ahd* (Beirut), 24 May 1985.
2. The biographical information, draws on the obituaries reproduced in *Al-Amaliyyat al-istishhadiyya: watha'iq wa-suwar: al-muqawama al-wataniyya al-lubnaniyya, 1982–1985* (Damascus: Al-Markaz al-arabi lil-ma'lumat, 1985), 22–35.
3. Details on Fahs and photographs, *Al-Amaliyyat al-istishhadiyya*, 68–81.
4. See Stephen Frederic Dale, "Religious Suicide in Islamic Asia: Anticolonial Terrorism in India, Indonesia, and the Philippines," *Journal of Conflict Resolution* (Beverly Hills) 32, no. 1 (March 1988): 37–59.
5. Interview with Shaykh Abd al-Karim Ubayd, *Al-Safir* (Beirut), 28 July 1986.
6. Al-Sayyid Muhammad Husayn Fadlallah, *Al-Muqawama al-Islamiyya: Afaq wa-tatallu'at* (Beirut: Lajnat Masjid al-Imam al-Rida, 1985), 118.
7. A photograph of this monument appears in the Lebanese weekly *Nouveau Magazine*, 17 June 1989, p. 60.
8. Dabbuq's obituary in *Al-Ahd*, 9 September 1988.
9. Speech by Sayyid Ibrahim al-Amin, *Al-Ahd*, 23 January 1987.
10. Speech by Fadlallah, *Al-Nahar* (Beirut), 27 September 1985.
11. Interview with Fadlallah, *Politique internationale*, no. 29 (Autumn 1985), 268.
12. Interview with Fadlallah, *Middle East Insight* (Washington) 4, no. 2 (June-July 1985), 10–11.
13. Al-Sayyid Muhammad Husayn Fadlallah, *Al-Muqawama al-Islamiyya fil-janub wal-Biqa al-Gharbi wa-Rashayya: tatallu'at wa-afaq; Nass al-muhadara allati alqaha samahat al-allama al-mujahid al-Sayyid Muhammad Husayn Fadlallah fi kulliyat idarat al-a'mal wal-iqtisad al-far' al-awwal, bi-ta'rikh 19 Shawwal 1404 al-muwafiq 18 Tammuz 1984* (n.p., n.d.), p. 18.
14. Interview with Fadlallah, *Monday Morning* (Beirut), 16 December 1985. Fadlallah specifically mentioned the operation undertaken by Ahmad Qusayr in Tyre, as well as a later operation near Metulla, as "successful."
15. Speech by Fadlallah, *Al-Nahar*, 14 May 1985.
16. Fadlallah interview, *Al-Nahar al-arabi wal-duwali*, 21 February 1988.
17. Fadlallah interview, *Nouveau Magazine*, 27 February 1988.
18. Fadlallah interview, *Kayhan* (Tehran), 3 March 1993.

14

France Held Hostage

In 1978, the Ayatollah Ruhollah Khomeini arrived in the Parisian suburb of Neauphle-le-Château following his expulsion from Iraq. The Shah of Shahs was threatened by a rising tide of dissent, and prevailed upon Iraq to eject the still obscure and aged cleric from his place of exile in the shrine city of Najaf. The Shah wished to distance Khomeini from Iran's borders, and France seemed sufficiently removed from the eye of the storm.

In fact, Parisian exile made Khomeini's appeal for revolution far more effective and audible. He and his disciples now had easy access to the international media and could direct-dial their supporters in Iran, carefully setting the cadence of escalation. Ultimately the Shah left for his own exile and Khomeini returned to Tehran on a triumphant direct flight from Paris. He descended to the tarmac on the supporting arm of an Air France pilot.

French policymakers had every cause to believe that their political hospitality had sowed the seeds of a privileged relationship with Iran. But the plant yielded bitter fruit. In the course of the subsequent decade, France and the Islamic Republic of Iran collided in spectacular and deadly ways. French aircraft and arms, sold in massive quantities to Iraq, took a daily toll in Iranian lives following the outbreak of the Iran-Iraq war in 1980. Iranian bombs, planted by Shi'ite operatives, claimed French lives in the rubble-strewn alleyways of Beirut and on the best shopping streets of Paris. Both sides took prisoners. Iran's agents in France were arrested, imprisoned, and expelled. Frenchmen in Lebanon—journalists, diplomats, bystanders—were abducted and held hostage by Iran's Shi'ite clients. By 1986, the hostage-holders in Lebanon had driven the French government into a corner, while bomb makers sent by Iran succeeded in placing the populace of Paris under virtual siege.

Five recent books bear witness to different aspects of the undeclared but dirty little war that raged between France and Iran in the 1980s. Two describe the frustration and growing desperation of the French official classes as they suffered blow after blow in a war they had failed to anticipate. Two other books are personal testimonies by two victimized bystanders, one a hostage, the other the wife of a hostage. The last, on the Lebanese Hizbullah, is an attempt to define an adversary whose power to elude definition was its greatest asset. While all of these books were written for a general audience (four of them by journalists), they are also bound to serve as grist for the busy mills of scholarship.

Between Baghdad and Tehran

Pierre Péan is an investigative journalist well known for his ability to ferret out information on the inner workings of the Élysée, government ministries, and intelligence agencies. Most of his book, *La menace*, is a painstaking reconstruction of French policy toward the Islamic Republic of Iran from the outbreak of the Gulf War until the so-called "war of the embassies" in 1987.[1]

Péan maps the principal corridors of policy, which he follows meticulously to a single conclusion: a powerful pro-Iraqi lobby compromised France's neutrality in the Gulf conflict. This lobby assured that the government approved massive arms sales and high technology transfers to Iraq (including nuclear reactor technology) largely on credit extended by France. An official embargo on sales to Iran accentuated the imbalance. Thus France unwittingly became a co-belligerent of Iraq in the Gulf War—unwittingly, because the architects of French policy assumed that such sales did not constitute acts of aggression. For Iran, however, the distinction between the sale and use of arms appeared arbitrary, despite its roots in the common law of Western nations. Péan himself seems to postulate a moral equivalence between Iran's spawning of deadly terror and France's dealing in deadly arms. It is an argument not without philosophical merit.

Péan thus claims to have uncovered what might be called an "Iraqgate." Private interests subverted France's declared policy of neutrality in the Gulf War, at the very moment when White House zealots subverted American neutrality by trading arms for hostages. (Péan is aware of the parallels, and a chapter is devoted to the arms-for-hostages escapades of the Americans.) Iran reacted by gradually escalating a campaign of intimidation, first in Lebanon, then in France itself. Péan does not excuse Iranian hostage-taking and terror bombing, which he clearly labels political extortion, but

French policy emerges from his narrative with scarcely more credit. The seemingly principled slogan that France would not become "hostage to the hostages" simply masked callous calculations made in favor of a blatantly pro-Iraqi policy.

In the end, of course, France did become "hostage to the hostages" who were taken at Iran's behest in Lebanon. Each night, the network news program of Antenne 2 reminded viewers of the French hostages' plight. Committees were organized on behalf of the journalists who had been seized, and they used their influence to keep the issue on front pages and television screens. The French government now had to take into account more than the demands of the pro-Iraqi lobbyists; it began a series of desultory negotiations with a bewildering array of intermediaries, both Iranian and Lebanese. Péan uses his unmatched sources to trace French diplomacy through the murkiest back channels to Iran's divided leadership.

During this trip through the looking glass, the French encountered a bizarre array of mediation impresarios as wondrous as the Iranian arms-dealer Manucher Ghorbanifar ("Gorba"), and as egotistical as Anglican superdealer Terry Waite. The most extraordinary of them all was Razah Raad, a Lebanese Shi'ite physician and naturalized Frenchman, formerly of Bidnayil in the Bekaa Valley, latterly of Argentan in Normandy, where he owned and inhabited a seventeenth-century château built by a duke. As the French hostages came to dominate the television news, it occurred to Dr. Raad that he might render his adopted country a service by mobilizing the extensive Raad clan to mediate among France, Iran, and the Shi'ite hostage-holders in Lebanon. Raad did have "fabulous contacts" in Shi'ite Lebanon, and disappeared for days into Beirut's southern suburbs, where he parleyed with representatives of the hostage-holders. Then he would reappear in West Beirut or Damascus, to deliver the latest terms. The mysterious missions of Raad clarified the demands of the hostage-holders, but produced no real progress. Neither did various French missions to Tehran and the mediation of several dubious Syrians—sometimes documented by Péan with leaked official documents.

When the holding of hostages failed to break French resolve, Iran finally moved to break the deadlock by inspiring an indiscriminate bombing campaign in Paris itself. There can be no doubt that these bombings, which killed eleven persons and wounded 275, finally broke the resolve of the French. It was one thing to suffer the embarrassment of impotence in the face of Shi'ite hostage-holders in Beirut, quite another to stand helpless before terror in Paris itself. The French government did not rush to surrender, as the "war of the embassies" demonstrated. (On that occasion, the French government launched a virtual siege of Iran's embassy in Paris, in order to force the surrender of an embassy employee suspected of involvement in the bombings. The effort failed when Iran retaliated in kind against the French embassy in Tehran.) In the final analysis, however, France lost the battle of wills, because it remained vulnerable to terror in its very capital. Faced with terror at home, Jacques Chirac opted for concessions to Iran. Iran, in turn, ordered an end to the bombing campaign and the release of French hostages in Lebanon.

Péan published his book shortly before this understanding was reached. Former Beirut correspondent Yves Loiseau has followed the story to its conclusion in *Le grand troc*, an extended chronology of the French hostage affair.[2] In a series of dated entries from 1985 to 1988, Loiseau follows the complex thread of statements, rumors, mediations, and negotiations which culminated in the "deal." While there are no startling revelations here, the presentation of the record could not be more systematic—and sobering.

With bombs going off on the Champs-Élysées and the Boulevard Saint-Michel, French officials concluded that victorious war could not be waged against terrorism, at least not by France. Moral posturing might suit the Americans, but the preservation of the very rhythm of life in France depended upon some compromise with the sponsors of terror. And did not France have a moral duty to negotiate for its citizens, held against their will simply because they were Frenchmen? In one of the more striking examples of Franco-American cultural divergence, the French public supported precisely the kind of dealing for hostages that absolutely scandalized the American public. Even the toughminded Loiseau, in a last section provocatively entitled "Lebanongate," indulges in the second thought that perhaps the freeing of the French hostages did justify "the means."

Yet only now is it becoming clear just how extraordinary those means were, involving direct negotiations with hostage-holders and the release of terrorists jailed in France for outrages. Mist still obscures the secret missions to Beirut of the famous "Stephani"—the false name of Jean-Charles Marchiani, former French intelligence operative and confidant of fellow Corsican Charles Pasqua, Chirac's interior minister. It was Marchiani who publicly delivered the French hostages from captivity. Was he a conduit for ransom to the hostage-holders? And just how far did the concessions to Iran go? In 1990, President François Mitterrand met a decade-old Iranian

demand for the pardon of four men convicted for their botched assassination attempt against Iranian opposition leader Shapour Bakhtiar in Paris. A
bystander and a policeman were killed in that attempt; another policeman
was paralyzed for life. Will that release ultimately serve as a precedent
for Fouad Ali Saleh, the Tunisian recruit to Iran's cause, whom a French
court sentenced to life in 1990 for masterminding the fatal bombings in
Paris? There are still loose ends to the "deal"—and room for a sequel to
these two books.

The Beirut Hostages

For one French hostage, the "deal" came too late. Michel Seurat, a young
sociologist of Islam, had done original work on Sunni fundamentalism in
Tripoli, and had begun researching Shi'ite fundamentalism in Beirut. In
May 1985, he flew back to Beirut from Morocco, where he had attended an
academic conference on "Terrorism, Violence, and the City." En route from
airport to city, Seurat (and French journalist Jean-Paul Kauffmann) were
dragged from their taxi and taken hostage by Islamic Jihad.

In Tripoli, Seurat had moved with ease among Sunni fundamentalists,
then locked in a struggle with Syria. His work on their movement combined
sociological insight with an understanding gained through direct experience,[3] but the Shi'ite neighborhoods of Beirut were not the quarter of Bâb
Tebbâné in Tripoli. Both were societies under siege, but Seurat's Shi'ite
captors played on a global stage, in a struggle that did not admit the neutrality of a sociologist of Islam. The "brethren" of Seurat's abductors had
been condemned in Kuwait for a series of bombings, including an attack
on the French embassy there. Seurat was seized in order to force France
to press for release of their "brethren."

Les corbeaux d'Alep is a brief but fascinating memoir written by
Seurat's Syrian wife, Marie.[4] It is really two books. One is an account
of her fruitless efforts on behalf of her husband—efforts that took her to
the chambers of Hizbullah's spiritual mentor, to the bases of Hizbullah in
the Bekaa Valley, and through the labyrinth of French officialdom. Marie
Seurat's insights cut to the bone: the dissembling Shi'ite clerics and militiamen, the ponderous French diplomats, the drama-mongers of the media,
are all portrayed with the blackest cynicism. This is a faithful guide to the
terrors of the purgatory inhabited by all families of hostages.

Yet this is also a book about personal transformation. Marie Seurat began her ordeal as a self-obsessed woman from a prosperous Syrian Christian family—a lady most at home in the world of Alfa Romeos, doting servants, and male suitors. Even her marriage to a leftist French sociologist with Palestinian sympathies was a kind of self-indulgence, not a true rebellion. With her husband's abduction, however, she was suddenly thrust into a violent labyrinth, without the compass of political savvy and without the rosary of religious faith carried by the wives of so many hostages. The absence of faith cost her dearly. When she reached the depths of her own despair, she turned to clairvoyants and astrologers, who promised to divine the fate of her husband. Ultimately she became so emotionally overwrought that she required some hospitalization. Yet for most of her ordeal, she not only kept her wits about her, but succeeded in penetrating the ritual posturing that surrounds every hostage affair.

The most remarkable passage in this remarkable book concerns the author's visit to her husband during his captivity. The visit was a privilege enjoyed by no other hostage of Islamic Jihad, and Michel Seurat, as a sympathetic student of Islam, did enjoy a privileged standing among the hostages. He received books of his choice and letters. During the visit, he told his wife that he wished to stay in Beirut even after his eventual release. "I still have many things to do here. My captors and the leader of the group have agreed to allow me to move about the southern suburbs. I could finish my study of the Shiʿite fundamentalists. . . . I must finish what I've started."

Seurat, alas, overestimated the value of his sympathetic scholarship to his captors. He could not escape categorization as a hostage, valued solely as a bargaining chip in a game played against the government of France. In his wife's view, media attention only raised the asking price for her husband's release, a view that put her at odds with the spouses of other hostages. (Nor did it help that in years past, Seurat had published a number of anti-Syrian articles under a pseudonym.) Islamic Jihad thus ignored an exceptional appeal on Seurat's behalf made by leading Lebanese Muslim figures, including the spiritual mentor of Hizbullah.

It was here that bad luck intervened. Seurat contracted viral hepatitis before Iran had asserted its prior claim to Islamic Jihad's French hostages. The illness reduced him to crawling on all fours, and the unavailability of proper treatment finally finished him. He reportedly lies buried in the cemetery of Rawdat al-Shahidayn, resting place of the martyrs of Hizbullah. For Marie Seurat, Islamic Jihad's refusal to release her husband, even as death hovered, was the final irony. Michel Seurat had showed the "Partisans of God" the sympathy of true fascination, and was rewarded with abduction and death. "The Arabist has been assassinated by the Arabs. The specialist who consults the Qur'an has been put to death by the fundamentalists. The Orientalist has been killed by his Orient. Even his death has betrayed him." The courage of this book lies in Marie Seurat's admission that her husband was blinded by his own "expertise"—that his sympathies conspired with his abductors to kill him.

The gods, in their unfathomable logic, looked down with greater favor upon Roger Auque. This journalist was abducted in January 1987 by the Revolutionary Justice Organization, a group of uncertain composition that enjoyed Iranian sanction. Auque spent over ten months in captivity before he was released as part of the "deal."

Published testimonies of former hostages are now quite numerous. The genre is not without literary potential, but no former hostage has effectively worked the experience into narrative. Yet in every such account, there are passages which do convey the overwhelming sense of loss that afflicts every hostage. There are quite a few such passages in Auque's memoir, *Un otage à Beyrouth*.[5] On one memorable page, he recreates his own reaction when the wife of a guard sprays perfume on his hand. "Anaïs, Cacherel," she confides to the blindfolded Auque. The rekindling of this sensation—a scent of femininity and freedom, introduced into the windowless, narrow space of a Beirut hostage—sets Auque's mind racing in every direction. Moments of fear, anger, despair, anticipation—Auque leaves us with a vivid impression of the intensity of a hostage's emotions, but for any hostage held over months or years, such moments are flashes in a dark expanse of boredom and isolation. No former hostage has yet found a way to convey the tyranny of that boredom without boring readers as well.

Nevertheless, Auque's account, like those of other hostages, does contain a rare kind of evidence. All foreign hostages were kept in the dark about the identity of their captors and their own place in the game. Foreign hostages spent most of their time behind blindfolds, sometimes alone, sometimes with other hostages. Yet the hostages had to be guarded, spinning threads of human contact between guard and hostage. Auque reports several conversations with his guards, and this table talk reveals much about the small cogs in the Revolutionary Justice Organization. Auque soon became convinced that his keepers were not fundamentalists at all. Most were preoccupied with money, women, and films. (According to testimony of other hostages, this was not the case with Islamic Jihad's gaolers, who had found true religion. Seurat reportedly described them as "neither human nor inhuman, but non-human.") Auque's reportage is telling evidence that Iran did not rely wholly upon religious zealots to supply it with French hostages. Iran discreetly created a demand for foreigners of certain nationalities; enterprising Lebanese answered that demand.

Captivity, though, is hardly the ideal vantage-point from which to view Iran's Lebanese involvement as a whole. One journalist who played the game carefully, got his information, and got out, has written the best single account of Hizbullah in French. Gilles Delafon arrived in Beirut in 1985, as a young journalist working for Europe 1 and the weekly magazine *Le Point*. The big story, of course, was the French hostages, and Delafon pursued it by making connections in the Shi'ite community. Delafon is a talented journalist, even if his style tends to the dramatic, and he has drawn a lively portrait of Hizbullah, entitled *Beyrouth: Les soldats de l'Islam*.[6] While the book tells the usual story of hostage-taking and hijacking, it also goes a step further in seeking to uncover the social foundations of Hizbullah.

In this respect, the chapter entitled "Les dollars de l'Iran" is the most valuable in the book. Elaborate rumors always circulated about Iranian financing of Hizbullah, especially regarding the sum total of the assistance. The oft-repeated figures were simple guesses. It is unlikely that even the Iranians knew how much they were spending in Lebanon, since the disbursements were made by different and often competing agencies. Delafon is not concerned with putting an arbitrary price tag on the value of Iranian aid, but instead seeks to illustrate the many ways in which this money reached and affected the Shi'ite community of Lebanon. Readers will wonder at the details in this chapter, for Delafon credits no sources. There is no need for bafflement. Delafon has gone through Hizbullah's own weekly newspaper, *Al-Ahd*, which is brimming with information about Iranian aid to university students and the activities of the Reconstruction Jihad and the Martyrs' Foundation.

The other chapters are rather less well grounded, if only because so many of Hizbullah's doings remain shrouded in secrecy and disinformation. Lots of livelihoods have been made over the years by providing "inside information" on the identities of clandestine operatives and the whereabouts of hostages. Yet Delafon shows discretion in sifting through what he hears, and he has avoided the usual traps laid by disinformants. His principal advantage seems to be that while other journalists often have relied on

(Christian) East Beirut sources for information on Hizbullah, Delafon had lots of leads in the Shi'ite Amal movement. Many of these leads had family members and acquaintances in Hizbullah, and so could provide Delafon with useful details and quotable opinions. These voices do not come from within Hizbullah, but they very much evoke the voices of Amal members who have crossed the line time and again into Hizbullah.

Still, much of this book relies on published sources, and it is unfortunate that Delafon does not cite them. No doubt this reflects the widespread aversion of French journalists to footnotes. (Péan has no use for them either.) A work of high journalism, though, should show its respect for serious readers—and acknowledge the author's own debts—by making explicit reference to sources. An example of the proper journalistic mode of citation was provided by Robin Wright in *Sacred Rage*—an example certainly known to Delafon, who relies extensively upon Wright at several points in his book. Since Delafon avers that it is impossible to thank his live informants by name, it is all the more regrettable that he did not reference his many published sources.

As it is, one never quite knows whether Delafon is reporting something he has seen, heard, or read. In one typical instance, he tells the story of the ceremony for laying the cornerstone of a new mosque in the obscure village of Zabbud, northeast of Baalbek in the Bekaa Valley (pp. 123–24). The vivid details given by Delafon leave the strong impression that he personally witnessed this (minor) event deep within Hizbullah's space, which would have been remarkable indeed. In fact his account is drawn completely from issue 173 of Hizbullah's weekly newspaper, which incorporates precisely the same details. (Another account also appeared in the Lebanese daily *Al-Nahar* on 12 October 1987). There is a minor deception at work here—one that detracts from the documentary value of Delafon's own personal testimony. For it is never clear where that testimony ends and reliance on others begins.

When these books were written, Iran still loomed in Western imaginations as an outlaw state, defiant of all international norms and supportive of terrorism. Since then, Khomeini has died, the Iran-Iraq war has ended in a cease-fire, and France's relationship with Iran has been "normalized." What, then, is the enduring significance of the outcome of Iran's unconventional war against France?

Precedents were set which may embolden other Middle Eastern states or movements to collect French hostages or bomb Paris shops. In the Gulf conflict of the 1980s, the occasional resort to terrorism became routinized;

so, too, did the occasional capitulation to terrorism. The 1990s now have ushered in other conflicts. France, having sowed the wind, may yet reap the whirlwind.

Notes

1. Pierre Péan, *La menace* (Paris: Fayard, 1987).
2. Yves Loiseau, *Le grand troc: Le labyrinthe des otages français au Liban* (Paris: Hachette, 1988).
3. His articles were collected and republished posthumously. See Michel Seurat, *L'État de barbarie* (Paris: Seuil, 1989).
4. Marie Seurat, *Les corbeaux d'Alep* (Paris: Gallimard/Lieu Commun, 1988). The book is now available in English as *Birds of Ill Omen*, trans. Dorothy S. Blair (London: Quartet, 1990).
5. Roger Auque (in collaboration with Patrick Forestier), *Un otage à Beyrouth* (Paris: Filipacchi, 1988).
6. Gilles Delafon, *Beyrouth: Les soldats de l'Islam* (Paris: Stock, 1989).

15

Islam and the West (including Manhattan)

On a weekend in New York in June 1993, the Middle East Institute at Columbia University convened a conference with the title, "Under Siege: Islam and Democracy." Invitations to the conference spoke of a "gathering atmosphere of crisis" that had "stimulated in this country a sense of confrontation between Islam and democracy," and that the organizers hoped their conference would help to "dispel." That ominous atmosphere of crisis, the invitation asserted, had "most recently been fueled by reactions to the bombing of the World Trade Center" the previous February.[1]

Thus, while downtown New York limped from a blast that had killed six, injured one thousand, and done half-a-billion-dollars' worth of damage, uptown New York anguished over the "reactions" to the blast—as if they, and not the terrorist act itself, were what had inflamed the "crisis." To the assembled academics, the worrisome "reactions" included, no doubt, any number of newspaper headlines in the style of "Muslim Arrested."

But in point of fact, Muslims *had* been arrested—men whose commitment to their understanding of Islam provided motive for their acts. Within days of the bombing, evidence collected by the FBI had produced a strong *prima facie* case against a number of recent immigrants from Arab countries, who were duly arrested and charged. Prior to their arrest, the suspects had frequented the Jersey City mosque of Shaykh Umar Abd al-Rahman, confidant of the assassins of Egyptian President Anwar al-Sadat, who had been using his American pulpit to lambaste the West and preach Islamic revolution in Egypt. The press, the public, and agencies of public order thus had every reason to ask whether the bombing had been intended, by some stretch of logic, to serve the interests of Islam.

Fortunately, even as the participants at Columbia's conference busily deconstructed the media's putative bias against Islam, the authorities understood that the most dangerous possible effect of the World Trade

Center bombing was not offensive headlines or attacks by bigots against innocent Arab-Americans. It was more bombings. Their hunch resulted in the arrest of eight more of the Shaykh's acolytes and translators, allegedly caught in the act of mixing fertilizer and diesel fuel, with which they intended to deconstruct U.N. and FBI headquarters, as well as the Lincoln and Holland tunnels. The Columbia conferees had hoped to "contribute to a *modus vivendi* between Islam and the West." A week later, the FBI's round of arrests made a more thorough contribution to just that end.

Through all this, it was hard to discern any serious effort to place the bombing and arrests in a credible context. Following the capture of the alleged conspirators in the U.N. bomb plot, New York Mayor David Dinkins adopted what by then had become the characteristic tone of evasion. In warning New Yorkers against projecting "outrage onto the whole community from which these individuals came," the mayor did his civic duty, but he leaped headlong into surmise when he determined that "these are individuals acting on their own, or in concert among other criminal collaborators." In fact, there was every likelihood that the bombing was political as well as criminal, and that its political context extended far beyond New York.

Dinkins could be excused—he was out of his depth—but many of America's academic interpreters of Islam, at the Columbia conference and elsewhere, seconded such evasions. Some simply averred that the bombing and foiled conspiracy, even if hatched by Muslims, had nothing to do with any extant reading of Islam. Some offered that the bombing was the work of "extremists," who could only be undermined by supporting "moderates." (On further elaboration, these "moderates" often turned out to be other Islamic fundamentalists, who may have drawn the line at blowing up skyscrapers and traffic tunnels but otherwise subscribed to the same principles as the "extremists.") One instant expert, writing in the pages of *Foreign Affairs*, confidently categorized the bombing as an "isolated event" which only "frustrated Cold Warriors," sold on an "Islamic conspiracy theory," could possibly tie to other events like terrorist attacks in Egypt.

In short, conventional wisdom decreed that the bombing occurred in a vacuum: it was pathological, not political. This abdication on the part of the professional interpreters of Islam left it to the investigative press to draw an outline of the suspects' murky world. Intensified reportage from New York, Khartoum, and Cairo began to untangle an informal but far-flung network of Islamic activism—a network that most academic experts had denied even existed. Many of the threads led by twists and turns back to Afghanistan, where Arab Muslim money and volunteers had contributed to the successful jihad against Soviet forces in the 1980s.

This reportage also raised an issue that has yet to be addressed: the extent to which the U.S., which also backed the Afghan jihad, coddled its Arab veterans with visas and other protection after the war ended. Shaykh Abd al-Rahman himself had been a fundraiser and meddler in Afghanistan. The State Department's lame explanation for his (repeated) entries into the U.S.—a computer error—suggested a preference for evasion in government as well.

In any case, were it not for the press, whose coverage of Islam is routinely maligned for its supposed bias, none of these fascinating lines of inquiry would have been opened up. A public hungry for analysis would have had to subsist only on the thin gruel of banalities served up by the scholars.

That which American academics and officials evaded, many Arab interpreters openly denied. They professed astonishment that anyone could attribute the planning or execution of such an attack to any Arab or Muslim. Rather than admit even the remote possibility, they did what they have long done: they blamed the Mossad, Israel's secret service, or they simply blamed the Jews.

This view was not confined to the fundamentalist fringe press (where it flourished). It also surfaced in some of the leading newspapers in the Arab world. The columnists of the Cairo daily *Al-Ahram*, which purports to be the most respected of Arab newspapers, led the charge. One writer announced with certainty that "the Islamic groups could not have carried out such an action," because it "would have such serious repercussions for them. Many of them could find no better place than the West, and particularly the United States, to take refuge in." Nor could any Palestinian have done it, for the same reason. But Israel, the writer went on, sought to tarnish the image of the Arabs, and to undermine Arab and Muslim communities in Europe and America through its agents. The conclusion: "Look for Israel's and the Mossad's hand in this dirty operation."

Another columnist in *Al-Ahram* called the plotters behind the bombing both "devilish and clever," since they had found in Muhammad Salameh, the principal suspect, someone combining the perfect features of a fall guy: he was a Palestinian, at one time he carried an Egyptian passport, and he belonged to a group of Muslim extremists. "Some widespread international planning must have gone into finding this needle in the haystack," the writer insinuated, and then supplied the clue:

> The only way to put the puzzle together is to resort to the Israeli Mossad. It alone is capable of deciphering the act, pinpointing the real culprits, and revealing the real objectives behind this terrorist action, which ultimately serves only one party—which is, coincidentally or not, Israel itself.

If the responsible Arab press fingered the Mossad, others in the Arab world glared accusingly at the inhabitants of New York, who deserved divine retribution. Hizbullah's radio in Lebanon offered this commentary: "We have the right to ask about the crazy and shameless residents of New York, its gangsters, nightclubs, and brothels. The answer emerges very clearly that the explosion that rocked New York merely expressed its identity." This apocalyptic vision gained respectability in a column in the Beirut daily *Al-Safir*, the newspaper that is supposed to represent the views of the serious, progressive left.

> New York is the city of crime, the Mafia, and organized gangsters who are stronger than armies. It is the jungle where one cannot move without fearing for one's life. New York is the capital of the Jews with all their perversions, including politics, sex, media, forgery, cinema, drugs, and money laundering. It is the greatest arena for crime, most terrible fortress of discrimination, and ugliest example of class and race oppression.

New Yorkers, the columnist concluded, were thus in no position to claim that terror came to their city only when the "dark-skinned and red-eyed Arabs appeared."

Migrants and Narratives

The press of Cairo and Beirut will continue to debate whether the bombing of the World Trade Center was a Mossad plot or a blast of hellfire, but for the people most at risk, the question is whether the bombing was indeed the disembodied work of individual criminals, cut loose from any known reading of Islam. Those who take this view may imagine that they are promoting interfaith understanding, but it is an approach that misses the bombing's import entirely—and perhaps helps to invite its repetition.

There *is* a wider context. The Al-Salaam mosque in Jersey City stands at the far edge of a vast pool of resentment in Islam, fed by a steady stream of fundamentalist complaint against the West in general and the United States in particular. The collapse of the Soviet Union, the survival of the United States as the sole great power, the slogan of a "new world order"—these developments have brought that pool of resentment to overflowing. The bombing should be read as a warning: that a part of Islam dissents from the new ascendancy of the United States. Evasion and denial will not make this animus disappear.

The first context to be grasped is the world inhabited by the defendants in the bombing and conspiracy. As fundamentalists and immigrants, they personify the discontent that afflicts much of Islam today. Fundamentalism and migration have been the two major avenues of escape from the desperate crisis that now besets Muslim countries. They are also the two major sources of friction between Islam and the West. It is at the points of overlap between them, in storefront mosques from Brooklyn, New York, to Bradford, England, that angry preaching wins an especially attentive hearing.

For growing numbers of the young, the poor, and the credulous in the lands of Islam, fundamentalism has provided both escape and hope in circumstances that grow more dire with each passing year. These movements express a widespread frustration at the inability of regimes to deliver on the promise of a quantum leap to power and prosperity, whether by imitation of the Soviet model or by mimicry of capitalism. In appealing to that frustration, fundamentalists propose to abandon all the political and social models of the West. Instead, raising the slogan "Islam is the solution," they offer the vague but alluring ideas of Islamic government and Islamic economics. Most importantly, they hold the West responsible for the present malaise of Islam—a malaise that is understood to be the result of a deliberate Western effort to destroy Islam.

So far, this brand of fundamentalism has seized power only in Islamic lands more distant from the West—Iran in the heart of Asia, Sudan in the heart of Africa. But recently Islamic fundamentalism has made impressive gains on the Muslim shores of the Mediterranean, especially in Algeria, Tunisia, Egypt, Lebanon, and Turkey. These are the Muslim societies closest to the West in geography and culture, and the spread of Islamic fundamentalism there is compelling evidence for the depth of the crisis in Islam. The zealots have yet to acquire power in a Mediterranean country, but they have come close in Algeria, and they may yet make a serious bid in Egypt.

Muslim immigration to the West has been an equally telling sign of crisis. This immigration, especially to Western Europe and North America, is a result of the vast asymmetry of opportunity between the economies of the West and Islam. Since decolonization, the movement of millions of Muslims has rapidly transformed Islam into the second religion in much of the West. The influx continues unabated, as the fast-growing populations of Muslim countries far outstrip productive capacity.

In recent years, this immigration has taken on a new character, drawing upon more traditional classes in Muslim societies. For the newer immigrants, seeking a livelihood in the lands of unbelief is not without social stigma. Many of them have justified their choice by renouncing acculturation—this, at a time when economic recession in the West has diminished the willingness of host societies to assimilate foreigners anyway. The result has been a backlash of bigotry, epitomized by the repeated and sometimes deadly attacks on Muslim foreigners in Germany.

The prevalence of fundamentalism among more recent Muslim immigrants has tempted fundamentalist states and movements to open a second front in their struggle for political and cultural domination at home. The Paris bomb attacks of 1985 and 1986, the agitation against Salman Rushdie in Britain, and the bombing of the World Trade Center have uncovered remote outposts of Muslim resentment in the West that are highly susceptible to suggestion by fundamentalists abroad.

To be sure, the vast majority of Muslim immigrants to the West, including fundamentalists, have come in search of opportunity, and would never imagine committing acts of political violence. Still there are those who simply await a word of encouragement or inspiration offered by a visiting cleric or foreign diplomat. This is an unpleasant truth, but one which must no longer be ignored by immigration services, law-enforcement agencies, and organized Muslim communities themselves.

The second, broader context of the bombing has to do with what might be called the fundamentalists' narrative of history. According to this narrative, the grand objective, first of Christendom and then of the West, has been the subordination, if not the destruction, of Islam. The medieval Crusades represented the first attempt, but Islam contained and repelled that aggression, which ultimately left no trace. Modern European imperialism, a far more dynamic force, constituted the next attempt; this proved far more successful, bringing nearly all of Islam under European rule. While Europe promptly stole the wealth and independence of Muslims, it did not, however, succeed in destroying their identity. This tenacious preservation of identity has given them the power to rise up in wars of resistance, to reclaim their formal independence and control of their resources.

But now—the narrative continues—Islam faces the most dangerous and insidious challenge yet: America, as heir to Europe and hence to the role of leader of unbelief against Islam, has produced a model of culture, society, and politics that pretends to universal validity. This model exercises so seductive an appeal that it threatens to bring about what one fundamentalist thinker has called "the extinction of the distinctive identity of the Islamic community." This final assault on Islam is now concealed beneath the American slogan of a "new world order."

Rashid al-Ghannushi, exiled leader of the Tunisian Islamic movement, puts the case most succinctly. The "new world order," he says,

> is even more oppressive and severe than the old world order, which tried to banish Islam and ruin it. For the first time, the United Nations has become a real international government with a president—none other than the president of the United States. It has a legal branch to endorse American decisions—the Security Council—and an executive branch, in the form of the U.S. military. It has a financial apparatus—the World Bank and other giant financial institutions—and it has a massive media machine. Government by the United Nations is really government by the United States, which is the main characteristic of the "new world order." This "new world order," from the point of view of its intellectual content, its ideology, and its religion, isn't new. It is simply American hegemony over the world, clothed in the ideology of human rights.

This kind of logic no doubt lay behind the choice of the United Nations as the target of the second bomb plot. Ghannushi, it should be added, is presented by his Western apologists as the most moderate and least anti-American fundamentalist leader.

In the fundamentalist narrative, Muslims are not without their defenses against the "new world order." The hope has been most effectively articulated by Sayyid Muhammad Husayn Fadlallah, mentor and oracle of Lebanon's Hizbullah. His purpose has been to persuade Muslims that "reports about the multifaceted and unrivaled strength of the United States are greatly exaggerated." While America looms large, "its shadow is greater than its substance. It possesses great military power, but that power is not supported by commensurate political or economic strength." Even its much-touted democracy is deeply flawed. Thus, the collapse of the Soviet Union, far from confirming American power, only presages its fall. Within a generation or two, America will lose its power, and Islam will begin to realize its own massive potential.

"Power is not the eternal destiny of the powerful," Fadlallah reminds the faithful. "Weakness is not the eternal destiny of the weak. We may not have the actual power the U.S. has, but we had the power previously and we have now the foundations to develop that power in the future." Islam might even end by bringing America and Europe into its fold; already, the spread of Islam into these areas

> represents a great problem for the arrogant powers that seek to preserve the status quo and their own character. We should remember that Hülegü [the Mongol conquerer of Baghdad in 1258] overwhelmed the lands of Islam, but Islam overwhelmed the minds of his descendants, who became Muslims. Their power became Islamic power. I believe it is possible that Islam will storm many of the bastions that are now a danger to Islam, turning them to the benefit of Islam.

America the Vulnerable

America's assault on Islamic identity, its bloated power cloaked as a "new world order," its hidden vulnerabilities, Islam's ultimate triumph, the final conversion of America—millions have been irradiated by this narrative, which might well have served as the underlying motif for the bombing of the World Trade Center. When the FBI arrested Muslims for the bombing, Fadlallah himself was quick to blame "Jewish circles in the United States." Yet he, and many other fundamentalist theoreticians, had been assuring Muslims repeatedly that if they looked, they would find "chinks in the armor of the United States, and we can penetrate these chinks and enlarge them." It could have come as no surprise to him that some Muslims living in the United States overheard these admonitions and acted upon them.

An Iranian commentator put the bombing precisely in the context of the fundamentalist narrative. Asadollah Badamchian, the deputy head of the Iranian judiciary for political affairs, and a well-known hardliner, wrote an analysis that was published the day *before* the arrest of Muhammad Salameh, when no one could make the damaging association between the bombing and Islam:

> If the United States cannot safeguard even one floor of the most important building in the heart of New York, how can it ever put into practice the foolish policy of Bush—the establishment of a new world order or a new chapter of U.S. domination?

And Badamchian concluded:

> Even though initially tyranny inflicts anguish on the oppressed, ultimately divine wrath gives the devout persons the upper hand and they annihilate the tyrant.

That the seemingly omnipotent U.S. was vulnerable at its heart, and that the "new world order" could be stopped—this was the message the fundamentalists were reading into the bombing before the evidence began to point precisely in their direction.

Paradoxically, of course, and thanks to the arrests, the bombing had the opposite of the intended effect. Fundamentalists who would have hammered home Badamchian's point about American vulnerability instead had to denounce the bombing, blame it on Israel, and declare the United States off-limits to their struggle. Even Shaykh Abd al-Rahman, who was later indicted for, among other things, conspiracy in the bombing, pronounced it incompatible with Islam. In the end, a chorus of fundamentalist voices affirmed the immunity of American soil.

The American response to the bombing also belied the fundamentalist portrayal of the United States as arch-foe of the Muslims. The Egyptian fundamentalist newspaper *Al-Nur* ran a commentary acknowledging that there was no popular wave of retribution against American Muslims, no random arrests, no mass interrogations, no storming of mosques in search of terrorists—the opposite, in fact, of what usually occurs in Egypt. Even the suspects "were treated in a civilized manner, and their lawyers were allowed to be present with them as soon as they were arrested." The simple workings of due process conveyed an image of immense power. So did the endless footage on Arab and Muslim television of the skyline of New York, unaltered by the bombing. In the end, ironically, one lasting effect of the bombing and trials may be to fill Arabian nights with many more dreams of Manhattan.

Yet Manhattan's own nightmare could recur. The fundamentalist struggle continues back in the capitals of Islam. It has lasted for nearly two decades, and its outcome is still far from decided. The Shah of Iran, one nemesis of the fundamentalists, is gone, but other secular kings and presidents rule on. Women are returning to the veil in Egypt, but a woman has become prime minister of Turkey. Islam, in short, remains divided against itself, and seems to be moving toward a civil war between two antagonistic blocs—social blocs within countries, and strategic blocs among states. The dividing issue is whether or not Islam should exist as a closed system, in constant tension with the world. The United States has obvious preferences in this struggle, and it is always possible that it may be threatened for holding them. It would therefore be foolish to rely on fundamentalist denunciations of this particular bombing. They were made under extreme duress.

Two bits of truth lying beneath the bomb rubble and should be embedded in the wall of Western defense. First, no one has the clairvoyance to sort the "moderates" from the "extremists." Those Arabs who waged jihad in Afghanistan, including some eventually convicted of the World Trade Center bombing, were supposed to be America's domesticated fundamentalists. They were often cited as prime evidence that not all Muslim fundamentalists are anti-American. But as the bombing suggests, the conduct even of those fundamentalists who were once American allies and clients cannot be predicted, even in the short term. In dealing with Islamic fundamentalism, the United States now has an obligation to its own citizenry to err on the side of caution.

Second, the systematic preaching of hatred eventually will produce violence. Even if others strike the detonator, the kind of vitriol against America so widely retailed by the likes of Shaykh Abd al-Rahman is the fuel. The bombers, regardless of whether they acted alone, are not lone men. They belong to a society with its own code, which they call true Islam, and whose interpreters have condemned America as the seat of evil.

In the bombing's wake, those who have made blithe assurances about Islamism would do well to reexamine the content and appeal of this code. The more they continue to evade hard truths, the more their credibility is bound to be questioned by the press and the public alike. As for government, the case of the Shaykh should also be a reminder that the preaching of hatred is still protected speech in America—which is why it is vital to keep such preachers at a safe distance from America's shores, even when they claim to bear the divine message of Islam.

Note

1. For the proceedings of the conference, see Richard W. Bulliet, ed., *Under Siege: Islam and Democracy*, Occasional Papers, no. 1 (New York: Middle East Institute of Columbia University, 1994).

16

Islam vs. Democracy

In the summer of 1881, the English poet Wilfrid Scawen Blunt wrote a series of essays subsequently published under the title, *The Future of Islam*. Blunt was a high-born patron of the downtrodden, a policy intellectual of sorts who enlivened the drawing rooms of Victorian ministers and viceroys. He had also fallen under the spell of the forerunners of modern Islamic fundamentalism. In his book, Blunt argued that these thinkers had carried Islam to the brink of a great religious reformation. Under their inspiration, he wrote,

> I committed myself without reserve to the Cause of Islam as essentially the "Cause of Good" over an immense portion of the world, and to be encouraged, not repressed, by all who cared for the welfare of mankind.

It fell upon England, as the world's greatest power, to "take Islam by the hand and encourage her boldly in the path of virtue."

More than a century later, a frantic quest for the "Cause of Good" in the Middle East and North Africa has again seized the West. In an era of democratization, these lands of Islam remain an anomaly—a zone of resistance to the ideals that have toppled authoritarian regimes of the left and the right. For several years now, political scientists and area experts, borne along by a tidal wave of research grants and federally funded initiatives, have scanned the horizons of Islam for signs of democracy. In a plethora of academic papers and conferences, they have speculated on the reasons for the absence of democratic movements, and suggested what should be done to encourage their emergence. Suddenly, many of them reached a stunning conclusion: these movements have already appeared, in the guise of Islamic fundamentalism.

It has been a time of fervent Western testimonials. Islam, avers a noted journalist in *Foreign Affairs*, is now "at a juncture increasingly equated with the Protestant Reformation," due to the growing number of Islamists

265

who "are now trying to reconcile moral and religious tenets with modern life, political competition, and free markets." What these "supposed fanatics" really want, writes a leading political scientist in *Ethics and International Affairs*, is "the end of corrupt, arbitrary, and unpredictable rule and the imposition of the rule of law and responsible government." The new Islamic fundamentalism should be seen "for what it is," concludes a former intelligence analyst in the *Washington Post*,

> a movement that is historically inevitable and politically "tamable." Over the long run it even represents ultimate political progress toward greater democracy and popular government.

These views have reverberated in the hearing rooms of Washington. The then-director of the CIA, Robert Gates, told the House Foreign Affairs Committee in February 1992:

> I'm not ready yet to concede that Islamic fundamentalism is, by its nature, anti-Western and anti-democratic. There are some fundamentalist elements in the region—they're not in power—that are not necessarily that way. And I think that it's also an evolution.

"I had made myself a romance about these reformers," Blunt confessed fifteen years after publication of *The Future of Islam*, "but I see that it has no substantial basis." Blunt was not the first Westerner to be swept off his feet, then left bewildered, by the promise of Islamic revival. Since the Enlightenment broke the lock of medieval prejudice against Islam, the reform of Islam has been declared inevitable, even imminent, by a parade of visionaries and experts. The current representation of Islamic fundamentalism as a portent of democracy has opened another chapter in this cyclical saga of hope and disillusionment. When that chapter comes to be written, it might begin by asking how Islamic fundamentalism, still loathing the West and loathed by it, yet became the hope of the democratizers.

"Islam is the Solution"

For most of the 1980s, those who saw Islamic fundamentalism for what it is saw groups as violent and dogmatic as any in the world. These were people who mixed nostalgia with grievance to produce a millenarian vision of an Islamic state—a vision so powerful that its pursuit justified any means. Angry believers invoked this Islam when they executed enemies of the revolution in Iran, assassinated a president in Egypt, and detonated themselves and abducted others in Lebanon. Their furious words complemented their deeds. They marched to chants of "Death to America" and intimidated all opponents with charges of espionage and treason. They did not expect to be understood, but they did want to be feared, and feared they were, by Muslims and non-Muslims alike.

Yet their violence failed to overturn the region. While fundamentalists did seize the state in Iran, in most Arab countries they lurked about the edges of politics. They were often dangerous, and always fascinating, but they posed no mortal threat to the established order.

By the decade's end, however, many of these same groups had managed to transform themselves into populist movements, and even win mass followings. They did so by riding a huge tide of discontent, fed by exploding populations, falling oil prices, and economic mismanagement by the state. While governments fumbled for solutions, the fundamentalists persuaded the growing numbers of the poor, the young, and the credulous that if they only returned to belief and implemented God's law, the fog of misery surrounding them would lift.

"Islam is the solution," ran the fundamentalist slogan. What that meant, no one would say. The treatises of those billed as first-rate theoreticians seemed vague, by design. Here and there, fundamentalists organized model communities. Although billed as successful experiments in self-reliance, they were actually Potemkin mosques, built and supported with money from oil-rich donors. Fundamentalists also organized Islamic investment banks, which were supposed to prove that market economics could flourish even under the Islamic prohibition of interest. The most extensive experiment in Islamic banking, in Egypt, produced Islamic financial scandal in fairly short order.

Most of the new followers, however, read no theory and lost no money. They stood mesmerized by the rhetorical brilliance of men like the Sudan's Hasan al-Turabi, Tunisia's Rashid al-Ghannushi, and Lebanon's Muhammad Husayn Fadlallah. These preachers did not intone musty Islamic polemics against the unbelievers. Often they sounded more like the tenured Left, venting professorial condemnations of the West's sins.

Indeed, many of them issued from the academy. Turabi, schooled at the University of London and the Sorbonne, had been a professor of law and a dean; Ghannushi, a teacher of philosophy. They had overheard the West's self-incrimination, uttered in Left Bank cafés and British and American faculty lounges. This they reworked into a double-edged argument for the superiority and inevitability of Islam, buttressed not only by familiar Islamic scripture but by the West's own doomsday prophets, from Toynbee onward. These wise men of the West had confessed to capital crimes: imperialism, racism, Zionism. If *they* felt the tremors of the coming quake, could Muslims not feel them? Those who listened long enough to words pumped from pulpit amplifiers did begin to feel a slight tremor, and the mosques filled to overflowing.

A great deal of solid scholarship on these movements appeared during the 1980s, making it difficult to view them benignly. Their theories of jihad and conspiracy, embedded in wordy tracts, received critical scrutiny. True, Edward Said, Columbia's part-time professor of Palestine, presented a contrary view in *Covering Islam,* a book that bemoaned the Western media's treatment of Islam. The book was much admired by the Islamic Jihad in Beirut, prolific deconstructionists (of U.S. embassies) who circulated it among Western hostages for their edification. But the violence of the fundamentalists made them a difficult sell, and when in 1989 they filled the streets to demand the death of Salman Rushdie, they bit the hands even of those few Western intellectuals who had tried to feed them. As the decade closed, Islamic fundamentalism could count on few foreign friends.

While Islam's fundamentalists demanded the death of Rushdie, a longing for democracy (and capitalism) swept across Latin America, Eastern Europe, and the Soviet Union. Throughout the Middle East and North Africa, rulers took fright at the scenes of revolution from Romania and East Germany, and proceeded to initiate tightly controlled experiments in political pluralism. At the time, the architects of these experiments had no sense of the fundamentalists' appeal; they thought that the openings would work to the benefit of parties advocating liberal reform.

It was the fundamentalists, though, who led the dash through the newly opened door. The first of a succession of surprises had occurred in Egypt's parliamentary elections in 1987, when a coalition dominated by the fundamentalist Muslim Brethren emerged as the biggest opposition party in a contest gerrymandered to assure victory for the ruling party. The fundamentalists also outdistanced all other opposition parties in the 1989 elections for Tunisia's parliament, although a winner-take-all system gave every seat to the ruling party. That same year, the fundamentalists nearly captured the lower house of Jordan's parliament, in that country's first general election since 1967. Then, in 1990, the fundamentalists swept the country-wide local elections in Algeria.

Given these successes, almost overnight fundamentalist movements became the most avid and insistent supporters of free elections—an un-patrolled route to the power that had hitherto eluded them. Liberal Arab intellectuals, who had lobbied for democratic reforms and human rights for much of the 1980s, now retreated in disarray, fearful that freer press and elections might play straight into the hands of fundamentalists.

For Western theorists of democracy, it was as if the Arabs had defied the laws of gravity. Few admitted the bind as frankly as Jeane Kirkpatrick, who said:

> The Arab world is the only part of the world where I've been shaken in my conviction that if you let the people decide, they will make fundamentally rational decisions. But there, they don't make rational decisions, they make fundamentalist ones.

Most theorists, however, refused to be shaken. In order to synchronize the Arab predicament with the march of democracy, they developed a convenient theory—the theory of initial advantage.

The fundamentalists, according to this theory, enjoyed an advantage in the first stage of democratization: they knew how to organize, to stir emotions, to get out the vote. But "as civil society is enlivened," announced one political scientist, "it is only natural that the influence of the Islamist groups will be challenged." Then their appeal would fade, once the people enjoyed a full range of options. In the privacy of the voting booth, the voters would become rational actors, and elect liberals and technocrats who proposed serious answers to the crisis of Arab society.

Algeria's parliamentary election, first scheduled for June 1991 and then postponed until December, was to have proved the point. According to the theorists, Algeria had the best chance of giving birth to a liberal democracy. More than any other Arab country, Algeria enjoyed an intimate connection with Europe, and its elites were at home with the ways of the West. True, the new Algerian voter had already given one sweeping victory to the Islamic Salvation Front (known by its French acronym, FIS) in local elections. But expert opinion declared the FIS victory a "protest" against the corruption of the ruling party, not a vote for a stern regime of Islamic mores. Anyway, ran the argument, the FIS had lost its initial advantage, first by mismanaging the muncipalities where it had assumed authority, then by backing Saddam Hussein in his Kuwait blunder.

"Saddam's defeat has turned the Algerian political situation upside down," announced *L'Express*, "leaving the FIS in the worst position of all." It was safely predicted that Algerians would turn away from the sheikhs in the upcoming parliamentary election—a fair and free ballot, structured in technical consultation with the best Parisian authorities in the *sciences politiques*. "The FIS can now count on only a die-hard bloc of unemployed urban youths," opined an American political scientist in the *Journal of Democracy*, who found it "unlikely that the FIS will gain enough votes to dictate the makeup of the new government." Such confident assurances anesthetized Algeria's elite, who secretly worshipped foreign expertise and looked surreptitiously to the foreign press to explain their own predicament to them.

Thus, Paris and Algiers were both astonished when the FIS won a landslide victory in the first round of the parliamentary election, nearly burying Algeria's regime and its Westernized elite. The Sudan's Turabi was right for once when he claimed that any observer with insight should have been able to predict the outcome: "The Western media wished this not to be so, so they hid the facts from everyone, so the results came as a surprise." But the self-deception went beyond the media, to the battery of democracy doctors who had ministered to the ailing Algerian polity. Their theory of initial advantage proved to be an immense blind spot, large enough to conceal a near-revolution.

Algeria confirmed something that had been demonstrated in study after study of fundamentalist movements: fundamentalism is no fad, but the preference of a generation. It will not stop on a dime—on the failure of Saddam's jihad, or the the scandal surrounding Islamic banks in Egypt, or haphazard garbage collection in fundamentalist-run towns in Algeria. Nor do the fundamentalists now need a detailed plan to alleviate suffering, because they possesses potent words, and those words vest suffering with meaning. In a Western polity, the pied pipers of the disaffected young could not hope to win power in a landslide vote. But the explosion of the young population in the Arab world has given the affected generation an immense electoral advantage. After Algeria's parliamentary election, the bleak reality could not be denied: free elections in the Middle East and North Africa were more likely to produce fundamentalist rule than not.

The failure to anticipate the FIS victory should have cut deeply into the credibility of Western democracy doctors, with their blithe promise that the fundamentalist appeal would fade in a truly free ballot. Instead, they have rebounded with a new discovery. Fundamentalism, they now claim, is not destined to disappear but to triumph, because *it* is the yearning for democracy in Islamic camouflage.

Those who claim credit for this discovery muster three arguments in support of their claim that Islamic fundamentalism has become the "Cause of Good," and that Islamic movements therefore deserve the sympathy the West has bestowed on democracy movements elsewhere. Paradoxically, each of these arguments has already been systematically refuted—by the fundamentalists themselves.

Islamist Contradictions

The first argument holds that Islamic fundamentalism, whatever its past, has entered upon an evolution, and has already started to reconcile Islam with democratic values. As one academic apologist claims:

> Many Islamic activists have "Islamized" parliamentary democracy, asserting an Islamic rationale for it, and appeal to democracy in their opposition to incumbent regimes.

The distortion here does not lie in the claim of compatibility between Islam and democracy. Although the dominant interpretation of Islam has historically sanctioned authoritarian rule, the reinterpretation of Islamic sources, done with enough imagination, could conceivably produce an opposing argument for Islamic democracy. Here and there, intrepid Muslims have searched the divine word of the Qur'an, the traditions of the Prophet, and the early history of Islam in order to establish the democratic essence of Islam, buried deep beneath the chronicles of despotism.

These are not, however, the Muslims leading the fundamentalist movements now bidding for power. Fundamentalists insist they have not demanded free elections to promote democracy or the individual freedoms that underpin it, but to promote Islam. Indeed, when leading fundamentalist thinkers do address the broader question of democracy, it is not to argue its compatibility with Islam but to demonstrate democracy's inferiority to Islamic government. Such a virtuous government, they affirm, can rest only on obedience to the divinely-given law of Islam, the *shari'a*.

A deception lurks in any description of the fundamentalists as being committed to the rule of law, for the *shari'a* is not legislated but revealed law. As such, in the eyes of the fundamentalists it has already achieved perfection, and while it is not above some reinterpretation, neither is it infinitely elastic. If anything, fundamentalist exegesis has rejected reformist attempts to stretch the law much beyond its letter, and has even magnified the differences between Islamic and universal law.

At the heart of these differences reside Islamic law's principled affirmations of inequality, primarily between Muslims and non-Muslims, secondarily between men and women. This has made fundamentalists into the most unyielding critics of the Universal Declaration of Human Rights, which guarantees the freedom to choose one's religion and one's spouse. Both freedoms indisputably contradict Islamic law, which defines conversion out of Islam as a capital offense, and forbids marriage between a Muslim woman and a non-Muslim man. (In 1981, the leading fundamentalists met in Paris and put out an Islamic Universal Declaration of Human Rights, which omits all freedoms that contradict the *shari'a*.)

The *shari'a*, as a perfect law, cannot be abrogated or altered, and certainly not by the shifting moods of an electorate. Accordingly, every major fundamentalist thinker has repudiated popular sovereignty as rebellion against God, the sole legislator. In the changed circumstances of the 1990s, some activists do allow that an election can serve a useful one-time purpose, as a collective referendum of allegiance to Islam, and as an act of submission to a regime of divine justice. But once such a regime gains power, its true measure is not how effectively it implements the will of the people but how efficiently it applies Islamic law.

The ideal of Islamic government most often evoked by the fundamentalists harks back to the rule of a just commander, ruling in consultation with experts in the law. There is a revulsion against the combat of parties and personalities in democratic politics, best expressed by the Sudan's Turabi, fundamentalism's best-known spokesman in the West. In a tract on the Islamic state, Turabi explains that such a state, once established, really has no need of party politics or political campaigns. While Islamic law does not expressly oppose a multiparty system,

> this is a form of factionalism that can be very oppressive of individual freedom and divisive of the community, and it is therefore, antithetical to a Muslim's ultimate responsibility to God.

As for election campaigns:

> In Islam, no one is entitled to conduct a campaign for themselves directly or indirectly in the manner of Western electoral campaigns. The presentation of candidates would be entrusted to a neutral institution that would explain to the people the options offered in policies and personalities.

Through this elaborate hedging, Turabi arrives at a tacit justification for one-party rule, which is the actual form of government he now justifies and supports in the Sudan.

Of the vast complex of democratic values and institutions offered by the West, the fundamentalists have thus seized upon only one, the free plebiscite, and even that is to be discarded after successful one-time use. They remain ambivalent, if not hostile, toward party politics, and they spend much of their intellectual energy arguing that the reckless expansion of freedom can only harm the collective security of Islam. When asked which existing regime most closely approximates an ideal Islamic order, fundamentalists most often cite the governments of the Sudan or Iran—the first a military regime, the second a hierocracy ruled by an increasingly autocratic cleric, and both first-order violators of human rights.

The second argument holds that Islamic fundamentalism drives many movements and represents a wide spectrum of views, not all of them extreme. Because of its diversity, the past or present performance of fundamentalism in one setting says nothing about its future performance in another. This diversity also rules out domino-like progress: the world does not face an Islamintern, but a variety of local movements.

The concept of a diverse fundamentalism has wound its way to Washington, where it achieved full flower in a June 1992 speech by Edward Djerejian, then assistant secretary of state for Near Eastern and South Asian affairs:

> In countries throughout the Middle East and North Africa, we thus see groups or movements seeking to reform their societies in keeping with Islamic ideals. There is considerable diversity in how these ideals are expressed. We detect no monolithic or coordinated international effort behind these movements. What we do see are believers living in different countries placing renewed emphasis on Islamic principles, and governments accommodating Islamist political activity to varying degrees and in different ways.

This claim for the diversity of fundamentalist movements—again labelled expectantly as movements of "reform"—is most convincingly countered by the fundamentalists themselves, with their uncanny knack for refuting every Western argument made on their behalf. The Sudan's Turabi again put it best, in an interview granted just after the FIS success in the first round of the Algerian parliamentary election. The awakening of Islam, he said, has produced a world movement notable for its *uniformity*. If there appear to be differences, it is because "God in His wisdom is varying and distributing the phenomenon to let people know that it is coming everywhere at all times."

The leading fundamentalists insist that their movement is pan-Islamic as a matter of principle. The borders that separate their countries, drawn up by European imperial fiat, do not bind them morally or limit them politically, and in practice, fundamentalist movements have an irresistible tendency to think and act across borders. Over the past decade, the international traffic among Islamic fundamentalists has grown intense. Fundamentalist leaders jet from conference to conference to open channels that will assure the rapid transmission of ideas and mutual aid. They learn from one another, imitate one another, and assist one another.

The greatest success of their joint efforts has been the aid they collectively mobilized for the Afghan *mujahidin* during the 1980s—aid that included money, material, and thousands of volunteers who fought in the Islamic jihad against the Soviet occupation. No less striking has been the success of the Islamic Republic of Iran in implanting the indomitable Hizbullah, a fundamentalist movement faithful to Iran's revolution, on Lebanese soil, where it has waged a largely successful jihad against American, French, and Israeli forces.

Thanks to the jet, the cassette, and the fax, pan-Islam is no longer a bogey but a growing reality. Turabi, for example, categorizes Islamic fundamentalism as a "pan-national movement," and the Sudan's policy reflects it. The Sudan has run Algerian voting data through its computers for the FIS, it has provided diplomatic passports for foreign fundamentalists, and it has brought the foremost fundamentalists to Khartoum to create an Islamic Arab Popular Conference, of which Turabi is secretary. Iran is still more active, and not only continues to finance Hizbullah in Lebanon, but includes a line item in its budget for support of the Palestinian intifada—monies that have gone largely to fundamentalists who battle the peace process. Visitors to Khartoum and Tehran are astonished at the odd mix of foreign fundamentalists who can be spotted in hotel lobbies and government ministries.

There is, in short, much ado about something, part of which is visible above-board in publicized visits and conferences, part of which is arranged in the conspiratorial fashion mastered by the fundamentalists during their long years underground. The apologists, preoccupied with imaginary changes in the substance of the fundamentalist message, overlook perhaps the most important transformation of all: the emergence of a global village of Islamic fundamentalism.

According to the final argument, fundamentalism, whatever the dangers it might pose to freedoms or borders, still constitutes no real threat to Western interests or to the stability of a new world order. The fundamentalists' goals cannot be achieved in defiance of the West. States that have sold oil to the West will still sell it; states that have needed Western aid will still need it. Once in power, promises another Western apologist, fundamentalists will

> generally operate on the basis of national interests and demonstrate a flexibility that reflects acceptance of the realities of a globally interdependent world.

But where their apologists see an interdependent world, the fundamentalists themselves see a starkly divided world. During the Gulf crisis, they championed the view that any partnership between believers and nonbelievers constituted a violation of divine order. Therefore, while Saddam may have done wrong when he invaded Kuwait, King Fahd, who depended on American "Crusaders" to defend Saudi Arabia, most certainly sinned. Ma'mun al-Hudaybi, official spokesman of the Egyptian Muslim Brotherhood, announced that "Islamic law does not permit any enlisting of assistance from polytheists [*mushrikun*]." According to Rashid al-Ghannushi, the exiled leader of the Tunisian fundamentalist movement, Saudi Arabia had committed a colossal crime. Of Saddam, no friend of Islam before the crisis, he said:

> We are not worshipping personalities, but anyone who confronts the enemies of Islam is my friend and anyone who puts himself in the service of the enemies of Islam is my enemy.

For fundamentalists, the identity of the enemy has remained constant since Islam first confronted unbelief. In *their* vision of interdependence, Islam will indeed sell its oil, provided that it is allowed to invest the proceeds in instruments of war which will enable Muslims to deter any form of Western intervention. This proliferation will eventually create a world order based not on American hegemony but on a restored balance of power—and terror. As Hizbullah's mentor, Fadlallah, says in a transparent reference to military might and the eventual acquisition of nuclear weapons:

> We may not have the actual power the U.S. has, but we had the power previously and we have now the foundations to develop that power in the future.

This restored balance between Islam and the West excludes the intrusive existence of Israel in the lands of Islam. Unlike several Arab regimes and the PLO, which have grudgingly accepted the reality of the Jewish state, the fundamentalists remain uncompromisingly theological in their understanding of the Arab-Israeli conflict. Palestine is a land sacred to Islam, a land stolen by the Jews. Not an inch may be alienated. Israel is a cancer in the Islamic world, implanted by imperialism and nurtured by the U.S. The Jewish state has to be fought, passively through nonrecognition, actively through jihad. Ibrahim Ghawsha, speaking for Hamas, the largest Palestinian fundamentalist movement, has drawn analogies that go beyond the usual parallel of Israel and the Crusaders:

> We think the conflict between the Arabs and Jews, between the Muslims and the Jews, is a cultural conflict that will continue to rage throughout all time.... Algeria fought for 130 years. Even the Baltic states, which were occupied by the Soviets, have had their independence recognized by world states 45 years after they were occupied. The Palestine question is only [about] 40 years old, considering that it came into being in 1948. We are at the beginning of the road. Our adversary needs to be dealt with through a protracted and continuous confrontation.

This view is shared by fundamentalists of all stripes, from the many Sunni movements in the Muslim Brethren tradition to the Shi‘ite movements that receive guidance and support from Iran.

Imagined Islamism

Democracy, diversity, accommodation—the fundamentalists have repudiated them all. In appealing to the masses who fill their mosques, they promise, instead, to institute a regime of Islamic law, make common cause with like-minded "brethren" everywhere, and struggle against the hegemony of the West and the existence of Israel. Fundamentalists have held to these principles through long periods of oppression, and will not abandon them now, at the moment of their greatest popular resonance.

These principles bear no resemblance to the ideals of Europe's democracy movements; if anything, they evoke more readily the atavism of Europe's burgeoning nationalist right. The refusal to see Islamic fundamentalism in this context, or to take seriously the discourse of the Islamists, is evidence of the persistent power of the West to create a wholly imaginary Islam. In this instance, the myth of fundamentalism as a movement of democratic reform assures the West that no society on earth has the moral resources to challenge the supremacy of Western values: even Islam's fundamentalists, cursing the ways of foreigners, will end up embracing them. This is a reassuring gospel, but it ignores Islam as actually believed and practiced by the fundamentalists, and this denial has sowed the seed of a future disillusionment.

As for the fundamentalists themselves, they and their apologists warn against the futility of resisting the fundamentalist surge. "Islam is a new force that is going to come anyway, because it's a wave of history," Turabi assures his Western listeners, and "superficial obstacles will certainly not stand in the way." In fact, fundamentalism will triumph no matter what the West does, because it "thrives" on repression.

Nevertheless, as governments do crack down on fundamentalist movements, their apologists and even their leaders have taken to pleading more vociferously for the *deus ex machina* of American intervention. The same fundamentalists who condemned Saudi Arabia's enlisting of assistance from "polytheists" would enlist some of it themselves, if they could. Their approach has been to tug at the conscience of the Western democracies. In particular, they ask that the United States intervene to protect the rights of free speech and assembly so precious to the West, and press for free elections throughout the region. "I am trying to tell my audiences that the values which are dear to them are also common to Islam," said a disingenuous Turabi in Washington, especially citing "free government based on consultation and participation."

Until now, the fundamentalists have offered nothing in exchange for this protection. In his policy speech on Islam in June 1992, Assistant Secretary Edward Djerejian expressed suspicion

of those who would use the democratic process to come to power, only to destroy that very process in order to retain power and political dominance.

Yet the speech left open the possibility of an accommodation if fundamentalists ceased to be "extreme," and so demonstrated that fundamentalism's apologists had won acceptance of their most essential point: fundamentalism is a movement of "reform," itself susceptible to reform. With Djerejian's speech, the United States moved, in Blunt's formulation, "to take Islam by the hand and encourage her boldly in the path of virtue."

If those hands are joined, the overture to fundamentalism promises to be the riskiest policy venture of the next decade in the Middle East and North Africa. According to one academic analyst,

The twenty-first century will test the ability of political analysts and policymakers to distinguish between Islamic movements that are a threat and those that represent legitimate indigenous attempts to reform and redirect their societies.

Would that these movements could be divided into two such broadly opposed categories. But every movement combines threat and "reform" in a seamless message, and much of the supposed "reform" is threatening as well—to women, minorities, and the occasional novelist who would write a book on Islam. Which of these movements could be trusted with power, and which would betray that trust at the first opportunity? No one can possibly know, because the threat that resides in fundamentalism is anchored to its foundations, and is liable to resurface at critical moments when the peace and stability of the region hang in the balance.

Political pluralism and peace do have true friends in the Middle East and North Africa. They are beleaguered and dazed by the generational surge of Islamic fundamentalism, and they are divided over the fate of Algeria and its implications. Some have been ridiculed by the democracy theorists as self-styled liberals, guilty of pedalling the view that existing governments are preferable to the anointed fundamentalists. Their forebodings, however, are as justified as those of Westerners who shudder at the rise of their own extreme right, and they remain democracy's only hope in the Arab world. In partnership with gradually liberalizing regimes they might just muddle through—provided they are not sacrificed on the alter of a bankrupt paradigm.

Conclusion

This volume has traced two ideas, one Arab nationalist, the other Islamist, that have dominated the Middle East for a century. While Arabs and Muslims continue to debate their identities, it is already evident that both these ideas, in their most widespread form, have disappointed. They have not made the Arabs and Muslims masters of their destinies. Indeed, despite the striking increase in population, the process of decolonization, and the advent of oil, it is doubtful whether Arabs and Muslims have mattered more to the twentieth century than they did to the nineteenth.

At various points in the twentieth century, it seemed to some observers that the "awakening" of the Arabs or the "revival" of Islam would overturn the absolute dominance of the West, that there would be an Arab-Muslim resurgence to global prominence. Such predictions became the stock-in-trade of Middle Eastern ideologues and their Western sympathizers. When Westerners made these predictions, they often made sweeping statements of self-reproach. "We Europeans have been lording it over the rest of the earth," announced Marshall G.S. Hodgson, the American historian of Islam, in 1944. "The other nations are already objecting, and their objections seem likely to increase. Is it not time that we wake up to the fact that we are not the only people in the world that matter?"[1] To buttress his point, he criticized modern map makers, and especially the Mercator projection, which seems to exaggerate Europe's land mass and diminishes India, China, and the lands of Islam. Through his indictment of Western cartography, Hodgson sought to humble his Western readers, to demonstrate a pervasive Eurocentrism even in the ostensibly scientific representation of the earth's surface.[2]

One wonders what Hodgson would have thought of today's thematic maps which magnify and shrink countries according to the size of their gross domestic products or per capita incomes. These maps are always striking to read, because they too are so at odds with the Mercator projection. North America and Europe loom as super-continents; East Asia's cats grow into tigers; little Israel seems to dominate the Middle East. These are arguably the most accurate maps of the contemporary world, the maps which people carry in their heads when they produce, consume, invest, and read. If maps are meant to guide, then these maps are far more reliable guides to real landscapes than any physical map. They trace the contours of a different kind of power, economic and social, to which land mass and population are largely irrelevant.

On such maps, the place occupied by the Arabs and Muslims is small, and it has continued to shrink through this century. There are Arabs and Muslims who might call this kind of mapping one more Eurocentric ruse to diminish them. But this is no ruse. It is an all-too-accurate measure of their diminished place in the world, which a century of ideological churning has done nothing to reverse.

Others have amassed the evidence. The Arab-Muslim world does not fare well in the U.S. State Department's annual *Patterns of Global Terrorism* or Freedom House's annual *Freedom in the World*. For anyone concerned with the present state and future of the Arab-Muslim world, perhaps it is UNESCO's annual *Statistical Yearbook* which makes the most sobering reading. In its dry pages of statistics, the grim realities of dependence become all too vivid.

By these indices, the Arab-Muslim world remains a great redoubt of poverty and illiteracy. There are approximately one billion Muslims in the world, a fifth of the world's population; 86 percent of them have annual incomes of less than $2,000; 76 percent less that $1,000; and 67 percent less than $500. Muslim illiteracy worldwide stands at about 51 percent for all age groups over fifteen. Despite a rapid increase in primacy school enrollment, only 45 percent of Muslim children aged six to eleven attend primary school.[3]

An even larger gap exists at higher levels of research. In the developed world, scientists and technologists employed in research and development number about 2,600 per million; the corresponding figure in the Muslim world is only 100 per million.[4] "The policymakers in the U.S. must be all too aware that Islam does not pose a threat to Western interests," concludes the Bangladeshi writer Bahauddeen Latif. "Certainly the numbers are large, but the technological base is pea-sized and littered all over Afro-Asia like a patchwork, with no center to hold."[5]

The Arab-Muslim world is also one of the most economically dependent zones in the world. Only about 10 percent of the trade of Muslim countries is conducted among themselves. For purposes of comparison, proportions of total intraregional trade are around 60 percent in Europe, 37 percent in East Asia and 36 percent in North America. The Muslim world exports a raw commodity, oil; it depends upon the outside world for everything from arms to food. An Islamist figure has complained that even the *ihram*, the pure white gown worn by the devout Muslim pilgrim as he circumambulates the Holy Ka'ba in Mecca, is today imported from Japan; the *sajada*, the prayer rug, is usually made in China. What do Muslims sell one another? Half of their paltry intraregional trade is in oil and gas; the rest is other raw materials. As imports have grown, the debts of the Arab-Muslim world have also spiralled upward. Both oil and non-oil producers have seen a rapid expansion of debt.

In short, the Muslim world, led by its Arab component, has grown more dependent on the West over the last half century, despite political independence. Whatever the causes of this dependence—and they are hotly debated—there is a broad consensus that it has deepened.

Visions of the Future

Will the place of the Arabs and Muslims shrink still further? Since the end of the Cold War, and with the approach of the twenty-first century, an industry has grown up in the United States around imagining history before it happens. Much of it is naturally focused upon the destiny of the West in general and the United States in particular—the hubs of the modern (and postmodern) world. At times, however, the new oracles have peered over the ramparts into the places where Arabic is spoken and Islam is professed. Not surprisingly, they are divided over what they see.

Francis Fukuyama, an American policy analyst whose vision came to be known as "Endism" after his 1989 article, "The End of History," assumes that the Arab-Muslim world will remain shrunken, despite the noise surrounding Islam's revival. For Fukuyama, that revival is an archaic remnant, a pocket of resentment against the triumph of the idea of liberal democracy. The Islamic world is out of synchronization with world time; its conflicts are waged in distant outposts that have yet to hear the news of liberalism's triumph. In this, as in so much else, Fukuyama replicates Hegel, who construed Islam as an antithesis to the Roman thesis, rendered irrelevant by the synthesis of modern Europe. ("Islam has long vanished from the stage of history," Hegel opined early in the last century, "and has retreated into oriental ease and repose.")[6]

For Fukuyama, Islam is first of all irrelevant as a cultural pole and ideological force in the wider world:

> Despite the power demonstrated by Islam in its current revival, it remains the case that this religion has virtually no appeal outside those areas that were culturally Islamic to begin with. The days of Islam's cultural conquests, it would seem, are over: it can win back lapsed adherents, but has no resonance for young people in Berlin, Tokyo, or Moscow. And while nearly a billion people are culturally Islamic—one-fifth of the world's population—they cannot challenge liberal democracy on its own territory on the level of ideas.

Fukuyama then goes one step beyond Hegel: Islam is increasingly irrelevant to Muslims themselves:

> Indeed, the Islamic world would seem more vulnerable to liberal ideas in the long run than the reverse, since such liberalism has attracted numerous and powerful Muslim adherents over the past century and a half. Part of the reason for the current, fundamentalist revival is the strength of the perceived threat from liberal, Western values to traditional Islamic societies.[7]

A pointed response to this vision of an irrelevant and embattled Islam comes from Ali Mazrui, the Kenyan Muslim historian who teaches at the State University of New York. Mazrui argues that Islam's role in the shaping of history, far from diminishing, is growing. True, in the first half of this century, Muslim peoples were "just passengers, sometimes passengers in chains." But in the second half, "we began to be members of the crew—at least some of us." In Algeria, the struggle against France profoundly altered French politics and European history; in Afghanistan, the struggle of the *mujahidin* precipitated the downfall of the Soviet Union. "The collapse of communism required the resistance of Islam," proclaims Mazrui, pointing out that communism never triumphed in any Muslim country.

Mazrui sees the possibility, over the next decade or two, for a Muslim "resumption of their role as makers of history." He dutifully notes that Muslims will become ever more numerous, but more important, their influence will run beyond simple numbers, to the realm of ideas. There are lacunae, Mazrui maintains, if not in democracy then certainly in capitalism. Their worst effects are mitigated by Islam, here understood not as a religion but as an egalitarian value system, and one which "has been the most resistant to the ultimate destructive forces of the twentieth century."[8] For Mazrui, the place of Islam in the world can only expand, as capitalism shrinks in the wash of its own contradictions.

The growing relevance of Islam can also be affirmed in a negative way. Harvard political scientist Samuel P. Huntington takes precisely this view of Islam's vitality in his 1993 article, "The Clash of Civilizations?" Huntington anticipates that the next global pattern of conflict will be a reversion to the age-old pattern that preceded the West's own "civil wars." The antagonists will be the old cultural formations known in the West as civilizations. Islam is one of eight civilizations in Huntington's reckoning, and it is central to his thesis: the division between Islam and the West is the world's oldest cultural fault-line, marked by conflict for 1,300 years.

Huntington sees the project of re-Islamization as a serious alternative to liberal democracy, and bolsters his argument for the salience of civilizational struggle largely by pointing to skirmishes already underway on the frontiers of Islam—in Bosnia to Islam's west, in Azerbaijan to its north, in Sudan to its south, and in Kashmir to its east. "Islam has bloody borders," writes Huntington; today's skirmishes are adduced as plain omens of the big clash to come. This return of history has enormous disruptive potential due to the proliferation of nonconventional weapons, permitting Islamic (and Confucian) civilization to pose a threat to the West at the pinnacle of its power. In the longer term, concludes Huntington, the economic and military strength of the West relative to the non-West—including Islam—will decline.[9]

Huntington's "descriptive hypotheses," the obverse of Fukuyama's, draws its most pointed response from a Muslim critic: Fouad Ajami, a Lebanese Shi'ite who teaches Middle Eastern politics at The Johns Hopkins University. For Ajami, Islam is no longer intact as a civilization; the real fault lines of conflict already run through its very core. Modernity and secularism have taken firm hold among Muslims; the "thrashing about" in the name of Islam must not be mistaken for the vitality of a battered tradition. Indeed, like Fukuyama, Ajami sees Islamic fundamentalism "less a sign of resurgence than of panic and bewilderment and guilt that the border with 'the other' has been crossed." As for the prospect of any kind of unified front among Muslims, it is a fantasy: "The world of Islam divides and subdivides," each state and society making a separate calculation of its interests as it scrambles for a place in the global economy. For Ajami, the Arabs and Muslims have chosen to join universal modernity on its own terms.[10]

In this *fin-de-siècle* American fascination with future speculation, Islam remains enigmatic. Fukuyama plays down the significance of Islam's resurgence; Huntington plays it up. Mazrui sees Muslims making history by relying upon Islam's ethos; Ajami sees them joining history by embracing the West's values. The Arab-Muslim world provides evidence to sustain all these contradictory hypotheses, which is another way of saying that it stands at a crossroads.

The Last Option

Of all Muslims, the Arabs face the most painful choices. The future cannot be divined, but one thing seems certain. The world will not wait for the Arabs in the twenty-first century—not the first world, not the second, nor even much of the third. Already the Western passions once excited by the Arab world are yielding to indifference. In the global marketplace, the Arabs produce nothing that threatens, and they consume so avidly that they have lost all romance. Even the phenomenon of the foreign friends is fading fast, an archaic remnant of the age of imperialism and guilt. At home, the Arabs are caught between regimes that will not reform and Islamists who cannot adapt.

Many Arab futurists are still dreaming of a solution through unification, attempting to revive pan-Arabism by arguing that the next century will be dominated by large, unified blocs of states. Some old-guard Arab intellectuals have done a massive futurological report calling for unification as the only solution. It rivals the fantasies of Islamists as a formula for future strife.[11] Blocs of states are indeed forming around the world, but they are doing so on the basis of shared interests, and these blocs bind together people of different nationalities. The project of Arab unity is a nineteenth-century relic, not a viable twenty-first-century program, and the intellectuals who propound it still prevent a thorough and honest reassessment of Arab prospects.

If, as this volume suggests, the politics of identity have failed, what then is left? The clearest option is a post-ideological Middle East, resting on a resolute pragmatism. This idea, drawing upon a vision of peace, development, and democratization, is offered as the West's alternative to Arabist fantasies and the Islamist ideology of retribution, sacrifice, and the rule of God. It is encapsulated in the phrase "new Middle East," that now trips off the tongues of many statesmen—Arab, Israeli, and American.

Ultimately, this "new Middle East" is also a promise of power—not the power to defeat enemies on battlefields, but to feed, house, and employ masses of people in cities. In many ways, this is a pledge more far-reaching than anything offered by Arabism or Islamism. The Nassers and Khomeinis could manipulate the language of authenticity, persuading millions to endure deprivation and forfeit freedoms for some distant redemption. The "new Middle East" must promise swifter, even instant gratification, because it speaks to interests, not identity. And it must produce results still faster, because it is linked to an alliance with the United States and peace with Israel, both regarded by critics as evidence of defeat.

Fast peace, fast democracy, and fast markets are a rude introduction to a fast-changing world. But other choices carry still greater risks, and a wrong choice might make the Arab world difficult to find on any map but Mercator's. "Awake, O Arabs, and arise!" These words formed a well-known ode in the last century, and a famous epigraph in this one. Without a thorough transformation, they might become a solemn epitaph in the next.

Notes

1. Marshall G.S. Hodgson, *Rethinking World History: Essays on Europe, Islam, and World History*, ed. Edmund Burke III (Cambridge: Cambridge University Press, 1993), 37.
2. Ibid., 4–5.
3. Islamic Educational, Scientific, and Cultural Organization (ISESCO) report, *Al-Sharq al-Awsat*, 25 December 1991. ISESCO figures are extracted from UNESCO's *Statistical Yearbook*.
4. ISESCO figures, *L'Opinion* (Rabat), 12 January 1992.
5. Bahauddeen Latif, "Chaos," in *For Rushdie: Essays by Arab and Muslim Writers in Defense of Free Speech* (New York: George Braziller, 1994), 210–11.
6. Quoted by Albert Hourani, "Islam in European Thought," in his *Islam in European Thought* (Cambridge: Cambridge University Press, 1991), 27.
7. Francis Fukuyama, *The End of History and the Last Man* (New York: Free Press, 1992), 46.
8. Ali A. Mazrui, "Islam and the End of History," *The American Journal of Islamic Social Sciences* 10, no. 4 (Winter 1993): 512–35. One is reminded of the similar verdict of a non-Muslim, the anthropologist Ernest Gellner: "[Islam's] sober and unrestrained unitarianism, its moralism and abstention from spiritual opportunism, manipulativeness and propiation, in brief its 'protestant' traits, give it an affinity with the modern world. It did not engender the modern world, but it may yet, of all the faiths, turn out to be the one best adapted to it." Ernest Gellner, "Forward," in *From Nationalism to Revolutionary Islam*, ed. Said Amir Arjomand (Albany: State University of New York Press, 1984), ix.
9. Samuel P. Huntington, "The Clash of Civilizations?" *Foreign Affairs* 72, no. 3 (Summer 1993): 22–49.
10. Fouad Ajami, "The Summoning," *Foreign Affairs* 72, no. 4 (September-October 1993): 2–9.

11. Centre for Arab Unity Studies, *The Future of the Arab Nation: Challenges and Options* (London: Routledge, 1991).

Index

Abbas Hilmi II, Khedive, 106–7
Abbasids, 94
Abd al-Rahman, Umar, 255–57, 263
Abdallah bin Husayn, Emir (later King), 25–27, 31
Abduh, Muhammad, 84n.23, 104
Abdülaziz, Sultan, 74
Abdülhamid II, Sultan, 61, 70, 72, 74–75, 84
Abu Sufyan (father of Yazid), 177, 186n.43
Abu Za'bal (prison), 35
Aden, 34, 117
Adrianople, 64
al-Afghani, Jamal al-Din, 104, 106, 108, 145–46, 151, 156; thought of, 143–44, 159n.27
Afghanistan, Afghans, 10, 40, 157, 212; war against Soviets in, 40, 150; *mujahidin* of, 257, 264, 274, 282
Aflaq, Michel, 39, 157
al-Ahmad, Sulayman, 195, 206n.11
Ajami, Fouad, 5, 46, 283–84
Akkar region (Lebanon), 199
Alawi Youth Movement, 201
Alawis: position under French, 191–94; Shi'ite view of, 11, 189–91, 193, 194–97, 199–205; status in Ottoman period, 191; Sunni view of, 194, 197–99, 203; theology of, 190–91
Aleppo, 65, 77, 79, 199
Alevis, 201
Alexandria, 55, 163
Algeria, , Algerians, 9, 13, 29, 33, 40, 127, 157, 227, 259, 276, 278, 282; elections in, 269–70, 273–74. *See also* Islamic Salvation Front
Ali (Muhammad's cousin), 190–91
Amal movement, 211–12, 253; Hiz-

bullah's conflict with, 12–13, 214–15, 220–21, 224, 232–35, 237–39, 241–43
American University of Beirut, 42, 133–35, 138
Anatolia, 76, 84
Anti-Semitism. *See* Jews
Antonius Lectures (Oxford), 7
Antonius, George, 4, 7–8, 19, 59; activities as author, 111–115; terms of employment, 121n.8; wartime liaisons of, 115–20
Antonius, Katy, 122n.18, 123n.37
Arab Awakening, The (Antonius). *See* Antonius, George
Arab caliphate, 5, 53–54, 59, 79, 89
Arab Centre (London), 115, 122n.17
Arab League, 30, 41
Arab National Movement, 3
Arab nationalism, 1, 15, 20–21, 189; anti-imperialism of, 26–27, 29, 115–19; apex of, 32–34; Arab resistance to, 27–28, 30–31, 189; articulation of, 7–8, 28–29; attempts to revive, 41–45, 46–48, 284; decline of, 3–4, 19–20, 35–37, 45, 279–81; foreign inspiration for, 4–7, 8–10, 53–54, 58–59, 63–64, 69–80, 82, 88–100, 133–35; Islamists on, 39–40, 47, 204, 217; origins of, 2–3, 21, 22–25, 69–78; relation to Alawis, 189, 195, 198; relation to Islam, 3, 23, 38–39, 70–71, 99–100, 105. *See also* Arabic language; Arab Revolt; Nasserism
Arab Revolt (1916), 5–6, 25–27, 39, 98, 100, 104
Arab socialism, 3, 32, 34
Arab unity, 5, 34, 46–48, 195, 284. *See also* Arab nationalism
Arab-Israeli peace process, 9, 20, 36, 45,

47, 225, 285; American role in, 135, 137–38
Arab-Israeli war (1948),31–32, 144, 146
Arab-Israeli war (1967), 3, 35, 37–38, 41, 44, 153
Arab-Israeli war (1973), 36–37, 135
Arabia, 21, 22, 23, 88, 94, 107, 112; Blunt's visits to, 54–55; early rumors of unrest in, 72–73. *See also* Arab Revolt; Pilgrimage; Saudi Arabia
Arabic language, 22, 79, 113, 119, 128, 136; and Arab nationalism, 3, 5–6, 21, 27–28, 45, 63–64; and Hartmann, 65–67, 70–71, 75–77; and pilgrims' slogans, 168; revival of, 23–24, 134
Arabic press, 24, 41, 46, 70, 90, 112; Hartmann on, 70, 76, 80, 85n.48; and spread of nationalism, 29, 53; subsidies for, 4, 53, 58–59. *See also individual newspapers, journalists*
Arabische Frage, Die (Hartmann), 4, 73
Arabischer Sprachführer für Reisende (Hartmann), 64, 66
Arabism. *See* Arab nationalism
Arabists (foreign), 9, 133–38. *See also individual persons*
Arabists, The (Kaplan), 133, 136–38
Arabs. *See* Arab nationalism
Arafat, Yasir, 128
Armenians, 65, 76, 79, 83, 91
Arslan, Shakib, 7, 99, 103–10
al-Asad, Hafiz, 11, 199, 202, 205
Ashura, 183, 239–40
Asir, 89
Assassins (medieval), 209
Assyrians (Nestorians), 29
Aswan Dam, 33
AUB. *See* American University of Beirut
Auque, Roger, 251
Axis powers: and Antonius, 116–17; and Arslan, 7, 108–9
Azerbaijan, 283
Azhar, 55, 197
Azoury, Nagib, 6, 84n.33, 88–89, 91, 98; Hartmann on, 71–72, 84n.34

Ba'th party, 33–35, 39, 41, 197, 221
Ba'thism, 21, 32
Baalbek, 253

Badamchian, Asadollah, 262
Baghdad railroad, 79
Baghdad, conquest by Mongols of, 262
Bahrain, 39, 212
Bakhtiar, Shapour, 249
Balcony, The (Genet), 127
Balfour Declaration, 26
Balkans, 3, 22, 24, 105
Banias, 196
al-Banna, Hasan, 144, 145–46, 153
Baram, Phillip J., 135
Bast (refuge),169
Becker, Carl Heinrich: on Hartmann, 68–69, 79, 80, 84n.24
Beirut Reform Committee, 78–79
Beirut: Antonius in, 115, 118–19, 122n.27, 123n.37; center of Arabism, 3, 23, 46, 63, 78–79; Hartmann in, 6, 64–66, 77–81, 83n.10; Palestinians massacred in, 125, 131; press of, 85n.48, 101n.36, 258; Shi'ites in, 211–12, 215, 220. *See also* American University of Beirut; Lebanon
Bekaa Valley, 152, 195, 210, 212, 214, 218, 220, 247, 249, 253
Belamri, Rabah, 15
Bell, Gertrude, 24, 136
Berber dahir, 105
Berbers, 29
Birri, Nabih, 234
Bismarck, 66
Black Panthers (America), 8, 127–28
Black September, 130
Blacks, The (Genet), 127
Bliss, Howard, 134
Blunt, Lady Anne, 53
Blunt, Wilfrid Scawen, 7; on Islamic reform, 143, 265–66; and Sabunji, 4–5, 53–61; support for Urabi, 55, 59–60
Borujerdi, Mohammad Husayn, 197
Bosnia, 283
Bradford (England), 259
Brazil, 96
Britain, British, 24, 54, 81, 88, 112, 136, 175; Antonius urges policy on, 115–19; Arab activism in, 20, 114–15, 120, 122n.17, 176; Arab criticism of, 104, 108; decline of, in Middle East, 9, 30, 32; and Egypt, 29, 55, 59, 74, 145; hostages, 220; Islamists in, 143, 153,

203, 259–60, 267; and Palestine, 115;
and partition of Middle East, 3, 26, 99;
promises to Arabs, 7, 39; Sabunji in,
53–54, 56–58, 60–61; support for Arab
nationalism, 4–5, 8, 20, 74, 96, 98,
129; support for Arab Revolt, 25–26,
93; support for Zionism, 27, 87, 95.
See also Blunt, Wilfrid Scawen
Brooklyn, 259
Budapest, 109
Buenos Aires, 90; bombing in, 230n.33
Burckhardt, John Louis, 163
Burroughs, William, 128
Burton, Richard Francis, 163
Bush, George, 137, 262
Butler, Nicholas Murray, 113–14

Cairo: Antonius in, 117, 119; Alawi stu-
dents in, 197–98; Arabic journalism in,
90, 100n.6, 104, 112, 143, 257–58
Caliphate. *See* Arab caliphate
Capitalism, 20, 68, 141, 259, 268, 282
Casablanca, 45
Caucasus, 22
Cavafy, Constantine, 120
Ceylon, 59, 60
Charles, Prince of Wales, 141, 143
Chile, 96
China, 42, 279, 281
Chirac, Jacques, 248
Christians: Alawis mistaken for, 191;
and American missionaries, 134; and
Arab nationalism, 6–7, 23, 39, 56,
75, 78, 92, 99, 134, 189, 195, 233;
Islamism and, 149, 250, 253; massa-
cred in Iraq, 29; subjects of Ottoman
Empire, 22, 25, 65, 70, 73, 88. *See
also* Maronites
Civilisation des arabes, La (Le Bon),
4, 63
"Clash of Civilizations?, The" (Hunting-
ton), 283
Clayton, Gilbert, 112
Cleveland, William, 103–10
Colombo, 60
Columbia University: Antonius ap-
pointment to, 113–14; conference at,
255–56
Comité Central Syrien, 91
Committee of Union and Progress. *See*
Young Turks

Communism, 1, 37, 48, 282
Congregationalists, 134
Corbeaux d'Alep, Les (Seurat), 249
Correspondance d'Orient (Paris), 92
Covering Islam (Said), 268
Crane, Charles, 4, 112–13
Crusades, 149–50, 154, 260

Da'wa party (Iraq), 151
Dabbuq, Haytham Subhi (bomber), 238
Damascus: as seat of Arabism, 23, 25–26;
Shi'ite shrines in, 185n.23
Darwish, Mahmoud, 19
Davis, Angela, 128
Decentralization party (Ottoman), 78, 90
Delafon, Gilles, 252–53
Democracy, 1, 20, 37, 255; and Arab
nationalism, 46–48; Hizbullah's view
of, 227; and Islam, 68, 70, 271; and
Islamism, 14, 138, 145–46, 148, 154,
157, 261, 265–66, 268–73, 276–78;
prospects for, 281–83, 285; resistance
to, 15, 37
*Department of State in the Middle East,
The* (Baram), 135
Deutsche Gesellschaft für Islamkunde,
80
Devotees of Islam (Iran), 144–45, 147
Dinkins, David, 256
Djaït, Hichem, 14, 43–44
Djerejian, Edward, 273, 277
Druze, 7, 27, 103, 105, 110, 195

Eagleton, William, 136
Eddy, William, 134–35
Egypt, Egyptians, 7, 20, 22, 37, 67, 70,
76, 143; Arab nationalism spreads
to, 29–30, 74, 78, 89; British in, 59,
118; Hartmann on "indolence" of, 65;
Islamists in, 39, 144–46, 148–52, 157,
227, 255–57, 259, 263, 267–68, 270;
and "Middle Easternism," 45; under
Nasser, 4, 31–35; under Sadat, 36;
Syrians in, 92, 96; Urabi revolt (1882)
in, 54–57, 60; and Yemen war, 34. *See
also* Cairo; Nasser
Elias, Edward, 84n.23
Emerson, Rupert, 21
"End of History, The" (Fukuyama), 281
Engert, Cornelius van, 119
Enver Pasha, 104

Ethics and International Affairs, 266
Europe, 42, 44, 46, 47, 96, 126–27, 269, 279, 281; Arab question in, 6, 24, 71, 75, 81, 87; compared to Middle East, 1–2, 19–21, 45, 92, 225, 276; critique of, 68, 260–62, 279; expansion of, 22, 260; Muslim communities in, 10, 147, 257, 259–60; scholarship in, 64; terrorism in, 14, 130–31, 220. *See also individual countries*
Express, L' (Paris), 270
Extremists: problem of defining, 141, 150, 256–57, 264
Égypte, L' (Cairo), 89

Fadlallah, Muhammad Husayn, 154, 157, 215, 267; on America, 261–62; on empowering Islam, 275–76; on Iranian revolution, 226; on Islamic Lebanon, 226; on "self-martyrdom" bombings, 223, 225, 239–41; on Shi'ite rivalries, 242; on violence, 218–19, 221
Fahd, King, 170, 175, 179, 181, 275
Fahs, Bilal (bomber), 232, 234–36, 238
Failure of Political Islam, The (Roy), 15
Fascism: inspires Arab nationalism, 28, 46; affinities to Islamism, 143, 148
Fatah, 41
Fatima (daughter of Prophet Muhammad), 164
Faysal, Emir (later King), 25–28, 98–99, 107
Fazy, Edmond, 84n.34, 85n.38
FBI, 255–56, 262
Fedayeen, 8, 42, 44, 125, 128–29. *See also* Palestine Liberation Organization
Finch, Edith, 55–56
FIS, see Islamic Salvation Front
Fleischer, Heinrich Leberecht, 64, 67
Fonda, Jane, 128
Foreign Affairs (New York), 256, 265
Fortnightly Review (London), 54, 61
Foucault, Michel, 9
Four Hours in Shatila (Genet), 131
France, French, 116, 154, 226; Arab intellectuals in, 20; Arslan's campaign against, 7, 104–5, 108–9; decolonization by, 30; influence of, in Arab world, 25, 28; Islamists (incl. Afghani, Khomeini) in, 143, 145, 153, 204, 245,

272; in Lebanon, 11, 151, 212, 219, 232–33, 245–54, 274; and North Africa, 29, 94, 270, 282; and partition of Middle East, 3, 26–27, 99; scholarship in, 67, 83n.21; and Suez war, 32–33; and Syria, 87–88, 94–100, 101n.36, 119, 123n.37, 189, 191–94; terrorism in, 13–14, 220, 224, 245–49, 254, 260. *See also* Jung; Genet
Frankfurter Zeitung, 77
Freedom in the World (Freedom House), 280
Front Islamique du Salut. *See* Islamic Salvation Front
Fukuyama, Francis, 15, 136, 281–83
Future of Islam, The (Blunt), 4, 54, 265–66

Gates, Robert, 266
Gaza, 35, 42
Gellner, Ernest, 285n.8
General Islamic Congress (Jerusalem), 194
General Syrian Congress (Damascus), 26
Genet, Jean, 4, 8–9, 42; attitude towards Israel, 129–30; literary activity, 125–27; political activism, 127–29; support for Palestinians, 128–31
Germany, Germans, 5, 90, 127, 130, 282; Arab attitudes to Nazi, 109, 116, 119; Azoury's view of, 72, 84n.33; Beirut consulate of, 64–66; hostages, 220; ideological influence of, 28; policy criticized by Hartmann, 78–79; pro-Ottomanism of, 6, 25, 73, 76, 79–81, 104; scholarship in, 66–68, 73. *See also* Hartmann
Geyer, August, 68
Ghanim, Shukri, 90–92
al-Ghannushi, Rashid, 153–54, 267; on "new world order," 261
Ghawsha, Ibrahim, 276
Ginsburg, Allen, 128
Gladstone, William, 60
Glaspie, April, 137
Glubb, John Bagot, 4, 129
Golan Heights, 35
Gottheil, Richard, 113
Grand troc, Le (Loiseau), 248

Great Mosque (Mecca), alleged Shi'ite pollution of, 163, 165; Iranian-Saudi clashes at, 167–70, 172–75, 179; seizure of (1979), 151. *See also* Pilgrimage
Gulf (Arab/Persian), 40, 151, 161, 171, 213, 227. *See also individual countries*
Gulf Cooperation Council, 178
Gulf War (1990–91), 19, 43–44, 46, 133, 137, 269, 275

Haifa, 77
al-Hakim, Muhsin, 195–97
Hamah, 77, 152, 199
Hamas, 12, 276
Hanafi, Hasan, 155–56
Harder, Ernst, 67
Hartmann, Martin, 4, 6–7; advocates Arab separatism, 70–74, 82; on Azoury, 71–72, 84n.34; Beirut years (1876–87), 65–66; education of, 64; on modernizing Arabic studies, 66–69, 79–80; Syrian visit (1913), 76–79; wartime pro-Ottomanism, 80–81, 86n.67; and Young Turk revolution, 74–76; and Zionism, 85n.50
Hebron, 183
Hegel, Georg, 281–82
Hijaz, 54, 73, 89–90, 92, 165. *See also* Arabia; Arab Revolt; Pilgrimage
Hizbullah, 11, 40, 185n.23, 258, 274; abductions and hijackings by, 220–21, 223–24, 246–47, 249–51; composition of, 214–15; ideology of, 215–19; origins of, 209–13; 249–51; political role of, 225–28, 230n.38, 252–53; and rivalry with Amal, 12–13, 214–15, 220–21, 224, 232–39, 241–43; "self-martyrdom" bombings by, 219, 221, 223, 231–33, 235–41. *See also* Fadlallah
Hodgson, Marshall G. S., 279
Homs, 77, 199
Horan, Hume, 136–37
Hourani, Albert, 7, 123n.39
Huntington, Samuel P., 15, 283–84
Hurgronje, Christiaan Snouck, 69, 81, 163
Husayn, Imam, 164, 186n.43, 239, 242

Husayn (of Jordan), King, 128
Husayn, Saddam. *See* Hussein, Saddam
Husayn, Sharif, 6, 25–26, 79, 87, 89, 91–92
al-Husayni, Haj Amin, 107, 109–10, 118–19, 194
al-Husri, Sati', 28
Husry, Khaldun S., 108
Hussein, Saddam, 41–44, 46, 133, 137, 269, 275
Huwaydi, Fahmi, 16n.3
Hülegü, 262

Ibn Sa'ud, King Abd al-Aziz, 92, 107–8, 134, 164–65
Ibrahim, Habib Al, 195–96
ICWA. *See* Institute for Current World Affairs
Immigrants, Muslim, 9, 255, 258–260
Indépendance arabe, L' (Paris), 89, 91
India, 70, 165, 279
Institute for Current World Affairs, 112, 114–15, 118, 121n.8, 123n.37
Iran, Iranians: and Afghani, 143; and Arab Shi'ites, 40; conflict with France, 13, 245–49; and Devotees of Islam, 144–49; influence of, on Islamists, 150–51, 273, 276; and pilgrimage to Mecca, 11, 161–83, 184 table 10.1, 185n.23; revolution in, 46, 149–50, 225, 259, 267; and Syria, 190, 203–5, 242; ties to Hizbullah of, 12, 212–21, 224–28, 237–38, 249–53, 274; war with Iraq, 13, 143, 220, 224; on World Trade Center bombing, 262–63. *See also* Khomeini
Iran-Iraq war, 13, 143, 167, 170–72, 204, 213, 220, 224–25, 227, 245–46, 254
Iraq, Iraqis, 27, 165, 166; American policy toward, 137; Alawi students in, 195–97; British rule in, 26, 28; invasion of Kuwait by, 43–45; Iranian pilgrims to, 170; Lebanese students in, 214; local nationalism in, 36, 42–43; military rule in, 31, 33, 35; Rashid Ali regime in, 118–19; Shi'ites in, 39, 151–52, 154, 164, 202, 212; under monarchy, 29–30, 107–8, 122n.16; war with Iran, 13, 167, 170, 204, 213, 220, 224–25, 227, 245–46. *See also* Hussein, Saddam; Mesopotamia; Najaf

Islam: and Arab nationalism, 3, 23, 38–39, 70–71, 99–100, 105; democracy and, 68, 70, 271; distinguished from Islamism, 10, 141, 277–78; and other identities, 27, 29, 32, 38, 105, 144, 264; Ottoman, 3, 22–23, 70, 72–73, 77–78, 104, 164; prospects in next century, 1, 15, 281–84; revival of, 38–40, 266–68; study of, 67, 79–80, 83n.21, 255–56, 268; tolerance of, 92; and underdevelopment, 279–81; unity of, 36, 70–71, 74, 77–78, 146–47, 227; view of Alawis, 190–91, 184, 197–98, 199, 203; in the West, 13–14, 255–56, 259–61. *See also* Islamic fundamentalism; Islamic law; Islamic reform; Islamic state; Shi'ism

Islamic Arab Popular Conference, 274

Islamic fundamentalism, Islamism, 1–2; accommodationism in, 156–57, 226–28, 277; actions against the West, 13–14, 133, 219–20, 245–51, 255–56, 262–64; anti-democratic bias of, 145–46, 271–73; apologists for, 14, 47, 99–100, 138, 141, 154, 158, 255–58, 265–66, 277; definition of, 141–42, 278; divisive effects of, 11–13, 183, 241–43; and elections, 268–70; as ideology, 10–11, 142, 147–50, 152–56, 215–19, 260–62, 267–68, 275–76; pan-Islamism of, 39, 105, 146–47, 150, 216–17, 273–75; revolutionary violence of, 150–52, 219–22, 266–67; self-restraints on, 222–25, 240–41; social bases of, 40, 210–15, 258–60; and suicide bombings, 12, 223, 231–40. *See also* Jihad; Shi'ism; *individual movements*

Islamic Jihad (Egypt), 151

Islamic Jihad (Lebanon), 215, 220, 222, 231, 238, 249, 250, 268

Islamic Jihad (Palestinian), 227

Islamic law: in Alawi courts, 192–93, 196, 200–1; in Islamist thought, 39–40, 47, 142, 147–49, 271–72, 275–76; regulates violence, 12, 222–25, 235, 239. *See also* Islamic state

Islamic reform, 23; absence of, 155, 266, 272, 278; Afghani and, 143–44, American expection of, 138, 155,

273; Blunt's search for, 54–55, 143, 265–66; Hartmann's view of, 71

Islamic Research Academy, 202

Islamic Resistance, 231, 233, 238. *See also* Hizbullah

Islamic Salvation Front (FIS), 269, 270, 273, 274

Islamic state, 47, 142, 157, 266, 272; in Hizbullah's program, 210, 212, 217, 227; nature of, in Islamist thought, 145–50, 152–55. *See also* Islamic law

Islamism. *See* Islamic fundamentalism

Isma'il, Khedive, 55, 56

Israel, Israelis, 19, 109, 279, 284; Arab-Muslim view of, 32, 36, 39, 42, 48, 147, 150, 257–58, 263, 276, 285; Arabist view of, 133, 135–36; Genet on, 129–30; Hizbullah's conflict with, 13, 217–20, 222, 224, 226, 230n.33, 231–35, 238–40, 274; and intervention in Lebanon, 38, 125, 211–12, 214–15; Iranian leaders on, 150, 166–67, 171, 176, 179–82. *See also* Arab-Israel peace process; Arab-Israel wars; Zionism

Istanbul, 22, 23, 61, 80, 90, 100n.6, 104, 143; Hartmann in, 64, 74–75. *See also* Ottoman Empire

Italy, Italians, 108–9, 116, 119

Ja'fari Society, 196

Jabla, 194, 196

Jerusalem, 67, 99, 101n.36, 183; anticipated liberation of, 175, 225; Antonius and, 115, 117, 119–20, 122n.18; Israeli occupation of East, 35, 39

Jews: alleged influence of, 95, 109, 258; American, 95, 113–14; in Arab countries, 29, 144; Genet on, 129–30; Islamist view of, 39, 146, 230n.33, 262, 276; in Ottoman Empire, 76; in Palestine, 24, 26, 71, 85n.50; Saudis alleged to be, 176. *See also* Israel; Zionism

Jibshit, 232, 234

Jidda, 92, 117

Jihad (precept of Islam), 14, 141, 145, 234; in Afghanistan, 257, 274; Hamas view of, 276; Hizbullah's view of,

215, 222–27, 238, 240. *See also* Islamic law
Jones, James Earl, 127
Jordan, 31, 34, 37, 42, 92, 147, 227; Genet with Palestinians in, 8, 128–29
Journal of Democracy, 270
Journalism. *See* Arabic press
Junbalat, Mayy, 103
Junbalat, Walid, 103
Jung, Eugène, 4, 6–7, 72; background of, 88–89; disillusionment of, 99–100; journalism of, 90–97; and Sharifians, 97–99

Ka'bah, 163. *See also* Pilgrimage
Kabul, 143
Kanafani, Ghassan, 42
Kaplan, Robert, 133–38
Karbala, 164, 166, 175, 202; in Shi'ite myth, 239–40
Karrubi, Mehdi, 172–73
Kashif al-Ghita, Muhammad al-Husayn Al, 194–95, 206n.11
Kashmir, 283
al-Kawakibi, Abd al-Rahman, 74
al-Kaylani, Rashid Ali, 118–19
Kedourie, Elie, 134
Kennedy, Paul, 1
Kerr, Malcom, 15, 133, 136–38
Khalid, King, 168–69
Khamene'i, Ali, 162, 178–79, 181–82
Khartoum, 256, 274
Kho'i, Abol Qasem, 203
Khoiniha, Musavi, 167, 171–72
Khomeini, Ahmad 156, 180
Khomeini, Ayatollah Ruhollah, 11, 13, 40, 145, 154–57, 204, 245, 253; contribution to Islamism by, 149–51, 159n.27; inspires Hizbullah, 212–14, 216–18, 234, 237, 239, 241; pilgrimage policy of, 167–79, 204; pilgrimage theory of, 166–67
Kiftaru, Ahmad, 203
Kirkpatrick, Jeane, 269
Kohn, Hans, 20
Kurd Ali, Muhammad, 77–79, 81
Kurdistan, 2
Kurds, 43
Kuwait, Kuwaitis, 2, 37, 151, 204; Hizbullah prisoners in, 220, 249; Iraqi

invasion of, 43–44, 133, 137, 269, 275; reflagging of tankers by, 161, 172; Shi'ites of, 177, 212–13

Lahad, Antoine, 220
Latakia, 77, 189, 191, 193, 196
Latif, Bahauddeen, 280
Law. *See* Islamic law
Lawrence, T. E., 4, 8, 98, 129, 131, 136, 137
Le Bon, Gustave, 4, 63
Le Chatelier, Alfred, 83n.21
League of Nations, 26, 29, 104
Lebanon, Lebanese 2, 7, 30, 36, 85n.48, 97, 112, 221, 259; Alawis of, 200–1; civil war in, 38, 211; Druze in, 103–4; elections in (1992), 230n.38; France in, 11, 151, 212, 219, 232–33, 245–54, 274; idea of, 27; Hizbullah's view of, 216–18, 227; Iranians in, 147, 204, 212–15, 274; Israeli intervention in, 11, 38, 125, 130, 211–12, 214–15; Palestinians in, 125, 136, 201, 211–12, 214–15; and rise of Arabism, 19, 23, 66; Shi'ites in, 11–12, 40, 151, 185n.23, 192–93, 195–97, 199–203, 210–12, 231–32, 237–39, 241–43, 283; Sunnis in, 134, 211, 213, 249; Syrian intervention in, 12, 38, 213, 237; U.S. intervention in, 11, 34, 151, 212, 219, 231–32, 274. *See also* Amal, Hizbullah, Maronites
Leipzig, 64
Libya, Libyans, 37, 46, 76, 108, 157
Loiseau, Yves, 248

MacMichael, Sir Harold 117
Mansur, Ali, 201
Maronites, 27, 38, 78, 211–12, 217
Marseille, 13
Martyrs' Foundation, 252
Marxism, 68, 156, 158
Mashhad, 183
Massignon, Louis, 4
Mawdudi, Abu al-Ala, 148, 151, 153, 154, 155
Mazrui, Ali, 282, 284
Mecca, 90, 161–83, 281. *See also* Great Mosque; Husayn, Sharif; Pilgrimage
Medina, 164, 167–72, 175–76. *See also* Pilgrimage

Menace, La (Péan), 246
Mercator projection, 279
Mesopotamia, 43, 72, 89, 92. *See also*
    Iraq
Mettray, 126
Mezze (prison), 35
Middle East Institute (Columbia University), 255
Middle East Institute (Washington), 138
Middle East: idea of, 45; "new," 284–85
Minorsky, Vladimir, 85n.42
Mitterrand, François, 249
Montazeri, Husayn Ali, 175
Morocco, Moroccans, 20, 21, 37, 95, 103, 105, 128, 249
Moscow, 104, 282
Mossad, 257–58
Mufti of Jerusalem. *See* al-Husayni, Haj Amin
Mughniyya, Imad, 215
Muhammad, Prophet, 22, 39, 142, 147,186n.43, 190, 210, 216, 271
Multinational Force, 233
Munich Olympics, 130
Murray, Wallace, 118
al-Musawi, Abbas, 214, 217–18, 220
Muscat, 179
Muslim Brethren, 144–47, 150–53, 204, 268, 275, 276. *See also* Islamic fundamentalism
Muslim World League, 175
Muslims. *See* Islam; *individual countries*
Mussolini, Benito, 108
Mutran, Rashid, 75

Nabatiyya, 232, 239–40
Naggiar, Ibrahim Salim, 90–92, 96–97, 99, 101n.36
Nahda. *See* Arab nationalism
Najaf, 152, 154, 166, 175, 183, 218, 245; Alawis viewed from, 192, 195–98, 201–4, 206n.11
Najjar, Ibrahim Salim al-. *See* Naggiar
Nasser, Gamal Abdul, 3, 31–35, 39, 41, 43, 144, 148
Nasserism, 9, 21, 32, 202
Nateq-Nuri, Ali Akbar, 182
Nation arabe, La (Geneva), 7, 103, 105, 109

National Bloc (Syria), 194
Nayif, Prince174
New York, 90, 178; an Arab view of, 258.
    See also Columbia University; Institute of Current World Affairs; World Trade Center bombing
Nihayyah Palace (prison), 35
Nile, 21
Nineteenth Century (London), 56
North Africa, North Africans, 2, 7, 9, 21, 22, 29, 105, 129, 146, 259, 265, 268, 270, 273, 278. *See also individual countries*

Oman, 179
Operation Moses, 136
Organization of the Islamic Conference, 176
Orient arabe, L' (Paris), 90, 92–97, 100n.7
Ottoman Empire, 1, 21, 29, 63, 134, 191; approach to Alawis of, 191–92; Arslan supports, 7, 104; collapse of, 25–26; Hartmann on, 6, 64–66, 70–82; Jung on, 87–89; and Muslim pilgrimage, 162–64; and rise of Arabism, 2–3, 22–25; Sabunji on, 5, 54, 57–59
Our Lady of the Flowers (Genet), 126
Oxford, 7, 113

Pahlavi, Mohammed Reza Shah, 167, 204, 216–17, 245, 263
Pakistan, 148
Palestine Liberation Organization (PLO), 37, 41, 131, 276
Palestine, Palestinians, 3, 7, 19, 27, 112; Arab involvement in, 36, 38; British in, 26, 87, 99, 115, 117; foreign Islamists for, 144, 146–47, 217; Genet's support for, 8–9, 127–29, 130–31; Islamists in, 12, 227, 257, 274, 276; journalism in, 101n.36; Jung on, 89, 94; in Lebanon, 125, 136, 201, 211–12, 214–15; Ottoman, 24, 71; partition of (1948), 31; resistance, 8–9, 41–42, 125. *See also* Antonius, George; Arab-Israel wars; Israel; Zionism
Party of God. *See* Hizbullah
Pasqua, Charles, 248
Patterns of Global Terrorism, 280

Peace process. *See* Arab-Israeli peace process
Permanent Mandates Commission, 104
Persians, 39, 72, 144. *See also* Iran
Péan, 246, 247, 248, 253
Phoenicians, 27
Pilgrimage to Mecca: bloodshed during (1987), 171–75; under Ibn Sa'ud, 164–66; Iranian-Saudi polemics over, 11, 161–62, 167–71, 175–83; Khomeini's concept of, 166–67; number of Iranians attending, 184 table 10.1; in Ottoman period, 162–64
PLO. *See* Palestine Liberation Organization
Political Islam. *See* Islamic fundamentalism
Popular Front for the Liberation of Palestine (PFLP), 42
Presbyterians, 9, 134
Prisoner of Love (Genet), 125, 129
Prophet's Mosque (Medina), 167, 170
Protestant Reformation, Islamic analogies to, 138, 155, 266, 285n.8
Puissances devant la révolte arabe, Les (Jung), 4, 72, 88

Qabbani, Nizar 19
Qardaha, 194–95, 197–198, 205
Qom, 195–97, 201–3, 205
Qur'an, 22, 147, 169, 212, 251, 271
Qusayr, Ahmad (bomber), 231, 233, 235–39
Qutb, Sayyid, 39, 148–49, 151, 153–55

Raad, Razah, 247
Rafsanjani, Ali Akbar Hashemi-, 175, 179–82
Razmara, Ali, 146
Reconstruction Jihad, 252
Reform. *See* Islamic reform
Reisebriefe aus Syrien (Hartmann), 77
Revolutionary Guards, 12, 151, 204, 212, 217–19
Revolutionary Justice Organization, 251
Reyshahri, Muhammad Muhammadi-, 179–82
Reza, Imam, 183
Réveil de la nation arabe dans l'Asie turque, Le (Azoury), 71

Révolte arabe, La (Jung), 99
Ribot, Alexandre, 96
Richard, Henry, 97, 101n.31
Rida, Rashid, 106–7
Rogers, Walter, 123n.37
Rome, 109, 131
Roosevelt, Franklin D., 134
Rushdie, Salman, 151, 260, 268
Russia, 44, 66, 81

Sa'ud al-Faysal, Prince, 178–79
Sabunji, John Louis, 5, 53–61
Sadat, Anwar, 36, 151
al-Sadr, Sayyid Musa, 199–202, 204
Safavi, Navvab, 144–47
Safavids, 162
Said, Edward, 8–9, 60, 268
Salameh, Muhammad (bomber), 257, 262
Saleh, Fouad Ali (bomber), 249
Salibi, Kamal, 36
Salonika, 75
Samné, Georges, 90, 92
San Remo conference, 26
Sanaa, 34
Sarkis, Khalil, 76
Sartre, Jean-Paul, 9, 125–27, 129
Saudi Arabia, 37, 233; and controversy over pilgrimage, 11, 152, 161, 164–82; Shi'ites in, 40, 151, 165, 212–13; U.S. support for, 134, 275, 277. *See also* Ibn Sa'ud, King Abd al-Aziz
Screens, The (Genet), 127
Seale, Bobby, 128
Secret History of the English Occupation of Egypt (Blunt), 55, 57
Seminar für Orientalische Sprachen, 66
Seurat, Marie, 249–51
Seurat, Michel, 249–52
Seven Pillars of Wisdom (Lawrence), 8, 129, 136
Shams al-Din, Muhammad Mahdi, 207n.29
Shams al-Din, Muhammad Rida, 196–97
Sharaf al-Din, Abd al-Husayn, 193
Shari'a. *See* Islamic law
Shariati, Ali, 166–67, 203
Shariatmadari, Ayatollah Kazem, 203–4
Shatila, 125

Shaykh, Abdallah bin Abd al-Rahman Al, 186n.30
Shi'ism, Shi'ites, 27, 210, 242; Alawis viewed by, 11, 190–97, 199–203, 205, 206n.11, 207n.29; as Arab underclass, 39–40, 151; Damascus shrines of, 185n.23; dissimulation in, 156, 167; impact of Iran's revolution upon, 212–13; and Iranian Sunnis, 183; and Islamic ecumenism, 147, 227; and Ottoman Sunnis, 161–64, 174–75; polemics with Saudis of, 165–66, 168–70, 174–77, 186n.43; reinterpretation of pilgrimage among, 166–67; themes of, evoked by Fadlallah, 240; veneration of Medina by 169–70; and Wahhabi movement, 164–65. See also Fadlallah; Hizbullah; Khomeini; individual countries
al-Shirazi, Ayatollah Hasan, 202–3
Shuf mountains, 103
Sidon, 66, 134
Sinai, 35–36
Society of the Muslim Brethren. See Muslim Brethren
Sokolov, 85n.50
Sorbonne, 113, 127, 153, 267
South Lebanon Army, 220–21
Soviet Union, Soviets, 33, 42, 48, 146, 156, 171, 258–59, 261, 268, 276; in Afghanistan, 40, 150, 257, 274, 282
St. Petersburg, 143
Stark, Freya, 4, 118–20, 136
Statistical Yearbook (UNESCO), 280
Storrs, Ronald, 136
Sudan, 2, 136, 153, 157, 259, 272–74, 283. See also Turabi
Suez War (1956), 32
Suez, 33, 45, 145
Supreme Islamic Shi'ite Council (SISC), 199–201, 207n.29
Sursuq, Jurji, 85n.48
Switzerland, Swiss, 7, 104–5, 109–10
Syria, Syrians, 128, 165, 247; Alawis of, 11, 189–205; and rise of Ba'thism, 32–33; constitution of, 198–99; and France, 87–88, 94–100, 101n.36, 119, 123n.37, 189, 191–94; "Greater," 30; and Iran, 190, 203–5, 242; in Lebanon, 12, 38, 213, 237; and Iraq, 107–8; Islamist uprising in, 151–52;

and Israel, 35, 221; Michel Seurat and, 249–50; military coups in, 31, 198; relations with Egypt, 33–34, 36; and rise of Arabism, 23–24, 65–66, 70–73, 75–80, 82, 90; Sharifian bid for, 6, 26, 28, 87–88, 98–99; Sunnis in, 4, 151, 189–90, 193–94, 198–99; throne of 106–7; U.S. and, 134, 136. See also Alawis; al-Asad, Hafiz
Syrian Protestant College, 134. See also American University of Beirut
Syrian Social Nationalist Party, 220–21
Syrie et la Guerre, La (Richards), 97, 101n.31

Tabbara, Ahmad, 81
Tarrazi, Philippe de, 57–58, 80
Tartus, 189, 191, 196
Tawhid Movement, 213
Tel Aviv, 85n.50
Thesiger, Wilfred, 136
"They Should Have Cared" (Cafavy), 120–21
Third Worldism, 20, 154
Thomas, Norman, 3
Toynbee, Arnold, 4, 20, 144, 268
Transjordan, 27, 30. See also Jordan
Tripoli (Lebanon), 66, 77, 199–201, 213, 249
Tripolitania, 67
Tunisia, Tunisians, 9, 29, 94, 153, 224, 227, 249, 259. See also Djaït; Ghannushi
Tura (prison), 35
al-Turabi, Hasan, 153–55, 157, 267, 270, 277; on pluralism, 272–74
Turkey, Turks, 45, 201, 259, 263; growth of nationalism among, 3, 24; Hartmann on, 65, 70–76, 78–81. See also Ottoman Empire
Tyre, 193, 231, 233, 238–39

Ubayd, Abd al-Karim, 222
Umayyads, 72, 94, 177, 186n.43
Un otage à Beyrouth (Auque), 251
"Under Siege: Islam and Democracy" (conference), 255
UNESCO, 280
United Arab Republic (1958–61), 33–34
United Nations, 31, 261
United States, Americans: Antonius and,

111–14, 118–20; Arabs in, 47, 96, 255, 259–60, 264; denounced by pilgrims, 166–67, 171–72, 179–82; and Egypt, 36; Genet on, 8, 127–28; Gulf policy of, 161, 275; and Iran arms sales, 246, 248; and Iranian revolution, 216; and Iraq, 137; Islamist view of, 149–50, 154, 156, 162, 177, 178, 217, 225, 258–59, 261, 263, 267, 277; and Israel, 135–36; Jews in, 95, 113–14; in Lebanon, 11, 34, 151, 212, 219, 231–32, 274; and Nasser, 33; promotes new order, 45; scholarship in, 137; support for Arab nationalism by, 9, 94, 133–37; targeted by Islamists, 14, 48, 151, 219–20, 231, 255–64; views of Islamism in, 138, 266, 273, 277–79, 281–84. *See also* Arabists; World Trade Center bombing

Universal Declaration of Human Rights, 272

University of California, 133

Unpolitische Briefe aus der Türkei (Hartmann), 75, 80

Urabi, Ahmad, 55, 57–58, 60

Velayati, Ali Akbar, 178–79, 181

Versailles (Paris) peace conference, 26, 98–99, 134

Vienna, 22

Wahhabism, 161, 164, 168, 177

Waite, Terry, 247

Washington Post, 266

Welt des Islams, Die (Berlin), 80

Wentworth, Judith, 57

West Bank, 31, 35, 42

West. *See* Europe; United States

White, Edmund, 125–27, 129

Wilhelm II, Kaiser, 73, 84

Women, 68, 263, Islamist view of, 148–49, 152, 173, 252, 272, 278; and jihad, 235–36

World Trade Center bombing (1993), 14, 255–58, 260, 263–64

Wright, Robin, 253

Yahya, Mahmud, 73

Yazid, 177, 186n.43

al-Yaziji, Ibrahim, 19, 44, 66, 83n.12

Yemen, Yemenis, 34, 36, 54, 73–74, 85n.38, 89

Young Turks, 74–75, 78, 81, 88–90

Zahedan, 183

Zaydan, Jurji, 76

Zionism, Zionists, 3, 20, 87, 114, 129, 205, Arab nationalists view, 8, 24, 26–27, 32; Hartmann discounts, 77, 85n.50; Islamist view of, 39, 144, 147, 268; Jung on, 95. *See also* Israel

Zurayk, Constantin, 31

Printed in the United States
202597BV00004B/34-48/P

9 781412 807678